Practical Religion

J.C. Ryle

Practical Religion

The present edition is a reproduction of previous publication of this classic work. Minor typographical errors may have been corrected without note, however, for an authentic reading experience the spelling, punctuation, and capitalization have been retained from the original text.

ISBN: 978-1-64439-137-2

CONTENTS

SELF-INQUIRY

"Let us go again and visit our brethren in every city where we have preached the word of the Lord — and see how they do." (Acts 15:36).

The text which heads this page contains a proposal which the Apostle Paul made to Barnabas after their first missionary journey. He proposed to revisit the Churches they had been the means of founding, and to see how the were getting on. Were their members *continuing* steadfast in the faith? Were they *growing* in grace? Were they going *forward* — or standing still? Were they prospering, or falling away? "Let us go again and visit our brethren in every city where we have preached the word of the Lord — and see how they do."

This was a wise and useful proposal. Let us lay it to heart, and apply it to ourselves in the nineteenth century. Let us search our ways, and find out how matters stand between ourselves and God. Let *us "see how we do."* I ask every reader of this volume to begin its perusal by joining me in *self-inquiry*. If ever self-inquiry about religion was needed — it is needed at the present day.

We live in an age of particular **spiritual privileges**. Since the world began, there never was such an opportunity for a man's soul to be saved, as there is in England at this time. There never were so many signs of religion in the land, so many *sermons* preached, so many services held in churches and chapels, so many *Bibles* sold, so many *religious books and tracts* printed, so many *Societies* for evangelizing mankind supported, so much *outward respect* paid to Christianity. Things are done everywhere now-a-days, which a hundred years ago would have been thought impossible. Bishops support the boldest and most aggressive efforts to reach the unconverted. Cathedrals are now opened for Sunday evening sermons! Clergy of the narrowest High Church School advocate special missions, and vie with the Evangelical brethren in proclaiming that going to church on Sunday is not enough to take a man to Heaven. In short, there is a *stir* about religion now-a-days, to which there has been nothing like since England was a nation, and which the cleverest skeptics and infidels cannot deny. If Romaine, and Venn, and Berridge, and Rowlands, and Grimshaw, and Hervey, had been told that such things would come to pass about a century after their deaths — they would have been tempted to say, with the Samaritan nobleman, "If the Lord should windows of heavens might such a thing be." (2 Kings 7:19).

But the Lord has opened the floodgates of Heaven. There is more taught now-a-days in England of the real Gospel, and of the way of salvation by faith in Jesus Christ, in one week — than there was in a year in Romaine's time. Surely I have a right to say that we live in an age of spiritual privileges. But are we any better for it? In an age like this it is well to ask, "How do we do about our souls?"

We live in an age of particular **spiritual danger**. Never perhaps since the world began, was there such an immense amount of mere *outward profession* of religion, as there is in the present day. A painfully large proportion of all the congregations in the land consists of unconverted people, who know nothing of heart-religion, never come to the Lord's Table, and never confess Christ in their daily lives. Myriads of those who are always running after preachers, and crowding to hear special sermons — are nothing better than empty tubs, and tinkling cymbals — without a bit of real vital Christianity at home. The parable of the sower is continually receiving most vivid and painful illustrations. The way-side hearers, the stony-ground hearers, the thorny-ground hearers — abound on every side!

The life of many religious people, I fear, in this age, is nothing better than a continual course of chasing after novelties. They are always morbidly craving fresh excitement; and they seem to care little what it is — if they only get it. All preaching seems to be the same to them; and they appear unable to "see differences" so long as they hear what is clever, have their ears tickled, and sit in a crowd. Worst of all, there are hundreds of young unestablished believers who are so infected with the same love of excitement, that they actually think it a duty to be always seeking it. Insensibly almost to themselves, they take up a kind of hysterical, sensational, sentimental Christianity — until they are never content with the "old paths;" and, like the Athenians, are always running after something new!

To see a calm-minded young believer, who is not stuck up, self-confident, self-conceited, and more ready to teach than learn — but content with a daily steady effort to grow up into Christ's likeness, and to do Christ's work quietly and unostentatiously, at home — is really becoming almost a rarity! Too many young professors, alas, behave like young recruits who have not spent all their bounty money. They show how little deep root they have, and how little knowledge of their hearts — by noise, forwardness, readiness to contradict and set down old Christians, and over-weaning trust in their own imagined soundness and wisdom! Well will it be for many young professors of this age if they do not end, after being tossed about for a while, and "carried to and fro by every wind of doctrine," by joining some petty, narrow-minded, censorious sect, or embracing some senseless, unreasoning crotchety heresy. Surely, in times like these there is great need for self-examination. When we look around us, we may well ask, "How do we do about our souls?"

In handling this question, I think the shortest plan will be to suggest a list of subjects for self-inquiry — and to get them in order. By so doing I shall hope to meet the case of every one into whose hands this volume may fall. I invite every reader of this paper to join me in calm, searching self-examination, for a few short minutes. I desire to speak to myself as well as to you. I approach you not as an enemy — but as a friend. "My heart's desire and prayer to God is that you may be saved" (Romans 10:1). Bear with me if I say things which at first sight look harsh and severe. Believe me — *he is your best friend, who tells you the most truth.*

(1) Let me ask, in the first place, "DO WE EVER *THINK* ABOUT OUR SOULS AT ALL?"

Thousands of English people, I fear, cannot answer that question satisfactorily. They never give the subject of religion any place in their thoughts. From the beginning of the year to the end — they are absorbed in the pursuit of business, pleasure, politics, money, or self-indulgence of some kind or another. Death, and judgment, and eternity, and Heaven, and Hell, and the world to come — are never calmly looked at and considered. They live on as if they were never going to die, or rise again, or stand at the bar of God, or receive an eternal sentence! They do not openly *oppose* religion, for they have not sufficient reflection about it to do so; but they eat and drink, and sleep, and get money, and spend money — -as if religion was a mere fiction, and not a reality. They are neither Romanists, nor Socinians, nor infidels, nor High Church, nor Low Church, nor Broad Church. They are just *nothing at all,* and do not take the trouble to have opinions.

A more senseless and unreasonable way of living cannot be conceived; but they do not pretend to *reason* about it. They *simply never think* about God — unless frightened for few minutes by sickness, death in their families, or an accident. Barring such *interruptions*, they appear to ignore religion altogether, and hold on to their way cool and undisturbed, as if there were nothing worth thinking of, except this poor world.

It is hard to imagine a life more unworthy of an immortal creature, than such a life as I have just described, for it reduces a man to the level of a beast! But it is literally and truly the life of multitudes in England; and as they pass away — their place is taken by multitudes like them. The picture, no doubt, is horrible, distressing, and revolting — but, unhappily, it is only too true. In every large town, in every market, on every stock-exchange, in every club — you may see specimens of this class by the scores — men who think of everything under the sun, except the one thing needful — the salvation of their souls. Like the Jews of old they do not "consider their ways," they do not "consider their latter end;" they do not "consider that they do evil" (Isaiah 1:3; Haggai 1:7; Deuteronomy 32:29; Ecclesiastes 5:1). Like Gallio they "care for none of these things," (Acts 18:17.)

If they prosper in the world, and get rich, and succeed in their line of life — they are praised, and admired by their contemporaries.

Nothing succeeds in England like success! But for all this, they cannot live forever. They will have to die and appear before the bar of God, and be judged; and *then* what will the end be? When a large class of this kind exists in our country — no reader need wonder that I ask whether he belongs to it. If you do, you ought to have a mark set on your door, as there used to be a mark on a plague-stricken house two centuries ago, with the words, *"Lord have mercy on us,"* written on it. Look at the class I have been describing, and then look at your own soul.

(2) Let me ask, in the second place, WHETHER WE EVER *DO* ANYTHING ABOUT OUR SOULS?

There are multitudes in England who think occasionally about religion — but unhappily never get *beyond thinking.* After a stirring sermon — or after a funeral — or under the pressure of illness — or on Sunday evening — or when things are going on badly in their families — or when they meet some bright example of a Christian — or when they fall in with some striking religious book or tract — they will at the time, think a good deal, and even talk a little about religion in a vague way. But they stop short, as if *thinking* and *talking* were enough to save them. They are always *meaning*, and *intending*, and *purposing*, and *resolving*, and *wishing*, and telling us that they "know" what is right, and "hope" to be found right in the end — but they never attain to any action. There is no actual *separation* from the service of the world and sin — no real *taking up the cross* and following Christ — no positive *doing* in their Christianity. Their life is spent in playing the part of the son in our Lord's parable, to whom the father said, "'Go and work today in the vineyard:' and he answered, 'I will, sir,' but he did not go" (Matthew 21:30).

They are like those whom Ezekiel describes, who *liked* his preaching — but never *practiced* what he preached: "They come unto you as the people comes, and they sit before you as my people, and they *hear* your words — but they will not *do* them . . . And lo, you are unto them as a very lovely song of one that has a pleasant voice, and can play well on an instrument: for they *hear* your words — but they *do* them not." (Ezekiel 33:31-32). In a day like this, when hearing and thinking without doing, is so common — no one can justly wonder that I press upon men the absolute need of self-examination. Once more, then, I ask my readers to consider the question of my text — "How do we do about our souls?"

(3) Let me ask, in the third place, WHETHER WE ARE TRYING TO SATISFY OUR CONSCIENCES WITH A MERE 'FORMAL' RELIGION?

There are myriads in England at this moment who are making *shipwreck* on this rock. Like the Pharisees of old, they make much ado about the *outward* part of Christianity, while the inward and spiritual part is totally neglected. They are careful to attend all the services of their place of worship, and regular in using all its forms and ordinances. They are never absent from Communion when the Lord's Supper is administered. Sometimes they are most strict in observing *Lent*, and attach great importance to *Saints' days*. They are often keen partisans of their own Church, or sect, or congregation, and ready to contend with anyone who does not agree with them.

Yet all this time there is no *heart* in their religion. Anyone who knows them intimately can see with half an eye — that their affections are set on things below, and not on things above; and that they are trying to make up for the lack of inward Christianity — by an excessive quantity of outward form. And this *formal religion* does them no real good. They are not satisfied. Beginning at the wrong end, by making the outward things first — they know nothing of inward joy and peace, and pass their days in a constant struggle, secretly conscious that there is something wrong, and yet not knowing why. Well, after all, if they do not go on from one stage of formality to another, until in despair they take a fatal plunge, and fall into *Popery!*

When professing Christians of this kind are so painfully numerous, no one need wonder if I press upon him the paramount importance of close self-examination. If you love life, do not be content with the *husk*, and *shell*, and *scaffolding* of religion. Remember our Savior's words about the Jewish formalists of His day: "These people draws near with their mouth, and honors Me with their lips — but their heart is far from Me. In vain do they worship." (Matthew 15:8-9). It needs something more than going diligently to church, and receiving the Lord's Supper — to take our souls to Heaven. *Means* of grace, and *forms* of religion, are useful in their way — and God seldom does anything for His church without them. But let us beware of making shipwreck on the very lighthouse which helps to show the channel into the harbor! Once more I ask, "How do we do about our souls?"

(4) Let me ask, in the fourth place, WHETHER WE HAVE RECEIVED THE FORGIVENESS OF OUR SINS?

Few reasonable Englishmen would think of denying that they are sinners. Many perhaps would say that they are not as bad as others, and that they have not been so very wicked, and so forth. But few, I repeat, would pretend to say that they had always lived like angels, and never done, or said, or thought a wrong thing all their days. In short, all of us must confess that we are more or less "sinners," and, as sinners, are guilty before God; and, as guilty, we must be forgiven — or be lost and condemned forever at the last day. Now it is the glory of the Christian religion that it provides for us the very *forgiveness* that we need — full, free, perfect, eternal, and complete. It is a leading article in that well-known creed, which most Englishmen learn when they are children. They are taught to say, "I believe in the forgiveness of sins." This forgiveness of sins has been purchased for us by the eternal Son of

God, our Lord Jesus Christ. He has *purchased* it for us by coming into the world to be our Savior, and by living, dying, and rising again, as our Substitute, in our behalf. He has *bought* it for us at the price of His own most precious blood, by suffering in our place on the cross, and making satisfaction for our sins.

But this forgiveness, as great, and full, and glorious as it is — does not become the property of every man and woman as a matter of course. It is not a privilege which every member of a Church possesses, merely because he is a Churchman. It is a thing which each individual must receive for himself by his own personal faith, lay hold on by faith, appropriate by faith, and make his own by faith; or else, so far as he is concerned, Christ will have died in vain. "He who believes on the Son has everlasting life, and he who believes not the Son shall not see life — but the wrath of God abides on him" (John 3:36). No terms can be imagined more simple, and more suitable to man. As good old Latimer said in speaking of the matter of justification, "It is but believe — and have." It is only *faith* that is required; and faith is nothing more than the humble, heartfelt trust of the soul which desires to be saved. Jesus is able and willing to save; but man must come to Jesus and believe. All that believe are at once justified and forgiven: but without believing there is no forgiveness at all.

Now here is exactly the point, I am afraid, where multitudes of English people fail, and are in imminent danger of being lost forever. They know that there is no forgiveness of sin excepting in Christ Jesus. They can tell you that there is no Savior for sinners, no Redeemer, no Mediator, excepting Him who was born of the Virgin Mary, and was crucified under Pontius Pilate, dead, and buried. But here they stop, and get no further! They never come to the point of actually laying hold of Christ by faith, and becoming one with Christ and Christ in them. They can say, He is a Savior — but not *my* Savior; a Redeemer — but not *my*Redeemer; a Priest — but not *my* Priest; an Advocate — but not *my* Advocate: and so they live and die unforgiven! No wonder that Martin Luther said, "Many are lost because they cannot use *possessive pronouns.*"

When this is the state of many in this day, no one need wonder that I ask men whether they have received the forgiveness of sins. An eminent Christian lady once said, in her old age, "The beginning of eternal life in my soul, was a conversation I had with an old gentleman who came to visit my father when I was only a little girl. He took me by the hand one day and said, 'My dear child, my life is nearly over, and you will probably live many years after I am gone. But never forget two things. One is, that there is such a thing as having our sins forgiven while we live. The other is, that there is such a thing as knowing and feeling that we are forgiven.' I thank God I have never forgotten his words."

How is it with us? Let us not rest until we "know and feel", as the Prayer Book says, that we are forgiven. Once more let us ask, in the matter of forgiveness of sins, "How do we do?"

(5) Let me ask, in the fifth place, WHETHER WE KNOW ANYTHING BY EXPERIENCE OF CONVERSION TO GOD.

Without conversion there is no salvation. "Except you be converted, and become as little children — you shall never enter the kingdom of Heaven." — "Except a man be born again — he cannot see the kingdom of God." — "If any man have not the Spirit of Christ — he is none of His." — "If any man be in Christ — he is a new creature." (Matthew 18:3, John 3:3, Romans 8:9, 2 Corinthians 5:17)

We are all by nature so weak, so worldly, so earthly-minded, so inclined to sin — that without a *thorough change* we cannot serve God in life, and could not enjoy Him after death. Just as ducks, as soon as they are hatched, take naturally to water — so do children, as soon as they can do anything, take to selfishness, lying, and deceit; and none pray or love God, unless they are taught. High or low, rich or poor, gentle or simple, we all need a complete change — a change which is the special office of the Holy Spirit to give us. Call it what you please — new birth, regeneration, renewal, new creation, quickening, repentance — the thing must be had if we are to be saved; and if we have the thing — it will be *seen.*

Sense of *sin* and deep hatred of it,
faith in *Christ* and love to Him,
delight in *holiness* and longing after more of it,
love for *God's people,* and
distaste for the things of the *world* —
these, these are the *signs* and *evidences* which always accompany conversion. Myriads around us, it may be feared, know nothing about it. They are, in Scripture language, dead, and asleep, and blind, and unfit for the kingdom of God. Year after year, perhaps, they go on repeating the words of the creed, "I believe in the Holy Spirit;" but they are utterly ignorant of His changing operations on the inward man. Sometimes they flatter themselves they are born again, because they have been baptized, and go to church, and receive the Lord's Supper; while they are totally destitute of the marks of the new birth, as described by John in his first Epistle. And all this time the words of Scripture are clear and plain — "Except you be converted, you shall in no case enter the kingdom." (Matthew 18:3).

In times like these, no reader ought to wonder that I press the subject of conversion on men's souls. No doubt there are plenty of *sham conversions* in such a day of religious excitement as this. But bad coin is no proof that there is no good money: no, rather it is a sign that there is some money current which is valuable, and is worth imitation. Hypocrites and sham Christians are indirect evidence that there is such a thing as real grace among men. Let us search our own hearts then, and see how it is with ourselves. Once more let us ask, in the matter of conversion, "How do we do?"

(6) Let me ask, in the sixth place, WHETHER WE KNOW ANYTHING OF PRACTICAL CHRISTIAN HOLINESS?

It is as certain as anything in the Bible, that "without holiness no one will see the Lord" (Hebrews 12:14). It is equally certain that holiness is . . . .
the invariable fruit of saving faith,
the real test of regeneration,
the only sound evidence of indwelling grace,
the certain consequence of vital union with Christ.

Holiness is not absolute perfection and freedom from all faults. Nothing of the kind! The wild words of some who talk of enjoying "unbroken communion with God for many months," are greatly to be deprecated, because they raise unscriptural expectations in the minds of young believers, and so do harm. *Absolute perfection* is for Heaven, and not for earth, where we have a weak body, a wicked world, and a busy devil continually near our souls. Nor is real Christian holiness ever attained, or maintained — without a constant fight and struggle. The great Apostle, who said "I fight — I labor — I keep under my body and bring it into subjection" (1 Corinthians 9:27), would have been amazed to hear of *sanctification without personal exertion,* and to be told that believers only need to sit still, and everything will be done for them!

Yet, as weak and imperfect as the holiness of the best saints may be, it is a real true thing, and has a character about it as unmistakable as light and salt. It is not a thing which begins and ends with noisy profession — it will be *seen* much more than *heard.* Genuine Scriptural holiness will make a man do his duty at home and by the fireside, and adorn his doctrine in the little trials of daily life. It will exhibit itself in *passive* graces — as well as in *active.* It will make a man humble, kind, gentle, unselfish, good-tempered, considerate of others, loving, meek, and forgiving. It will not constrain him to go out of the world, and shut himself up in a cave, like a hermit. But it will make him do his duty in that state to which God has called him, on Christian principles, and after the pattern of Christ.

Such holiness, I know well, is not common. It is a style of *practical Christianity* which is painfully rare in these days. But I can find no other standard of holiness in the Word of God — no other which comes up to the pictures drawn by our Lord and His Apostles. In an age like this, no reader can wonder if I press this subject also on men's attention. Once more let us ask — In the matter of holiness, how is it with our souls? "How do we do?"

(7) Let me ask, in the seventh place, WHETHER WE KNOW ANYTHING OF ENJOYING THE MEANS OF GRACE?

When I speak of the means of grace, I have in my mind's eye, five principal things:
the reading of the Bible,
private prayer,
public worship,
the sacrament of the Lord's Supper,
and the rest of the Lord's day.

They are *means* which God has graciously appointed in order to convey grace to man's heart by the Holy Spirit, or to keep up the spiritual life after it has begun. As long as the world stands, the state of a man's soul will always depend greatly on the *manner* and *spirit* in which he uses means of grace. The manner and spirit, I say deliberately and of purpose. Many English people use the means of grace regularly and formally — but know nothing of *enjoying* them: they attend to them as a matter of *duty* — but without a jot of feeling, interest, or affection. Yet even common sense might tell us that this *formal*, mechanical use of holy things — is utterly worthless and unprofitable. Our feeling about them is just one of the many tests of the state of our souls.

How can that man be thought to love God — who reads about Him and His Christ as a mere matter of duty, content and satisfied if he has just moved his bookmark onward over so many chapters? How can that man suppose he is ready to meet Christ — who never takes any trouble to pour out his heart to Him in private as a Friend, and is satisfied with saying over a string of words every morning and evening, under the name of "prayer", scarcely thinking what he is about? How could that man be happy in Heaven forever — who finds Sunday a dull, gloomy, tiresome day — who knows nothing of hearty prayer and praise, and cares nothing whether he hears truth or error from the pulpit, or scarcely listens to the sermon? What can be the spiritual condition of that man whose heart never "burns within him," when he receives that bread and wine which specially remind us of Christ's death on the cross, and the atonement for sin?

These inquiries are very serious and important. If *means of grace* had no other use, and were not mighty helps toward Heaven — they would be useful in supplying a test of our real state in the sight of God. Tell me what a man does in the matter of Bible reading and praying, in the matter of public worship and the Lord's Supper — and I will soon tell you what he is, and on which road he is traveling. How is it with ourselves? Once more let us ask — In the matter of means of grace, "How do we do?"

(8) Let me ask, in the eighth place, WHETHER WE EVER TRY TO DO ANY GOOD IN THE WORLD?

Our Lord Jesus Christ was continually "going around doing good," while He was on earth (Acts 10:38). The Apostles, and all the disciples in Bible times, were always striving to walk in His steps. A Christian who was content to go to Heaven himself and cared not what became of others, whether they lived happy and died in peace or not — would have been regarded as a kind of *monster* in primitive times, who did not have the Spirit of Christ. Why should we suppose for a moment that a lower standard will suffice in the present day? Why should fig trees which bear no fruit be spared in the present day, when in our Lord's time they were to be cut down as "cumberers of the ground"? (Luke 13:7). These are serious inquiries, and demand serious answers.

There is a generation of professing Christians now-a-days, who seem to know nothing of caring for their neighbors, and are completely swallowed up in the concerns of *number one* — that is, their own and their family's. They eat, and drink, and sleep, and dress, and work, and earn money, and spend money, year after year; and whether others are happy or miserable, well or ill, converted or unconverted, traveling towards Heaven or toward Hell — appear to be questions about which they are totally indifferent. Can this be right? Can it be reconciled with the religion of Him who spoke the parable of the good Samaritan, and bade us "go and do likewise"? (Luke 10:37). I doubt it altogether.

There is much to be done everywhere. There is not a place in England where there is not a field for work and an open door for being useful — if anyone is willing to enter it. There is not a Christian in England who cannot find some good work to do for others, if he has only a heart to do it. The poorest man or woman, without a single penny to give, can always show his deep sympathy to the sick and sorrowful, and by *simple good-nature* and *tender helpfulness,* can lessen the misery and increase the comfort of somebody in this troubled world. But alas, the vast majority of professing Christians, whether rich or poor, Churchmen or Dissenters — seem possessed with a devil of detestable *selfishness*, and do not know *the luxury of doing good.* They can argue by the hour about baptism, and the Lord's supper, and the forms of worship, and the union of Church and State, and such-like *dry-bone* questions. But all this time they seem to care nothing for their neighbors. The plain practical point, whether they love their neighbor, as the Samaritan loved the unfortunate traveler in the parable, and can spare any time and trouble to do him good — is a point they never touch with one of their fingers.

In too many English parishes, both in town and country, true love seems almost dead, both in church and chapel — and wretched *party-spirit* and *controversy* are the only fruits that Christianity appears able to produce. In a day like this, no reader should wonder if I press this plain old subject on his conscience. Do we know anything of genuine *Samaritan love* to others? Do we ever try to do any good to any one beside our own friends and relatives, and our and our own party or cause? Are we living like disciples of Him who always "went about doing good," and commanded His disciples to take Him for their "example"? (John 13:15). If not, with what face shall we meet Him in the judgment day? In this matter also, how is it with our souls? Once more I ask, "How do we do?"

(9) Let me ask, in the ninth place, WHETHER WE KNOW ANYTHING OF LIVING THE LIFE OF HABITUAL COMMUNION WITH CHRIST?

By "communion," I mean that habit of "abiding in Christ" which our Lord speaks of, in the fifteenth chapter of John's Gospel, as essential to Christian fruitfulness (John 15:4-8). Let it be distinctly understood that *union* with Christ is one thing — and *communion* is another thing. There can be no communion with the Lord Jesus without union first; but unhappily there may be union with the Lord Jesus, and afterwards little or no communion at all. The difference between the two things is not the difference between two distinct steps — but the higher and lower ends of an inclined plane.

Union is the common privilege of all who feel their sins, and truly repent, and come to Christ by faith, and are accepted, forgiven, and justified in Him. Too many believers, it may be feared, never get beyond this stage!

Partly from ignorance,
partly from laziness,
partly from the fear of man,
partly from secret love of the world,
partly from some unmortified besetting sin
— they are content with a little faith, and a little hope, and a little peace, and a little measure of holiness. And they live on all their lives in this condition — doubting, weak, hesitant, and bearing fruit only "thirty-fold" to the very end of their days!

Communion with Christ is the privilege of those who are continually striving to grow in grace, and faith, and knowledge, and conformity to the mind of Christ in all things — who "forget what is behind," and "do not consider themselves yet to have taken hold of it — but "press on toward the goal to win the prize for which God has called me heavenward in Christ Jesus." (Philippians 3:13-14)

Union is the bud — but communion is the flower.
Union is the baby — but communion is the strong man.

He who has union with Christ does well; but he who enjoys communion with Him does far better. Both have one life, one hope, one heavenly seed in their hearts — one Lord, one Savior, one Holy Spirit, one eternal home: but union is not as good as communion!

The grand secret of communion with Christ is to be continually "living the life of faith in Him," and drawing out of Him every hour, the supply that every hour requires. To me, said Paul, "to live is Christ." "I live: yet not I — but Christ lives in me!" (Galatians 2:20; Philippians 1:21). Communion like this, is the secret of the abiding "joy and peace in believing," which eminent saints like Bradford and Rutherford notoriously possessed. None were ever more humble, or more deeply convinced of their own infirmities and corruption. They would have told you that the seventh chapter of Romans precisely described their own experience. They would have said continually, "The remembrance of our sins is grievous to us; the burden of them is intolerable."

But they were ever looking unto Jesus, and in Him they were ever able to rejoice. Communion like this is the secret of the splendid victories which such men as these won over sin, the world, and the fear of death. They did not sit still idly, saying, "I leave it all to Christ to do for me," but, strong in the Lord, they used the Divine nature He had implanted in them, boldly and confidently, and were "more than conquerors through Him who loved them." (Romans 8:37). Like Paul, they would have said, "I can do all things through Christ who strengthens me." (Philippians 4:13).

Ignorance of this *life of communion* is one among many reasons why so many in this age are hankering after the Confessional, and strange views of the "real presence" in the Lord's Supper. Such errors often spring from imperfect knowledge of Christ, and obscure views of the life of faith in a risen, living, and interceding Savior. Is communion with Christ like this a common thing? Alas! It is very rare indeed! The greater part of believers seem content with the barest elementary knowledge of justification by faith, and half-a-dozen other doctrines — and go doubting, limping, halting, groaning along the way to Heaven, and experience little of the sense of victory or of joy.

The Churches of these latter days are full of weak, powerless, and uninfluential believers, saved at last, "but so as by fire," but never shaking the world, and knowing nothing of an "abundant entrance." (1 Corinthians 3:15; 2 Peter 1:11). *Despondency* and *Feeble-mind* and *Much-afraid*, in "Pilgrim's Progress," reached the celestial city as really and truly as V*aliant-for-the-truth* and *Great-heart*. But they certainly did not reach it with the same comfort, and did not do a tenth part of the same good in the world! I fear there are many like them in these days! When things are so in the Churches, no reader can wonder that I inquire how it is with our souls. Once more I ask — In the matter of communion with Christ, "How do we do?

(10) Let me ask, in the tenth and last place, WHETHER WE KNOW ANYTHING OF BEING READY FOR CHRIST'S SECOND COMING?

That He will come again the second time, is as certain as anything

in the Bible. The world has not yet seen the last of Him. As surely as He went up visibly and in the body on the Mount of Olives before the eyes of His disciples — so surely will he come again in the clouds of Heaven, with power and great glory (Acts 1:11). He will come . . .
to raise the dead,
to change the living,
to reward His saints,
to punish the wicked,
to renew the earth, and take the curse away,
to purify the world —
and to set up a kingdom where sin shall have no place, and holiness shall be the universal rule.

The early Christians made it a part of their religion to look for His return.

Backward they looked to the *cross* and the atonement for sin, and rejoiced in Christ crucified.

Upward they looked to Christ at the right hand of God, and rejoiced in Christ interceding.

Forward they looked to the promised return of their Master, and rejoiced in the thought that they would see Him again.

And we ought to do the same. What have we really *received* from Christ? And what do we *know* of Him? And what do we *think* of Him? Are we living as if we long to see Him again, and love His appearing? Readiness for that appearing is nothing more than being a real, consistent Christian. It requires no man to cease from his daily business. The *farmer* need not give up his farm, nor the *shopkeeper* his counter, nor the *doctor* his patients, nor the *carpenter* his hammer and nails, nor the *bricklayer* his mortar and trowel, nor the *blacksmith* his smithy. Each and all can do no better than be found doing his duty — but doing it as a Christian, and with a heart packed up and ready to be gone. In the face of truth like this no reader can feel surprised if I ask, How is it with our souls in the matter of Christ's second coming?

The world is growing old and running to seed. The vast majority of Christians seem like the men in the time of Noah and Lot, who were eating and drinking, marrying and giving in marriage, planting and building, up to the very day when flood and fire came. Those words of our Master are very solemn and heart-searching, "Remember Lot's wife." "Take heed lest at any time your heart be overcharged with the cares of this life, and that day come upon you unawares." (Luke 17:32; 21:34). Once more I ask — In the matter of readiness for Christ's second coming, "How are we doing?

I end my *inquiries* here. I might easily add to them; but I trust I have said enough, at the beginning of this volume, to stir up self-inquiry and self-inquiry and self-examination in many minds. God is my witness that I have said nothing that I do not feel of paramount importance to my own soul. I only want to do good to others.

Let me now conclude all with a few words of **Practical Application**.

(A) IS ANY READER OF THIS PAPER ASLEEP AND UTTERLY THOUGHTLESS ABOUT CHRISTIANITY?

Oh, awake and sleep no more! Look at the churchyards and cemeteries. One by one the people around you are dropping into them — and *you* must lie there one day. Look forward to a world to come, and lay your hand on your heart, and say, if you dare, that you ready to die and meet God. Ah! You are like one sleeping in a boat drifting down the stream towards the falls of Niagara! "What do you mean, oh sleeper! Arise and call on your God!" "Awake you that sleep, and arise from the dead, and Christ shall give you light!" (Jonah 1:6; Ephesians 5:14).

(B) IS ANY READER OF THIS PAPER FEELING SELF-CONDEMNED, AND AFRAID THAT THERE IS NO HOPE FOR HIS SOUL?

Cast aside your fears, and accept the offer of our Lord Jesus Christ to sinners. Hear Him saying, "Come unto me, all you who labor and are heavy laden, and I will give you rest." (Matthew 11:28). "If any man thirsts — let him come unto me and drink." (John 7:37). Him that comes unto me — I will never cast out." (John 6:37).

Do not doubt that these words are for you as well as for anyone else. Bring all your sins, and unbelief, and sense of guilt, and unfitness, and doubts, and infirmities — bring all to Christ! "This man receives sinners," and He will receive you (Luke 15:2). Do not stand still, wavering between two opinions, and waiting for a convenient season. On your feet! He's calling you. Come to Christ this very day (Mark 10:49).

(C) IS ANY READER OF THIS PAPER A PROFESSING BELIEVER IN CHRIST — BUT A BELIEVER WITHOUT MUCH JOY AND PEACE AND COMFORT?

Take advice this day. Search your own heart, and see whether the fault is not entirely your own. Very likely you are sitting at ease, content with a little faith, and a little repentance, a little grace, and a little sanctification — and unconsciously shrinking back from extremes. You will never be a very happy Christian at this rate, if you live to the age of Methuselah. Change your plan, if you love life and would see good days, without delay. Come out boldly, and act decidedly. Be thorough, thorough, very through in your Christianity, and set your face fully towards the sun. Lay aside every weight, and the sin that so easily besets you. Strive to get nearer to Christ, to abide in Him, to cleave to Him, and to sit at His feet like Mary, and drink full draughts out of the fountain of life. "These things," says John, "we write unto you, that your joy may be full." (1 John 1:4). "If we walk in the light, as He is in the light, we have fellowship with one another." (1 John 1:7).

(D) IS ANY READER OF THIS PAPER A BELIEVER OPPRESSED WITH DOUBTS AND FEARS, ON ACCOUNT OF HIS FEEBLENESS, INFIRMITY, AND SENSE OF SIN?

Remember the text that says of Jesus, "A bruised reed will He not break, and smoking flax shall he not quench." (Matthew 12:20). Take comfort in the thought that this text is for you. What though your faith is weak? It is better than no faith at all. The least grain of life is better than death. Perhaps you are expecting too much in this world. Earth is not Heaven. You are yet in the body. Expect little from self — but much from Christ. Look more to Jesus — and less to self.

(D) FINALLY, IS ANY READER OF THIS PAPER SOMETIMES DOWNCAST BY THE TRIALS HE MEETS WITH ON THE WAY TO HEAVEN — BODILY TRIALS, FAMILY TRIALS, TRIALS OF CIRCUMSTANCES, TRIALS FROM NEIGHBORS, AND TRIALS FROM THE WORLD?

Look up to a sympathizing Savior at God's right hand, and pour out your heart before Him. He can be touched with the feelings of your trials, for He Himself suffered when He was tempted. Are you alone? So was He. Are you misrepresented and slandered? So was He. Are you forsaken by friends? So was He. Are you persecuted? So was He. Are you wearied in body and grieved in spirit? So was He. Yes! He can *feel* for you, and He can *help* as well as feel. Then learn to draw nearer to Christ. The time is short. Yet in a little while, and all will be over: we shall soon be "with the Lord". "There is an end, and your expectation shall not be cut off." (Proverbs 23:18). "You have need of patience, that, after you have done the will of God, you might receive the promise. For yet a little while, and He who shall come will come and will not tarry." (Hebrews 10:36-37).

SELF-EXERTION

*"**Strive** to enter in at the narrow gate: for many, I say unto you, will seek to enter in, and shall not be able!"* Luke 13:24

There was once a man who asked our Lord Jesus Christ a very deep question. He said to Him, *"Lord, are there few that will be saved?"*

Who this man was, we do not know. What his *motive* was for asking this question, we are not told. Perhaps he wished to gratify an idle curiosity; perhaps he wanted an excuse for not seeking salvation himself. The Holy Spirit has kept back all this from us — the name and motive of the inquirer are both hidden.

But one thing is very clear, and that is the vast importance of the saying of our Lord to which the question gave rise. Jesus seized the opportunity to direct the minds of all around Him to their own plain duty. He knew the train of thought which the man's inquiry had set moving in their hearts: He saw what was going on within them. "Strive," He cries, "to enter in at the narrow gate!" Whether there be few saved or many, your course is clear — strive to enter in. Now is the accepted time. Now is the day of salvation. A day shall come when many will seek to enter in and shall not be able. "Strive to enter in *now*."

I desire to call the serious attention of all who read this paper to the *solemn lessons* which this saying of the Lord Jesus is meant to teach. It is one which deserves special remembrance in the present day. It teaches unmistakably that mighty truth — our own personal responsibility for the salvation of our souls. It shows the immense danger of putting off the great business of religion, as so many unhappily do. On both these points, the witness of our Lord Jesus Christ in the text is clear. He, who is the eternal God, and who spoke the words of perfect wisdom, says to the sons of men, "Strive to enter in at the narrow gate — for many, I say unto you, will seek to enter in, and shall not be able!"

(I) Here is *a description* of the way of salvation. Jesus calls it "the narrow gate."

(II) Here is a plain *command*. Jesus says, "Strive to enter in."

(III) Here is an solemn *prophecy*. Jesus says, "Many will seek to enter in, and shall not be able."

May the Holy Spirit apply the subject to the hearts of all into whose hands this paper may fall! May all who read it *know* the way of salvation experimentally, *obey* the command of the Lord practically, and be found *safe* in the great day of His second coming!

I. Here is *a description* of the way of salvation. Jesus calls it "*the narrow gate.*"

There is a gate which leads to pardon, peace with God, and Heaven. Whoever goes in by that gate, shall be saved. Never, surely, was a gate more needed. Sin is a *vast mountain* between man and God. How shall a man climb over it? Sin is a *high wall* between man and God. How shall man get through it? Sin is a *deep gulf* between man and God. How shall man cross over it? *God* is in Heaven — holy, pure, spiritual, undefiled, light without any darkness at all — a Being who cannot bear that which is evil, or look upon iniquity. *Man* is a poor fallen worm, crawling on earth for a few years — sinful, corrupt, erring, defective — a being whose imagination is only evil, and whose heart is deceitful above all things, and desperately wicked. *How shall man and God be brought together?* How shall man ever draw near to his Maker without fear and shame? Blessed be God, there is a way! There is a road. There is a path. There is a door. It is the *gate* spoken of in the words of Christ, "the narrow gate."

This gate was *made for sinners by the Lord Jesus Christ.* From all eternity He covenanted and engaged that He would make it. In the fullness of time He came into the world and made it, by His own atoning death on the cross. By that death He made satisfaction for man's sin, paid man's debt to God, and bore man's punishment. He built a great gate at the cost of His own body and blood. He reared a ladder on earth whose top reached to Heaven. He made a door by which the chief of sinners may enter into the holy presence of God, and not be afraid. He opened a road by which the vilest of men, believing in Him, may draw near to God and have peace. He cries to us, "I am the door: by Me if any man enter in, he shall be saved." (John 10:9.) "I am the way: no man comes unto the Father but by Me." (John 14:6.) "By Him," says Paul, "we have boldness and access with confidence." (Ephesians 3:12.) Thus was the gate of salvation formed.

This gate is called *the narrow gate,* and it is not called so without cause. It is always narrow, and difficult to pass through to some people, and it will be so as long as the world stands. It is narrow to all who *love sin* — and are determined not to part with it. It is narrow to all who set their affection on this *world* — and seek first its pleasures and rewards. It is narrow to all who dislike *trouble* — and are unwilling to take pains and make sacrifices for their souls. It is narrow to all who like *company* — and want to keep in with the crowd. It is narrow to all who are *self-righteous* — and think they are good people, and deserve to be saved. To all such, the great gate which Christ made, is narrow and strait. In vain they seek to pass through. The gate will not admit them. God is not unwilling to receive them; their sins are not too many to be forgiven: but they are not willing to be *saved in God's way.*

Thousands, for the last eighteen centuries, have tried to make the gate *wider!* Thousands have worked and toiled to get to Heaven on lower terms. But the gate never alters. It is not elastic — it will not stretch to accommodate one man more than another. It is still the *narrow* gate.

As narrow as this gate is, it is *the only one by which men can get to Heaven.* There is no side door; there is no bye-path; there is no gap or low-place in the wall. All who are ever saved — will he saved only by Christ, and only by simple faith in Him. Not one will be saved by *repentance.* Today's sorrow, does not wipe off yesterday's sin. Not one will be saved by his own *works.* The best works that any man can do — are little better than *splendid sins.* Not one will be saved by his formal regularity in the use of the outward means of grace. When we have done all — we are poor "unprofitable servants." Oh, no! it is mere waste of time to seek any other road to eternal life.

Men may look right and left, and weary themselves with their own devices — but they will never find another door. *Proud* men may dislike the gate if they will. *Profligate* men may scoff at it, and make a jest of those who use it. *Lazy* men may complain that the way is hard. But men will discover no other salvation than that of faith in the blood and righteousness of a crucified Redeemer. There stands between us and Heaven, one great gate: it may be narrow; but it is the only one. We must either enter Heaven by the narrow gate — or not at all.

As narrow as this gate is, it is *a gate ever ready to open.* No sinners of any kind are forbidden to draw near: whoever will, may enter in and be saved. There is but one condition of admission: that condition is that you really feel your sins and desire to be saved by Christ in His own way. Are you really sensible of your guilt and vileness? Have you a truly broken and contrite heart? Behold the gate of salvation — and come in! He who made it declares, "Him that comes unto Me, I will never cast out." (John 6:37.)

The question to be considered is not whether you are a *great* sinner or a *little* sinner — whether you are elect or not — whether you are converted or not. The question is simply this, "Do you feel your sins? Do you feel laboring and heavy-laden? Are you willing to put your soul into Christ's hand?" Then if that is the case, the gate will open to you at once. Come in this very day. "Why do you stand outside?" (Genesis 24:31.)

As narrow as this gate is, it is *one through which thousands have gone in and been saved.* No sinner was ever turned back, and told he was too bad to be admitted, if he came really sick of his sins. Thousands of all sorts have been received, cleansed, washed, pardoned, clothed, and made heirs of eternal life. Some of them seemed very unlikely to be admitted: you and I might have thought that they were too bad to be saved. But He who built the gate did not refuse them. As soon as they knocked — He gave orders that they should be let in.

Manasseh, the wicked King of Judah, went up to this gate. None could have been worse than he. He had despised his good father Hezekiah's example and advice. He had bowed down to idols. He had filled Jerusalem with bloodshed and cruelty. He had slain his own children. But as soon as his eyes were opened to his sins, and he fled to the gate for pardon — the gate flew wide open, and he was saved.

Saul the Pharisee went up to this gate. He had been a great offender. He had been a blasphemer of Christ, and a persecutor of Christ's people. He had labored hard to stop the progress of the Gospel. But as soon as his heart was touched, and he found out his own guilt and fled to the gate for pardon — at once the gate flew wide open, and he was saved.

Many of the *Jews* who crucified our Lord went up to this gate. They had been grievous sinners indeed. They had refused and rejected their own Messiah. They had delivered Him to Pilate, and entreated that He might be slain. They had desired Barabbas to be released, and the Son of God to be crucified. But in the day when they were pricked to the heart by Peter's preaching — they fled to the gate for pardon, and at once the gate flew open, and they were saved.

The *jailer* at Philippi went up to this gate. He had been a cruel, hard, godless man. He had done all in his power to ill-treat Paul and his companion. He had thrust them into the inner prison, and made their feet fast in the stocks. But when his conscience was aroused by the earthquake, and his mind enlightened by Paul's teaching — he fled to the gate for pardon, and at once the gate flew open, and he was saved.

But why need I stop short in Bible examples? Multitudes have gone to "the narrow gate "since the days of the Apostles, and have entered in by it and been saved! Thousands of all ranks, classes, and ages — learned and unlearned, rich and poor, old and young — have tried the gate and found it ready to open — have gone through it and found peace to their souls. Yes, thousands of people yet living have made proof of the gate, and found it the way to real happiness. Noblemen and commoners, merchants and bankers, soldiers and sailors, farmers and tradesmen, laborers and workmen, are still upon earth, who have found the narrow gate to be "a way of pleasantness and a path of peace." They have found Christ's yoke to be easy, and His burden to be light. Their only regret has been that so few enter in, and that they themselves did not enter in before.

This is the gate which I want every one to enter, into whose hand this paper may fall. I want you not merely to go to church or chapel — but to go with heart and soul to the *gate of life*. I want you not merely to believe there is such a gate, and to think it a good thing — but to enter by faith and be saved.

Think *what a privilege* it is to have a gate at all. The *angels*, who kept not their first estate — fell, never to rise again. To them there was no door of escape opened. The *heathen* never heard of any way to eternal life. What would not many a black man and many a red man give, if he only heard one plain sermon about Christ? The *Jews* in Old Testament times only saw the gate dimly and far away. "The way into the holiest was not made manifest, while the first tabernacle was standing." (Hebrews 9:8.)

But you have the gate set plainly before you — you have Christ and full salvation offered to you, without money and without price. You never need be at a loss which way to turn. Oh, consider what a mercy this is! Beware that you do not *despise* the gate and *perish* in unbelief! Better a thousand times not to know of the gate — than to know of it and yet tarry outside! How indeed will you escape — if you neglect so great salvation?

Think *what a thankful man* you ought to be if you have really gone in at the narrow gate. To be a pardoned, forgiven, justified soul — to be ready for sickness, death, judgment and eternity — to be ever provided for in both worlds — surely this is matter for daily praise. True Christians ought to be more full of thanksgivings than they are. I fear that few sufficiently remember what they were by nature, and what *debtors to grace* they are. Singing hymns of praise, was one special mark of the early Christians. Well would it be for Christians in the present day, if they knew more of this frame of mind. It is no mark of a healthy state of soul, when there is much complaining and little praise. It is an amazing mercy that there is any gate of salvation at all; but it is a still greater mercy when we are taught to enter in by it and be saved.

II. In the second place, here is a plain *command*. Jesus says to us, "*Strive to enter in at the narrow gate.*" There is often much to be learned in a single word of Scripture. The words of our Lord Jesus in particular, are always full of matter for thought. Here is a word which is a striking example of what I mean. Let us see what the great Teacher would have us gather out of the word *"Strive."*

"STRIVE" teaches that a man must use *means* diligently, if he would have his soul saved. There are means which God has appointed to help man in his endeavors to approach Him. There are ways in which a man must walk, if he desires to be found of Christ. Public worship, reading the Bible, hearing the Gospel preached — these are the kind of things to which I refer. They lie, as it were, in the middle, between man and God. Doubtless no one can change his own heart, or wipe away one of his sins, or make himself in the least degree acceptable to God; but I do say that if man could do nothing but sit still — Christ would never have said "Strive."

"STRIVE" teaches that man is a free agent, and will be dealt with by God as a responsible being. The Lord Jesus does not bid us to wait, and wish, and feel, and hope, and desire. He says, "Strive." I call that miserable religion, which teaches people to be content with saying, "We can do nothing of ourselves," and makes them continue in sin. It is as bad as teaching people that it is not their fault if they are not converted, and that God only is to blame if they are not saved. I find no such theology in the New Testament. I hear Jesus saying to sinners, "Come — repent — believe — labor — ask — seek — knock." I see plainly that our *salvation*, from first to last — is entirely *of God*. But I see with no less plainness that our *ruin*, if lost — is wholly and entirely *of ourselves*. I maintain that sinners are always addressed as accountable and responsible; and I need no better proof of this than is contained in the word "Strive."

"STRIVE" teaches that a man must expect many *adversaries* and a hard *battle* — if he would have his soul saved. And this, as a matter of experience, is strictly true. There are no "gains without pains" in spiritual things — any more than in temporal things. That roaring lion, the *devil* — will never let a soul escape from him without a struggle. The *heart* which is naturally sensual and earthly — will never be turned to spiritual things without a daily fight. The *world*, with all its opposition and temptations — will never be overcome without a conflict.

But why should all this surprise us? What great and good thing was ever done without trouble?

Wheat does not grow without ploughing and sowing;
riches are not obtained without care and attention;
success in life is not won without hardships and toil; and *Heaven*, above all, is not to be reached without the cross and the battle. The "violent take the kingdom by force." (Matt 11:12.) A man must "strive."

"STRIVE" teaches that it is worth while for a man to seek salvation. That may well be said. If there is anything that deserves a struggle in this world — it is the prosperity of the soul. The objects for which the great majority of men strive are comparatively *poor* and *trifling* things. Riches, and greatness, and rank, and learning, are "a corruptible crown." The *incorruptible* things are all within the narrow gate. The peace of God which passes all understanding — the bright hope of good things to come — the sense of the Spirit dwelling in us — the consciousness that we are pardoned, safe, ready, insured, provided for in time and eternity, whatever may happen — these are *true gold*, and *durable riches*. Well may the Lord Jesus call on us to "strive."

"STRIVE" teaches that *laziness in religion* is a great sin. It is not merely a misfortune, as some imagine — a thing for which people are to be pitied, and a matter for regret. It is something far more than this. It is a breach of a plain commandment. What shall be said of the man who transgresses God's law, and does something which God clearly forbids? There can be but one answer. He is a sinner. "Sin is the transgression of the law." (1 John 3:4.) And what shall be said of the man who neglects his soul, and makes no effort to enter the narrow gate? There can be only one reply. He is omitting a positive duty. Christ says to him, "Strive" — and behold, he sits still.

"STRIVE" teaches that all who are outside the narrow gate are in great danger! They are in danger of being lost forever. There is but a step between them and death! If death finds them in their present condition — they will eternally perish without hope. The Lord Jesus saw that clearly. He knew the uncertainty of life and the shortness of time: He would gladly have sinners make haste and delay not, lest they put off soul-business too late. He speaks as one who saw the devil drawing near to them daily, and the days of their life gradually ebbing away. He would have them take heed they be not too late: therefore He cries, "Strive."

That word "Strive," raises solemn thoughts in my mind. It is brimful of condemnation for thousands of *baptized* people. It condemns the ways and practices of multitudes who profess and call themselves Christians. Many there are who neither swear, nor murder, nor commit adultery, nor steal, nor lie; but one thing unhappily cannot be said of them: they cannot be said to "strive" to be saved. The "spirit of slumber" possesses their hearts in everything that concerns religion. About the things of the world — they are active enough: they rise early, and late take rest; they labor; they toil; they are busy; they are careful. But about the *one thing needful* — they never "strive" at all.

What shall I say of those who are irregular about public worship on Sundays? There are thousands all over Great Britain who answer this description. Sometimes, if they feel disposed, they go to some church or chapel, and attend a religious service; at other times they stay at home and read the paper, or idle about, or look over their accounts, or seek some amusement. *Is this "striving"?* I speak to men of common sense. Let them judge what I say.

What shall I say of those who come regularly to a place of worship — but come entirely as a matter of form? There are many in every parish of Great Britain in this condition. Their fathers taught them to come; their custom has always been to come: it would not be respectable to stay away. But they care nothing for the worship of God when they do come. Whether they hear law or Gospel, truth or error — it is all the same to them. They remember nothing afterwards. They put off their *form of religion* with their Sunday clothes, and return to the world. And *is this "striving"?* I speak to men of common sense. Let them judge what I say.

What shall I say of those who seldom or never read the Bible? There are thousands of people, I fear, who answer this description. They know the Book by name; they know it is commonly regarded as the only Book which teaches us how to live and how to die — but they can never find time for reading it! Newspapers, reviews, novels, romances, they can read — but not the Bible! And *is this "striving"* to enter in? I speak to men of common sense. Let them judge what I say.

What shall I say of those who never pray? There are multitudes, I firmly believe, in this condition. Without God they rise in the morning, and without God they lie down at night. They *ask* nothing; they *confess* nothing; they return *thanks* for nothing; they *seek* nothing. They are all dying creatures — and yet they are not even on speaking terms with their Maker and their Judge! And *is this striving"?* I speak to men of common sense. Let them judge what I say.

It is a solemn thing to be a *minister* of the Gospel. It is a painful thing to look on, and notice the ways of mankind in spiritual matters. We hold in our hands that great statute Book of God, which declares that without repentance, and conversion, and faith in Christ, and holiness — no man living can be saved. In discharge of our office, we urge on men to repent, believe, and be saved; but, alas, how frequently we have to lament that our labor seems all in vain. Men attend our churches, and listen, and approve — but do not "strive" to be saved.

We show the *sinfulness of sin*;
we unfold the *loveliness of Christ*;
we expose the *vanity of the world*;
we set forth the *happiness of Christ's service*;
we offer the *living water* to the wearied and heavy laden sons of toil — but, alas, how often we seem to speak to the winds! Our words are patiently heard on Sundays; our arguments are not refuted: but we see plainly in the week that men are not "striving" to be saved. There comes the *devil* on Monday morning — and offers his countless snares; there comes the *world* — and holds out its seeming prizes: our hearers follow them greedily. They work hard for this world's goods; they toil at Satan's bidding! But for the *one thing needful* they will not "strive" at all!

I am not writing from hearsay. I speak what I have *seen*. I write down the result of thirty-seven years experience in the ministry. I have learned lessons about human nature during that period which I never knew before. I have seen how true are our Lord's words about the *narrow way*. I have discovered how few there are that "strive" to be saved.

Earnestness about *temporal* matters is common enough. Striving to be *rich* and *prosperous* in this world is not rare at all. Pains about *money*, and *business*, and *politics* — pains about *trade*, and *science*, and *fine arts*, and *amusements* — pains about *rent*, and *wages*, and *labor*, and *land* — pains about such matters I see in abundance both in town and country! But I see few who take pains about their souls. I see few anywhere who "strive" to enter in at the narrow gate!

I am not surprised at all this. I read in the Bible that it is only what I am to expect. The parable of the *great supper* is an exact picture of things that I have seen with my own eyes ever since I became a minister. (Luke 14:16.) I find, as my Lord and Savior tells me, that "men make excuse." One has his piece of *land* to see; another has his *oxen* to prove; a third has his *family* hindrances. But all this does not prevent my feeling deeply grieved for the souls of men. I grieve to think that they should have eternal life so close to them — and yet be lost because they will not "strive" to enter in and be saved.

I know not in what state of soul many readers of this paper may be. But I warn you to take heed that you do not perish forever for lack of "striving." Do not suppose that it needs some *great scarlet sin* to bring you to the pit of eternal destruction! You have only to sit still and do nothing — and you will find yourself there at last. Yes! Satan does not ask you to walk in the steps of Cain, and Pharaoh, and Ahab, and Belshazzar, and Judas Iscariot. There is another road to Hell quite as sure — the road of spiritual indolence, spiritual laziness, and spiritual sloth! Satan has no objection to your being a respectable member of the Christian Church. He will let you pay your tithes; he will allow you to sit comfortably in church every Sunday you live. He knows full well, that so long as you do not "strive" — that you must come at last to the worm that never dies, and the fire that is never quenched. Take heed that you do not come to this end. I repeat it, *you have only to do nothing — and you will be eternally lost!*

If you have been taught to "strive" for your soul's prosperity, I entreat you never to suppose you can go too far. Never give way to the idea that you are taking too much trouble about your spiritual condition, and that there is no need for so much carefulness. Settle it rather in your mind that "in all labor there is profit," and that no labor is so profitable as that bestowed on the soul. It is a maxim among good farmers that the more they do for the land — the more the land does for them. I am sure it should be a maxim among Christians that the more they do for their religion — the more their religion will do for them. Watch against the slightest inclination to be careless about any means of grace. Beware of shortening your prayers, your Bible reading, your private communion with God. Take heed that you do not give way to a thoughtless, lazy manner of using the public services of God's house. Fight against any rising disposition to be sleepy, critical, and fault-finding, while you listen to the preaching of the Gospel. Whatever you do for God — do it with all your heart and mind and strength. In other things be moderate — and dread running into extremes. In soul matters fear *moderation* just as you would fear the plague! Care not what *men* think of you. Let it be enough for you that your Master says, "STRIVE!"

III. The last thing I wish to consider in this paper is the *solemn prophecy which the Lord Jesus delivers.* He says, "Many will seek to enter in, and shall not be able." When shall this be? At what period shall the gate of salvation be shut forever? When shall "striving" to enter be of no use? These are serious questions. The gate is now ready to open to the chief of sinners; but a day comes when it shall open no more.

The time foretold by our Lord is the time of His own second coming to judge the world. The long-suffering of God will at last have an end. The throne of *grace* will at length be taken down — and the throne of *judgment* shall be set up in its place. The *fountain of living waters* shall at length be closed. The *narrow gate* shall at last be barred and bolted. The *day of grace* will be passed and over. The *day of reckoning* with a sin-laden world shall at length begin. And then shall be brought to pass the solemn prophecy of the Lord Jesus, "Many will seek to enter in, and shall not be able."

All prophecies of Scripture that have been fulfilled hitherto, have been fulfilled to the very letter. They have seemed to many unlikely, improbable, impossible, up to the very time of their accomplishment; but not one word of them has ever failed.

The promises of *good things* have come to pass, in spite of difficulties that seemed insuperable. Sarah had a son when she was past bearing age; the children of Israel were brought out of Egypt and planted in the promised land; the Jews were redeemed from the captivity of Babylon, after seventy years, and enabled once more to build the temple; the Lord Jesus was born of a pure virgin, lived, ministered, was betrayed, and crucified — precisely as Scripture foretold. The Word of God was pledged in all these cases, that it should be. *And so it was.*

The predictions of *judgments* on cities and nations have come to pass, though at the time they were first spoken, they seemed incredible. Egypt is the basest of kingdoms; Edom is a wilderness; Tyre is a rock for drying nets; Nineveh, that "exceeding great city," is laid waste, and become a desolation; Babylon is a dry land and a wilderness — her broad walls are utterly broken down; the Jews are scattered over the whole earth as a separate people. In all these cases, the Word of God foretold that it should be so. *And so it was.*

The prophecy of the Lord Jesus Christ which I press on your attention this day, shall be fulfilled in like manner. Not one word of it shall fail when the time of its accomplishment is due. "Many will seek to enter in — and shall not be able."

There is a time coming, when seeking God shall be useless. Oh, that men would remember that! Too many seem to imagine that the hour will never arrive when they shall seek and not find: but they are sadly mistaken. They will discover their mistake one day to their own confusion, except they repent. When Christ comes, "many shall seek to enter in, and *not be able."*

There is a time coming when many shall be shut out from Heaven forever. It shall not be the lot of a few — but of a great multitude; it shall not happen to one or two in this parish, and one or two in that — it shall be the miserable end of a vast crowd. *"Many* will seek to enter in, and shall not be able."

Knowledge shall come to many too late. They shall see at last the value of an immortal soul, and the happiness of having it saved. They shall understand at last their own sinfulness and God's holiness, and the glorious fitness of the Gospel of Christ. They shall comprehend at last why ministers seemed so anxious, and preached so long, and entreated them so earnestly to be converted. But, alas, they shall know all this — *too late!*

Repentance shall come to many too late. They shall discover their own exceeding wickedness and be thoroughly ashamed of their past folly. They shall be full of bitter regret and unavailing lamentations, of keen convictions and of piercing sorrows. They shall weep, and wail, and mourn — when they reflect on their sins. The remembrance of their lives will be grievous to them; the burden of their guilt will seem intolerable. But, alas, like Judas Iscariot, they will repent *too late!*

Faith shall come to many too late. They will no longer be able to deny that there is a God, and a devil, a Heaven, and a Hell. Deism, and scepticism, and infidelity shall be laid aside forever! Scoffing, and jesting, and free-thinking shall cease! They will *see* with their own eyes, and *feel* in their own bodies, that the things of which ministers spoke were not cunningly devised fables — but great real truths! They will find out to their cost, that evangelical religion was not mere religious cant, extravagance, fanaticism, and enthusiasm! They will discover that it was the one thing needful, and that for lack of it they are lost forever. Like the devil, they will at length believe and tremble — but *too late!*

A *desire of salvation* shall come to many too late. They shall long after pardon, and peace, and the favor of God — when they can no more be had. They will wish they might have one more Sunday over again, have one more offer of forgiveness, have one more call to prayer. But it will matter nothing what they think, or feel, or desire then — the day of grace will be over; the gate of salvation will be bolted and barred! It will be *too late!*

I often think what a change there will be one day, in the estimation at which things are *valued.* I look round this world in which my lot is cast; I mark the current price of everything this world contains; I look forward to the coming of Christ, and the great day of God. I think of the new order of things, which that day will bring in; I read the words of the Lord Jesus, when He describes the master of the house rising up and shutting the door; and as I read, I say to myself, "There will be a great change soon!"

What are the *dear things* now? Gold, silver, precious stones, bank notes, mines, ships, lands, houses, horses, carriages, furniture, food, drink, clothes, and the like. These are the things that are thought valuable; these are the things that command a ready market; these are the things which you can never get below a certain price. He who has much of these things — is counted a *wealthy* man. Such is the world!

And what are the *cheap things* now?

The knowledge of God,
the free salvation of the Gospel,
the favor of Christ,
the grace of the Holy Spirit,
the privilege of being God's son,
the title to eternal life,
the right to the tree of life,
the promise of a mansion in Heaven,
the promises of an incorruptible inheritance,
the offer of an unfading crown of glory!

These are the things that no man hardly cares for. They are offered to men without money and without price — they may be had for nothing — freely and gratuitously. Whoever will, may take his portion. But, alas, there is no *demand* for these things! They go a begging. They are scarcely looked at. They are offered in vain. Such is the world!

But a day is coming upon us all, when the value of everything shall be altered. A day is coming when *bank-notes* shall be as useless as rags, and *gold* shall be as worthless as the dust of the earth! A day is coming when thousands shall care nothing for the things for which they once lived — and shall desire nothing so much as the things which they once despised. The halls and palaces will be forgotten in the desire of a "house not made with hands." The favor of the rich and great will be no more remembered, in the longing for the favor of the King of kings. The silks, and satins, and velvets, and laces, will be lost sight of — in the anxious lack of the robe of Christ's righteousness. All shall be *altered*, all shall be *changed* in the great day of the Lord's return. "Many will seek to enter in, and shall not be able."

It was a weighty saying of some wise man, that *"Hell is truth known too late."* I fear that thousands of *professing* Christians in this day will find this out by sad experience. They will discover the value of their souls — when it is too late to obtain mercy; and see the beauty of the Gospel — when they can derive no benefit from it. Oh, that men would be wise early!

I often think there are few passages of Scripture more solemn than that in the first chapter of Proverbs, "But since you rejected me when I called and no one gave heed when I stretched out my hand, since you ignored all my advice and would not accept my rebuke, I in turn will laugh at your disaster; I will mock when calamity overtakes you — when calamity overtakes you like a storm, when disaster sweeps over you like a whirlwind, when distress and trouble overwhelm you. Then they will call to me but I will not answer; they will look for me but will not find me. Since they hated knowledge and did not choose to fear the LORD, since they would not accept my advice and spurned my rebuke — they will eat the fruit of their ways and be filled with the fruit of their schemes! For the waywardness of the simple will kill them, and the complacency of fools will destroy them!" Proverbs 1:24-32

Some reader of this paper may be one of those who neither like the *faith* nor *practice* which the Gospel of Christ requires. You think us extreme when we beseech you to repent and be converted. You think we ask too much when we urge you to come out from the world, and take up the cross, and follow Christ. But take notice that you will one day confess *that we were right*. Sooner or later, in this world or the next — you will acknowledge that you were wrong. Yes! it is a melancholy consideration for the faithful minister of the Gospel, that all who hear him will one day allow that his counsel was good. Mocked, despised, scorned, neglected as his testimony may be on earth — a day is coming which shall prove effectually that *truth* was on his side. The *rich man* who hears us and yet makes a god of this world; the *tradesman* who hears us and yet makes his ledger his Bible — the *farmer* who hears us and yet remains as cold as the clay on his land — the *laborer* who hears us and feels no more for his soul than a stone — all, all will at length acknowledge before the world, that they were wrong. All will at length desire earnestly that very mercy which we now set before them in vain. "They will seek to enter in — and shall not be able."

Some reader of this paper may be one of those who love the Lord Jesus Christ in sincerity. Such a one may well take comfort when he looks forward. You often suffer persecution now for your religion's sake. You have to bear *hard words* and *unkind insinuations*. Your *motives* are often misrepresented, and your *conduct* slandered. The *reproach of the cross* has not ceased. But you may well take courage when you look forward and think of the Lord's second coming. *That day shall make amends for all.*

You will see those who now laugh at you because you read the Bible, and pray, and love Christ — in a very different state of mind. They will come to you as the foolish virgins came to the wise, saying, "Give us some of your oil, because our lamps are gone out." (Matthew 25:8.) You will see those who now hate you and call you *fools* because, like Caleb and Joshua, you bring up a good report of Christ's service — altered, changed, and no longer like the same men. They will say, "Oh, that we had taken part with you! You have been the truly wise — and we the foolish."

Then fear not the reproach of men. Confess Christ boldly before the world. Show your colors, and be not ashamed of your Master. Time is short! Eternity hastens on! The *cross* is only for a little season — the *crown* is forever! Make sure work about that crown — leave nothing uncertain. "Many will seek to enter in — and shall not be able."

And now let me offer to every one who reads this paper, a few parting words, in order to apply the whole subject to his soul. You have heard the words of the Lord Jesus unfolded and expounded. You have seen the picture of the *way of salvation* — it is a narrow gate. You have heard the *command* of the King: "Strive to enter in." You have been told of His *solemn warning*: "Many shall seek to enter in, and shall not be able." Bear with me a little longer while I try to *impress the whole matter on your conscience*. I have yet something to say on God's behalf.

(1) For one thing, I will ask you a plain question. *Have you entered in at the narrow gate, or not?* Old or young, rich or poor, churchman or dissenter, I repeat my question, Have *you* entered in at the narrow gate?

I ask not whether you have *heard* of it, and *believe* there is a gate. I ask not whether you have *looked* at it, and *admired* it, and *hope* one day to go in. I ask whether you have gone up to it, knocked at it, been admitted, and *are now inside?*

If you are not inside, what good have you got from your religion? You are not pardoned and forgiven. You are not reconciled to God. You are not born again, sanctified, and fit for Heaven. If you die as you are — the devil will have you forever, and your soul will be eternally miserable!

Oh, think, think what a state this is to *live* in! Think, think above all things, what a state this is to *die* in! Your life is but a vapor. A few more years at most — and you are gone! Your place in the world will soon be filled up; your house will be occupied by another. The sun will go on shining; the grass and daises will soon grow thick over your grave; your body will be food for worms, and your soul will be lost to all eternity!

And all this time there stands open before you a gate of salvation. God invites you. Jesus Christ offers to save you. All things are ready for your deliverance. One thing only is lacking, and that is that you should be *willing* to be saved.

Oh think of these things, and be wise!

(2) For another thing, I will give plain advice to all who are not yet inside the narrow gate. That advice is simply this: *to enter in without a day's delay.*

Tell me, if you can, of anyone who ever reached Heaven except through "the narrow gate." I know of none. From Abel, the first who died, down to the end of the list of Bible names — I see none saved by any way, but that of *faith in Christ.*

Tell me, if you can, of anyone who ever entered in at the narrow gate without "striving." I know of none! He who would win Heaven — must be content to fight for it.

Tell me, if you can, of anyone who ever strove earnestly to enter, and failed to succeed. I know of none. I believe that however weak and ignorant men may be, they never seek life heartily and conscientiously, at the right door — and are left without an answer of peace.

Tell me, if you can, of anyone who ever entered in at the narrow gate, and was afterwards sorry. I know of none. I believe the *footsteps* on the threshold of that gate are all *one way.* All have found it a good thing to serve Christ, and have never regretted taking up His cross.

If these things are so, seek Christ without delay, and enter in at the gate of life while you can! Make a beginning this very day. Go to that merciful and mighty Savior in prayer, and pour out your heart before Him. Confess to Him your guilt and wickedness and sin. Unbosom yourself freely to Him — keep nothing back. Tell Him that you cast yourself and all your soul's affairs wholly on His hands, and ask Him to save you according to His promise, and put His Holy Spirit within you.

There is everything *to encourage you to do this.* Thousands as bad as you have applied to Christ in this way — and not one of them has been sent away and refused. They have found a peace of conscience which they never knew before, and have gone on their way rejoicing. They have found strength for all the trials of life — and none of them have been allowed to perish in the wilderness. Why should not you also seek Christ?

There is everything to encourage you to do what I tell you *at once.* I know no reason why your repentance and conversion should not be as immediate as that of others before you. The Samaritan woman came to the well an ignorant sinner — and returned to her home a new creature. The Philippian jailor turned from darkness to light — and became a professed disciple of Christ in a single day. And why should others not do the same? Why should *you* not give up your sins, and lay hold on Christ this very day?

I know that the advice I have given you is good. The grand question is, *Will you take it?*

(3) The last thing I have to say, shall be a *request* to all who have really entered in at the narrow gate. That request is, that you will *tell others* of the blessings which you have found.

I want all converted people to be *missionaries*. I do not want them all to go out to foreign lands, and preach to the heathen; but I do want all to be of a missionary spirit, and to strive to do good at home. I want them to testify to all around them — that the narrow gate is the way to happiness, and to persuade them to enter in by it.

When *Andrew* was converted — he found his brother Peter, and said to him, "We have found the Messiah! And he brought him to Jesus." (John 1:41, 42.) When *Philip* was converted — he found Nathaniel, and said to him, "We have found Him, of whom Moses in the law, and the prophets wrote, Jesus of Nazareth! And Nathaniel said unto him, Can there any good thing come out of Nazareth? Philip said unto him, Come and see!" (John 1:45, 46.) When the *Samaritan* woman was converted. "Then, leaving her water jar, the woman went back to the town and said to the people: Come, see a man who told me everything I ever did. Could this be the Christ?" (John 4:28, 29.) When Saul the Pharisee was converted, "*Immediately* he preached Christ in the synagogues, that He is the son of God." (Acts 9:20.)

I long to see this kind of spirit among Christians in the present day. I long to see more zeal to commend the *narrow gate* to all who are yet outside, and more desire to persuade them to enter in and be saved. Happy indeed is that Church whose members not only desire to reach Heaven *themselves* — but desire also to take *others* with them!

The great gate of salvation is yet ready to open — but the hour draws near when it will be closed forever. Let us work while it is called today, for "the night comes when no man can work." (John 9:4.) Let us tell our relatives and friends, that we have *proved* the way of life — and found it pleasant, that we have *tasted* the bread of life — and found it good.

I have heard it calculated that if every believer in the world were to bring one soul to Christ each year, the whole human race would be converted in less than twenty years. I make no comment on such a calculation. Whether such a thing might be or not, one thing is sure: that many more *souls might probably be converted to God, if Christians were more zealous to do good.*

This, at least, we may remember, that God is "not willing that any should perish — but that all should come to repentance." (2 Peter 3:9.) He who endeavors to show his neighbor the *narrow gate* is doing a work which God approves. He is doing a work which *angels* regard with interest, and with which the building of a pyramid will not compare in importance. What says the Scripture? "He who converts a sinner from the error of his way, shall save a soul from death, and shall hide a multitude of sins." (James 5:20.)

Let us all awaken to a deeper sense of our responsibility in this matter. Let us look round the circle of those among whom we live, and consider their state before God. Are there not many of them yet *outside* the gate, unforgiven, unsanctified, and unfit to die? Let us watch for opportunities of speaking to them. Let us tell them of the narrow gate, and entreat them to "*strive* to enter in."

Who can tell what "a word spoken in due season" may do? Who can tell what it may do when spoken in faith and prayer? It may be the turning-point in some man's history. It may be the beginning of thought, prayer, and eternal life. Oh, for more *love* and *boldness* among believers! Think what a blessing to be allowed to speak one converting word!

I know not what the feelings of my readers may be on this subject. My heart's desire and prayer is that you may daily remember Christ's solemn words, "Many will seek to enter in — and shall not be able." Keep these words in mind — and then be careless about the souls of others, if you can!

REALITY!

"Reprobate silver." Jeremiah 6:30

"Nothing but leaves." Mark 11:13

"Let us not love in word, neither in tongue — but in deed and in truth!" 1 John 3:18.

"You have a name that you live — and are dead!" Revelation 3:1

If we profess to have any religion at all, let us take care that it is *real.* I say it emphatically, and I repeat the saying: Let us mind that our religion is *real.*

What do I mean when I use the word "real." I mean that which is genuine, and sincere, and honest, and thorough. I mean that which is not base, and hollow, and formal, and false, and counterfeit, and sham, and nominal. "Real "religion is not mere show, and pretense, and skin-deep feeling, and temporary profession, and *outside* work. It is something inward, solid, substantial, intrinsic, living, lasting. We know the difference between base coin and good money, between solid gold and tinsel, between plated metal and silver, between real stone and plaster imitation. Let us think of these things as we consider the subject of this paper. What is the character of our religion? Is it real? It may be *weak*, and *feeble*, and *mingled* with many infirmities. That is not the point before us today. Is our religion real? Is it true?

The times in which we live demand attention to the subject. A lack of reality is a striking feature of a vast amount of religion in the present day. Scientists have sometimes told us that the world has passed through different states or conditions. We have had a golden age, and a silver age, a brazen age, and an iron age. How far this is true, I do not stop to inquire. But I fear there is little doubt as to the character of the age in which we live. It is universally an age of *base metal and alloy.*

If we measure the religion of the age by its apparent *quantity* — there is much of it. But if we measure it by its *quality* — there is very little indeed. On every side we want MORE REALITY.

I ask your attention, while I try to bring home to your consciences the question of this paper. There are two things which I propose to do:

I. In the first place, I will show the **importance** of reality in religion.

II. In the second place, I will supply some **tests** by which we may prove whether our own religion is real.

Has any reader of this paper the least desire to go to Heaven when he dies? Do you wish to have a religion which will comfort you in life, give you good hope in death, and abide the judgment of God at the last day? Then, do not turn away from the subject before you. Sit down, and consider calmly, whether your Christianity is real and true — or base and hollow.

I. I have to show the IMPORTANCE of reality in religion.

The point is one which, at first sight, may seem to require very few remarks to establish it. All men, I shall be told, are fully convinced of the importance of reality. But is this true? Can it be said indeed that reality is rightly esteemed among professing Christians? I deny it entirely.

The greater part of people who profess to admire reality, seem to think that *everyone* possesses it! They tell us "that all have got *good hearts* at bottom," that all are sincere and true in the main, though they may make mistakes. They call us uncharitable, and harsh, and censorious, if we doubt anybody's goodness of heart. In short, they destroy the *value* of reality, by regarding it as a thing which almost everyone has.

This wide-spread delusion is precisely one of the causes why I take up this subject. I want men to understand that reality is a far more *rare* and *uncommon* thing than is commonly supposed. I want men to see that unreality is one of the great dangers of which professing Christians ought to beware.

What says the Scripture? This is the only *judge* that can try the subject. Let us turn to our Bibles, and examine them fairly, and then deny, if we can, the importance of reality in religion, and the danger of not being real.

(1) Let us look then, for one thing, at the *parables* spoken by our Lord Jesus Christ. Observe how many of them are intended to put in strong contrast the true believer and the mere nominal disciple. The parables of the sower, of the wheat and tares, of the draw-net, of the two sons, of the wedding garment, of the ten virgins, of the talents, of the great supper, of the pounds, of the two builders — have all one great point in common. They all bring out in striking colors the *difference* between reality and unreality in religion. They all show the uselessness and danger of any Christianity which is not real, thorough, and true.

(2) Let us look, for another thing, at the language of our Lord Jesus Christ about the *scribes* and the *Pharisees*. Eight times over in one chapter, we find Him denouncing them as "hypocrites," in words of almost fearful severity.

"You serpents, you generation of vipers," He says, "How can you escape the damnation of Hell!" What may we learn from these tremendously strong expressions? How is it that our gracious and merciful Savior used such *cutting* words about people who at any rate were more moral and decent than the publicans and harlots? It is meant to teach us the *exceeding abominableness of false profession* and mere *external religion* in God's sight.

Open profligacy and willful obedience to fleshly lusts are no doubt ruinous sins, if not given up. But there seems nothing which is so displeasing to Christ — as *hypocrisy* and *unreality!*

(3) Let us look, for another thing, at the startling fact, that there is hardly a *grace* in the character of a true Christian of which you will not find a *counterfeit* described in the Word of God. There is not a feature in a believer's countenance, of which there is not an imitation. Give me your attention, and I will show you this in a few particulars.

Is there not an *unreal repentance?* Beyond doubt there is. Saul and Ahab, and Herod, and Judas Iscariot had many feelings of sorrow about sin. But they never really repented unto salvation.

Is there not an *unreal faith?* Beyond doubt there is. It is written of Simon Magus, at Samaria, that he "believed," and yet his heart was not right in the sight of God. It is even written of the devils that they "believe and tremble." (Acts 8:13; James ii. 19.)

Is there not an *unreal holiness?* Beyond doubt there is. Joash, king of Judah, became to all appearance very holy and good, so long as Jehoiada the priest lived. But as soon as he died, the religion of Joash died at the same time! (2 Chronicles 24:2.) Judas Iscariot's outward life was as correct as that of any of the apostles, up to the time that he betrayed his Master. There was nothing *suspicious* about him. Yet in reality he was "a thief" and a traitor! (John 12:6.)

Is there not an unreal *love* and *charity?* Beyond doubt there is. There is a love which consists in words and tender expressions, and a great show of affection, and calling other people "dear brethren" — while the heart does not love at all. It is not for nothing that John says, "Let us not love in word, neither in tongue — but in deed and in truth!" It was not without cause that Paul said: "Let love be sincere." (1 John 3:18; Romans 12:19.)

Is there not an *unreal humility?* Beyond doubt there is. There is a pretended lowliness of demeanor, which often covers over a very proud heart. Paul warns us against a "voluntary humility," and speaks of "things which had a *show* of wisdom in will-worship and humility." (Colossians 2:18, 23.)

Is there not *unreal praying?* Beyond doubt there is. Our Lord denounces it as one of the special sins of the Pharisees that for a "pretense they made long prayers." (Matt, 23:14.) He does not charge them with *not* praying, or with praying too shortly. Their sin lay in this, that their prayers were not *real.*

Is there not *unreal worship?* Beyond doubt there is. Our Lord says of the Jews: "This people draw near to Me with their mouths, and honor Me with their lips — but their *heart* is far from Me." (Matthew 15:8.) They had plenty of *formal services* in their temples and their synagogues. But the *fatal defect* about them was lack of reality and lack of heart.

Is there not *unreal talking* about religion? Beyond doubt there is. Ezekiel describes some professing Jews who talked and spoke like God's people "while their hearts went after their covetousness." (Ezekiel 33:31.)

Paul tells us that we may "speak with the tongue of men and angels," and yet be no better than sounding brass and a tinkling cymbal. (1 Corinthians 13:1.)

What shall we say to these things? To say the least, they ought to set us thinking. To my own mind they seem to lead to only one conclusion. They show clearly the immense *importance* which Scripture attaches to *reality in religion.* They show clearly what need we have to take heed, lest our Christianity turn out to be merely nominal, formal, unreal, and base.

The subject is of deep importance in every age. There has never been a time, since the Church of Christ was founded, when there has not been a vast amount of unreality and mere nominal religion among professing Christians. I am sure it is the case in the present day.

Wherever I turn my eyes I see abundant cause for the warning, "Beware of base metal in religion. Be genuine. Be thorough. Be real. Be true."

How much religion among some members of the **Church of England** consists of nothing but church rituals! They belong to the Established Church. They are baptized at her fonts, married at her communion rails, buried in her churchyards, preached to on Sundays by her ministers. But the great doctrines laid down in her Articles and Liturgy have no place in their *hearts*, and no *influence* on their *lives.* They neither think, nor feel, nor care, nor know anything about them. And is the religion of these people *real* Christianity? It is nothing of the kind. It is mere base metal. It is not the Christianity of Peter, and James, and John, and Paul. It is *Churchianity* — and no more!

How much religion among some **Dissenters** from the Church of England consists of nothing but *dissent!* They pride themselves on having nothing to do with the Anglican church. They rejoice in having no liturgy, no forms, no bishops. They glory in the exercise of their private judgment, and the absence of everything like ceremonial in their public worship. But all this time they have neither grace, nor faith, nor repentance, nor holiness, nor spirituality of conduct or conversation. The experimental and practical piety of the old Nonconformists is a thing of which they are utterly destitute. Their Christianity is as sapless and fruitless as a dead tree, and as dry and marrowless as an old bone! And is the Christianity of these people real? It is nothing of the kind. It is base metal. It is not the Christianity of

Owen, and Manton, and Goodwin, and Baxter, and Traill. It is *Dissentianity* — and nothing more.

How much **Ritualistic** religion is utterly unreal! You will sometimes see men boiling over with zeal about vestments, and gestures, and postures, and church decorations, and daily services, and frequent communions — while their hearts are manifestly in the world.

Of the inward work of the Holy Spirit,
of living faith in the Lord Jesus,
of delight in the Bible and pious conversation,
of separation from worldly follies and amusements,
of zeal for the conversion of souls to God
of all these things they are profoundly ignorant! And is such
Christianity as this real? It is nothing of the kind. It is a *mere name.*

How much **Evangelical** religion is completely unreal? You will sometimes see men professing great affection for the pure "Gospel," while they are practically inflicting on it the greatest injury. They will talk loudly of soundness in the faith, and have a keen nose for heresy. They will run eagerly after popular preachers, and applaud Protestant speakers at public meetings to the very echo. They are familiar with all the *phrases* of evangelical religion, and can converse fluently about its leading *doctrines*. To see their faces at public meetings, or in church — you would think them eminently godly. To hear them *talk* — you would suppose their *lives* were bound up in religious Societies. And yet these people in private will sometimes do things of which even some *heathen* would be ashamed! They are neither truthful, nor straightforward, nor honest, nor manly, nor just, nor good-tempered, nor unselfish, nor merciful, nor humble, nor kind! And is such Christianity as this real? It is not. It is a *miserable imposture*, a base cheat and caricature!

How much **Revivalist** religion in the present day is utterly unreal! You will find a crowd of false professors bringing discredit on the work of God wherever the Holy Spirit is poured out. You will see a mixed multitude of Egyptians accompanying the Israel of God, and doing it harm, whenever Israel goes out of Egypt. How many now-a-days will profess to be suddenly convinced of sin, to find peace in Jesus, to be overwhelmed with joys and ecstasies of soul — while in reality they have *no grace* at all. Like the stony-ground hearers — they endure but for a season. "In the time of temptation they fall away." (Luke 8:13) As soon as the first *excitement* wears off — they return to their old ways, and resume their former sins. Their religion is like Jonah's gourd, which came up in a night — and perished in a night. They have neither root nor vitality. They only injure God's cause and give occasion to God's enemies to blaspheme. And is Christianity like this real? It is nothing of the kind. It is *base metal from the devil's mint*, and is worthless in God's sight!

I write these things with sorrow. I have no desire to bring any *section* of the Church of Christ into contempt. I have no wish to cast any slur on any movement which begins with the Spirit of God. But the times demand very *plain speaking* about some points in the prevailing Christianity of our day. And one point, I am quite persuaded, that demands attention, is the abounding lack of reality which is to be seen on every side.

No reader, at any rate, can well deny that the subject of the paper before him is of vast importance. I pass on now to the second thing which I propose to do.

II. I will supply some TESTS by which we may try the reality of our religion.

In approaching this part of my subject, I ask every reader of this paper to deal fairly, honestly, and reasonably with his soul. Dismiss from your mind the common idea, that *of course all is right if you go to church or to chapel.* Cast away such vain notions forever. You must look further, higher, deeper than this, if you would find out the truth. Listen to me, and I will give you a few hints. Believe me, it is no light matter. It is your life.

(1) For one thing, if you would know whether your religion is real — try it by *the place which it occupies in your* ***INNER MAN***.

It is not enough that it is in your *HEAD*. You may *know* the truth, and *assent* to the truth, and *believe* the truth — and yet be wrong in God's sight!

It is not enough that it is on your *LIPS*. You may repeat the creed daily. You may say "Amen" to public prayer in church — and yet have nothing more than an outward religion.

It is not enough that it is in your *FEELINGS*. You may weep under preaching one day, and be lifted to the third Heaven by joyous excitement another day — and yet be dead to God.

Your religion, if it is real, and given by the Holy Spirit — must be in your *HEART*. It must occupy the *citadel*. It must hold the *reins*. It must sway the *affections*. It must lead the *will*. It must direct the *tastes*. It must influence the *choices* and *decisions*. It must fill the deepest, lowest, inmost seat in your soul. Is this your religion? If not, you may well doubt whether it is "real" and true. (Acts 8:21; Romans 10:10.)

(2) In the next place, if you would know whether your religion is real — try it by the feelings towards ***SIN*** which it produces. The Christianity which is from the Holy Spirit, will always have a very deep view of the *sinfulness of sin*. It will not merely regard sin as a *blemish* and *misfortune*, which makes men and women objects of pity and compassion. It will see in sin, the abominable thing which God hates, the thing which makes man guilty and lost in his Maker's sight —

the thing which deserves God's wrath and condemnation. It will look on sin as the cause of all sorrow and unhappiness, of strife and wars, of quarrels and contentions, of sickness and death — the *blight* which has blighted God's fair creation, the *accursed thing* which makes the whole earth groan and travail in pain! Above all, it will see in sin the thing which will . . . ruin us eternally — unless we can find a ransom;
lead us captive — unless we can get its chains broken; and
destroy our happiness, both here and hereafter — unless we fight against it, even unto death.

Is this your religion? Are these your feelings about sin? If not, you may well doubt whether your religion is "Real."

(3) For another thing, if you would know whether your religion is real, try it by the feelings toward ***CHRIST*** which it produces. *Nominal* religion may believe that such a person as Christ existed, and was a great benefactor to mankind. It may show Him some external respect, attend His outward ordinances, and bow the head at His name. But it will go no further.

Real religion will make a man glory in Christ, as the Redeemer, the Deliverer, the Priest, the Friend — without whom he would have no hope at all.

It will produce . . .
confidence in Him,
love towards Him,
delight in Him,
comfort in Him —
as the mediator, the food, the light, the life, the peace of the soul.

Is this your religion? Do you know anything of feelings like these toward Jesus Christ? If not, you may well doubt whether your religion is "real"

(4) For another thing, if you would know whether your religion is real, try it by the ***FRUIT*** it bears in your heart and life. The Christianity which is from above — will always be known by its fruits. It will produce in the man who has it: repentance, faith, hope, charity, humility, spirituality, kind temper, self-denial, unselfishness, forgivingness, temperance, truthfulness, brotherly-kindness, patience, and forbearance. The *degree* in which these various graces appear, may *vary* in different believers. The germ and seeds of them will be found in all who are the children of God. By their *fruits* — they may be known.

Is this your religion? If not, you may well doubt whether it is "real"

(5) In the last place, if you would know whether your religion is real, try it by your feelings and habits about ***MEANS OF GRACE***. Prove it by the Sunday. Is that day a season of weariness and constraint — or a delight and a refreshment, and a sweet foretaste of the rest to come in Heaven? Prove it by the public means of grace. What are your feelings about public prayer and public praise, about the public preaching of God's Word, and the administration of the Lord's Supper? Are they things to which you give a *cold assent*, and *tolerate* them as proper and correct? Or, are they things in which you take pleasure, and without which you could not live happy?

Prove it, finally, by your feelings about *private* means of grace. Do you find it essential to your comfort to read the Bible regularly in private, and to speak to God in prayer? Or, do you find these practices irksome, and either slur them over, or neglect them altogether? These questions deserve your attention. If means of grace, whether public or private, are not as *necessary* to your soul as food and drink are to your body — you may well *doubt* whether your religion is "real."

I press on the attention of all my readers the five points which I have just named. There is nothing like coming to *particulars* about these matters. If you would know whether your religion is "real," genuine, and true — measure it by the five particulars which I have now named. Measure it fairly — test it honestly. If your heart is right in the sight of God — you have no cause to flinch from examination. If it is wrong — the sooner you find it out the better.

And now I have done what I proposed to do. I have shown from Scripture, the unspeakable *importance* of reality in religion, and the *danger* in which many stand of being lost forever — for lack of it. I have given *five plain tests*, by which a man may find out whether his Christianity is real. I will conclude all by a direct application of the whole subject to the souls of all who read this paper. I will draw my bow at a venture, and trust that God will bring an *arrow* home to the *hearts* and *consciences* of many.

(1) My first word of *application* shall be an INQUIRY.

Is *your own* religion real or unreal? Genuine or base? I do not ask what you think about *others*. Perhaps you may see many hypocrites around you. You may be able to point to many who have no "reality "at all. This is not the question. You may be right in your opinion about others. But I want to know about *yourself*. Is your own Christianity real and true — or nominal and base?

If you love life, do not turn away from the question which is now before you. The time must come when the whole truth will be known. The judgment day will reveal every man's religion, of what sort it is. The parable of the wedding-garment will receive a solemn fulfillment Surely it is a thousand times better to find out your condition *now*, and to repent — than to find it out too late in the next world, when there will be no space for repentance.

If you have common prudence, sense, and judgment, consider what I say. Sit down quietly this day, and examine yourself. Find out the real character of your religion. With the *Bible* in your hand,

and *honesty* in your heart — the thing may be known. Then resolve to find out.

(2) My second word of application shall be a WARNING.

I address it to all who know, in their own consciences, that their religion is *not* real. I ask them to remember the greatness of their *danger*, and their exceeding *guilt* in the sight of God.

An unreal Christianity is specially offensive to that Great God with whom we have to do. He is continually spoken of in Scripture as the God of Truth. Truth is peculiarly one of His attributes. Can you doubt for a moment that He abhors everything that is not genuine and true? Better, I firmly believe, to be found an *ignorant heathen* at the last day — than to be found with nothing better than a *nominal religion!* If your religion is of this sort — beware!

An unreal Christianity is sure to fail a man at last. It will wear out; it will break down; it will leave its possessor like a *wreck on a sandbank*, high and dry and forsaken by the tide; it will supply *no comfort* in the hour when comfort is most needed, in the time of affliction, and on the bed of death. If you want a religion to be of any use to your soul — then beware of unreality! If you would not be comfortless in death, and hopeless in the judgment day — be genuine, be real, be true!

(3) My third word of application shall be ADVICE. I offer it to all who feel pricked in conscience by the subject of this paper. I advise them to cease from all *trifling* and *playing* with religion, and to become honest, thoroughgoing, whole-hearted followers of the Lord Jesus Christ.

Apply without delay to the Lord Jesus, and ask Him to become your Savior, your Physician, your Priest, and your Friend. Let not the thought of *your unworthiness* keep you away; let not the recollection of *your great sins* prevent your application. Never, never forget that Christ can cleanse you from any quantity of sins, if you only commit your soul to Him. But one thing He does ask of those who come to Him: He asks them to be real, honest, and true!

Let reality be one great mark of your approach to Christ — and there is everything to give you hope.

Your *repentance* may be feeble — but let it be real;
your *faith* may be weak — but let it be real;
your desires after *holiness* may be mingled with much infirmity — but let them be real.

Let there be nothing of reserve, of double-dealing, of part-acting, of dishonesty, of sham, of counterfeit — in your Christianity. Never be content to wear a *cloak of religion*. Be all that you profess.

Though you may *err* — be *real*. Though you may *stumble* — be *true*. Keep this principle continually before your eyes, and it will be well with your soul throughout your journey from grace to glory.

(4) My last word of application shall be ENCOURAGEMENT.

I address it to all who have manfully taken up the cross, and are honestly following Christ. I exhort them to persevere, and not to be moved by difficulties and opposition.

You may often find *few* with you — and *many* against you. You may often hear hard things said of you. You may often be told that you *go too far,* and that you are *extreme.* Heed it not. Turn a deaf ear to remarks of this kind. Press on.

If there is anything which a man ought to do thoroughly, really, truly, honestly, and with all his heart — it is the business of his soul. If there is any work which he ought never to slur over, and do in a slovenly fashion — it is the great work of "working out his own salvation." (Philippians 2:12.) Believer in Christ, remember this! Whatever you do in religion — do it well. Be real. Be thorough. Be honest. Be true.

If there is anything in the world of which a man need not be ashamed, it is the service of Jesus Christ. Of sin, of worldliness, of levity, of trifling, of time-wasting, of pleasure-seeking, of bad temper, of pride, of making an idol of money, dress, dancing, hunting, shooting, card-playing, novel-reading, and the like — of all this a man may well be ashamed. Living after this fashion — he makes the angels sorrow, and the devils rejoice.

But of living for his soul, caring for his soul, thinking of his soul, providing for his soul, making his soul's salvation the principal and chief thing in his daily life — of all this a man has no cause to be ashamed at all.

Believer in Christ, remember this! Remember it in your Bible-reading and your private praying. Remember it in your worship of God. In all these things never be ashamed of being whole-hearted, real, thorough, and true!

The years of our life are fast passing away. Who knows but this year may be the last in his life? Who can tell but that he may be called this very year to *meet his God?* As ever you would be found *ready* — be a real and true Christian. Do not be *base metal.*

The time is fast coming, when nothing but *reality* will stand the fire. Real *repentance* towards God, real *faith* towards our Lord Jesus Christ, real *holiness* of heart and life — these, these are the things which will alone pass current at the last day! It is a solemn saying of our Lord Jesus Christ, "Many shall *say* in that day: Lord, Lord, have we not prophesied in Your name, and in Your name have cast out devils, and in Your name done many wonderful works? And then will I profess to them: I never knew you. Depart from Me, you who work iniquity!" (Matt 7:22, 23.)

A CALL TO PRAYER

"Men ought always to pray." Luke 18:1

I have a question to offer you. It is contained in three words, **DO YOU PRAY?**

The question is one that none but you can answer. Whether you attend public worship or not, your minister knows. Whether you have family prayers in your house or not, your relations know. But whether you pray in private or not, is a matter between yourself and God.

I beseech you in all affections to attend to the subject I bring before you. Do not say that my question is too close. If your heart is right in the sight of God, there is nothing in it to make you afraid. Do not turn off my question by replying that you say your prayers. It is one thing to say your prayers and another to pray. Do not tell me that my question is unnecessary. Listen to me for a few minutes, and I will show you good reasons for asking it.

Prayer is the most important subject in practical religion. All other subjects are second to it. Reading the Bible, listening to sermons, attending public worship, going to the Lord's Table—all these are very important matters. But none of them are so important as *private prayer*.

I propose in this paper to offer *seven clear reasons* why I use such strong language about prayer. I draw to these reasons the attention of every thinking man into whose hands this paper may fall. I venture to assert with confidence that they deserve serious consideration.

I. I ASK WHETHER YOU PRAY, BECAUSE PRAYER IS ABSOLUTELY NEEDFUL TO A PERSON'S SALVATION.

I say, absolutely needful, and I say so advisedly. I am not speaking now of infants or idiots. I am not settling the state of the heathen. I know where little is given, there little will be required. I speak especially of those who call themselves Christians, in a land like our own. And of such I say, no man or woman can expect to be saved who does not pray.

I hold to *salvation by grace* as strongly as anyone. I would gladly offer a free and full pardon to the greatest sinner that ever lived. I would not hesitate to stand by his dying bed, and say, "Believe on the Lord Jesus Christ even now, and you shall be saved." (Acts 16:31.) But that a person can have salvation without asking for it, I cannot see in the Bible. That a person will receive pardon of their sins, who will not so much as lift up their heart inwardly, and say, "Lord Jesus, give it to me," this I cannot find. I can find that nobody will be saved by their prayers, but I cannot find that without prayer anybody will be saved.

It is not absolutely needful to salvation that a person should read the Bible. A person may have no learning, or be blind, and yet have Christ in their heart. It is not absolutely needful that a person should hear public preaching of the gospel. They may live where the gospel is not preached, or they may be bedridden, or deaf. But the same thing cannot be said about prayer. It is absolutely needful to salvation that a person should pray.

There is no royal road either to health or learning. Prime ministers and kings, poor men and peasants, all alike must attend to the needs of their own bodies and their own minds. No person can eat, drink, or sleep, by proxy. No person can get the alphabet learned for them by another. All these are things which everybody must do for themselves, or they will not be done at all.

Just as it is with the mind and body, so it is with the soul. There are certain things absolutely needful to the soul's health and well-being. Each must attend to these things for himself. Each must repent for himself. Each must apply to Christ for himself. And for himself each must speak to God and pray. You must do it for yourself, for by nobody else it can be done.

To be prayerless is to be without God, without Christ, without grace, without hope, and without heaven. It is to be in the road to hell. Now can you wonder that I ask the question, DO YOU PRAY?

II. I ASK AGAIN WHETHER YOU PRAY, BECAUSE A HABIT OF PRAYER IS ONE OF THE SUREST MARKS OF A TRUE CHRISTIAN.

All the children of God on earth are alike in this respect. From the moment there is any life and reality about their religion, they pray. Just as the first sign of the life of an infant when born into the world is the act of breathing, so the first act of men and women when they are born again is praying.

This is one of the common marks of all the elect of God, "They cry unto him day and night." (Luke 18:7.) The Holy Spirit who makes them new creatures, works in them a feeling of adoption, and makes the cry, "Abba, Father." (Romans 8:15.) The Lord Jesus, when He quickens them, gives them a voice and a tongue, and says to them, "Be dumb no more." God has no dumb children. It is as much a part of their new nature to pray, as it is of a child to cry. They see their need of mercy and grace. They feel their emptiness and weakness. They cannot do other wise than they do. They must pray.

I have looked carefully over the lives of God's saints in the Bible. I cannot find one whose history much is told us, from Genesis to Revelation, who was not a person of prayer. I find it mentioned as a characteristic of the godly, that "they call on the Father," that "they call upon the name of the Lord Jesus Christ." I find it recorded as a characteristic of the wicked, that "they call not upon the Lord." (1 Peter 1:17; 1 Corinthians 1:2; Psalm 14:4.)

I have read the lives of many eminent Christians who have been on earth since the Bible days. Some of them, I see, were rich, and some poor. Some were learned, and some were unlearned. Some of them were Episcopalians, and some were Christians of other names. Some were Calvinists, and some were Arminians. Some have loved to use liturgy, and some to use none. But one thing, I see, they all had in common. They have all been people of prayer.

I study reports of missionary societies in our own times. I see with joy that lost men and women are receiving the gospel in various parts of the globe. There are conversions in Africa, in New Zealand, in India, in China. The people converted are naturally unlike one another in every respect. But one striking thing I observe at all the missionary stations: the converted people always pray.

I do not deny that a person may pray without heart and without sincerity. I do not for a moment pretend to say that the mere fact of a person's praying proves everything about their soul. As in every other part of religion, so also in this, there may be deception and hypocrisy.

But this I do say, that not praying is a clear proof that a person is not yet a true Christian. They cannot really feel their sins. They cannot love God. They cannot feel themselves a debtor to Christ. They cannot long after holiness. They cannot desire heaven. They have yet to be born again. They have yet to be made a new creature. They may boast confidently of election, grace, faith, hope and knowledge, and deceive ignorant people. But you may rest assured it is all vain talk if they do not pray.

And I say furthermore, that of all the evidences of the real work of the Spirit, a habit of hearty private prayer is one of the most satisfactory that can be named. A person may preach from false motives. A person may write books and, make fine speeches and seem diligent in good works, and yet be a Judas Iscariot. But a person seldom goes into their closet and pours out their soul before God in secret, unless they are in earnest. The Lord Himself has set his stamp on prayer as the best proof of true conversion. When He sent Ananias to Saul in Damascus, He gave him no other evidence of his change of heart than this, "Behold he prays." (Acts 9:11.)

I know that much may go on in a person's mind before they are brought to pray. They may have many convictions, desires, wishes, feelings, intentions, resolutions, hopes, and fears. But all these things are very uncertain evidences. They are to be found in ungodly people, and often come to nothing. In many a case they are not more lasting than the morning cloud, and dew that passes away. A real hearty prayer, flowing from a broken and contrite spirit, is worth all these things put together.

I know that the Holy Spirit, who calls sinners from their evil ways, does in many instances lead them by very slow degrees to acquaintance with Christ. But the eye of man can only judge by what it sees. I can not call anyone justified until they believe. I dare not say that anyone believes until they pray. I cannot understand a dumb faith. The first act of faith will be to speak to God. Faith is to the soul what life is to the body. Prayer is to faith what breath is to the body. How a person can live and not breathe is past my comprehension, and how a person can believe and not pray is past my comprehension too.

Never be surprised if you hear ministers of the gospel dwelling much on the importance of prayer. This is the point they want to bring to you. They want to know that you pray. Your views of doctrine may be correct. Your love of Protestantism may be warm and unmistakable. But still this may be nothing more than head knowledge and party spirit. They want to know whether you are actually acquainted with the throne of grace, and whether you can speak to God as well as speak about God.

Do you wish to find out whether you are a true Christian? Then rest assured that my question is of the very first importance—DO YOU PRAY?

III. I ASK WHETHER YOU PRAY, BECAUSE THERE IS NO DUTY IN RELIGION SO NEGLECTED AS PRIVATE PRAYER.

We live in days of abounding religious profession. There are more places of public worship than there ever was before. There are more people attending them than there ever was before. And yet in spite of all this public religion, I believe there is a vast neglect of private prayer. It is one of those private transactions between God and our souls which no eye sees, and therefore one which people are tempted to pass over and leave undone.

I believe that thousands never utter a word of prayer at all. They eat. They drink. They sleep. They rise. They go forth to their work. They return to their homes. They breathe God's air. They see God’s sun. They travel on God's earth. They enjoy God's mercies. They have dying bodies. They have judgment and eternity before them. But they never speak to God. They live like the animals that perish. They behave like creatures without souls. They have not one word to say to Him in whose hand are their life and breath, and all things, and from whose mouth they must one day receive their everlasting sentence. How dreadful this seems; but if the secrets of men were only known, how common.

I believe there are tens of thousands whose prayers are nothing but mere form, a set of words repeated by rote, without a thought about there meaning. Some say over a few hasty sentences picked up in the nursery when they were children. Some content themselves with repeating the Creed, forgetting that there is not a request in it. Some add the Lord's Prayer, but without the slightest desire that its solemn petitions may be granted.

Many, even those who use good forms, mutter their prayers over after they have gotten into bed, or while they wash or dress in the morning. People may think what they please, but they may depend upon it that in the sight of God this is not praying. Words said without heart are as utterly useless to our souls as the drum beating of savages before their idols. Where there is no heart, there may be lip-work and tongue-work, but there is nothing that God listens to; there is no prayer. Saul, I have no doubt, said many a long prayer before the Lord met him on the way to Damascus. But it was not until his heart was broken that the Lord said, "He prays."

Does this surprise you? Listen to me, and I will show you that I am not speaking as I do without reason. Do you think that my assertions are extravagant and unwarrantable? Give me your attention, and I will soon show you that I am only telling you the truth.

Have you forgotten that it is not natural to anyone to pray? "The carnal mind is enmity against God." (Romans 8:7.) The desire of a person's heart is to get far away from God, and have nothing to do with Him. Their feeling towards Him is not love, but fear. Why then should a person pray when they have no real sense of sin, no real feeling of spiritual needs, no thorough belief in unseen things, no desire after holiness and heaven? Of all these things the vast majority of people know and feel nothing. The multitudes walk in the broad way. I cannot forget this. Therefore I say boldly, I believe that few pray.

Have you forgotten that it is not fashionable to pray? It is one of those things that many would be rather ashamed to admit. There are hundreds who would rather storm a breach, or lead a forlorn hope then confess publicly that they make a habit of prayer. There are thousands who, if obliged to sleep in the same room with a stranger, would lie down in bed without a prayer. To dress well, to go to theaters, to be thought clever and agreeable, all this is fashionable, but not to pray. I cannot forget this. I cannot think a habit is common which so many seem ashamed to admit. Thus I believe that few pray.

Have you forgotten the lives that many live? Can we really believe that people are praying against sin night and day, when we see them plunging into it? Can we suppose they pray against the world, when they are entirely absorbed and taken up with its pursuits? Can we think they really ask God for grace to serve Him, when they do not show the slightest interest to serve Him at all? Oh, no, it is plain as daylight that the great majority of people either ask nothing of God or do not mean what they say when they do ask, which is just the same thing. Praying and sinning will never live together in the same heart. Prayer will consume sin, or sin will choke prayer. I cannot forget this. I look at people's lives. I believe that few pray.

Have you forgotten the deaths that many die? How many, when they draw near death, seem entirely strangers to God. Not only are they sadly ignorant of His gospel, but sadly lacking in the power of speaking to Him. There is a terrible awkwardness and shyness in their endeavors to approach Him. They seem to be taking up a fresh thing. They appear as if they want an introduction to God, and as if they have never talked with Him before. I remember having heard of a lady who was anxious to have a minister to visit her in her last illness. She desired that he would pray for her. He asked her what he should pray for. She did not know, and could not tell. She was utterly unable to name any one thing which she wished him to ask God for her soul. All she seemed to want was the form of a minister's prayers. I can quite understand this. Death-beds are great revealers of secrets. I cannot forget what I have seen of sick and dying people. This also leads me to believe that few people pray.

I cannot see your heart. I do not know your private history in spiritual things. But from what I see in the Bible and in the world, I am certain I cannot ask you a more necessary question than that before you—DO YOU PRAY?

IV. I ASK WHETHER YOU PRAY, BECAUSE PRAYER IS AN ACT OF RELIGION TO WHICH THERE IS GREAT ENCOURAGEMENT.

There is everything on God's part to make prayer easy if people will only attempt it. All things are ready on His side. Every objection is anticipated. Every difficulty is provided for. The crooked places are made straight and the rough places made smooth. There is no excuse left for the prayerless person.

There is a way by which any person, however sinful and unworthy, may draw near to God the Father. Jesus Christ has opened that way by the sacrifice He made for us upon the cross. The holiness and justice of God need not frighten sinners and keep them back. Only let them cry to God in the name of Jesus, only let them plead the atoning blood of Jesus, and they shall find God upon the throne of grace, willing and ready to hear. The name of Jesus is a never-failing passport for our prayers. In that name a person may draw near to God with boldness, and ask with confidence. God has engaged to hear him. Think of this. Is this not an encouragement?

There is an Advocate and Intercessor always waiting to present the prayers of those who come to God through Him. That advocate is Jesus

Christ. He mingles our prayers with the incense of His own almighty intercession. So mingled, they go up as a sweet savor before the throne of God. Poor as they are in themselves, they are mighty and powerful in the hand of our High Priest and Elder Brother. The bank-note without a signature at the bottom is nothing but a worthless piece of paper. The stroke of a pen confers on it all its value. The prayer of a poor child of Adam is a feeble thing in itself, but once endorsed by the hand of the Lord Jesus it avails much. There was an officer in the city of Rome who appointed to have his doors always open, in order to receive any Roman citizen who applied to him for help. Just so the ear of the Lord Jesus is ever open to the cry of all who need mercy and grace. It is His office to help them. Their prayer is His delight. Think of this. Is this not an encouragement?

There is the Holy Spirit ever ready to help our infirmities in prayer. It is one part of His special office is assist us in our endeavors to speak to God. We need not be cast down and distressed by the fear of not knowing what to say. The Spirit will give us words if we seek His aid. The prayers of the Lord's people are the inspiration of the Lord's Spirit, the work of the Holy Spirit who dwells within them as the Spirit of grace and supplication. Surely the Lord's people may well hope to be heard. It is not merely those who pray, but the Holy Spirit pleading in them. Think of this. Is not this an encouragement?

There are exceeding great and precious promises to those who pray. What did the Lord Jesus mean when he spoke such words as these: "Ask and it shall be given you; seek, and you shall find; knock, and the door shall be opened unto you: for every one that asks, receives; and he that seeks, finds; and to him who knocks, it shall be opened." (Matthew 7:7, 8.) "All things whatever you shall ask in prayer believing, you shall receive ." (Matthew 21:22.) "Whatever you shall ask in my name, that I will do, that the Father may be glorified in the Son. If you shall ask anything in my name I will do it." (John 14:13, 14.) What did the Lord mean when He spoke the parables of the Friend at Midnight and the Importunate Widow? (Luke 11:5, 18:1.) Think over these passages. If this is not an encouragement to pray, words have no meaning.

There are wonderful examples in the Scripture of the power of prayer. Nothing seems to be too great, too hard, or too difficult for prayer to do. It has obtained things that seemed impossible and out of reach. It has won victories over fire, air, earth, and water. Prayer opened up the Red Sea. Prayer brought water from the rock and bread from heaven. Prayer made the sun stand still. Prayer brought fire from the sky on Elijah's sacrifice. Prayer turned the counsel of Ahithophel into foolishness. Prayer overthrew the army of Sennacherib. Well might Mary Queen of Scots say, "I fear John Knox's prayers more than an army of ten thousand men." Prayer has healed the sick. Prayer has raised the dead. Prayer has procured the conversion of souls. "The child of many prayers," said an old Christian to Augustine's mother, "shall never perish." Prayer, pains, and faith can do anything. Nothing seems impossible when a person has the spirit of adoption. "Let me alone," is the remarkable saying of God to Moses when Moses was about to intercede for the children of Israel. (Exodus 32:10.) So long as Abraham asked mercy for Sodom, the Lord went on giving. He never ceased to give until Abraham ceased to pray. (Genesis 18:17-33.) Think of this. Is this not an encouragement?

What more can people need to lead them to take any step in religion, than the things I have just told you about prayer? What more could be done to make the path to the mercy seat easy, and to remove all occasions of stumbling from the sinners way? Surely if the devils in hell had such a door set before them, they would leap for gladness and make the very pit ring with joy.

But where will the person hide their head at the last who neglects such glorious encouragements? What can possibly be said for the person who, after all, dies without prayer? Surely I may feel anxious that you should not be that person. Surely I may well ask—DO YOU PRAY?

V. I ASK WHETHER YOU PRAY, BECAUSE DILIGENCE IN PRAYER IS THE SECRET OF EMINENT HOLINESS.

Without controversy there is a vast difference among true Christians. There is an immense interval between the foremost and the hindermost in the army of God.

They are all fighting the same good fight but how much more valiantly some fight than others. They are all doing the Lord's work; but how much more some do than others. They are all light in the Lord; but how much more brightly some shine than others. They are all running the same race; but how much faster some get on than others. They all love the same Lord and Savior; but how much more some love Him than others. I ask any true Christian whether this is not the case. Are these things not so?

There are some of the Lord's people who seem never able to get on from the time of their conversion. They are born again, but they remain babies all their lives. You hear from them the same old experience. You remark in them the same lack of spiritual appetite, the same lack of interest in anything beyond their own little circle, which you remarked ten years ago. They are pilgrims indeed, but pilgrims like the Gibeonites of old; their bread is always dry and moldy, their shoes always old, and their garments always rent and torn. (Joshua 9:3-15.) I say this with sorrow and grief; but I ask any real Christian: is it not true?

There are others of the Lord's people who seem to be always advancing. They grow like grass after rain; they increase like Israel in Egypt; they press on like Gideon, though sometimes faint, yet always pursuing. (Judges 8:4.) They are ever adding grace to grace, and faith to faith, and strength to strength. Every time you meet them their hearts seems larger, and their spiritual stature taller and stronger. Every year they appear to see more, and, and know more, and believe more, and feel more in their religion. They not only have good works to prove the reality of their faith, but they are zealous of them. They not only do well, but they are unwearied in well doing. They attempt great things, and they do great things. When they fail they try again, and when they fall they are soon up again. And all this time they think themselves poor, unprofitable servants, and fancy that they do nothing at all. These are those who make religion lovely and beautiful in the eyes of all. They wrest praise even from the unconverted and win golden opinions even from the selfish people of the world. It does one good to see, to be with them, and to hear them. When you meet them, you could believe that like Moses, they had just come out from the presence of God. (Exodus 34:29-35.) When you part with them you feel warmed by their company, as if your soul had been near a fire. I know such people are rare. I only ask: are there not many such?

Now how can you account for the difference which I have just described? What is the reason that some believers are so much brighter and holier than others? I believe the difference, in nineteen cases out of twenty, arises from different habits about private prayer. I believe that those who are not eminently holy pray little, and those who are eminently holy pray much.

I dare say this opinion will startle some readers. I have little doubt that many look on eminent holiness as a kind of special gift, which none but a few must pretend to aim at. They admire it at a distance in books. They think it beautiful when they see an example near themselves. But as to its being a thing within the reach of any but a very few, such a notion never seems to enter their minds. In short, they consider it a kind of monopoly granted to a few favored believers, but certainly not to all.

Now I believe that this is a most dangerous mistake. I believe that spiritual as well as natural greatness depends in a high degree on the faithful use of means within everybody's reach. Of course I do not say we have a right to expect a miraculous grant of intellectual gifts; but I do say, that when a person is once converted to God, his progress in holiness will be much in accordance with his own diligence in the use of God's appointed means. And I assert confidently that the principle means by which most believers have become great in the church of Christ is the habit of diligent private prayer.

Look through the lives of the brightest and best of God's servants, whether in the Bible or not. See what is written of Moses and David and Daniel and Paul. Mark what is recorded of Luther and Bradford the Reformers. Observe what is related of the private devotions of Whitefield and Cecil and Venn and Bickersteth and McCheyne. Tell me of one of all the goodly fellowship of saints and martyrs, who has not had this mark most prominently—they were men of prayer. Depend on it, prayer is power.

Prayer obtains fresh and continued outpourings of the Spirit. He alone begins the work of grace in a person's heart. He alone can carry it forward and make it prosper. But the good Spirit loves to be entreated. And those who ask most will have most of His influence.

Prayer is the surest remedy against the devil and besetting sins. That sin will never stand firm which is heartily prayed against. The devil will never long keep dominion over us which beseech the Lord to cast forth. But then we must spread out all our case before our heavenly Physician, if He is to give us daily relief.

Do you wish to grow in grace and be a devoted Christian? Be very sure, if you wish it, you could not have a more important question than this—DO YOU PRAY?

VI. I ASK WHETHER YOU PRAY, BECAUSE NEGLECT OF PRAYER IS ONE OF THE GREATEST CAUSES OF BACKSLIDING.

There is such a thing as going back in religion after making a good profession. People may run well for a season, like the Galatians, and then turn aside after false teachers. People may profess loudly while their feelings are warm, as Peter did, and then in the hour of trial deny their Lord. People may lose their first love as the Ephesians did. People may cool down in their zeal to do good, like John Mark the companion of Paul. People may follow an apostle for a season, and like Demas go back to the world. All these things people may do.

It is a miserable thing to be a backslider. Of all unhappy things that can befall a person, I suppose it is the worst. A stranded ship, a broken-winged eagle, a garden overrun with weeds, a harp without strings, a church in ruins, all these are sad sights, but a backslider is a sadder still. A wounded conscience—a mind sick of itself—a memory full of self-reproach—a heart pierced through with the Lord's arrows—a spirit broken with the inward accusation—all this is a taste of hell. It is a hell on earth. Truly that saying of the wise man is solemn and weighty, "The backslider in heart shall be filled with his own ways." (Proverbs 14:14.)

Now what is the case of most backslidings? I believe, as a general rule, one of the chief causes is neglected private prayer. Of course the secret history of falls will not be known until the last day. I can only give my opinion as a minister of Christ and a student of the heart. That opinions, I repeat distinctly, that backsliding generally first begins with neglect of private prayer.

Bibles read without prayer; sermons heard without prayer; marriages contracted without prayer; journeys undertaken without prayer; residences chosen without prayer; friendships formed without prayer; the daily act of prayer itself hurried over, or gone through without heart: these are the kind of downward steps by which many a Christian descends to a condition of spiritual palsy, or reaches the point where God allows them to have a tremendous fall.

This is the process which forms the lingering Lots, the unstable Samsons, the wife-idolizing Solomons, inconsistent Asas, the pliable Jehoshaphats, the over-careful Marthas, of whom so many are to be found in the church of Christ. Often the simple history of such cases is this: they became careless about private prayer.

You may be very sure people fall in private long before they fall in public. They are backsliders on their knees long before they backslide openly in the eyes of the world. Like Peter, they first disregard the Lord's warning to watch and pray, and then like Peter, their strength is gone, and in the hour of temptation they deny their Lord. (Matthew 26:40-75.)

The world takes notice of their fall, and scoffs loudly. But the world knows nothing of the real reason. The heathen succeeded in making a well-known Christian offer incense to an idol, by threatening him with a punishment worse than death. They triumphed greatly in the sight of his cowardice and apostasy. But the heathen did not know the fact of which history informs us, that on that very morning he had left his bedchamber hastily, and without finishing his usual prayers.

If you are a Christian indeed, I trust you will never be a backslider. But if you do not want to be a backsliding Christian, remember the question I ask you: DO YOU PRAY?

VII. I ASK, LASTLY, WHETHER YOU PRAY BECAUSE PRAYER IS ONE OF THE BEST MEANS OF HAPPINESS AND CONTENTMENT.

We live in a world where sorrow abounds. This has always been the state since sin came in. There cannot be sin without sorrow. And until sin is driven out from the world, it is vain for any one to suppose they can escape sorrow.

Some without doubt have a larger cup of sorrow to drink than others. But few are to be found who live long without sorrows or cares of one sort or another. Our bodies, our property, our families, our children, our relations, our servants, our friends, our neighbors, our worldly callings, each and all of these are fountains of care. Sickness, deaths, losses, disappointments, partings, separations, ingratitude, slander, all these are common things. We cannot get through life without them. Some day or other they find us out. The greater are our affections the deeper are our afflictions, and the more we love the more we have to weep.

And what is the best means of cheerfulness in such a world as this? How shall we get through this valley of tears with the least pain? I know no better means than the habit of taking everything to God in prayer.

This is the plain advice that the Bible gives, both in the Old Testament and the New. What says the Psalmist? "Call upon me in the day of trouble, and I will deliver you and you shall glorify me." (Psalm 50:15.) "Cast your burden upon the Lord and He shall sustain you: He shall never suffer the righteous to be moved." (Psalm 55:22.) What says the apostle Paul? "Be careful for nothing; but in everything, by prayer and supplication with thanksgiving, let your requests be made known unto God. And the peace of God, which passes all understanding shall keep your hearts and minds through Christ Jesus." (Philippians 4:6, 7.) What says the apostle James: "Is any afflicted among you? Let him pray." (James 5:13.)

This was the practice of all the saints whose history we have recorded in the Scriptures. This is what Jacob did when he feared his brother Esau. This is what Moses did when the people were ready to stone him in the wilderness. This is what Joshua did when Israel was defeated before the men of Ai. This is what David did when he was in danger in Keliah. This what Hezekiah did when he received the letter from Sennacherib. This is what the church did when Peter was put in prison. This is what Paul did when he was cast into the dungeon at Philippi.

The only way to really be happy in such a world as this, is to be ever casting all our cares on God. It is trying to carry their own burdens which so often makes believers sad. If they will tell their troubles to God, He will enable them to bear them as easily as Samson did the gates of Gaza. (Judges 16:3.) If they are resolved to keep them to themselves, they will one day find that the very grasshopper is a burden.

There is a friend ever waiting to help us, if we will unbosom to Him our sorrow—a friend who pitied the poor and sick and sorrowful, when He was upon earth—a friend who knows the heart of man, for He lived thirty-three years as a man among us—a friend who can weep with the weepers, for He was a man of sorrows and acquainted with grief—a friend who is able to help us, for there never was earthly pain He could not cure. That friend is Jesus Christ. The way to be happy is to be always opening our hearts to Him. Oh that we were all like that poor Christian slave who only answered when threatened and punished, "I must tell the Lord."

Jesus can make those happy who trust Him and call Him,

whatever be their outward condition. He can give them peace of heart in a prison, contentment in the midst of poverty, comfort in the midst of bereavements, joy on the brink of the grave. There is a mighty fullness in Him for all His believing members—a fullness that is ready to be poured out on everyone that will ask in prayer. Oh that people would understand that happiness does not depend on outward circumstances, but on the state of the heart.

Prayer can lighten crosses for us, however heavy. It can bring down to our side One who will help us to bear them. Prayer can open a door for us when our way seems hedged up. It can bring down One who will say, "This is the way, walk in it." (Isaiah 30:21.) Prayer can let in a ray of hope when all our earthly prospects seem darkened. It can bring down One who will say, "I will never leave you, nor forsake you." (Hebrews 13:5) Prayer can obtain relief for us when those we love most are taken away, and the world feels empty. It can bring down One who can fill the gap in our hearts with himself, and say to the waves within, "Peace, be still." (Mark 4:39.) Oh that people were not so like Hagar in the wilderness, blind to the well of living waters close beside them. (Genesis 21:14-19.)

I want you to be happy. I know I cannot ask you a more useful question than this: DO YOU PRAY?

And now it is high time for me to bring this tract to an end. I trust I have brought before you things that will be seriously considered. I heartily pray God that this consideration may be blessed to your soul.

Let me speak **a parting word to THOSE WHO DO NOT PRAY**. I dare not suppose that all those who read these pages are praying people. If you are a prayerless person, suffer me to speak to you this day on God's behalf.

Prayerless reader, I can only warn you but I do warn you most solemnly. I warn you that you are in a position of fearful danger. If you die in your present state, you are a lost soul. You will only rise again to be eternally miserable. I warn you that all professing Christians you are utterly without excuse. There is not a single good reason that you can show for living without prayer.

It is useless to say you know not how to pray. Prayer is the simplest act in all religion. It is simply speaking to God. It needs neither learning nor wisdom nor book-knowledge to begin it. It needs nothing but heart and will. The weakest infant can cry when he is hungry. The poorest beggar can hold out their hand for alms, and does not wait to find fine words. The most ignorant person will find something to say to God, if they have only a mind.

It is useless to say you have no convenient place to pray in. Any person can find a place private enough, if they are disposed. Our Lord prayed on a mountain; Peter on the housetop; Isaac in the field;

Nathaniel under the fig tree; Jonah in the whale's belly. Any place may become a closet, an oratory, and a Bethel, and be to us the presence of God.

It is useless to say you have no time. There is plenty of time, if people will employ it. Time may be short, but time is always long enough for prayer. Daniel had the affairs of a kingdom on his hands, and yet he prayed three times a day. (Daniel 2:48; 6:10.) David was the ruler over a mighty nation, and yet he says, "Evening and morning and at noon will I pray." (Psalm 55:17.) When time is really wanted, time can always be found.

It is useless to say you cannot pray until you have faith and a new heart, and that you must sit still and wait for them. This is to add sin to sin. It is bad enough to be unconverted and going to hell. It is even worse to say, "I know it, but will not cry for mercy." This is a kind of argument for which there is no warrant in Scripture. "Call you upon the Lord," says Isaiah, "while He is near." (Isaiah 55:6.) "Take with you words, and turn unto the Lord," says Hosea. (Hosea 14:2.) "Repent and pray," says Peter to Simon Magus. (Acts 8:22.) If you want faith and a new heart, go and cry to the Lord for them. The very attempt to pray has often been the quickening of a dead soul.

Oh, prayerless reader, who and what are you that you will not ask anything of God? Have you made a covenant with the dead and hell? Are you at peace with the worm and fire? Have you no sins to be pardoned? Have you no fear of eternal torment? Have you no desire after heaven? Oh that you would awake from your present folly. Oh that you would consider your latter end. Oh that you would arise and call upon God. Alas, there is a day coming when many shall pray loudly, "Lord, Lord, open to us," but all too late; when many shall cry to the rocks to fall on them and the hills to cover them, who would never cry to God. (Matthew 25:11; Revelation 6:16.) In all affection, I warn you, beware lest this be the end of your soul. Salvation is very near you. Do not lose heaven for want of asking.

Let me speak TO THOSE WHO HAVE REAL DESIRES FOR SALVATION, but know not what steps to take, or where to begin. I cannot but hope that some readers may be in this state of mind, and if there be but one such I must offer them affectionate counsel.

In every journey there must be a first step. There must be a change from sitting still to moving forward. The journeyings of Israel from Egypt to Canaan were long and wearisome. Forty years pass away before they crossed the Jordan. Yet there was someone who moved first when they marched from Ramah to Succoth. When does a person really take their first step in coming out of sin and the world? They do it the day when they first pray with their heart.

In every building the first stone must be laid, and the first blow must be struck. The ark was one hundred and twenty years in the building. Yet there was a day when Noah laid his axe to the first tree he cut down to form it. The temple of Solomon was a glorious building. But there was a day when the first huge stone was laid deep in mount Moriah. When does the building of the Spirit really begin to appear in a person's heart? It begins, so far as we can judge, when they first pour out their heart to God in prayer.

If you desire salvation, and want to know what to do, I advise you to go this very day to the Lord Jesus Christ, in the first private place you can find, and earnestly and heartily entreat him in prayer to save your soul.

Tell him that you have heard that He receives sinners, and has said, "Him that comes unto me I will in nowise cast out." (John 6:37.) Tell Him that you are a poor vile sinner, and that you come to Him on the faith of His own invitation. Tell him you put yourself wholly and entirely in His hands: that you feel vile and helpless, and hopeless in yourself: and that except He saves you, you have no hope of being saved at all. Beseech Him to deliver you from guilt, the power, and the consequences of sin. Beseech Him to pardon you, and wash you in his own blood. Beseech Him to give you a new heart, and plant the Holy Spirit in your soul. Beseech Him to give you grace and faith and will and power to be His disciple and servant from this day forever. Oh, reader, go this very day, and tell these things to the Lord Jesus Christ, if you really are in earnest about your soul.

Tell him in your own way, and your own words. If a doctor came to see you when you were sick you could tell him where you felt pain. If your soul feels its disease indeed, you can surely find something to tell Christ.

Doubt not His willingness to save you, because you are a sinner. It is Christ's office to save sinners. He says Himself, "I came not to call the righteous, but sinners to repentance." (Luke 5:32.)

Wait not because you feel unworthy. Wait for nothing. Wait for nobody. Waiting comes from the devil. Just as you are, go to Christ. The worse you are, the more need you have to apply to Him. You will never mend yourself by staying away.

Fear not because your prayer is stammering, your words feeble, and your language poor. Jesus can understand you. Just as a mother understands the first lispings of her infant, so does the blessed Savior understand sinners. He can read a sigh, and see a meaning in a groan.

Despair not because you do not get an answer immediately. While you are speaking, Jesus is listening. If He delays an answer, it is only for wise reasons, and to try if you are in earnest. The answer will surely come. Though it tarry, wait for it. It will surely come.

Oh, reader, if you have any desire to be saved, remember the advice I have given to you this day. Act upon it honestly and heartily, and you shall be saved.

Let me speak, lastly, TO THOSE WHO DO PRAY. I trust that some who read this tract know well what prayer is, and have the Spirit of adoption. To all such, I offer a few words of brotherly counsel and exhortation. The incense offered in the tabernacle was ordered to be made in a particular way. Not every kind of incense would do. Let us remember this, and be careful about the matter and manner of our prayers.

Brethren who pray, if I know anything of a Christian's heart, you are often sick of your own prayers. You never enter into the apostle's words, "When I would do good, evil is present with me." so thoroughly as you sometimes do upon your knees. (Romans 7:21.) You can understand David's words, "I hate vain thoughts." (Psalm 119:113.) You can sympathize with that poor converted Hottentot who was overheard praying, "Lord, deliver me from all my enemies, and above all, from that bad man—myself." There are few children of God who do not often find the season of prayer a season of conflict. The devil has special wrath against us when he sees us on our knees. Yet, I believe that prayers which cost us no trouble, should be regarded with great suspicion. I believe we are very poor judges of the goodness of our prayers, and that the prayer which pleases us least, often pleases God most. Suffer me then, as a companion in the Christian warfare, to offer a few words of exhortation. One thing, at least, we all feel: we must pray. We cannot give it up. We must go on.

I commend then to your attention, the importance of reverence and humility in prayer. Let us never forget what we are, and what a solemn thing it is to speak with God. Let us beware of rushing into His presence with carelessness and levity. Let us say to ourselves: "I am on holy ground. This is no other than the gate of heaven. If I do not mean what I say, I am trifling with God. If I regard iniquity in my heart, the Lord will not hear me." (Exodus 3:5; Genesis 28:17; Psalm 66:18.) Let us keep in mind the words of Solomon, "Do not be rash with your mouth, and let not your heart be hasty to utter anything before God; for God is in heaven, and you on earth." (Ecclesiastes 5:2.) When Abraham spoke to God, he said, "I am dust and ashes." When Job spoke to God, he said, "I am vile." Let us do likewise. (Genesis 18:27; Job 40:4.)

I commend to you the importance of praying spiritually. I mean by that, that we should labor always to have the direct help of the Spirit in our prayers, and beware above all things of formality. There is nothing so spiritual that it may become a form, and this is especially true of private prayer. We may insensibly get into the habit of using the fittest possible words, and offering the most scriptural petitions, and yet do it all by rote without feeling it, and walk daily round an old beaten path. I desire to touch this point with caution and delicacy. I know that there are certain things we daily want, and that there is nothing necessarily formal in asking for these things in the same words. The world, the devil, and our hearts are daily the same. Of necessity we must daily go over old ground. But this I say, we must be very careful on this point. If the skeleton and outline of our prayers be by habit almost form, let us strive that the clothing and filling up of our prayers, be as far as possible of the Spirit. As to praying of a book in our private devotions, it is a habit I cannot praise. If we can tell our doctors the state of our bodies without a book, we ought to be able to tell the state of our souls to God. I have no objection to a person using crutches when they are first recovering from a broken limb. It is better to use crutches, than not to walk at all. But if I saw them all their life on crutches, I should not think it matter for congratulation. I should like to see them strong enough to throw their crutches away.

I commend to you the importance of making prayer a regular business of life. I might say something of the value of regular times in the day for prayer. God is a God of order. The hours for morning and evening sacrifice in the Jewish temple were not fixed as they were without a meaning. Disorder is eminently one of the fruits of sin. But I would not bring any under bondage. This only I say, that it is essential to your soul's health to make praying a part of the business of every twenty-four hours of your life. Just as you allot time to eating, sleeping, and business, so also allot time to prayer. Choose your own hours and seasons. At the very least, speak with God in the morning, before you speak with the world: and speak with God at night, after you have done with the world. But settle it in your minds, that praying is one of the great things of every day. Do not drive it into a corner. Do not give it the scraps and parings of your duty. Whatever else you make a business of, make a business of prayer.

I commend to you the importance of perseverance in prayer. Once having begun the habit, never give it up. Your heart will sometimes say, "You will have had family prayers: what mighty harm if you leave private prayer undone?" Your body will sometimes say, "You are unwell, or sleepy, or weary; you need not pray." Your mind will sometimes say, "You have important business to attend to today; cut short your prayers." Look on all such suggestions as coming direct from Satan. They are all as good as saying, "Neglect your soul." I do not maintain that prayers should always be of the same length; but I do say, let no excuse make you give up prayer. Paul said, "Continue in prayer" and, "Pray without ceasing." (Colossians 4:2; 1 Thessalonians 5:17.) He did not mean that people should be always on their knees, but he did mean that our prayers should be like the continual burned-offering, steadily preserved in every day; that it should be like seedtime and harvest, and summer and winter, unceasingly coming round at regular seasons; that it should be like the fire on the altar, not always consuming sacrifices, but never completely going out. Never forget that you may tie together morning and evening devotions, by an endless chain of short ejaculatory prayers throughout the day. Even in company, or business, or in the very streets, you may be silently sending up little winged messengers to God, as Nehemiah did in the very presence of Artaxerxes. (Nehemiah 2:4.) And never think that time is wasted which is given to God. A nation does not become poorer because it loses one year of working days in seven, by keeping the Sabbath. A Christian never finds he is a loser, in the long run, by persevering in prayer.

I commend to you the importance of earnestness in prayer. It is not that a person should shout, or scream, or be very loud, in order to prove that they are in earnest. But it is desirable that we should be hearty and fervent and warm, and ask as if we were really interested in what we were doing. It is the "effectual fervent" prayer that "avails much." (James 5:16.) This is the lesson that is taught us by the expressions used in Scripture about prayer. It is called, "crying, knocking, wrestling, laboring, striving." This is the lesson taught us by scripture examples. Jacob is one. He said to the angel at Penuel, "I will not let You go, except You bless me." (Genesis 32:26.) Daniel is another. Hear how he pleaded with God: "O Lord, hear; O Lord, forgive; O Lord, hearken and do; defer not, for Your own sake, O my God." (Daniel 9:19.) Our Lord Jesus Christ is another. It is written of Him, "In the days of His flesh, He offered up prayers and supplications with strong crying and tears." (Hebrews 5:7.) Alas, how unlike is this to many of our supplications! How tame and lukewarm they seem by comparison. How truly might God say to many of us, "You do not really want what you pray for." Lets us try to amend this fault. Let us knock loudly at the door of grace, like Mercy in Pilgrim's Progress, as if we must perish unless heard. Let us settle it in our minds, that cold prayers are a sacrifice without fire. Let us remember the story of Demosthenes the great orator, when one came to him, and wanted to plead his cause. He heard him without attention, while he told his story without earnestness. The man saw this, and cried out with anxiety that it was all true. "Ah," said Demosthenes, "I believe you now."

I commend to you the importance of praying in faith. We should endeavor to believe that our prayers are heard, and that if we ask things according to God's will, we shall be answered. This is the plain command of our Lord Jesus Christ: "Whatever things you desire, when you pray, believe that you receive them, and you shall have them." (Mark 11:24.) Faith is to prayer what the feather is to the arrow: without it prayer will not hit the mark. We should cultivate the habit of pleading promises in our prayers.

We should take with us some promises, and say, "Lord, here is Your own word pledged. Do for us as You have said." This was the habit of Jacob and Moses and David. The 119th Psalm is full of things asked, "according to your word." Above all, we should cultivate the habit of expecting answers to our prayers. We should do like the merchant who sends his ships to sea. We should not be satisfied, unless we see some return. Alas, there are few points on which Christians come short so much as this. The church at Jerusalem made prayer without ceasing for Peter in prison; but when the prayer was answered, they would hardly believe it. (Acts 12:15.) It is a solemn saying of Robert Traill, "There is no surer mark of trifling in prayer, than when men are careless what they get in prayer."

I commend to you the importance of boldness in prayer. There is an unseemly familiarity in some people's prayers which I cannot praise. But there is such a thing as a holy boldness, which is exceedingly to be desired. I mean such boldness as that of Moses, when he pleads with God not to destroy Israel. "Wherefore," says he, "should the Egyptians speak and say, 'For mischief did He bring them out, to slay them in the mountains'? Turn from Your fierce anger." (Exodus 32:12.) I mean such boldness as that of Joshua, when the children of Israel were defeated before men of Ai: "What," says he, "will You do unto Your great name?" (Joshua 7:9.) This is the boldness for which Luther was remarkable. One who heard him praying said, "What a spirit, what a confidence was in his very expressions. With such a reverence he sued, as one begging of God, and yet with such hope and assurance, as if he spoke with a loving father or friend." This is the boldness which distinguished Bruce, a great Scottish divine of the seventeenth century. His prayers were said to be "like bolts shot up into heaven." Here also I fear we sadly come short. We do not sufficiently realize the believer's privileges. We do not plead as often as we might, "Lord, are we not Your own people? Is it not for Your glory that we should be sanctified? Is it not for Your honor that Your gospel should increase?"

I commend to you the importance of fullness in prayer. I do not forget that our Lord warns us against the example of the Pharisees, who, for pretense, made long prayers; and commands us when we pray not to use vain repetitions. But I cannot forget, on the other hand, that He has given His own sanction to large and long devotions by continuing all night in prayer to God. At all events, we are not likely in this day to err on the side of praying too much. Might it not rather be feared that many believers in this generation pray too little? Is not the actual amount of time that many Christians give to prayer, in the aggregate, very small? I am afraid these questions cannot be answered satisfactorily. I am afraid the private devotions of many are painfully scanty and limited; just enough to prove they are alive and no more. They really seem to want little from God. They seem to have little to confess, little to ask for, and little to thank Him for. Alas, this is altogether wrong. Nothing is more common than to hear believers complaining that they do not get on. They tell us that they do not grow in grace as they could desire. Is it not rather to be suspected that many have quite as much grace as they ask for? Is it not the true account of many, that they have little, because they ask little? The cause of their weakness is to be found in their own stunted, dwarfish, clipped, contracted, hurried, narrow, diminutive prayers. They have not, because they ask not. Oh, we are not straitened in Christ, but in ourselves. The Lord says, "Open your mouth wide, and I will fill it." (Psalm 8:10.) But we are like the King of Israel who smote on the ground thrice and stayed, when he ought to have smitten five or six times. (2 Kings 13:14-19.)

I commend to you the importance of particularity in prayer. We ought not to be content with general petitions. We ought to specify our needs before the throne of grace. It should not be enough to confess we are sinners; we should name the sins of which our conscience tells us we are most guilty. It should not be enough to ask for holiness; we should name the graces in which we feel most deficient. It should not be enough to tell the Lord we are in trouble; we should describe our trouble and all its peculiarities. This is what Jacob did when he feared his brother Esau. He tells God exactly what it is that he fears. (Genesis 32:11.) This is what Eleazar did, when he sought a wife for his master's son. He spreads before God precisely what he needs. (Genesis 24:12.) This is what Paul did when he had a thorn in the flesh. He besought the Lord. (2 Corinthians 12:8.) This is true faith and confidence. We should believe that nothing is too small to be named before God. What should we think of the patient who told his doctor he was ill, but never went into particulars? What should we think of the wife who told her husband she was unhappy, but did not specify the cause? What should we think of the child who told their father that he was in trouble, but nothing more? Christ is the true bridegroom of the soul, the true physician of the heart, the real father of all His people. Let us show that we feel this by being unreserved in our communications with Him. Let us hide no secrets from Him. Let us tell Him all our hearts.

I commend to you the importance of intercession in our prayers. We are all selfish by nature, and our selfishness is very apt to stick to us, even when we are converted. There is a tendency in us to think only of our own souls, our own spiritual conflicts, our own progress in religion, and to forget others. Against this tendency we all have need to watch and strive, and not the least in our prayers. We should study to be of a public spirit. We should stir ourselves up to name other names besides our own before the throne of grace. We should try to bear in our hearts the whole world, the heathen, the Jews, the Roman Catholics, the body of true believers, the professing Protestant churches, the country in which we live, the congregation to which we belong, the household in which we sojourn, the friends and relations we are connected with. For each and all of these we should plead. This is the highest charity. They love me best who loves me in their prayers. This is for our soul's health. It enlarges our sympathies and expands our hearts. This is for the benefit of the church. The wheels of all machinery for extending the gospel are moved by prayer. They do as much for the Lord's cause who intercede like Moses on the mount, as they who fight like Joshua in the thick of the battle. This is to be like Christ. He bears the names of His people, as their High Priest, before the Father. Oh, the privilege of being like Jesus! This is to be a true helper to ministers. If I must choose a congregation, give me a people that pray.

I commend to you the importance of thankfulness in prayer. I know well that asking God is one thing and praising God is another. But I see so close a connection between prayer and praise in the Bible, that I dare not call that true prayer in which thankfulness has no part. It is not for nothing that Paul says, "By prayer and supplication, with thanksgiving, let your requests be made known unto God." (Philippians 4:6.) "Continue in prayer, and watch in the same with thanksgiving." (Colossians 4:2.) It is of mercy that we are not in hell. It is of mercy that we have the hope of heaven. It is of mercy that we live in a land of spiritual light. It is of mercy that we have been called by the Spirit, and not left to reap the fruit of our own ways. It is of mercy that we still live and have opportunities of glorifying God actively or passively. Surely these thoughts should crowd on our minds whenever we speak with God. Surely we should never open our lips in prayer without blessing God for that free grace by which we live, and for that loving kindness which endures forever. Never was there an eminent saint who was not full of thankfulness. Paul hardly ever writes an epistle without beginning with thankfulness. Men like Whitefield in the last century, and Bickersteth in our own time, abounded in thankfulness. Oh, reader, if we would be bright and shining lights in our day, we must cherish a spirit of praise. Let our prayers be thankful prayers.

I commend to you the importance of watchfulness over your prayers. Prayer is the point in religion at which you must be most of all on your guard. Here it is that true religion begins; here it flourishes, and here it decays. Tell me what a person's prayers are, and I will soon tell you the state of their soul. Prayer is the spiritual pulse. By this the spiritual health may be tested. Prayer is the spiritual weather-glass. By this we may know whether it is fair or foul with our hearts. Oh, let us keep an eye continually upon our private devotions. Here is the heart of the matter of our practical Christianity. Sermons and books and tracts, and committee-meetings and the company of good people are all good in their way, but they will never make up for the neglect of private prayer. Mark well the places and society and companions that unhinge your hearts for communion with God and make your prayers drive heavily. There be on your guard. Observe narrowly what friends and what employment leave your soul in the most spiritual frame, and most ready to speak with God. To these cleave and stick fast. If you will take care of your prayers, nothing shall go very wrong with your soul.

I offer these points for your private consideration. I do it in all humility. I know no one who needs to be reminded of them more than I do myself. But I believe them to be God's own truth, and I desire myself and all I love to feel them more.

I want the times we live in to be praying times. I want the Christians of our day to be praying Christians. I want the church to be a praying church. My Heart's desire and prayer in sending forth this tract is to promote a spirit of prayerfulness. I want those who never prayed yet, to arise and call upon God, and I want those who do pray, to see that they are not praying amiss.

BIBLE READING

"Search the Scriptures." John 5:39

"How do you read it?" Luke 10:26

Next to *praying*, there is nothing so important in practical religion as *Bible-reading*. God has mercifully given us a book which is "able to make us wise unto salvation through faith which is in Christ Jesus." (2 Tim. 3:15.) By reading that book, we may learn . . .
what to *believe*,
what to *be*,
what to *do*;
how to *live* with comfort,
and how to die in peace.

Happy is that man who *possesses* a Bible! Happier still is he who *reads* it! Happiest of all is he who not only reads it—but *obeys* it, and makes it the rule of his faith and practice!

Nevertheless, it is a sorrowful fact that man has an unhappy skill in abusing God's gifts. His privileges, and power, and faculties, are all ingeniously perverted to other ends than those for which they were bestowed. His speech, his imagination, his intellect, his strength, his time, his influence, his money—instead of being used as *instruments for glorifying his Maker*—are generally wasted, or employed for his own selfish ends. And just as man naturally makes a bad use of his other mercies, so he does of the written Word. One sweeping charge may be brought against the whole of Christendom, and that charge is *neglect and abuse of the Bible.*

To prove this charge we have no need to look abroad: the proof lies at our own doors. I have no doubt that there are more Bibles in Great Britain at this moment than there ever were since the world began. There is more Bible buying and Bible selling, more Bible printing and Bible distributing—than ever was since England was a nation. We see Bibles in every bookseller's shop—Bibles of every size, price, and style; Bibles great, and Bibles small—Bibles for the rich, and Bibles for the poor. There are Bibles in almost every house in the land. But all this time I fear we are in danger of forgetting, that to *have* the Bible is one thing—and to *read* it quite another.

This neglected Book is the subject about which I address the readers of this paper today. Surely it is no light matter what you are doing with the Bible. Surely, when the plague is abroad, you should search and see, whether the plague-spot is on you. Give me your attention while I supply you with a few plain reasons why everyone who cares for his soul ought to *value* the Bible highly, to *study* it regularly, and to make himself *thoroughly acquainted* with its contents.

1. In the first place, there is no book in existence written in such a manner as the Bible.

The Bible was "given by inspiration of God." (2 Timothy 3:16.) In this respect, it is utterly unlike all other writings. God taught the writers of it what to say. God put into their minds thoughts and ideas. God guided their pens in setting down those thoughts and ideas. When you read it—you are not reading the self-taught compositions of poor imperfect *men* like yourself—but the words of the eternal *God*. When you hear it, you are not listening to the erring opinions of short-lived mortals—but to the unchanging mind of the King of kings. The men who were employed to compose the Bible, spoke not of themselves. They "spoke as they were moved by the Holy Spirit." (2 Peter 1:21.) *All other books* in the world, however good and useful in their way, are more or less *defective*. The more you look at them—the more you see their defects and blemishes. The Bible alone is *absolutely perfect*. From beginning to end, it is "the Word of God."

I shall not waste time by attempting any long and labored proof of this. I say boldly, that the Book itself is the best witness of its own inspiration. It is utterly inexplicable and unaccountable in any other point of view. It is the greatest standing miracle in the world. He who dares to say the Bible is not inspired, let him give a reasonable account of it, if he can. Let him explain the peculiar nature and character of the Book in a way that will satisfy any man of common sense. The burden of proof seems to my mind to lie on him.

It proves nothing against inspiration, as some have asserted, that the writers of the Bible have each a different style. Isaiah does not write like Jeremiah, and Paul does not write like John. This is perfectly true—and yet the works of these men are not a whit less equally inspired. The waters of the sea have many different shades. In one place they look blue, and in another green. And yet the difference is owing to the depth or shallowness of the part we see, or to the nature of the bottom. The water in every case is the same salt sea. The breath of a man may produce different sounds, according to the character of the instrument on which he plays. The flute, the pipe, and the trumpet, have each their peculiar note. And yet the breath that calls forth the notes, is in each case one and the same. The light of the planets we see in the skies is very various. Mars, and Saturn, and Jupiter, have each a peculiar color. And yet we know that the light of the sun, which each planet reflects, is in each case one and the same. Just in the same way the books of the Old and New Testaments are all inspired truth—and yet the aspect of that truth varies according to the mind through which the Holy Spirit makes it flow. The handwriting and style of the writers differ enough to prove that each had a distinct individual being; but the *Divine Guide* who dictates and directs the whole, is always one. All is alike inspired. Every *chapter*, and *verse*, and *word*—is from God.

Oh, that men who are troubled with doubts, and questionings, and skeptical thoughts about inspiration, would calmly examine the Bible for themselves! Oh, that they would act on the advice which was the first step to Augustine's conversion, "Take it up and read it!—take it up and read it!" How many *Gordian knots* this course of action would cut! How many *difficulties* and *objections* would vanish away at once like mist before the rising sun! How many would soon confess, "The finger of God is here! God is in this Book, and I knew it not!"

This is the Book about which I address the readers of this paper. Surely it is no light matter what you are doing with this Book. It is no light thing that God should have caused this Book to be "written for your learning," and that you should have before you "the oracles of God." (Romans 3:2; 15:4.) I charge you, I summon you to give an honest answer to my question. *What are you doing with the Bible? Do you read it at all? How do you read it?*

2. In the second place, there is no knowledge absolutely needful to a man's salvation, except a knowledge of the things which are to be found in the Bible.

We live in days when the words of Daniel are fulfilled before our eyes, "Many run to and fro, and knowledge is increased." (Dan. 12:4.) Schools are multiplying on every side. New colleges are set up. Old Universities are reformed and improved. New books are continually coming forth. More is being taught—more is being learned—more is being read—than there ever was since the world began.

It is all well. I rejoice at it. An *ignorant population* is a perilous and expensive burden to any nation. It is a ready prey to the first Absalom, or Catiline, or Wat Tyler, or Jack Cade, who may arise to entice it to do evil. But this I say—-we must never forget that all the education a man's *head* can receive, will not save his soul from Hell, unless he knows the truths of the Bible.

A man may have prodigious learning—and yet never be saved. He may be master of half the languages spoken round the globe. He may be acquainted with the highest and deepest things in Heaven and earth. He may have read books until he is like a *walking encyclopaedia*. He may be familiar with the stars of skies—the birds of the air—the beasts of the earth, and the fish of the sea. He may be able, like Solomon, to "speak of trees, from the cedar of Lebanon to the hyssop that grows on the wall, of beasts also, and fowls, and creeping things, and fish." (1 King 4:33.) He may be able to discourse of all the secrets of fire, air, earth, and water. And yet, if he dies ignorant of Bible truths—he dies a miserable man!

Chemistry never silenced a guilty conscience. Mathematics never healed a broken heart. All the sciences in the world never smoothed a dying pillow. No earthly philosophy ever supplied hope in death, or gave peace in the prospect of meeting a holy God. All these things are of the earth, earthy, and can never raise a man above the earth's level. They may enable a man to strut and fret his little season here below with a more dignified gait than his fellow-mortals—but they can never give him wings, and enable him to soar towards Heaven. He who has the largest share of them, will find at length that without Bible knowledge—he has got no lasting possession. Death will make an end of all his attainments, and after death they will do him no good at all.

A man may be a very ignorant man—and yet be saved. He may be unable to read a word, or write a letter. He may know nothing of geography beyond the bounds of his own town, and be utterly unable to say which is nearest to England, Paris or New York. He may know nothing of arithmetic, and not see any difference between a million and a thousand. He may know nothing of history, not even of his own land, and be quite ignorant whether his country owes most to Semiramis, Boadicea, or Queen Elizabeth. He may know nothing of the affairs of his own times, and be incapable of telling you whether the Chancellor of the Treasury, or the Commander-in-Chief, or the Archbishop of Canterbury is managing the national finances. He may know nothing of science, and its discoveries. Whether Julius Caesar won his victories with gunpowder, or the apostles had a printing press, or the sun goes around the earth—may be matters about which he has not an idea! And yet if that very man has heard Bible truth with his ears, and believed it with his heart, he knows enough to save his soul. He will be found at last with Lazarus in Abraham's bosom, while his well-taught scientific fellow-man, who has died unconverted, is lost forever.

There is much talk in these days about science and "useful knowledge." But after all, a knowledge of the Bible is the one knowledge that is needful and eternally useful. A man may get to Heaven without money, without learning, without health, or without friends—but without Bible knowledge he will never get there at all. A man may have the mightiest of minds, and a memory stored with all that mighty mind can grasp—and yet, if he does not know the things of the Bible, he will make shipwreck of his soul forever. Woe! woe! woe to the man who dies in ignorance of the Bible! This is the Book about which I am addressing the readers of these pages today. It is no light matter what you do with such a book. It concerns the life of your soul. I *summon* you—I *charge* you to give an honest answer to my question. *What are you doing with the Bible? Do you read it? How do you read it?*

3. In the third place, no book in existence contains such important matter as the Bible.

The time would fail me if I were to enter fully into all the great things which are to be found in the Bible—and *only* in the Bible. It is not by any sketch or outline, that the treasures of the Bible can be displayed. It would be easy to fill this volume with a list of the peculiar truths it reveals—and yet the half of its riches would be left untold.

How glorious and soul-satisfying is the description it gives us of *God's plan of salvation*, and the way by which our sins can be forgiven! The coming into the world of Jesus Christ, the God-man, to save sinners—the atonement He has made by suffering in our stead, the just for the unjust—the complete payment He has made for our sins by His own blood—the justification of every sinner who simply believes on Jesus—the readiness of Father, Son, and Holy Spirit, to receive, pardon, and save to the uttermost—how unspeakably grand and cheering are all these truths! We would know nothing of them without the Bible.

How comforting is the account it gives us of the great **Mediator** of the New Testament—the *God-man* Christ Jesus! Four times over His picture is graciously drawn before our eyes. Four separate witnesses tell us of . . .
His miracles and His ministry,
His sayings and His doings,
His life and His death,
His power and His love,
His kindness and His patience,
His ways, His words, His works, His thoughts, His heart!

Blessed be God, there is one thing in the Bible which the most prejudiced reader can hardly fail to understand—and that is the character of Jesus Christ!

How encouraging are the examples the Bible gives us of **godly** people! It tells us of many who were of like passions with ourselves—men and women who had cares, crosses, families, temptations, afflictions, diseases, like ourselves—and yet "by faith and patience inherited the promises," and got safely home. (Hebrews 6:12.) It keeps back nothing in the history of these people. Their mistakes, their infirmities, their conflicts, their experience, their prayers, their praises, their useful lives, their happy deaths—all are fully recorded. And it tells us the God and Savior of these men and women still waits to be gracious, and is altogether unchanged.

How instructive are the examples the Bible gives us of **evil** people! It tells us of men and women who had light, and knowledge, and opportunities, like ourselves—and yet hardened their hearts, loved the world, clung to their sins, would have their own way, despised reproof, and ruined their own souls forever! And it warns us that the God who punished Pharaoh, and Saul, and Ahab, and Jezebel, and Judas, and Ananias and Sapphira—is a God who never alters, and that there is a Hell!

How precious are the **promises** which the Bible contains for the use of those who love God! There is hardly any possible emergency or condition, for which it has not some "word in season." And it tells men that God loves to be put in remembrance of these promises, and that if He has said He will do a thing—His promise shall certainly be performed.

How blessed are the **hopes** which the Bible holds out to the believer in Christ Jesus!
Peace in the hour of death,
rest and happiness on the other side of the grave,
a glorious body in the morning of the resurrection,
a full and triumphant acquittal in the day of judgment,
an everlasting reward in the kingdom of Christ,
a joyful meeting with the Lord's people in the day of gathering together.
These, these are the future prospects of every true Christian. They are all written in the book—in the book which is all true!

How striking is the light which the Bible throws on the character of **man**! It teaches us what men may be expected to be and do in every position and station of life. It gives us the deepest insight into the secret springs and motives of human actions, and the ordinary course of events under the control of human agents. It is the true "discerner of the thoughts and intents of the heart." (Hebrews 4:12.)

How deep is the **wisdom** contained in the books of Proverbs and Ecclesiastes! I can well understand an old divine saying, "Give me a candle and a Bible, and shut me up in a dark dungeon—and I will tell you all that the whole world is doing!"

All these are things which men could find nowhere except in the Bible. We have probably not the least idea how little we would know about these things, if we had not the Bible. We hardly know the value of the *air* we breathe, and the *sun* which shines on us—because we have never known what it is to be without them. We do not value the truths on which I have been just now dwelling—because we do not realize the darkness of men to whom these truths have not been revealed. Surely no tongue can fully tell the value of the treasures which this one volume contains. Well might old John Newton say that some books were *copper* books in his estimation, some were *silver*, and some few were *gold*—but the Bible alone was like a book all made up of bank notes!

This is the Book about which I address the reader of this paper this day. Surely it is no light matter what you are doing with the Bible. It is no light matter in what way you are using this treasure. I charge you, I summon you to give an honest answer to my question: *What are you doing with the Bible? Do you read it? How do you read it?*

4. In the fourth place, no book in existence has produced such wonderful effects on mankind at large as the Bible.

(a) This is the Book whose doctrines turned the world upside down in the days of the Apostles.

Eighteen centuries have now passed away since God sent forth a few Jews from a remote corner of the earth, to do a work which according to man's judgment must have seemed impossible. He sent them forth at a time when the whole world was full of superstition, cruelty, lust, and sin. He sent them forth to proclaim that the *established religions* of the earth were false and useless, and must be forsaken. He sent them forth to persuade men to give up old habits and customs, and to live different lives. He sent them forth to do battle with the most groveling *idolatry*, with the vilest and most disgusting *immorality*, with vested interests, with old associations, with a bigoted priesthood, with sneering philosophers, with an ignorant population, with bloody-minded emperors, with the whole influence of imperial Rome. Never was there an enterprise to all appearance less likely to succeed!

And how did God *arm* them for this battle? He gave them *no carnal weapons*. He gave them *no worldly power* to compel assent, and *no worldly riches* to bribe belief. He simply put the Holy Spirit into their hearts—and the Scriptures into their hands! He simply bade them to expound and explain, to enforce and to publish the doctrines of the Bible. The preacher of Christianity in the first century was not a man with a sword and an army to frighten people, like Mahomet—or a man with a license to be sensual, to allure people, like the priests of the shameful idols of Hindustan. No! he was nothing more than one holy man—with one holy book.

And how did these *men of one book* prosper? In a few generations they entirely changed the face of society by the doctrines of the Bible. They emptied the temples of the *heathen gods*. They famished *idolatry*, or left it high and dry like a stranded ship. They brought into the world a higher tone of *morality* between man and man. They raised the character and position of *woman*. They altered the standard of *purity* and *decency*. They put an end to many *cruel* and bloody *customs*, such as the gladiatorial fights. There was no stopping the change. Persecution and opposition were useless. One victory after another was won. One bad thing after another melted away. Whether people liked it or not, they were insensibly affected by the movement of the new religion, and drawn within the *whirlpool of its power*. The earth shook, and their rotten refuges fell to the ground. The flood rose, and they found themselves obliged to rise with it. The tree of Christianity swelled and grew, and the chains they had cast around it to arrest its growth, snapped like thread!

And all this was done by the doctrines of the Bible! Talk of victories indeed! What are the victories of Alexander, and Caesar, and Marlborough, and Napoleon, and Wellington—compared with those I have just mentioned? For extent, for completeness, for results, for permanence—there are no victories like the victories of the Bible.

(b) This is the Book which turned Europe upside down in the days of the glorious *Protestant Reformation*.

No man can read the history of Christendom as it was five hundred years ago, and not see that darkness covered the whole professing Church, even a darkness that might be felt. So great was the change which had come over Christianity that if an apostle had risen from the dead—he would not have recognized it, and would have thought that *heathenism* had revived again! The doctrines of the Gospel lay buried under a dense mass of human traditions. Penances, and pilgrimages, and indulgences, relic-worship, and image-worship, and saint-worship, and worship of the Virgin Mary—formed the sum and substance of most people's religion. The *Church* was made an idol. The priests usurped the place of Christ. And by what means was all this miserable darkness cleared away? By none so much as by bringing forth once more the Bible.

It was not merely the preaching of Luther and his friends, which established Protestantism in Germany. The grand lever which overthrew the Pope's power in that country was Luther's translation of the Bible into the German tongue. It was not merely the writings of Cranmer and the English Reformers which cast down popery in England. The seeds of the work thus carried forward were first sown by Wycliffe's translation of the Bible many years before. It was not merely the quarrel of Henry VIII and the Pope of Rome, which loosened the Pope's hold on English minds. It was the royal permission to have the Bible translated and set up in churches—so that every one who liked might read it.

Yes! it was the reading and circulation of Scripture which mainly established the cause of Protestantism in England, in Germany, and Switzerland. Without it, the people would probably have returned to their former bondage when the first reformers died. But by the reading of the Bible, the public mind became gradually pervaded with the principles of true religion. Men's eyes became thoroughly open. Their spiritual understandings became thoroughly enlarged. The abominations of popery became distinctly visible. The excellence of the pure Gospel became a rooted idea in their hearts. It was then in vain for Popes to thunder forth excommunications. It was useless for Kings and Queens to attempt to stop the course of Protestantism by fire and sword. It was all too late. The people knew too much. They had seen the light. They had heard the joyful sound. They had tasted the truth. The sun had risen on their minds. The scales had fallen from their eyes. The Bible had done its appointed work within them, and that work was not to be overthrown. The people would not return to *Egypt*. The clock could not be turned back. A mental and moral revolution had been effected, and mainly effected by God's Word.

Those are the true revolutions which the Bible effects. What are all the revolutions which France and England have gone through, compared to these? No revolutions are so bloodless, none so satisfactory, none so rich in lasting results, as the revolutions accomplished by the Bible!

The Bible is the book on which the well-being of nations has always hinged, and with which the best interests of every nation in Christendom at this moment are inseparably bound up. Just in proportion as the Bible is honored or not—light or darkness, morality or immorality, true religion or superstition, liberty or despotism, good laws or bad—will be found in a land.

Come with me and open the pages of *history*, and you will read the proofs in time past. Read it in the history of Israel under the Kings. How great was the wickedness that then prevailed! But who can wonder? *The Word of God* had been completely lost sight of, and was found in the days of Josiah thrown aside in a corner of the temple! (2 Kings 22:8.) Read it in the history of the Jews in our Lord Jesus Christ's time. How solemn the picture of Scribes and Pharisees, and their religion! But who can wonder? The Scripture was "made of none effect by man's traditions." (Matthew 15:6.) Read it in the history of the Church of Christ in the middle ages. What can be worse than the accounts we have of its ignorance and superstition? But who can wonder? The times might well be dark, when men had not the light of the Bible.

This is the Book to which the *civilized* world is indebted for many of its best and most praise-worthy *institutions*. Few probably are aware how many are the good things that men have adopted for the public benefit, of which the origin may be clearly traced up to the Bible. It has left lasting marks wherever it has been received. From the Bible are drawn many of the best *laws* by which society is kept in order. From the Bible has been obtained the *standard of morality* about truth, honesty, and the relations of man and wife, which prevails among Christian nations, and which—however feebly respected in many cases—makes so great a difference between Christians and heathen. To the influence of the Bible we owe nearly every humane and charitable institution in existence. The sick, the poor, the aged, the orphan, the lunatic, the idiot, the blind, were seldom or never thought of—before the Bible leavened the world. You may search in vain for any record of institutions for their aid in the histories of Athens or of Rome.

Alas! there are many who sneer at the Bible, and say the world would get on well enough without it, who little think how great are their own obligations to the Bible. Little does the infidel workman think, as he lies sick in one of our great hospitals, that he owes all his present comforts to the very book he affects to despise. Had it not been for the Bible, he might have died in misery—uncared for, unnoticed and alone. Truly the world we live in is fearfully unconscious of its debts to the Scripture. The last day alone, I believe, will tell the full amount of benefit conferred upon it by the Bible.

This wonderful book is the subject about which I address the reader of this paper this day. Surely it is no light matter what you are doing with the Bible. The swords of conquering Generals—the ship in which Nelson led the fleets of England to victory—the hydraulic press which raised the tubular bridge at the Menai—each and all of these are objects of interest as instruments of mighty power. The Book I speak of this day is an instrument a thousand-fold mightier still. Surely it is no light matter whether you are paying it the attention it deserves. I charge you, I summon you to give me an honest answer this day: *What are you doing with the Bible? Do you read it? How do you read it?*

5. In the fifth place, no book in existence can do so much for every one who reads it rightly, as the Bible.

The Bible does not profess to teach the *wisdom of this world.* It was not written to explain geology or astronomy. It will neither instruct you in mathematics, nor in philosophy. It will not make you a doctor, or a lawyer, or an engineer.

But there is another world to be thought of, beside that world in which man now lives. There are other ends for which man was created, beside making money and working. There are other interests which he is meant to attend to, beside those of his body—and those interests are the interests of his soul. It is the interests of the immortal soul which the Bible is especially able to promote. If you would know law—you may study Blackstone or Sugden. If you would know astronomy or geology—you may study Herschel and Lyell. But if you would know how to have your soul saved—you must study the written Word of God.

The Bible is "able to make a man wise unto salvation, through faith which is in Christ Jesus." (2 Timothy 3:15.) It alone can . . .
show you the way which leads to Heaven,
teach you everything you need to *know*,
point out everything you need to *believe*,
and explain everything you need to *do*.
It alone can show you . . .
what you are—a sinner,
what God is—perfectly holy,
the great giver of pardon, peace, and grace—Jesus Christ.

I have read of an Englishman who visited Scotland in the days of Blair, Rutherford, and Dickson, three famous preachers—and heard all three in succession. He said that the first showed him the *majesty of God*—the second showed him the *beauty of Christ*—and the third showed him *all his heart*. It is the glory and beauty of the Bible that it is always teaching these three things more or less, from the first chapter of it to the last.

The Bible applied to the heart by the Holy Spirit, is the grand instrument by which souls are first **converted** to God. That mighty change is generally begun by some text or doctrine of the Word, brought home to a man's conscience. In this way the Bible has worked moral miracles by thousands! It has made . . .
drunkards become sober,
unchaste people become pure,
thieves become honest, and
violent people become meek!

It has wholly altered the course of men's lives. It has caused their old things to pass away, and made all their ways new. It has taught worldly people—to seek first the kingdom of God. It has taught lovers of pleasure—to become lovers of God. It has taught the stream of men's affections—to run upwards instead of running downwards. It has made men think of Heaven—instead of always thinking of earth; and live by faith—instead of living by sight. All this it has done, in every part of the world.

All this it is doing still. What are the *Romish* miracles which weak men believe, compared to all this, even if they were true? Those are the truly great miracles which are yearly worked by the Word.

The Bible applied to the heart by the Holy Spirit, is the chief means by which men are **built up** and **established** in the faith, after their conversion. It is able to cleanse them, to sanctify them, to instruct them in righteousness, and to thoroughly furnish them for all good works. (Psalm 119:9; John 17:17; 2 Timothy 3:16, 17.) The Spirit ordinarily does these things by the *written* Word; sometimes by the Word *read*, and sometimes by the Word *preached*—but seldom, if ever, without the Word. The Bible can show a believer how to walk in this world so as to please God. It can teach him how to glorify Christ in all the relations of life—and can make him a good master, servant, subject, husband, father, or son. It can enable him to bear *afflictions* and privations without murmuring, and say, "It is well." It can enable him to look down into the *grave*, and say, "I fear no evil." (Psalm 23:4.) It can enable him to think on *judgment* and *eternity*, and not feel afraid. It can enable him to bear *persecution* without flinching, and to give up liberty and life rather than deny Christ's truth.

Is he drowsy in soul? The Bible can awaken him.
Is he mourning? The Bible can comfort him.
Is he erring? The Bible can restore him.
Is he weak? The Bible can make him strong.
Is he in company? The Bible can keep him from evil.
Is he alone? The Bible can talk with him. (Proverbs 6:22.)

All this the Bible can do for all believers—for the least as well as the greatest—for the richest as well as the poorest. It has done it for thousands already—and is doing it for thousands every day!

The man who has the *Bible*, and the *Holy Spirit* in his heart—has everything which is absolutely needful to make him spiritually wise and mature. He needs no *priest* to break the bread of life for him. He needs no ancient *traditions*, no writings of the Fathers, no *voice of the Church*—to guide him into all truth. He has the *well of truth* open before him—and what more can he want? Yes! though he is shut up alone in a prison, or cast on a desert island, though he never see a church, or minister, or sacrament again—if he has but the Bible, he has got the infallible guide, and needs no other. If he has but the will to read that Bible rightly, it will certainly teach him the road that leads to Heaven. It is here alone that *infallibility* resides. It is not in any *church*. It is not in the *Councils*. It is not in *ministers*. It is only in the *written Word*.

(a) I know well that many say they have found no saving power in the Bible. They tell us they have tried to read it, and have learned nothing from it. They can see in it nothing but hard and deep things. They ask us what we mean by talking of its *power*.

I answer, that the Bible no doubt contains hard things, or else it would not be the *book of God*. It contains things hard to comprehend—but only hard because we have not grasp of *mind* to comprehend them. It contains things *above* our reasoning powers—but nothing that might not be explained if the eyes of our understanding were not feeble and dim. But is not an acknowledgment of our own ignorance, the very corner-stone and foundation of all knowledge? Must not many things be taken for granted in the beginning of every science—before we can proceed one step towards acquaintance with it? Do we not require our children to learn many things of which they cannot see the meaning at first? And ought we not then to expect to find "deep things" when we begin studying the Word of God—and yet to believe that if we persevere in reading it, the meaning of many of them will one day be made clear? No doubt we ought so to expect, and so to believe.

We must read with *humility*. We must take much on *trust*. We must believe that what we do not know now—we shall know hereafter; some *part* in this world—and *all* in the world to come.

But I ask that man who has given up reading the Bible because it contains hard things, whether he did not find many things in it easy and plain? I put it to his conscience whether he did not see great *landmarks* and *principles* in it all the way through?

And what ought we to say to the man who gives up reading the Bible because it contains hard things, when his own state, and the path to Heaven, and the way to serve God—are all written down clearly and unmistakably, as with a sunbeam? Surely we ought to tell that man that his objections are no better than lazy excuses, and do not deserve to be heard.

(b) I know well that many raise the objection, that thousands read the Bible and are not a whit the better for their reading. And they ask us, when this is the case, what becomes of the Bible's boasted power? I answer, that the reason why so many read the Bible without benefit is plain and simple—they do not read it in the *right way*. There is generally a right way and a wrong way of doing everything in the world; and just as it is with other things, so it is in the matter of reading the Bible. The Bible is not so entirely different from all other books, as to make it of no importance in what *spirit* and *manner* you read it. It does not do good, as a matter of course, by merely *running our eyes over the print*, any more than the sacraments do good by mere virtue of our receiving them. It does not ordinarily do good, unless it is read with *humility* and *earnest prayer*. The best steam-engine that was ever built is useless—if a man does not know how to work it. The best sun-dial that was ever constructed will not tell its owner the time of day—if he is so ignorant as to put it up in the shade. Just as it is with that steam-engine, and that sun-dial—so it is with the Bible. When men read it without profit, the fault is not in the Book—but in themselves.

I tell the man who doubts the power of the Bible, because many read it, and are no better for the reading—that the *abuse* of a thing is no argument against the *use* of it. I tell him boldly, that never did man or woman read that book in a childlike persevering spirit, like the Ethiopian eunuch, and the Bereans (Acts 8:28; 17:11)—and miss the way to Heaven. Yes, many a broken cistern will be exposed to shame in the day of judgment; but there will not rise up one soul who will be able to say, that he went *thirsting* to the Bible, and found in it no *living water*—that he searched for truth in the Scriptures, and searching, did not find it. The words which are spoken of Wisdom in the Proverbs are strictly true of the Bible: "If you *call out* for insight and *cry aloud* for understanding, and if you *look* for it as for silver and *search* for it as for hidden treasure—*then* you will understand the fear of the Lord and find the knowledge of God!" (Proverbs 2:3-5.)

This wonderful Book is the subject about which I address the readers of this paper this day. Surely it is no light matter what you are *doing* with the Bible. What would you think of the man who in time of cholera, despised a sure remedy for preserving the health of his body? What must be thought of you, if you despise the only sure remedy for the everlasting health of your soul? I charge you, I entreat you, to give an honest answer to my question. *What do you do with the Bible? Do you read it? How do you read it?*

6. In the sixth place, the Bible is the only rule by which all questions of *doctrine* or of *duty* can be tried.

The Lord God knows the weakness and infirmity of our poor fallen understandings. He knows that, even after conversion, *our perceptions* of right and wrong are exceedingly indistinct. He knows how artfully Satan can *gild error* with an appearance of truth, and can dress up wrong with plausible arguments—until it looks like right. Knowing all this, He has mercifully provided us with an *unerring standard* of truth and error, right and wrong, and has taken care to make that standard a written book—even the Scripture.

No one can look around the world, and not see the wisdom of such a provision. No one can live long, and not find out that he is constantly in need of a counselor and adviser—of a *rule of faith and practice,* on which he can depend. Unless he lives like a beast, without a soul and conscience, he will find himself constantly assailed by difficult and puzzling questions. He will be often asking himself: What must I believe? What must I do?

(a) The world is full of difficulties about points of doctrine. The house of *error* lies close alongside the house of *truth.* The door of one is so like the door of the other—that there is continual risk of mistakes.

Does a man read or travel much? He will soon find the most opposite opinions prevailing among those who are called Christians. He will discover that different people give the most different answers to the important question: What shall I do to be saved? The Roman Catholic and the Protestant—the Neologian and the Tractarian—the Mormonite and the Swedenborgian—each and all will assert that he alone has the truth. Each and all will tell him that safety is only to be found in his party. Each and all say, "Come with us!" All this is puzzling. What shall a man do?

Does he settle down quietly in some English or Scotch parish? He will soon find that even in our own land, the most conflicting views are held. He will soon discover that there are serious differences among Christians as to the comparative importance of the various parts and articles of the faith. One man thinks of nothing but Church government—another of nothing but sacraments, services, and forms—a third of nothing but preaching the Gospel. Does he apply to ministers for a solution? He will perhaps find one minister teaching one doctrine, and another another. All this is puzzling. What shall a man do? There is only one answer to this question. A man must make the *Bible alone* his *rule.* He must *receive* nothing, and *believe* nothing, which is not according to the Word. He must try all religious teaching by one simple test—Does it square with the Bible? What says the Scripture?

I wish that the eyes of the laity of this country were more open on this subject. I wish that they would learn to weigh sermons, books, opinions, and ministers—in the scales of the Bible, and to value all according to their conformity to the Word. I wish that they would see that it matters little *who* says a thing, whether he be Father or Reformer—Bishop or Archbishop—Priest or Deacon—Archdeacon or Dean. The only question is: Is the thing said Scriptural? If it is—it ought to be received and believed. If it is not—it ought to be refused and cast aside. I fear the consequences of that servile acceptance of everything which "the pastor" says, which is so common among many English laymen. I fear lest they be led they know not where, like the blinded Syrians, and awake some day to find themselves in the power of Roman Catholicism! (2 Kings 6:20.) Oh, that men in England would only remember for what purpose the Bible was given them!

Some say that it is presumptuous to judge a minister's teaching by the Word. But when one doctrine is proclaimed in one parish, and another in another—people must read and judge for themselves. Both doctrines cannot be right, and both ought to be tried by the Word. I charge them, above all things, never to suppose that any true minister of the Gospel will dislike his people measuring all that he teaches, by the Bible. On the contrary, the more they read the Bible, and prove all he says by the Bible—the better he will be pleased. A false minister may say, "You have no right to use your private judgment: leave the Bible to us who are ordained." A true minister will say, "Search the Scriptures, and if I do not teach you what is Scriptural—do not believe me." A false minister may cry, "Hear the Church," and "Hear me." A true minister will say, "Hear the Word of God."

(b) But the world is not only full of difficulties about points of *doctrine*—it is equally full of difficulties about points of *practice*. Every professing Christian, who wishes to act conscientiously, must know that it is so. The most puzzling questions are continually arising. He is tried on every side by doubts as to the line of *duty*, and can often hardly see what is the right thing to do.

He is tried by questions connected with the management of his *worldly calling*, if he is in business or in trade. He sometimes sees things going on of a very doubtful character—things that can hardly be called fair, straightforward, and truthful. But then, everybody in the trade does these things. They have always been done in the most respectable businesses. There would be no carrying on a profitable business, if they were not done. They are not things that are distinctly named and prohibited by God. All this is very puzzling. What is a man to do?

He is tried by questions about *worldly amusements*. Races, and balls, and operas, and theaters, and card parties, are all very doubtful methods of spending time. But then he sees numbers of great people taking part in them. Are all these people wrong? Can there really be such mighty harm in these things? All this is very puzzling. What is a man to do?

He is tried by questions about the *education of his children*. He wishes to train them up morally and religiously, and to remember their souls. But he is told by many sensible people, that *young people will be young*—that it does not do to check and restrain them too much, and that he ought to attend children's parties, and give children's balls himself. He is informed that this nobleman, or that lady of rank, always does so—and yet they are reckoned religious people. Surely it cannot be wrong. All this is very puzzling. What is he to do?

There is only one answer to all these questions. A man must make the Bible alone his rule of conduct. He must make its leading principles the *compass* by which he steers his course through life. By the letter or spirit of the Bible—he must test every difficult point and question. "To the law and to the testimony! What do the Scriptures say?" He ought to care nothing for what other people may think right. He ought not to set his watch by the clock of his *neighbor*—but by the sun-dial of the *Word*.

I charge my readers solemnly to act on the maxim I have just laid down, and to adhere to it rigidly all the days of their lives. You will never repent of it. Make it a leading principle never to act contrary to the Word. Do not regard the charge of over-strictness, and needless precision. Remember that you serve a strict and holy God. Do not listen to the common objection, that the rule you have laid down is impossible, and cannot be observed in such a world as this. Let those who make such an objection speak out plainly—and tell us for what purpose the Bible was given to man. Let them remember that by the Bible we shall all be judged at the last day, and let them learn to judge themselves by it here—lest they be judged and condemned by it hereafter.

This mighty *rule of faith and practice* is the book about which I am addressing the readers of this paper this day. Surely it is no light matter what you are doing with the Bible. Surely when danger is abroad on the right hand and on the left—you should consider what you are doing with the safe-guard which God has provided. I charge you, I beseech you, to give an honest answer to my question. *What are you doing with the Bible? Do you read it? How do you read it?*

7. In the seventh place, the Bible is the book which all true servants of God have always lived on and loved. Every living thing which God creates, requires food. The life that God imparts, needs sustaining and nourishing. It is so with animal and vegetable life—with birds, beasts, fish, reptiles, insects, and plants. It is equally so with spiritual life. When the Holy Spirit raises a man from the death of sin and makes him a new creature in Christ Jesus—the *new principle* in that man's heart requires food, and the only food which will sustain it is the Word of God.

There never was a man or woman truly converted, from one end of the world to the other—who did not love the Word of God. Just as a child born into the world desires naturally the milk provided for its nourishment, so does a "born again" soul desire the sincere milk of the Word. This is a common mark of all the children of God—they "delight in the law of the Lord." (Psalm 1:2.) Show me a person who despises Bible reading, or thinks little of Bible preaching, and I hold it to be a certain fact that he is not yet "born again." He may be zealous about forms and ceremonies. He may be diligent in attending sacraments and daily services. But if these things are more precious to him than the Bible, I cannot think he is a converted man.

Tell me what the Bible is to a man—and I will generally tell you what he is. This is the spiritual pulse—if we would know the state of the heart. I have no notion of the Spirit dwelling in a man and not giving clear evidence of His presence. And I believe it to be a signal evidence of the Spirit's presence—when the Word is really precious to a man's soul.

Love to the Word is one of the characteristics we see in *Job*. As little as we know of this Patriarch and his age, this at least stands out clearly. He says, "I have esteemed the words of His mouth more than my necessary food." (Job 23:12.)

Love to the Word is a shining feature in the character of *David*. Mark how it appears all through that wonderful part of Scripture, the 119th Psalm. He might well say, "Oh, how I love your law! "(Psalm 119:97.)

Love to the Word is a striking point in the character of *Paul*. What were he and his companions, but men "mighty in the Scriptures?" What were his sermons, but expositions and applications of the Word?

Love to the Word appears pre-eminently in our Lord and Savior *Jesus Christ*. He read it publicly. He quoted it continually. He expounded it frequently. He advised the Jews to "search" it. He used it as His weapon to resist the devil. He said repeatedly, "The Scripture must be fulfilled." Almost the last thing He did was to "open the understanding of His disciples, that they might understand the Scriptures." (Luke 24:45.) I am afraid that man can be no true servant of Christ, who has not something of his Master's mind and feeling towards the Bible.

Love to the Word has been a prominent feature in the history of all the *saints*, of whom we know anything, since the days of the Apostles. This is the *lamp* which Athanasius and Chrysostom and Augustine followed. This is the *compass* which kept the Waldenses and Albigenses from making shipwreck of the faith. This is the *well* which was re-opened by Wycliffe and Luther, after it had been long stopped up. This is the *sword* with which Latimer, and Jewell, and Knox won their victories. This is the *manna* which fed Baxter and Owen, and the noble host of the Puritans, and made them strong to battle. This is the *armory* from which Whitefield and Wesley drew their powerful weapons. This is the *mine* from which Bickersteth and M'Cheyne brought forth rich gold. Differing as these holy men did in some matters, on one point they were all agreed—they all delighted in the Word.

Love to the Word is one of the first things that appears in the converted heathen, at the various Missionary stations throughout the world. In hot climates and in cold—among savage people and among civilized—in New Zealand, in the South Sea Islands, in Africa, in Hindustan—it is always the same. They enjoy hearing it read. They long to be able to read it themselves. They wonder why Christians did not send it to them before. How striking is the picture which Moffat draws of African, the fierce South African chieftain, when first brought under the power of the Gospel! "Often have I seen him," he says, "under the shadow of a great rock nearly the whole day, eagerly perusing the pages of the Bible." How touching is the expression of a poor converted Negro, speaking of the Bible! He said, "It is never old—and never cold." How affecting was the language of another old negro, when some would have dissuaded him from learning to read, because of his great age. "No!" he said, "I will never give it up until I die. It is worth all the labor to be able to read that one verse: God so loved the world, that he gave his only begotten Son, that whoever believes in him should not perish—but have eternal life."

Love to the Bible is one of the grand points of agreement among all converted men and women in our own land. Episcopalians and Presbyterians, Baptists and Independents, Methodists and Plymouth Brethren—all unite in honoring the Bible, as soon as they are real Christians. This is the *manna* which all the tribes of our Israel feed upon, and find satisfying food. This is the *fountain* round which all the various portions of Christ's flock meet together, and from which no sheep goes thirsty away.

Oh, that believers in this country would learn to cleave more closely to the written Word! Oh, that they would see that the more the Bible, and the Bible only, is the substance of men's religion—the more they will agree. It is probable there never was an uninspired book more universally admired than Bunyan's *Pilgrim's Progress*. It is a book which all denominations of Christians delight to honor. It has won praise from all parties. Now what a striking fact it is, that the author was pre-eminently *a man of one book!* He had read hardly anything but the Bible.

It is a blessed thought that there will be "many people" in Heaven at last. As few as the Lord's people undoubtedly are at any one given time or place—yet all gathered together at last, they will be "a multitude that no man can number." (Rev. 7:9; 19:1.) They will be of one heart and mind. They will have passed through like experience. They will all have repented, believed, lived holy, prayerful, and humble. They will all have washed their robes and made them white in the blood of the Lamb. But one thing beside all this they will have in common: they will all love the texts and doctrines of the Bible. The Bible will have been their food and delight in the days of their pilgrimage on earth. And the Bible will be a common subject of joyful meditation and retrospect, when they are gathered together in Heaven.

This Book, which all true Christians live upon and love, is the subject about which I am addressing the readers of this paper this day. Surely it is no light matter what you are doing with the Bible. Surely it is matter for serious inquiry, whether you know anything of this *love* to the Word, and have this mark of walking "in the footsteps of the flock." (Song 1:8.) I charge you, I entreat you to give me an honest answer. *What are you doing with the Bible? Do you read it? How do you read it?*

8. In the last place: the Bible is the only book which can comfort a man in the last hours of his life. Death is an event which is before us all. There is no avoiding it. It is the *river* which each of us must cross. I who write, and you who read, have each one day to die. It is good to remember this. We are all sadly apt to put away the subject from us. "Each man thinks each man mortal, but himself." I want every one to do his duty in life—but I also want every one to think of death. I want everyone to know how to *live*—but I also want everyone to know how to *die*.

Death is a solemn event to all. It is the winding up of all earthly plans and expectations. It is a separation from all that we have loved and lived with. It is often accompanied by much bodily pain and distress. It brings us to the grave, the worm, and corruption. It opens the door to judgment and eternity—to Heaven or to Hell. It is an event after which there is no change, or space for repentance. Other mistakes may be corrected or retrieved—but not a mistake on our death-beds. As the tree falls—there it must lie. No conversion in the coffin! No new birth *after* we have ceased to breathe! And death is before us all. It may be close at hand. The time of our departure is quite uncertain. But sooner or later we must each lie down alone and die. All these are serious considerations.

Death is a solemn event even to the believer in Christ. For him no doubt, the "sting of death" is taken away. (1 Corinthians 15:55.) Death has become one of his *privileges*, for he is Christ's. Living or dying, he is the Lord's. If he lives—Christ lives in him; and if he dies—he goes to live with Christ. To him "to live is Christ, and to die is gain." (Philippians 1:21.)

Death frees him from many trials—from . . .
a weak and sick body,

a sinful and corrupt heart,
a tempting and deceitful devil, and
an ensnaring and persecuting world.

Death admits him to the enjoyment of many blessings. He rests from his labors; the *hope* of a joyful resurrection is changed into a *certainty*; he has the company of holy redeemed spirits; he is "with Christ." All this is true—and yet, even to a believer, death is a *solemn* thing. Flesh and blood naturally shrink from it. To part from all we love, is a wrench and trial to the feelings. The world we go to, is a world *unknown*, even though it is our *home*. As friendly and harmless as death is to a believer, it is not an event to be treated lightly. It always must be a very solemn thing.

It befits every thoughtful and sensible man to consider calmly how he is going to meet death. Gird up your loins, like a man, and look the subject in the face. Listen to me, while I tell you a few things about the *end* to which we are coming.

The good things of the world cannot comfort a man when he draws near death. All the *gold* of California and Australia will not provide light for the *dark valley*. Money can buy the best medical advice and attendance for a man's body; but money cannot buy *peace* for his conscience, heart, and soul.

Relatives, loved friends, and servants, cannot comfort a man when he draws near death. They may minister affectionately to his bodily needs. They may watch by his bed-side tenderly, and anticipate his every wish. They may smooth his dying pillow, and support his sinking frame in their arms. But they cannot stop the *achings of a troubled heart*. They cannot screen an uneasy conscience from the *eye of God*.

The *pleasures of the world* cannot comfort a man when he draws near death. The brilliant ball-room; the merry dance—the midnight revel—the party to races, the card table—the box at the opera—the voices of singing men and singing women—all these are at length *distasteful* things. To hear of hunting and shooting engagements gives him no pleasure. To be invited to feasts, and sports, and fancy-fairs, gives him no ease. He cannot hide from himself, that these are hollow, empty, powerless things. They jar upon the ear of his conscience. They are out of harmony with his condition. They cannot stop one gap in his heart, when the *last enemy* is coming in like a flood. They cannot make him calm in the prospect of meeting a holy God.

Books and newspapers cannot comfort a man, when he draws near death. The most brilliant writings of Macaulay or Dickens will pall on his ear. The most able article in *the Times* will fail to interest him. The Edinburgh and Quarterly Reviews will give him no pleasure. The last new *novel* will lie unopened and unheeded. Their time will be past. Their vocation will be gone. Whatever they may be in health—they are *useless in the hour of death*.

There is but one *fountain of comfort* for a man drawing near to at his end—and that is the Bible. Chapters out of the Bible—texts out of the Bible—statements of truth taken out of the Bible, books containing matter drawn from the Bible—these are a man's only chance of comfort when he comes to die. I do not at all say that the Bible will do good, as a matter of *course*, to a dying man—if he has not valued it before. I know, unhappily, too much of *death-beds* to say that. I do not say whether it is probable that he who has been unbelieving and neglectful of the Bible in life—will at once believe and get comfort from it in death. But I do say positively, that no dying man will ever get real comfort—except from the contents of the Word of God. All comfort from any other source, is a house built upon sand.

I lay this down as a rule of universal application. I make no exception in favor of any class on earth. Kings and poor men, learned and unlearned—all are on a level in this matter. There is not a jot of real consolation for any dying man, unless he gets it from the Bible. Chapters, passages, texts, promises, and doctrines of Scripture—heard, received, believed, and rested on—these are the only *comforters* I dare promise to any one, when he leaves the world. Taking the sacrament will do a man no more good than the Popish extreme unction, so long as the Word is not received and believed. Priestly absolution will no more ease the conscience than the incantations of a heathen magician, if the poor dying sinner does not receive and believe Bible truth. I tell every one who reads this paper, that although men may seem to get on comfortably without the Bible while they live, they may be sure that without the Bible they cannot comfortably die. It was a true confession of the learned Selden, "There is no book upon which we can rest in a dying moment but the Bible."

I might easily confirm all I have just said by examples and illustrations. I might show you the death-beds of men who have affected to despise the Bible. I might tell you how Voltaire and Paine, the famous infidels, died in misery, bitterness, rage, fear, and despair. I might show you the happy death-beds of those who have loved the Bible and believed it, and the blessed effect the sight of their death-beds had on others.

I have seen many dying people in my time. I have seen great varieties of manner and deportment among them. I have seen some die sullen, silent, and comfortless. I have seen others die ignorant, unconcerned, and apparently without much fear. I have seen some die so wearied out with long illness that they were quite willing to depart—and yet they did not seem to me at all in a fit state to go before God. I have seen others die with professions of hope and trust in God, without leaving satisfactory evidences that they were on the rock. I have seen others die who, I believe, were "in Christ," and safe—and yet they never seemed to enjoy much sensible comfort. I have seen some few dying in the full assurance of hope, and like Bunyan's "Standfast," giving glorious testimony to Christ's faithfulness, even in the *river of death*. But one thing I have never seen. I never saw anyone enjoy what I should call real, solid, calm, reasonable peace on his death bed—who did not draw his peace from the Bible. And this I am bold to say, that the man who thinks to go to his death-bed without having the Bible for his comforter, his companion, and his friend—is one of the greatest madmen in the world. There are no comforts for the soul but Bible comforts, and he who has not got hold of these, has got hold of nothing at all, unless it be a broken reed.

The only comforter for a death-bed is the *book* about which I address the readers of this paper this day. Surely it is no light matter whether you read that book or not. Surely a dying man, in a dying world, should seriously consider whether he has got anything to comfort him when his turn comes to die. I charge you, I entreat you, for the last time, to give an honest answer to my question. *What are you doing with the Bible? Do you read it? How do you read it?*

I have now given the reasons why I press on every reader the duty and importance of reading the Bible. I have shown that no book is written in such a manner as the Bible—that knowledge of the Bible is absolutely necessary to salvation—that no book contains such matter—that no book has done so much for the world generally—that no book can do so much for every one who reads it aright—that this book is the only rule of faith and practice—that it is, and always has been, the food of all true servants of God—and that it is the only book which can comfort men when they die. All these are ancient things. I do not pretend to tell anything new. I have only gathered together old truths, and tried to mold them into a new shape. Let me finish all by addressing a few plain words to the conscience of every class of readers.

(a) This paper may fall into the hands of some who can read—but **never do read the Bible** at all. Are you one of them? If you are, I have something to say to you.

I cannot comfort you in your present state of mind. It would be mockery and deceit to do so. I cannot speak to you of peace and Heaven, while you treat the Bible as you do. You are in danger of losing your soul.

You are in danger, because your neglected Bible is a plain evidence that you do not love God. The health of a man's body may generally be known by his appetite. The health of a man's soul may be known by his treatment of the Bible. Now you are manifestly laboring under a sore soul-disease. Will you not repent? I know I cannot reach your heart. I cannot make you see and feel these things. I can only enter my solemn protest against your present treatment of the Bible, and lay that protest before your conscience. I do so with all my soul. Oh, beware lest you repent too late! Beware lest you put off reading the Bible until you send for the doctor in your last illness, and then find the Bible a sealed book, and dark, as the cloud between the hosts of Israel and Egypt, to your anxious soul! Beware lest you go on saying all your life, "Men do very well without all this Bible-reading," and find at length, to your cost, that men do very ill, and end up in Hell! Beware lest the day comes when you will feel, "Had I but honored the Bible as much as I have honored the newspaper—I would not have been left without comfort in my last hours!" Bible neglecting reader, I give you a plain warning. The plague-mark is at present on your door. May the Lord have mercy upon your soul!

(b) This paper may fall into the hands of someone who is willing to begin reading the Bible—but **wants advice** on the subject. Are you that man? Listen to me, and I will give a few short hints.

(i) For one thing, begin reading your Bible *this very day*. The way to do a thing—is to do it; and the way to read the Bible—is actually to read it! It is not merely *meaning*, or *wishing*, or *resolving*, or *intending*, or *thinking* about it—which will advance you one step. You must positively read. There is no *royal road* in this matter, any more than in the matter of prayer. If you cannot read yourself, you must persuade somebody else to read it to you. But one way or another, through *eyes* or *ears*—the words of Scripture must actually pass before your mind.

(ii) For another thing, read the Bible with an earnest desire to *understand* it. Do not think for a moment, that the great object is to *turn over a certain quantity of printed paper*, and that it matters nothing whether you understand it or not. Some ignorant people seem to imagine, that all is done if they *advance so many chapters every day*, though they may not have a notion what they are all about, and only know that they have pushed on their bookmark ahead so many pages. This is turning Bible reading into a *mere ritual form*. It is almost as bad as the *Popish* habit of 'buying indulgences'—by saying an astounding number of 'Ave-Marias' and 'Pater-nosters' (*Hail-Mary's* and *Our-Father's*—on their 'rosary beads'.) It reminds one of the poor Hottentot who ate up a Dutch hymn-book because he saw it comforted his neighbors' hearts! Settle it down in your mind as a general principle, that a Bible not understood—is a Bible that does no good! Say to yourself often as you read, "What is this all about?" Dig for the meaning like a man digging for gold.

(iii) For another thing, read the Bible with *child-like faith* and *humility*. Open your *heart*—as you open God's book, and say, *"Speak, Lord, for your servant is listening!"* Resolve to believe implicitly whatever you find there, however much it may run counter to your own desires and prejudices. Resolve to receive heartily every statement of truth—whether you like it or not. Beware of that miserable habit into which some readers of the Bible fall—they *receive* *some* doctrines because they like them; and they *reject others* because they are condemning to themselves, or to some relation, or friend. At this rate, the Bible is useless! Are *we* to be judges of what ought to be in God's Word? Do we know better than God? Settle it down in your mind—that you will *receive* all and *believe* all, and that what you cannot understand—you will take on trust. Remember, when you pray—that you are speaking to God, and God hears you. But, remember, when you read Scripture—that God is speaking to you, and you are not to "dictate," but to *listen!*

(iv) For another thing, read the Bible in a spirit of *obedience* and *self-application*. Sit down to the study of it with a daily determination that you will . . .
live by its rules,
rest on its statements,
and act on its commands.

Consider, as you travel through every chapter, "How does this affect my *thinking* and *daily conduct?* What does this *teach* me?" It is poor work to read the Bible from mere *curiosity*, and for speculative purposes—in order to fill your head and store your mind with *mere opinions;* while you do not allow the book to influence your *heart* and *life*. That Bible is *read* best—which is *practiced* most!

(v) For another thing, read the Bible *daily*. Make it a part of every day's business to *read* and *meditate* on some portion of God's Word. Private means of grace are just as needful every day for our souls—as food and clothing are for our bodies. Yesterday's food will not feed the laborer today; and today's food will not feed the laborer tomorrow. Do as the Israelites did in the wilderness. Gather your *manna fresh* every morning. Choose your own seasons and hours. Do not scramble over and hurry your reading. Give your Bible the *best*, and not the worst part of your time! But whatever plan you pursue, let it be a rule of your life to visit the *throne of grace* and *God's Word* every day.

(vi) For another thing, read *all* of the Bible—and read it in an *orderly* way. I fear there are many parts of the Word which some people never read at all. This is to say at the least, a very presumptuous habit. "*All* Scripture is profitable." (2 Timothy 3:16.) To this habit may be traced that lack of *well-proportioned views of truth*, which is so common in this day. Some people's Bible-reading is a system of perpetual 'dipping and picking'. They do not seem to have an idea of regularly going through the whole book.

This also is a great mistake. No doubt in times of sickness and affliction, it is allowable to search out seasonable portions. But with this exception, I believe it is by far the best plan to begin the Old and New Testaments at the same time—to read each straight through to the end, and then begin again. This is a matter in which every one must be persuaded in his own mind. I can only say it has been my own plan for nearly forty years, and I have never seen cause to alter it.

(vii) For another thing, read the Bible *fairly* and *honestly*. Determine to take everything in its plain, obvious meaning—and regard all *forced* interpretations with great suspicion. As a general rule, whatever a verse of the Bible *seems* to mean—it *does* mean! Cecil's rule is a very valuable one, "The right way of interpreting Scripture is to take it as we find it, without any attempt to force it into any particular theological system."

(viii) In the last place, read the Bible with *Christ* continually in view. The grand primary object of all Scripture, is to testify of Jesus! Old Testament *ceremonies* are shadows of Christ. Old Testament *deliverers* are types of Christ. Old Testament *prophecies* are full of Christ's *sufferings*, and of Christ's *glory* yet to come.
The first coming and the second;
the Lord's humiliation and His glorious kingdom;
His *cross* and the *crown*—
shine forth everywhere in the Bible. Keep fast hold on this *clue*, if you would read the Bible aright!

I might easily add to these *hints*, if space permitted. Few and short as they are—you will find them most profitable when implemented.

The 'book' satisfies and feeds his soul. A poor Christian woman once said to an infidel, "I am no scholar. I cannot argue like you. But I know that honey is honey, because it leaves a sweet taste in my mouth. And I know the Bible to be *God's book*, because of the *taste* it leaves in my heart!"

(3) This paper may fall into the hands of someone who loves and believes the Bible—and yet reads it but *little*. I fear there are many such in this day. It is a day of hustle and bustle. It is a day of talking, and committee meetings, and public work. These things are all very well in their way—but I fear that they sometimes clip and cut short the private reading of the Bible. Does your conscience tell you that you are one of the people I speak of? Listen to me, and I will say a few things which deserve your serious attention.

You are the man who is likely to get little comfort from the Bible in time of *need*. Trial is a sifting season. Affliction is a searching wind, which strips the leaves off the trees, and brings to light the bird nests. Now I fear that your *stores of Bible consolations* may one day run very low. I fear lest you should find yourself at last on very short allowance, and come into harbor weak, worn and thin!

You are the man that is likely never to be established in the truth. I shall not be surprised to hear that you are troubled with *doubts* and *questionings* about assurance, grace, faith, perseverance, and the like. The devil is an old and cunning enemy. Like the Benjamites, he can "throw stones at a hair-breadth, and not miss." (Judges 20:16.) He can quote Scripture readily enough when he pleases. Now you are not sufficiently ready with your *weapons* to be able to fight a good fight with him. Your *armor* does not fit you well. Your *sword* sits loosely in your hand.

You are the man that is likely to make mistakes in life. I shall not wonder if I am told that you have . . .
erred about your own *marriage*,
erred about your *children's* education,
erred about the conduct of your *household*,
erred about the *company* you keep.

The world you steer through is full of rocks, and shoals, and sandbanks! You are not sufficiently familiar either with the *lights* or *charts*.

You are the man who is likely to be carried away by some specious false teacher for a season. It will not surprise me if I hear that one of those clever, eloquent men, who can "make the worse appear the better cause," is leading you into many follies! You are lacking in *ballast*. No wonder if you are *tossed to and fro*, like a cork on the waves!

All these are uncomfortable things. I want every reader of this paper to escape them all. Take the advice I offer you this day. Do not merely read your Bible *a little*—but read it a great deal. "Let the Word of Christ dwell in you *richly*." (Coloss. 3:16.) Do not be a mere *babe* in spiritual knowledge. Seek to become "well-instructed in the kingdom of Heaven," and to be continually adding new things to old. A religion of *mere feeling* is an uncertain thing. It is like the tide—sometimes high, and sometimes low. It is like the moon, sometimes bright, and sometimes dim. A religion of deep Bible knowledge, is a firm and lasting possession! It enables a man not merely to say," I *feel* hope in Christ,"—but "I *know* whom I have believed." (2 Timothy 1:12.)

(4) This paper may fall into the hands of someone who reads the Bible much—and yet imagines that he is no better for his reading. This is a crafty temptation of the devil. At one stage he says, "Do not read the Bible at all." At another be says, "Your reading does you no good—give it up!" Are you that man? I feel for you from the bottom of my soul. Let me try to do you good.

Do not think you are getting no good from the Bible, merely because you do not see that good *day by day*. The greatest *effects* are by no means those which make the most noise, and are most easily observed. The greatest effects are often silent, quiet, and hard to detect at the time they are being produced. Think of the influence of the *moon* upon the earth—and of the *air* upon the human lungs. Remember how silently the *dew* falls—and how imperceptibly the grass grows.

There may be far more happening than you think in your soul by your Bible-reading. The Word may be gradually producing deep impressions on your heart, of which you are not at present aware. Often when the *memory* is retaining no facts, the *character* of a man is receiving some everlasting impression.

Is *sin* becoming every year more hateful to you?

Is *Christ* becoming every year more precious?

Is *holiness* becoming every year more lovely and desirable in your eyes?

If these things are so—take courage. The Bible is doing you good—though you may not be able to trace it out day by day.

The Bible may be *restraining you from some sin or delusion* into which you would otherwise run. It may be daily keeping you back, and hedging you up, and preventing many a false step! Ah, you might soon find this out to your cost, if you were to cease reading the Word! The very *familiarity* of blessings sometimes makes us *insensible* to their value. Resist the devil. Settle it down in your mind as an established rule, that, whether you feel it at the moment or not, you are *inhaling spiritual health* by reading the Bible, and insensibly becoming more strong!

(5) This paper may fall into the hands of some who really *love* the Bible, *live* upon the Bible, and *read it much*. Are you one of these? Give me your attention, and I will mention a few things which we shall do well to lay to heart for time to come.

Let us resolve to **read** the Bible *more and more* every year we live. Let us try to get it rooted in our memories, and engrafted into our hearts. Let us be thoroughly well-provisioned with it, against the *voyage of death*. Who knows but we may have a very stormy passage? Sight and hearing may fail us, and we may be in *deep waters*. Oh, to have the Word "hidden in our hearts" in such an hour as that! (Psalm 119:11.)

Let us resolve to be more ***watchful*** over our Bible reading every year that we live. Let us be jealously careful about the *time* we give to it, and the *manner* that time is spent. Let us beware of *omitting* our daily reading, without sufficient cause. Let us not be gaping, and yawning, and dozing over God's book, while we read. Let us read like a wife reading a husband's Letter from a distant land.

Let us be very careful that we never exalt any minister, or sermon, or book, or tract, or friend—*above* the Word. Cursed be that book, or tract, or human counsel—which creeps in between us and the Bible, and hides the Bible from our eyes! Once more I say, let us be very watchful. The moment we open the Bible—the devil sits down by our side. Oh, to read with a hungry spirit, and a simple desire for edification!

Let us resolve to ***honor*** the Bible more in our families. Let us read it morning and evening to our families, and not be ashamed to let others see that we do so.

Let us not be discouraged by seeing no good arise from it. The Bible-reading in a family has kept many a one from the jail, the workhouse, and the hospital—if it has not kept him from Hell.

Let us resolve to ***meditate*** more on the Bible. It is good to take with us two or three texts when we go out into the world, and to turn them over and over in our minds whenever we have a little leisure time. It keeps out many vain thoughts. It *clenches the nail* of daily reading. It preserves our souls from stagnating and breeding corrupt things. It sanctifies and quickens our memories; and prevents them becoming like those foul ponds where the *reptiles* live, but the *fish* die.

Let us resolve to ***talk*** more to believers about the Bible when we meet them. Alas, the conversation of Christians, when they do meet, is often sadly unprofitable! How many frivolous, and trifling, and uncharitable things are said! Let us bring out the Bible more, and it will help to drive the devil away, and keep our hearts in tune. Oh, that we may all strive so to walk together in this evil world; that Jesus may often draw near, and go with us, as He went with the two disciples journeying to Emmaus!

Last of all, let us resolve to ***live*** by the Bible more and more every year we live. Let us frequently take account of . . .
all our opinions and practices,
all our habits and tempers,
all our behavior in public and in private
—in the world, and by our own firesides.

Let us *measure* all by the Bible, and resolve, by God's help, to *conform* to it. Oh that we may learn increasingly to "cleanse our ways" by the Word! (Psalm 119:9.)

I commend all these things to the serious and prayerful attention of every one into whose hands this paper may fall. I want the *ministers* of my beloved country—to be Bible-reading ministers; the *congregations*—to be Bible-reading congregations; and the *nation*—to be a Bible-reading nation. To bring about this desirable end I cast in my mite into God's treasury. The Lord grant that it may prove not to have been in vain!

THE LORD'S SUPPER

"But let a man *examine himself*— and so let him eat of that bread, and drink of that cup." 1 Corinthians 11:28

The words which form the title of this paper refer to the subject of vast importance. That subject is the Lord's Supper.

Perhaps no part of the Christian religion is so *thoroughly misunderstood* as the Lord's Supper. On no point have there been so many disputes, strifes, and controversies for almost 1800 years. On no point have mistakes done so much harm. The very ordinance which was meant for our *peace* and *profit* has become the cause of *discord* and the occasion of sin! These things ought not to be!

I make no excuse for including the Lord's Supper among the leading points of "practical" Christianity. I firmly believe that ignorant views or false doctrine about this ordinance lie at the root of some of the present divisions of professing Christians. Some *neglect* it altogether; some completely *misunderstand* it; some *exalt* it to a position it was never meant to occupy, and turn it into an idol. If I can throw a little *light* on it, and clear up the doubts in some minds, I will feel very thankful. It is hopeless, I fear, to expect that the controversy about the Lord's Supper will ever be finally closed until the Lord comes. But it is not too much to hope that the *fog* and *mystery* and *obscurity* with which it is surrounded in some minds — may be cleared away by plain Bible truth.

In examining the Lord's Supper I will be content with asking four practical questions, and offering answers to them.

I. Why was the Lord's Supper ordained?

II. Who ought to go to the Table and be communicants?

III. What may communicants expect from the Lord's Supper?

IV. Why do many professing Christians never go to the Lord's Table?

I think it will be impossible to handle these four questions fairly, honestly, and impartially, without seeing the subject of this paper more clearly, and getting some distinct and practical ideas about some leading errors of our day. I say "practical" emphatically. My chief aim in this volume is to promote *practical Christianity*.

I. WHY was the Lord's Supper ordained? It was ordained for the continual remembrance of the sacrifice of the death of Christ, and of the benefits which we thereby receive. The *bread* which in the Lord's Supper is broken, given, and eaten, is meant to remind us of Christ's body given on the cross for our sins. The *wine* which is poured out and received, is meant to remind us of Christ's blood shed on the cross for our sins. He who eats that bread and drinks that wine is reminded, in the most striking and forcible manner — of the benefits Christ has obtained for his soul, and of the death of Christ as the hinge and turning point on which all those benefits depend.

Is this view, the doctrine of the New Testament? If it is not, forever let it be rejected, cast aside, and refused by men. If it is, let us never be ashamed to hold it close, profess our belief in it, pin our faith on it, and steadfastly refuse to hold any other view, no matter who teaches it.

In subjects like this, we must call no man master. It matters little what great theologians and learned preachers have thought fit to put forth about the Lord's Supper. If they teach more than the Word of God contains — they are not to be believed. I take up my Bible and turn to the New Testament. There I find no less than four separate accounts of the first appointment of the Lord's Supper. Matthew, Mark, Luke, and Paul — all four describe it — all four agree in telling us what our Lord did on this memorable occasion. Only two tell us the reason why our Lord commanded that His disciples were to eat the bread and drink the cup. Paul and Luke both record the remarkable words, *"Do this in remembrance of me."* Paul adds his own inspired comment: *"For whenever you eat this bread and drink this cup, you proclaim the Lord's death until he comes."* (Luke 22:19; 1 Corinthians 11:25-26). When Scripture speaks so clearly — why can't men be content with it? Why should we mystify and confuse a subject which in the New Testament is so simple?

The "continual remembrance of Christ's death" was the one grand object for which the Lord's Supper was ordained. He who goes further than this is adding to God's Word, and does so to the great peril of his soul.

Now, is it reasonable to suppose that our Lord would appoint an ordinance for so simple a purpose as "remembering His death?" It most certainly is! Of all the facts in His earthly ministry none are equal in importance to that of His death. It was the great settlement for man's sin, which had been appointed in God's promise from the foundation of the world. It was the great redemption of almighty power, to which every sacrifice of animals, from the fall of man, continually pointed. It was the grand end and purpose for which the Messiah came into the world. It was the cornerstone and foundation of all man's hopes of pardon and peace with God. In short, Christ would have lived, and taught, and preached, and prophesied, and performed miracles in vain — if He had not *crowned it all by dying for our sins as our Substitute on the Cross!* His death was our life. His death was the payment of our sin-debt to God. Without His death we would have been the most miserable of all creatures!

No wonder that an ordinance was specially appointed to remind us of our Savior's death. It is the one thing which poor, weak, sinful man needs to be continually reminded. Does the New Testament authorize men to say that the Lord's Supper was ordained to be a *sacrifice*, and that in it Christ's *literal* body and blood are present under the forms of bread and wine? Most certainly not! When the Lord Jesus said to the disciples, "This is my Body," and "this is my Blood," He clearly meant, "This *bread* in my hand is an symbol of my Body, and this cup of *wine* in my hand contains a symbol of my Blood." The disciples were accustomed to hear Him use such language. They remembered His saying, "The *field* is the world, and the *good seed* stands for the sons of the kingdom. The *weeds* are the sons of the evil one" (Matthew 13:38). It never entered into their minds that He meant to say He was holding His own body and His own blood in His hands, and literally giving them His literal body and blood to eat and drink! Not one of the writers of the New Testament ever speaks of the Lord's Supper as a *sacrifice*, or calls the Lord's Table an *altar*, or even hints that a Christian minister is a *sacrificing priest*. The universal doctrine of the New Testament is that after the *one* offering of Christ on the cross, there remains no more need of sacrifice.

If anyone believes that Paul's words to the Hebrews, *"We have an altar"* (Hebrews 13:10), are a proof that the Lord's table is an altar, I remind him "Christians have an altar where they partake. That altar is Christ our Lord — who is Altar, Priest, and Sacrifice, all in One." Throughout the Communion Service the one idea of the ordinance continually pressed on our attention is that of a "remembrance" of Christ's death. As to any *presence of Christ's natural body* and blood under the forms of bread and wine, the clear answer is that "the natural body and blood of Christ are in Heaven, and not here." Those Roman Catholics who delight in talking of the "altar," the "sacrifice," the "priest," and the "real presence" in the Lord's Supper — would do well to remember that they are using language which is entirely non-Biblical.

The point before us is one of vast importance. Let us lay hold upon it firmly, and never let it go. It is the very point on which our Reformers had their sharpest controversy with the Roman Catholics, and went to the stake, rather than give way. Sooner than admit that the Lord's Supper was a sacrifice, they cheerfully laid down their lives. To bring back the doctrine of the "real presence," and to turn the communion into the Roman Catholic "mass," is to pour contempt on our Martyrs, and to upset the first principles of the Protestant Reformation. No, rather, it is to ignore the plain teaching of God's Word, and do dishonor to the priestly office of our Lord Jesus Christ! The Bible teaches expressly that the Lord's Supper was ordained to be "a remembrance of Christ's body and blood," and not a sacrificial offering. The Bible teaches that Christ's substituted death on the cross was the *perfect* sacrifice for sin, which never needs to be *repeated.* Let us stand firm in these two great principles of the Christian faith. A clear understanding of the intention of the Lord's Supper is one of the soul's best safeguards against the delusions of false doctrine.

II. WHO ought to receive the Lord's Supper? What kind of people were meant to go to the Table and receive the Lord's Supper?

I will first show, **who ought NOT to be partakers of this ordinance**. The ignorance which prevails on this, as well as on every part of the subject, is vast, lamentable, and appalling. If I can contribute anything that may throw light upon it, I will feel very thankful. The principal giants whom John Bunyan describes, in "Pilgrim's Progress," as dangerous to Christian pilgrims, were two, *Pope* and *Pagan.* If the good old Puritan had foreseen the times we live in, he would have said something about the giant *Ignorance*!

(a.) It is *not* right to urge **all *professing* Christians** to go to the Lord's Table. There is such a thing as fitness and preparedness for the ordinance. It does not work like a medicine, independently of the state of mind of those who receive it. The teaching of those who urge all their congregation to come to the Lord's Table, as if the coming must necessarily do everyone good — is entirely without warrant of Scripture. No, rather, it is a teaching which is calculated to do immense harm to men's souls, and to turn the reception of the Lord's Supper into a mere *religious form. Ignorance* can never be the mother of acceptable worship, and an ignorant communicant who comes to the Lord's Table without knowing *why* he comes — is altogether in the wrong place!

"A man ought to examine himself before he eats of the bread and drinks of the cup." "Recognizing the body of the Lord" — that is to understand what the elements of bread and wine represent, and why they are appointed, and what is the particular use of remembering Christ's death — is an essential qualification of a true communicant. God commands *all* people everywhere to *repent* and *believe* the Gospel (Acts 17:30) — but He does not in the same way, or in the same manner, command everybody to come to the Lord's Table. No! this thing is not to be taken lightly, or carelessly! It is a solemn ordinance, and solemnly it ought to be used!

(b.) But this is not all. **Sinners living in open sin**, and determined not to give it up, ought never to come to the Lord's Table. To do so is a positive insult to Christ, and to pour contempt on His Gospel. It is nonsense to profess we desire to remember Christ's death, while we cling to sin — the accursed thing which made it needful for Christ to die! The mere fact that a man is continuing in sin is clear evidence that he does not care for Christ, and feels no gratitude for the offer of redemption. The ignorant Roman Catholic who goes to the priest's confessional and receives absolution, may think he is fit to go to the Roman Catholic mass — and after mass may return to his sins. He never reads the Bible — and knows no better! But the professing Christian who habitually breaks any of God's commandments — and yet goes to the Lord's Table, as if it would do him good and wipe away his sins — is very guilty indeed. So long as he chooses to continue his wicked habits — he cannot receive the slightest benefit from the Lord's Table — and is only adding sin to sin! To carry unrepented sin to the Lord's Table, and there receive the bread and wine, knowing in our own hearts that we and wickedness are yet friends — is one of the worst things man can do, and one of the most hardening to the conscience. If a man must have his sins, and can't give them up, let him by all means stay away from the Lord's Supper! There is such a thing as "eating and drinking in an unworthy manner" and to our own "judgment." To no one do these words apply so thoroughly, as to an unrepentant sinner.

(c.) Self-righteous people who think that they will be saved by their own works, have no business to come to the Lord's Table. Strange as it may sound at first, these people are the *least* qualified of all to receive the Lord's table. They may be outwardly correct, moral and respectable in their lives — but so long as they trust in their own goodness for salvation they are entirely in the wrong place at the Lord's Supper. For what do we declare at the Lord's Supper? We publicly profess that we have no goodness, righteousness, or worthiness of our own, and that all our hope is in Christ. We publicly profess that we are guilty, sinful, corrupt — and naturally deserve God's wrath and condemnation. We publicly profess that Christ's merit and not ours; Christ's righteousness and not ours — is the only cause why we look for acceptance with God. Now what has a self-righteous man to do with an ordinance like this? Clearly nothing at all.

One thing at any rate, is very clear: a self-righteous man has no business to receive the Lord's Supper. The Communion Service of the Church bids all communicants declare that "they do not presume to come to the Table trusting in their own righteousness — but in God's numerous and great mercies." It tells them to say, "We are not worthy so much as to gather up the crumbs under Your table," "the memory of our sins is grievous to us; the burden of them is intolerable." How many self-righteous professing Christians can ever go to the Lord's Table, and take these words into his mouth — is beyond my understanding! It only shows that many professing Christians use the "forms" of worship without taking the trouble to consider what they mean.

The plain truth is that the Lord's Supper was not meant for dead souls — but for living ones. The *careless*, the *ignorant*, the willfully *wicked*, the *self-righteous*, are no more fit to come to the Lord's Table than a dead corpse is fit to sit down at a king's feast! To enjoy a spiritual feast we must have a spiritual heart, and taste, and appetite. To suppose that the Lord's Table can do any good to an unspiritual man — is as foolish as to put bread and wine into the mouth of a dead person! The careless, the ignorant, and the willfully wicked, so long as they continue in that state, are utterly unfit to come to the Lord's Supper. To urge them to partake is not to do them good — but harm.

The Lord's Supper is not a *converting* or *justifying* ordinance. If a man goes to the Table unconverted or unforgiven, he will be *no better* when he comes away (actually *worse* due to the associated judgments for coming unworthily).

But, after all, the ground having been cleared of error, the question still remains to be answered: **Who are the sort of people who *ought* to receive the Lord's Supper?** I answer that by saying, people who have "examined themselves to see whether they have truly repented of their former sins, steadfastly purposing to lead a new life — have a true faith in God's mercy through Christ, with a thankful remembrance of His death — they are in love with all men."

In a word, I find that a worthy communicant is one who possesses three simple marks and qualifications — repentance, faith, and love. Does a man truly *repent* of sin and hate it? Does a man put his *trust* in Jesus Christ as his only hope of salvation? Does a man live in *love* towards others? He who can truly answer each of these questions, "I do," he is a man that is Scripturally qualified for the Lord's Supper. Let him come boldly. Let no barrier be put in his way. He comes up to the Bible standard of communicants. He may draw near with confidence, and feel assured that the great Master of the banquet is not displeased.

Such a man's **repentance** may be very much *imperfect*. Never mind! Is it real? Is he *truly* repentant? His **faith** in Christ may be very weak. Never mind! Is it real? A penny is as much true currency as is a one hundred dollar bill. His **love** may be very defective in quantity and degree. Never mind! Is it genuine? The grand test of a man's Christianity is not the *quantity* of holiness he has — but whether he has any true holiness all. The first twelve communicants, when Christ Himself gave the bread and wine, were weak indeed — weak in knowledge, weak in faith, weak in courage, weak in patience, weak in love! But eleven of them had something about them which outweighed all defects — they were real, genuine, sincere, and true!

Forever let this great principle be rooted in our minds — that the only worthy communicant is the man who has demonstrated *repentance* toward God, *faith* toward our Lord Jesus Christ, and practical *love* toward others. Are you that man? Then you may draw near to the table, and take the ordinance to your comfort. Anything less than this I dare not change in my standard of a communicant. I will never encourage someone to receive the Lord's Supper — who is careless, ignorant, and self-righteous! I will never tell anyone to keep away until he is perfect, and to wait until his heart is as holy as an angel's. I will not do so, because I believe that neither my Master nor His Apostles would have done so. Show me a man that really feels his sins, really leans on Christ, really struggles to be holy — and I will welcome him in My Master's name. He may feel weak, erring, empty, feeble, doubting, wretched, and poor. But what does that matter? Paul, I believe, would have received him as a right communicant, and I will do likewise.

III. What BENEFIT communicants may expect to get by receiving the Lord's Supper. This is a point of grave importance, and one on which many mistakes abound. On no point, perhaps, connected with this ordinance are the views of Christians so vague and indistinct and undefined. One common idea among men is that "receiving the Lord's Supper must do them some good." Why, they can't explain. What good, they can't exactly say. But they have a loose general notion that it is the right thing to be a communicant, and that somehow or other it is of value to their souls! This is of course nothing better than ignorance. It is unreasonable to suppose that such communicants can please Christ, or receive any real benefit from what they do.

If there is any principle clearly laid down in the Bible about any act of religious worship, it is this that it must be with *understanding*. The worshiper must at least understand *something* about what he is doing. Mere bodily worship, unaccompanied by mind or heart — is utterly worthless. The man who eats the bread and drinks the wine, as a mere matter of form, because it is the "right" thing to do, without any clear idea of what it all means, derives no benefit. He might just as well stay at home!

Another common idea among men is that, "taking the Lord's Supper will help them get to Heaven, and take away their sins." To this false idea you may trace up the habit in some churches of going to the Lord's Table once a year, in order, as an old farmer once said, "to wipe off the year's sins." To this idea again, you may trace the too common practice of *sending for a minister in time of sickness*, in order to receive the ordinance before death. Yes, how many take comfort about their relatives, after they have lived a most ungodly life, for no better reason than this, that they took the Lord's Supper when they were dying! Whether they repented and believed and had new hearts — they neither seem to know or care. All they know is that "they took the Lord's Supper before they died."

My heart sinks within me when I hear people resting on such evidence as this. Ideas like these are sad proofs of the ignorance which fills the minds of men about the Lord's Supper. They are ideas for which there is not the slightest warrant in Scripture. The sooner they are cast aside and given up — the better for the Church and the world. Let us settle it firmly in our minds — that the Lord's Supper was not given to be a means either of *justification* or of *conversion*. It was never meant to give grace — where there is no grace already; or to provide pardon — when pardon is not already enjoyed. It cannot possibly provide what is lacking, with the absence of repentance to God, and faith toward the Lord Jesus Christ. It is an ordinance for the penitent, not for the impenitent; for the believing, not for the unbelieving; for the converted, not for the unconverted.

The unconverted man, who fancies that be can find a "shortcut" to Heaven by taking the Lord's Supper, without treading the well-worn steps of *repentance* and faith — will find to his cost one day, that he is totally deceived! The Lord's Supper was meant to *increase* and help the grace that a man has — but not to *impart* the grace that he does not have. It was certainly never intended to make our peace with God, to justify, or to convert. The simplest statement of the benefit which a truehearted communicant may expect to receive from the Lord's Supper, is the strengthening and refreshing of our souls — clearer views of Christ and His atonement, clearer views of all the offices which Christ fills, as our Mediator and Advocate, clearer views of the complete redemption Christ has obtained for us by His substituted death on the cross, clearer views of our full and perfect acceptance in Christ before God, fresh reasons for deep repentance for sin, fresh reasons for lively faith — these are among the leading returns which a believer may confidently expect to get from his attendance at the Lord's Table. He who eats the bread and drinks the wine in a right spirit — will find himself drawn into closer communion with Christ, and will feel to know Him more, and understand Him better.

(a) Right reception of the Lord's Supper has a "**humbling**" effect on the soul. The sight of the bread and wine as emblems of Christ's body and blood, reminds us how sinful sin must be, if nothing less than the death of God's own Son could make satisfaction for it, or redeem us from its guilt. Never should we be so "clothed with humility," as when we receive the Lord's Supper.

(b) Right reception of the Lord's Supper has a "**cheering**" effect on the soul. The sight of the bread broken, and the wine poured out, reminds us how full, perfect, and complete is our salvation! Those vivid emblems remind us what an enormous price has been paid for our redemption. They press on us the mighty truth — that believing on Christ, we have nothing to fear, because a sufficient payment has been made for our debt. The "precious blood of Christ" answers every charge that can be brought against us. God can be "just and the one who justifies, those who have faith in Jesus" (Romans 3:26).

(c) Right reception of the Lord's Supper has a "**sanctifying**" effect on the soul. The bread and wine remind us how great is our debt of gratitude to our Lord, and how thoroughly we are bound to live for Him who died for our sins. They seem to say to us, "Remember what Christ has done for you — and ask yourself whether there is anything too great to do for Him!"

(d) Right reception of the Lord's Supper into hearts, has a "**restraining**" effect on the soul. Every time a believer receives the bread and the wine, he is reminded what a serious thing it is to be a Christian, and what an obligation is laid on him to lead a consistent life. Bought with such a price as that which the bread and wine call to his recollection, ought he not to glorify Christ in body and spirit, which are His? The man that goes regularly and intelligently to the Lord's Table finds it increasingly hard to yield to sin and conform to the world.

Such is a brief account of the benefits which a right-hearted communicant may expect to receive from the Lord's Supper. In eating that bread and drinking that cup, such a man will have his *repentance* deepened, his *faith* increased, his *knowledge* enlarged, his habit of *holy living* strengthened. He will realize more of the "real presence" of Christ in his heart. Eating, that bread by faith, he will feel closer communion with the body of Christ. Drinking that wine by faith, he will feel closer communion with the blood of Christ. *He will see more clearly what Christ is to him, and what he is to Christ.* He will understand more thoroughly what it is to be "one with Christ, and Christ one with him." He will feel the roots of his soul's spiritual life watered, and the work of grace in his heart established, built up, and carried forward.

All these things may seem and sound like foolishness to a natural man — but to a true Christian these things are light, and health, and life, and peace. No wonder that a true Christian finds the Lord's Supper a source of blessing! Remember, I do not pretend to say that all Christians experience the full blessing of the Lord's Supper, which I have just attempted to describe. Nor do I say that the same believer will always find his soul in the same spiritual frame, and always receive the same amount of benefit from the ordinance. But I boldly say this: you will rarely find a true believer who will not say that he believes the Lord's Supper is one of his best helps and highest privileges. He will tell you that if he were deprived of the Lord's Supper on a regular basis he would find the loss of it a great detriment to his soul. There are some things of which we never know the value of, until they are taken from us. So I believe it is with the Lord's Supper. The weakest and humblest of God's children gets a blessing from this ordinance, to an extent of which he is not aware.

IV. Why so many *professin* Christians never come to the Lord's Supper. It is a simple matter of fact, that myriads of people who *call* themselves Christians never come to the Table of the Lord. They would not endure to be told that they deny the faith, and are not in communion with Christ. When they worship, they attend a place of Christian worship; when they hear religious teaching, it is the teaching of Christianity; when they are married, they use a Christian service. Yet all this time they never come to the Lord's Supper! They often live on in this state of mind for many years, and to all appearance are not ashamed. They often die in this condition without ever having received the ordinance — and yet profess to feel hope at the last, and their friends express a hope about them. And yet they live and die in open disobedience to a plain command of Christ! These are simple facts. Let anyone look around him, and deny them if he can.

Now why is this? What explanation can we give? Our Lord Jesus Christ's last injunctions to His disciples are clear, plain, and unmistakable. He says to all, "Eat, drink: do this in remembrance of Me." Did He leave it to our discretion whether we would obey His injunction or not? Did He mean that it was not significant whether His disciples did or did not keep up the ordinance He had just established? Certainly not! The very idea is absurd, and one certainly never dreamed of in apostolic times. Paul evidently takes it for granted that every Christian would go to the Lord's Table when it was available. A class of Christian worshipers who never came to the Table, was a class whose existence was unknown to him.

What, then, are we to say of that number which fail to receive the Lord's Supper, unabashed, unhumbled, not afraid, not the least ashamed? Why is it? How is it? What does it all mean? Let us look these questions fairly in the face, and endeavor to give an answer to them.

(1) For one thing, many fail to go to the Table because they are utterly careless and thoughtless about true religion, and ignorant of very first principles of Christianity. They go to church, as a matter of form — but they neither know, nor care anything about what is done at church! Christianity has no place either in their hearts, or heads, or consciences, or wills, or understandings. It is a mere affair of "words and names," about which they know little — and have little concern. There were very few such false Christians in Paul's times, if indeed there were any. There are far too many in these last days of the world. They are the dead-weights of the Churches, and the scandal of Christianity. What such people need is light, knowledge, grace, a renewed conscience, a changed heart. In their present state they have no part of Christ; and dying in this state they are thrown into Hell. Do I wish them to come to the Lord's Supper? Certainly not, until they are converted. No one can enter the kingdom of God unless he is born again.

(2) For another thing, many *professing* Christians do not receive the Lord's Supper because they know they are living in the habitual practice of some sin, or in the neglect of some Christian duty. Their conscience tells them so long as they live in this state, and do not turn away from their sins, they are unfit to come to the Table of the Lord. Well, they are so far quite right! I wish no man to be a communicant if he cannot give up his sins. But I warn these people not to forget that if they are unfit for the Lord's Supper in that condition, they will be lost eternally. The same sins which disqualify them for the ordinance, most certainly disqualify them for Heaven. Do I want them to come to the Lord's Supper as they are? Certainly not! But I do want them to repent and be converted, to cease to do evil, and to break off from their sins. Forever let it be remembered, that the man who is unfit for the Lord's Supper — is unfit to die!

(3) For another thing, some are not communicant because they imagine that it will add to their responsibility. They are not, as many, ignorant and careless about religion. They even attend church regularly and listen to the preaching of the gospel. But they say they dread coming to the Lord's Table and making a confession and a profession. They fear that they might afterwards fall away, and bring scandal on the cause of Christianity. They think it wisest to be on the *safe* side, and not commit themselves at all. Such people would do well to remember, that if they avoid responsibility of one kind by not coming to the Lord's Table, they incur responsibility of another kind, quite as grave, and quite as injurious to the soul. They are responsible for *open disobedience* to a command from of Christ. They are shrinking from doing that which their Master continually commands His disciples — confessing Him before men.

No doubt it is a serious step to come to the Lord's Table and receive the bread and the wine. It is a step that none should take lightly and without self-examination. But it is "no less a serious step to walk away and refuse the ordinance," when we remember Who invites us to receive it, and for what purpose it was appointed! I warn the people I am now dealing with — to be careful what they are doing. Let them not flatter themselves that *it can ever be a wise, a prudent, a safe line of conduct to neglect a plain command of Christ!* They may find at length, to their cost, that they have only increased their guilt and forsaken their mercies!

(4) For another thing, some false Christians stay away from the Lord's Supper because they believe they are not yet worthy. They wait and stand still, under the mistaken notion that no one is qualified for the Lord's Supper unless he feels within him, something like perfection. They pitch their idea of a communicant so high that they despair of attaining to it. Waiting for inward perfection they live, and waiting for it they die. Now such people would do well to understand that they are completely mistaken in their estimate of what "worthiness" really is.

They are forgetting that the Lord's Supper was not intended for *unsinning angels* — but for men and women subject to weakness, living in a world full of temptations, and needing mercy and grace every day they live! *A sense of our own utter unworthiness is the best worthiness that we can bring to the Lord's Table.* A deep feeling of our own entire indebtedness to Christ for all we have and hope for, is the best feeling we can bring with us. The people I now have in view, ought to consider seriously whether the ground they have taken up is defensible. If they are waiting until they feel in themselves perfect hearts, perfect motives, perfect feelings, perfect repentance, perfect love, perfect faith — they will wait forever. There never were such communicants in any age — certainly not in the days of our Lord and of the Apostles — there never will be as long as the world stands. No, rather, the very thought that we feel literally worthy, is a symptom of secret self-righteousness, and proves us unfit for the Lord's Table in God's sight. Sinners we are, when we first are saved — sinners we will be — until we die! Converted, changed, renewed, sanctified — but sinners still (though not like before — sin is not the *pattern* of a believer's new life). In short, no man is really worthy to receive the Lord's Supper who does not deeply feel that he is a "miserable sinner."

(5) In the last place, some object going to the Lord's Table because they see others partaking who are not worthy, and not in a right state of mind. Because others eat and drink unworthily, they refuse to eat and drink at all. Of all the reasons taken up by those refusing to come to the Lord's Supper to justify their own neglect of Christ's ordinance, I must plainly say — I know none which seems to me so foolish, so weak, so unreasonable, and so unscriptural as this. It is as good as saying that we will never receive the Lord's Supper at all! When will we ever find a body of communicants on earth, of which all the members are converted and living perfect lives? It is setting up ourselves in the most unhealthy attitude of judging others. "Who are you, that you judge another person?" "What is that to you? You must follow me" (John 21:22). It is depriving ourselves of a great privilege, because others profane it and make a bad use of it. It is pretending to be wiser than our Master Himself. It is taking up ground for which there is no warrant in Scripture.

Paul rebukes the Corinthians sharply, for the irreverent behavior of some of the communicants; but I cannot find him giving a single hint that when some came to the Table unworthily, others ought to draw back or stay away. Let me advise the non-communicants I have now in view, to beware of being wise above that which was written. Let them study the parable of the Wheat and Tares, and mark how both were to "grow together *until* the harvest" (Matthew 13:30). Perfect Churches, perfect congregations, perfect bodies of communicants, are all unattainable in this world of confusion and sin. Let us covet the best gifts, and do all we can to check sin in others; but let us not starve our own selves, because others are ignorant sinners, and turn their food into poison. If others are foolish enough to eat and drink unworthily, let us not turn our backs on Christ's ordinance, and refuse to eat and drink at all.

Such are the five common excuses why myriads in the present day, though *professing* themselves Christians, never come to the Lord's Supper. One common remark may be made about them — there is not a single *reason* among the five, which deserves to be called "good," and which does not condemn the man who gives it. I challenge anyone to deny this. I have said repeatedly that I want no one to come to the Lord's Table who is not properly qualified. But I ask those who stay away never to forget that the very reasons they assign for their conduct, are their condemnation. I tell them that they stand convicted before God of either being very ignorant of what a communicant is, and what the Lord's Supper is; or else of being people who are not *living* right — and are unfit to *die*.

In short, to say, I am a non-communicant, is as good as saying one of three things — I am living in sin — and cannot come; I know Christ commands me — but I will not obey Him; I am an ignorant man — and do not understand what the Lord's Supper means.

I know not in what state of mind this book may find the reader of this paper, or what his opinions may be about the Lord's Supper. But I will *conclude* the whole subject by offering to all some **WARNINGS**, which I venture to think are highly required by the times.

(A) In the first place, "do not neglect" the Lord's Supper. The man who coolly and deliberately refuses to use an ordinance which the Lord Jesus Christ appointed for his profit — may be very sure that his soul is in a very wrong state. There is a judgment to come; there is an account to be rendered of all our conduct on earth. How any one can look forward to that judgment day, and expect to meet Christ with comfort and in peace, if he has refused all his life to commune with Christ at His Table, is a thing that I cannot understand. Does this hit home to you? Be careful what you are doing!

(B) In the second place, do not receive the Lord's Supper "carelessly, irreverently, and as a matter of form." The man who goes to the Lord's Table, and eats the bread and drinks the wine, while his heart is far away — is committing a great sin, and robbing himself of a great blessing. In receiving the Lord's Table, as in every other means of grace, everything depends on the state of mind and heart, in which the ordinance is used. He who draws near without repentance, faith, and love — and with a heart full of sin and the world — will certainly be nothing better — but rather worse! Does this hit home to you? Be careful what you are doing!

(C) In the third place, "do not make an idol" of the Lord's Supper. The man who tells you that it is the first, foremost, chief, and principal precept in Christianity, is telling you that which he will find it hard to prove. In the great majority of the books of the New Testament the Lord's Supper is not even named. In the letter to Timothy and Titus, about a minister's duties, the subject is not even mentioned. To repent and be converted, to believe and be holy, to be born again and have grace in our hearts — all these things are of far more importance than to be a communicant. Without them we cannot be saved. Without the Lord's Supper we can be saved. Are you tempted to make the Lord's Supper override and overshadow everything in Christianity, and place it above prayer and preaching? Be careful. Pay attention what you are doing!

(D) In the fourth place, "do not use the Lord's Supper irregularly." Never be absent when the Lord's Supper is administered. Make every effort to be in attendance. Regular habits are essential to the maintenance of the health of our bodies. Regular use of the Lord's Supper is essential to the well-being of our souls. The man who finds it a burden to attend on every occasion when the Lord's Table is spread, may well doubt whether all is right within him, and whether he is ready for the Marriage Supper of the Lamb. If Thomas had not been absent when the Lord appeared the first time to the assembled disciples, he would not have said the foolish things he did. Absence made him miss a blessing. Does this hit home to you? Be careful what you are doing!

(E) In the fifth place, "do not do anything to bring discredit" on your profession as a communicant. The man who after attending the Lord's Table runs into sin — does more harm perhaps than any unsaved sinner. *He is a walking sermon on behalf of the devil!* He gives opportunity to the enemies of the Lord to blaspheme. He helps to keep people away from Christ. Lying, drinking, immoral, dishonest, selfish communicants — are the helpers of the devil, and the worst enemies of the Gospel. "For the grace of God that brings salvation has appeared to all men. It teaches us to say "No" to ungodliness and worldly passions, and to live self-controlled, upright and godly lives in this present age!" Titus 2:11-12. Does this hit home to you? Be careful what you are doing!

(F) In the last place, "do not despair" and be cast down, if with all your desires you do not feel that you get a lot of good from the Lord's Supper. Very likely you are expecting too much. Very likely you are a poor judge of your own state. Your soul's *roots* may be strengthening and growing — while you *think* that you are not growing. Very likely you are forgetting that earth is not Heaven, and that here we walk by *sight* and not by *faith*, and must expect nothing perfect. Lay these things to heart. Do not think harsh things about yourself without cause.

To every reader into whose hands this paper may fall, I commend the whole subject of it as deserving of serious and solemn consideration. I am nothing better than a poor or fallible man myself. But if I have made up my mind on any point it is this — that there is no truth which demands such plain speaking, as truth about the Lord's Supper!

CHRISTIAN LOVE!

"And now these three remain: faith, hope and love. But the *greatest* of these is love!" 1 Corinthians 13:13

"The end of the commandment is love." 1 Timothy 1:5

Love is rightly called "the Queen of Christian graces." It is a grace which all people profess to admire. It seems a plain practical thing which everybody can understand. It is none of "those troublesome doctrinal points" about which Christians are disagreed. Thousands, I suspect, would not be ashamed to tell you that they knew nothing about justification or regeneration, about the work of Christ or the Holy Spirit. But nobody, I believe, would like to say that he knew nothing about "love!" If men possess nothing else in religion, they always flatter themselves that they possess "love."

A few *plain thoughts* about love may not be without use. There are *false notions* abroad about it which require to be dispelled. There are *mistakes* about it which require to be rectified. In my admiration of love, I yield to none. But I am bold to say that in many minds, the whole subject seems completely misunderstood.

I. Let me show, firstly, the place which the Bible gives to love.

II. Let me show, secondly, what the love of the Bible really is.

III. Let me show, thirdly, where true love comes from.

IV. Let me show, lastly, why love is "the greatest" of the graces.

I ask the best attention of my readers to the subject. My heart's desire and prayer to God is, that the growth of love may be promoted in this sin-burdened world. In nothing does the fallen condition of man show itself so strongly, as in the *scarcity of Christian love.* There is little *faith* on earth, little *hope*, little *knowledge* of Divine things. But nothing, after all, is so *scarce* as real love!

I. Let me show the PLACE which the Bible gives to love.

I begin with this point in order to establish the *immense practical importance* of my subject. I do not forget that there are many high-flying Christians in this present day, who almost refuse to look at anything *practical* in Christianity. They can talk of nothing but two or three favorite doctrines. Now I want to remind my readers that the Bible contains much about *practice* as well as about *doctrine*, and that one thing to which it attaches great weight, is "love."

I turn to the New Testament, and ask men to observe what it says about love. In all religious inquiries there is nothing like letting the Scripture speak for itself. There is no surer way of finding out truth, than the old way of *turning to plain texts.* Texts were our

Lord's *weapons*, both in answering Satan, and in arguing with the Jews. Texts are the *guides* we must never be ashamed to refer to in the present day. "What do the Scriptures say? What is written? How do you read?"

Let us hear what Paul says to the Corinthians: "If I speak in the tongues of men and of angels, but have not love—I am only a resounding gong or a clanging cymbal. If I have the gift of prophecy and can fathom all mysteries and all knowledge, and if I have a faith that can move mountains, but have not love—I am nothing. If I give all I possess to the poor and surrender my body to the flames, but have not love—I gain nothing!" 1 Corinthians 13:1-3

Let us hear what Paul says to the Colossians: "Above all these things put on love, which is the bond of perfectness." (Colossians 3:14.)

Let us hear what Paul says to Timothy: "The end of the commandment is love out of a pure heart" (1 Timothy 1:5.)

Let us hear what Peter says: "Above all things, have fervent love among yourselves: for love shall cover the multitude of sins." (1 Peter 4:8.)

Let us hear what our Lord Jesus Christ Himself says, "A new command I give you: Love one another. As I have loved you, so you must love one another. By this all men will know that you are my disciples, if you love one another." (John 13:34, 35.)

Above all, let us read our Lord's account of the last judgment, and mark that lack of love will condemn millions. "Then He will say to those on the left: Depart from Me, you who are cursed, into the eternal fire prepared for the Devil and his angels! For I was hungry and you gave Me nothing to eat; I was thirsty and you gave Me nothing to drink; I was a stranger and you did not take Me in; I was naked and you did not clothe Me, sick and in prison and you did not take care of Me." (Matthew 25:41-43.)

Let us hear what Paul says to the Romans: "Owe no man anything—but to love another: for he who loves another has fulfilled the law." (Romans 13:9.)

Let us hear what Paul says to the Ephesians: "Walk is love, as Christ also has loved us." (Ephesians 5:2.)

Let us hear what John says: "Beloved, let us love one another, because love is from God, and everyone who loves has been born of God and knows God. The one who does not love does not know God, because God is love." (1 John 4:7, 8.)

I shall make *no comment* upon these texts. I think it better to place them before my readers in their *naked simplicity*, and to let them speak for themselves. If anyone is disposed to think the subject of this paper a matter of light importance, I will only ask him to look at these texts, and to think again. He who would take down "love" from the high and holy place which it occupies in the Bible, and treat it as a matter of *secondary* consequence, must settle his account with God's Word. I certainly shall not waste time in arguing with him.

To my own mind, the evidence of these texts appears clear, plain, and incontrovertible. They show the *immense importance* of love, as one of the "things that accompany salvation." They prove that it has a right to demand the serious attention of all who call themselves Christians, and that those who despise the subject are only exposing their own ignorance of Scripture.

II. Let me show, secondly, WHAT the love of the Bible really is.

I think it of great importance to have clear views on this point. It is precisely here that mistakes about love begin. Thousands delude themselves with the idea that they have "love," when they have not, from downright ignorance of Scripture. Their love is not the love described in the Bible.

(a) The love of the Bible does not consist in *giving to the poor*. It is a common delusion to suppose that it does. Yet Paul tells us plainly, that a man may "bestow all his goods to feed the poor "(1 Corinthians 13:8)—and not have love! That a charitable man will "remember the poor," there can be no question. (Galatians 2:10.) That he will do all he can to assist them, relieve them, and lighten their burdens—I do not for a moment deny. All I say is, that this does not make up "love." It is easy to spend a fortune in giving away money, and soup, and milk, and and bread, and coals, and blankets, and clothing—and yet to be utterly destitute of Bible love!

(b) The love of the Bible does not consist in never disapproving anybody's conduct. Here is another very common delusion! Thousands pride themselves on never *condemning* others, or calling them *wrong*, whatever they may do. They convert the precept of our Lord, "do not judge," into an excuse for having no unfavorable opinion at all of anybody! They pervert His prohibition of *rash* and *censorious* judgments, into a prohibition of *all* judgment whatever.

Your neighbor may be a drunkard, a liar, and a violent man. Never mind! "It is not love," they tell you, "to pronounce him, wrong!" You are to believe that he has a *good heart at the bottom!* This idea of love is, unhappily, a very common one. It is full of mischief. To *throw a veil over sin*, and to refuse to call things by their right names, to talk of "hearts" being good, when "lives" are flatly wrong, to shut our eyes against wickedness, and say smooth things of immorality—this is not Scriptural love!

(c) The love of the Bible does not consist in never *disapproving anybody's religious opinions*. Here is another most serious and growing delusion. There are many who pride themselves on never pronouncing others mistaken, whatever views they may hold. Your neighbor may be an Atheist, or a Buddhist, or a Roman Catholic, or a Mormonite, a Deist, or a Skeptic, a mere Formalist, or a thorough Antinomian. But the "love" of many says that you have no right to think him wrong! "If he is sincere, it is uncharitable to think unfavorably of his spiritual condition!"

From such love—may I ever be delivered!

At this rate, the Apostles were wrong in going out to preach to the Gentiles!

At this rate, there is no use in missions!

At this rate, we had better close our Bibles, and shut up our churches!

At this rate, everybody is right—and nobody is wrong!

At this rate, everybody is going to Heaven—and nobody is going to Hell!

Such *love* is a monstrous caricature! To say that all are equally right in their opinions—though their opinions flatly contradict one another; to say that all are equally in the way to Heaven—though their doctrinal sentiments are as opposite as black and white—this is not Scriptural love. Love like this, pours contempt on the Bible, and talks as if God had not given us a written standard of truth. Love like this, confuses all our notions of Heaven, and would fill it with a discordant inharmonious rabble. True love does not think everybody right in doctrine. True love cries, "Do not believe every spirit, but test the spirits to see whether they are from God, because many false prophets have gone out into the world!" 1 John 4:1. "If anyone comes to you and does not bring this teaching, do not take him into your house or welcome him!" 2 John 1:10

I leave the *negative* side of the question here. I have dwelt upon it at some length because of the days in which we live and the strange notions which abound. Let me now turn to the *positive* side. Having shown what love is not, let me now show what it is.

Christian love is that "love," which Paul places first among those fruits which the Spirit causes to be brought forth in the heart of a believer. "The fruit of the Spirit is love." (Galatians 5:22.)

Love to **God**, such as Adam had before the fall, is its first feature. He who has love, desires to love God with heart, and soul and mind, and strength.

Love to **man** is its second feature. He who has Christian love, desires to love his neighbor as himself.

Christian love will show itself in a believer's **doings**. It will make him ready to do kind acts to everyone within his reach, "both to their bodies and souls. It will not let him be content with soft words and kind wishes. It will make him diligent in doing all that lies in his power to lessen the sorrow and increase the happiness of others. Like his

Master, he will care more for ministering than for being ministered to, and will look for nothing in return. Like his Master's great apostle, he will very willingly "spend and be spent" for others, even though they repay him with hatred, and not with love. True love does not want *wages*. Its work is its reward.

Christian love will show itself in a believer's **readiness to bear evil** as well as to do good. It will make him . . .
patient under provocation,
forgiving when injured,
meek when unjustly attacked,
quiet when slandered.

It will make him bear much and forbear much, put up with much and look over much, submit often and deny himself often—all for the sake of peace. It will make him put a strong *bit* on his temper, and a strong *bridle* on his tongue.

True love is not always asking, "What are *my* rights? Am *I* treated as I deserve?" but, "How can I best promote peace? How can I do that which is most edifying to others?"

Christian love will show itself in the general spirit and demeanor of a believer. It will make him kind, unselfish, good-natured, good-tempered, and considerate for others. It will make him gentle, affable, and courteous, in all the daily relations of private life. It will make him thoughtful for others' comfort, tender for others' feelings, and more anxious to give pleasure than to receive.

True love never *envies* others when they prosper, nor rejoices in the calamities of others when they are in trouble. At all times, it will believe, and hope, and try to put a good construction on others' actions. And even at the worst, it will be full of pity, mercy, and compassion.

Would we like to know where the **true Pattern** of love like this can be found? We have only to look at the life of our Lord Jesus Christ, as described in the Gospels, and we shall see it perfectly exemplified. Love shone forth in all His *doings*. His *daily life* was an incessant "going about" doing good. Love shone forth in all His *bearing*. He was continually hated, persecuted, slandered, misrepresented. But He patiently endured it all. No angry word ever fell from His lips. No ill-temper ever appeared in His demeanor. "When they hurled their insults at him, he did not retaliate; when he suffered, he made no threats." (1 Peter 2:23.) Love shone forth in all His *spirit* and *deportment*. The *law of kindness* was ever on His lips. Among weak and ignorant disciples, among sick and sorrowful petitioners for help and relief, among publicans and sinners, among Pharisees and Sadducees—He was always one and the same—kind and patient to all.

And yet, be it remembered, our blessed Master never *flattered sinners*, or *connived at sin*. He never shrank from *exposing wickedness* in its true colors, or from rebuking those who would cleave to it. He never hesitated to *denounce false doctrine*, by whoever it might be held, or to exhibit *false practice* in its true colors, and the certain end to which it tends. He called things by their right names. He spoke as freely of Hell and the fire that is never quenched, as of Heaven and the kingdom of glory. He has left on record an everlasting proof that perfect love does not require us to approve everybody's life or opinions, and that it is quite possible to condemn false doctrine and wicked practice—and yet to be full of love at the same time.

I have now set before my readers the *true nature of Christian love*. I have given a slight and very brief account of what it is *not*, and what it *is*. I cannot pass on without suggesting **two practical thoughts**, which press home on my mind with weighty force, and I hope may press home on others.

Think, for a moment, how deplorably little love there is upon earth! How w conspicuous is the absence of true love among professing Christians! I speak not of *heathen* now, I speak of professing Christians! What angry tempers, what passions, what selfishness, what bitter tongues—are to be found in private families! What strifes, what quarrels, what spitefulness, what malice, what revenge, what envy between neighbors and fellow-parishioners! What jealousies and contentions between Churchmen and Dissenters, Calvinists and Arminians, High Churchmen and Low Churchmen! "Where is love?" we may well ask, "Where is love? Where is the mind of Christ?"—when we look at the spirit which reigns in the world. No wonder that Christ's cause stands still, and infidelity abounds—when men's hearts know so little of love! Surely, we may well say, "When the Son of man comes, shall He find *love* upon earth?"

Think, for another thing, what a happy world this would be—if there was more love. It is the lack of love which causes half the misery which there is upon earth. Sickness, and death, and poverty, will not account for more than half the sorrows. The rest come from ill- temper, ill-nature, strifes, quarrels, lawsuits, malice, envy, revenge, frauds, violence, wars, and the like. It would be one great step towards doubling the happiness of mankind, and halving their sorrows—if all men and women were full of Scriptural love.

III. Let me show, thirdly—*where* the love of the Bible comes from.

Love, such as I have described, is certainly not *natural* to man. Naturally, we are all more or less selfish, envious, ill-tempered, spiteful, ill-natured, and unkind! We have only to observe children, when left to themselves, to see the proof of this. Let boys and girls grow up without proper training and education—and you will not see one of them possessing Christian love! Mark how some of them think first of themselves, and their own comfort and advantage! Mark how others are full of pride, passion, and evil tempers! How can we account for it? There is but one reply. The *natural heart* knows nothing of true love.

Christian love will never be found except in a heart prepared by the Holy Spirit. It is a tender plant, and will never grow except in one soil. You may as well expect grapes on thorns, or figs on thistles—as look for love when the heart is not right.

The heart in which love grows, is a heart changed, renewed, and transformed by the Holy Spirit. The image and likeness of God, which Adam lost at the fall, has been restored to it, however feeble and imperfect the restoration may appear. It is a "partaker of the Divine nature," by union with Christ and sonship to God; and one of the first features of that nature is *love.* (2 Peter I. 4.)

Such a heart is deeply convinced of *sin*—hates it, flees from it, and fights with it from day to day. And one of the prime motions of sin which it daily labors to overcome, is *selfishness* and *lack of love.*

Such a heart is deeply sensible of its *mighty debt to our Lord Jesus Christ.* It feels continually that it owes to Him who died for us on the cross, all its present comfort, hope, and peace. How can it show forth its gratitude? What can it render to its Redeemer? If it can do nothing else, it strives to be like Him, to drink into His spirit, to walk in His footsteps, and, like Him—to be full of love. "The love of Christ shed abroad in the heart by the Holy Spirit" is the surest *fountain* of Christian love. Love will produce love.

I ask my reader's special attention to this point. It is one of great importance in the present day. There are many who profess to admire love—while they care nothing about *vital Christianity.* They like some of the *fruits* and results of the Gospel—but not the *root* from which these fruits alone can grow, or the doctrines with which they are inseparably connected.

Hundreds will praise love—who hate to be told of man's corruption, of the blood of Christ, and of the inward work of the Holy Spirit. Many a parent would like his children to grow up unselfish and good tempered—who would not be much pleased if conversion, and repentance, and faith, were pressed home on their attention.

Now I desire to protest against this notion, that you can have the *fruits* of Christianity, without the *roots*—that you can produce Christian tempers, without teaching Christian doctrines—that you can have love which will wear and endure, without grace in the heart.

I grant, most freely, that every now and then one sees a person who seems very charitable and amiable, without any distinctive Christian religion. But such cases are so rare and remarkable, that, like *exceptions*—they only prove the truth of the general rule. And often, too often, it may be feared in such cases the love is only *apparent*, and in private it completely fails. I firmly believe, as a general rule, you will not find such love as the Bible describes, except in the *soil* of a heart thoroughly imbued with Bible religion. Holy *practice* will not flourish without sound *doctrine*. What God has joined together, it is useless to expect to have separate.

The delusion which I am trying to combat, is helped forward to a most mischievous degree by the vast majority of novels, romances, and tales of fiction. Who does not know that the heroes and heroines of these works are constantly described as patterns of perfection? They are always doing the right thing, saying the right thing, and showing the right temper! They are always kind, and amiable, and unselfish, and forgiving! And yet you never hear a word about their religion! In short, to judge by the generality of works of fiction, it is possible to have . . .

excellent practical religion—without doctrine,
the *fruits* of the Spirit—without the *grace* of the Spirit,
and the *mind* of Christ—without *union* with Christ!

Here, in short, is the great danger of reading most novels, romances, and works of fiction. The greater part of them give a false or incorrect view of human nature. They paint their model men and women as they *ought* to be, and not as they *really are*. The readers of such writings get their minds filled with wrong conceptions of what the world is. Their notions of mankind become *visionary* and *unreal*. They are constantly looking for men and women such as they never meet—and expecting what they never find.

Let me entreat my readers, once for all, to draw their ideas of human nature from the Bible, and not from novels. Settle it down in your mind, that there cannot be true love without a heart renewed by grace. A certain degree of kindness, courtesy, amiability, good nature—may undoubtedly be seen in many who have no vital religion. But the glorious plant of *Bible love*, in all its fullness and perfection, will never be found without union with Christ, and the work of the Holy Spirit. Teach this to your children, if you have any. Hold it up in schools, if you are connected with any. Lift up love. Make much of love. Give place to none in exalting the grace of kindness, love, good nature, unselfishness, good temper.

But never, never forget, that there is but one *school* in which these things can be thoroughly learned—and that is the school of Christ. Real love comes down from above. True love is the *fruit of the Spirit*. He who would have it—must sit at Christ's feet, and learn of Him.

IV. Let me show, lastly—*why* love is called the "greatest" of the graces.

The words of Paul, on this subject, are distinct and unmistakable. He winds up his wonderful chapter on love in the following manner:

"And now these three remain: faith, hope and love. But the *greatest* of these is love!" 1 Corinthians 13:13

This expression is very remarkable. Of all the writers in the New Testament, none, certainly, exalts "faith" so highly as Paul. The Epistles to the Romans and Galatians abound in sentences showing its vast importance. By faith, the sinner lays hold on Christ and is saved. Through faith, we are justified, and have peace with God. Yet here the same Paul speaks of something which is even *greater than faith!* He puts before us the three leading Christian graces, and pronounces the following judgment on them, "The greatest is love!" Such a *sentence* from such a *writer* demands special attention. What are we to understand, when we hear of love being greater than faith and hope?

We are not to suppose, for a moment, that love can *atone* for our sins, or make our *peace* with God. Nothing can do that for us, but the blood of Christ; and nothing can give us a saving interest in Christ's blood, but faith. It is Scriptural ignorance not to know this. The office of justifying and joining the soul to Christ, belongs to *faith alone*. Our love, and all our other graces, are all more or less imperfect, and could not stand the severity of God's judgment. When we have done all—we are "unprofitable servants." (Luke 17:10.)

We are not to suppose that Christian love can exist independently of faith. Paul did not intend to set up one grace in *rivalry* to the other. He did not mean that one man might have faith, another hope, and another love—and that the best of these, was the man who had love. *The three graces are inseparably joined together.* Where there is faith, there will always be love; and where there is love, there will be faith. Sun and light, fire and heat, ice and cold, are not more intimately united than faith and love!

The reasons why love is called the greatest of the three graces, appear to me plain and simple. Let me show what they are.

(a) Love is called the greatest of graces, because it is the one in which there is some **likeness between the believer and his God**. God has no need of faith. He is dependent on no one. There is none superior to Him in whom He must trust. God has no need of hope. To Him all things are certain, whether past, present, or to come. But "God is love" and the more love His people have—the more similar they are to their Father in Heaven.

(b) Love, for another thing, is called the greatest of the graces, because it is most **useful to others**. Faith and hope, beyond doubt, however precious, have special reference to a believer's own private individual benefit. *Faith* unites the soul to Christ, brings peace with God, and opens the way to Heaven. *Hope* fills the soul with cheerful expectation of things to come, and, amid the many discouragements of things seen, comforts with visions of the things unseen.

But *love* is pre-eminently the grace which makes a man useful. It is the *spring* of good works and kindnesses. It is the *root* of missions, schools, and hospitals. Love made apostles spend and be spent for souls. Love raises up workers for Christ, and keeps them working. Love smooths quarrels, and stops strife—and in this sense, "covers a multitude of sins." (1 Peter 4:8.) Love adorns Christianity, and recommends it to the world. A man may have real faith, and feel it—and yet his faith may be invisible to others. But a man's love cannot be hidden.

(c) Love, in the last place, is the greatest of the graces, because it is the one which **endures the longest**. In fact, it will never die. *Faith* will one day be swallowed up in sight—and *hope* in certainty. Their office will be useless in the morning of the resurrection; and, like old almanacs, they will be laid aside. But love will live on through the endless ages of eternity! Heaven will be the abode of love. The inhabitants of Heaven will be full of love. One *common feeling* will be in all their hearts, and that will be *love*.

I leave this part of my subject here, and pass on to a **CONCLUSION**. On each of the three points of comparison I have just named, between love and the other graces, it would be easy to enlarge. But time and space both forbid me to do so. If I have said enough to guard men against mistakes about the *right meaning*, of the *greatness* of love—I am content. Love, be it ever remembered, cannot justify and put away our sins. It is neither Christ, nor faith.
But love makes us somewhat *like* God.
Love is of mighty *use* to the world.
Love will live and flourish when faith's work is done.
Surely, in these points of view—love well deserves the crown!

(1) And now let me ask every one into whose hands this paper may come a simple question. Let me press home on your conscience the whole subject of this paper. Do you know anything of the grace of which I have been speaking? Do you have Christian love?

The strong language of the Apostle Paul must surely convince you that the inquiry is not one that ought to be lightly put aside. The grace, without which that holy man could say, "I am nothing," the grace which the Lord Jesus says expressly is the great mark of being His disciple—such a grace as this, demands the serious consideration of every one who is in earnest about the salvation of his soul. It should set him thinking, "How does this affect me? Do I have Christian love?"

You have some *knowledge*, it may be, of religion. You know the difference between true and false doctrine. You can, perhaps, even quote texts, and defend the opinions you hold. But, remember the knowledge which is barren of practical results in life and temper—is a useless possession! The words of the Apostle are very plain: "If I can fathom all mysteries and all knowledge—but have not love, I am nothing!" (1 Corinthians 13:3.)

You think you have *faith*, perhaps. You trust you are one of God's elect, and rest in that. But surely you should remember that there is a faith of *devils*, which is utterly unprofitable—and that the faith of God's elect is a "faith which works by love." It was when Paul remembered the "love" of the Thessalonians, as well as their faith and hope, that he said, "I know your election of God." (1 Thessalonians 1:4.)

Look at your own *daily life*, both at home and abroad, and consider what place Christian love has in it. What is your temper? What are your ways of *behaving* toward all around you in your own family? What is your manner of *speaking*, especially in seasons of vexation and provocation? Where is your good-nature, your courtesy, your patience, your meekness, your gentleness, your forbearance? Where are your *practical actions of love* in your dealing with others? What do you know of the mind of Him who "went about doing good"—who loved all, though specially His disciples—who returned good for evil, and kindness for hatred, and had a heart wide enough to feel for all?

What would you do in Heaven, I wonder, if you got there without love? What comfort could you have in an abode where love was the law, and selfishness and ill-nature completely shut out? Alas! I fear that Heaven would be no place for an uncharitable and ill-tempered man! A little boy said, "If *grandfather* goes to Heaven—I hope my brother and I will not go there." "Why do you say that?" he was asked. He replied, "If he sees us there, I am sure he will say, as he does now—'What are these boys doing here? Get them get out of the way!' He does not like to see us on earth, and I suppose he would not like to see us in Heaven!"

Give yourself no rest, until you know something by experience of real Christian love. Go and learn of Him who is meek and lowly of heart, and ask Him to teach you how to love. Ask the Lord Jesus to put His Spirit within you, to take away the old heart, to give you a new nature, to make you know something of His mind. Cry to Him night and day for grace, and give Him no rest until you feel something of what I have been describing in this paper. Happy indeed will your life be, when you really understand "walking in love."

(2) But I do not forget that I am writing to some who are not ignorant of the love of Scripture, and who long to feel *more* of it every year. I will give you two simple words of exhortation. They are these:

Practice love diligently. It is one of those graces, above all, which *grow* by constant *exercise*. Strive more and more to carry it into every little detail of daily life. Watch over your own tongue and temper throughout every hour of the day, and especially in your dealings with children and spouse. Remember the character of the excellent woman: "In her tongue is the *law of kindness*." (Proverbs 31:26.)

Remember the words of Paul: "Let ALL your things be done with love." (1 Corinthians 16:14.) Love should be seen in *little* things, as well as in great ones.

Remember, not least, the words of Peter: "Have fervent love among yourselves;" not a love which just keeps alight, but a burning shining fire, which all around can see! (1 Peter 4:8.) It may cost pains and trouble to keep these things in mind. There may be little encouragement from the example of others. But persevere. Love like this brings its own reward!

Finally, **teach love to others**. Press it continually on your *children*. Tell them the great duty of kindness, helpfulness, and considerateness, one for another. Remind them constantly that kindness, good nature, and good temper, are among the first *evidences* which Christ requires in children. If they cannot know much, or explain doctrines—they can understand love. A child's religion is worth very little if it only consists in repeating texts and hymns. As useful as they are, they are often . . .
learned without thought,
remembered without feeling,
repeated without consideration of their meaning,
and forgotten when childhood is gone!

By all means let children be taught texts and hymns; but let not such teaching be made *everything* in their religion. Teach them to keep their tempers, to be kind one to another, to be unselfish, good-natured, obliging, patient, gentle, forgiving. Tell them never to forget to their dying day, if they live as long as Methuselah, that *without love*, the Holy Spirit says, "we are nothing." Tell them "above all things—to put on love, which is the bond of perfectness." (Colos. 3:14.)

ZEAL

"It is good to be zealously affected always in a good thing." Galatians 4:18

Zeal is a subject, like many others in religion, most sadly misunderstood. Many would be ashamed to be thought "zealous" Christians. Many are ready to say of zealous people what Festus said of Paul: "They are beside themselves — they are mad!" (Acts 26:24.)

But zeal is a subject which no reader of the Bible has any right to pass over. If we make the Bible our rule of faith and practice, we cannot turn away from it. We must look it in the face. What says the Apostle Paul to Titus? "Christ gave Himself for us that He might redeem us from all iniquity, and purify unto Himself a peculiar people, zealous of good works." (Titus 2:14.) What says the Lord Jesus to the Laodicean Church? "Be zealous and repent!" (Rev. 3:19.)

My object in this paper is to plead the cause of zeal in religion. I believe we ought not to be afraid of it — but rather to love and admire it. I believe it to be a mighty blessing to the world, and the origin of countless benefits to mankind. I want to strike a blow at the lazy, easy, sleepy Christianity of these latter days, which can see no beauty in zeal, and only uses the word "zealot" as a word of reproach. I want to remind Christians that "Zealot" was a name given to one of our Lord Jesus Christ's Apostles, and to persuade them to be zealous men.

I ask every reader of this paper to give me his attention while I tell him something about zeal. Listen to me for your own sake — for the sake of the world — for the sake of the Church of Christ. Listen to me, and by God's help I will show you that to be "zealous" is to be wise.

I. Let me show, in the first place, what is zeal in religion.

II. Let me show, in the second place, when a man can be called rightly zealous in religion?

III. Let me show, in the third place, why it is a good thing for a man to be zealous in religion?

I. First of all, I propose to consider this question: "**WHAT is zeal in religion?"**

Zeal in religion is a burning desire to please God, to do His will, and to advance His glory in the world in every possible way. It is a desire which no man feels by nature — which the Spirit puts in the heart of every believer when he is converted — but which some believers feel so much more strongly than others, that they alone deserve to be called "zealous" Christians.

This desire is so strong, when it really reigns in a man, that it impels him to make any sacrifice — to go through any trouble — to deny himself to any amount — to suffer, to work, to labor, to toil — to spend himself and be spent, and even to die — if only he can please God and honor Christ.

A zealous man in religion is pre-eminently a man of one thing. It is not enough to say that he is earnest, hearty, uncompromising, thorough-going, whole-hearted, fervent in spirit. He sees one thing, he cares for one thing, he lives for one thing, he is swallowed-up in one thing — and that one thing is to please God.

Whether he lives — or whether he dies;
whether he has health — or whether he has sickness;
whether he is rich — or whether he is poor;
whether he pleases man — or whether he gives offence;
whether he is thought wise — or whether he is thought foolish;
whether he gets blame — or whether he gets praise;
whether he gets honor, or whether he gets shame
— for all this the zealous man cares nothing at all. He burns for one thing — and that one thing is to please God, and to advance God's glory. If he is consumed in the very burning — he is content. He feels that, like a lamp, he is made to burn, and if consumed in burning — he has but done the work for which God appointed him. Such a one will always find a sphere for his zeal. If he cannot preach, and work, and give money — he will cry, and sigh, and pray. Yes, if he is only a pauper, on a perpetual bed of sickness — he will make the wheels of sin around him drive heavily, by continually interceding against it. If he cannot fight in the valley with Joshua — then he will do the prayer-work of Moses, Aaron, and Hur, on the hill. (Exod. 17:9-13.) If he is cut off from working himself — he will give the Lord no rest until help is raised up from another quarter, and the work is done. This is what I mean when I speak of "zeal" in religion.

We all know the habit of mind that makes men ***great*** in this world — that makes such men as Alexander the Great, or Julius Caesar, or Oliver Cromwell, or Napoleon. We know that, with all their faults, they were all *men of one thing*. They threw themselves into *one grand pursuit*. They cared for nothing else. They put everything else aside. They counted everything else as second-rate, and of subordinate importance, compared to the one thing that they put before their eyes every day they lived. I say that the same habit of mind applied to the service of the Lord Jesus Christ, becomes *religious zeal.*

We know the habit of mind that makes men great in the ***sciences*** of this world — that makes such men as Archimedes, or Sir Isaac Newton, or Galileo, or Ferguson the astronomer, or James Watt. All these were men of one thing. They brought the powers of their minds into one single focus. They cared for nothing else beside. And this was the secret of their success. I say that this same habit consecrated to the service of God, becomes religious zeal.

We know the habit of mind that makes men ***rich*** – that makes men amass mighty fortunes, and leave millions behind them. What kind of people were the bankers, and merchants, and tradesmen, who have left a name behind them, as men who acquired immense wealth and became rich from being poor? They were all men that threw themselves entirely into their business, and neglected everything else for the sake of that business. They gave their first *attention*, their first *thoughts*, the best of their *time*, and the best part of their *mind* – to pushing forward the transactions in which they were engaged. They were men of one thing. Their hearts were not divided. They devoted themselves, body, soul, and mind to their business. They seemed to live for nothing else. I say that if you turn that habit of mind to the service of Christ, it makes religious zeal.

(a) Now this habit of mind — this zeal was the characteristic of all the *Apostles*. See for example the Apostle Paul. Hear him when he speaks to the Ephesian elders for the last time: "None of these things move me, neither count I my life dear unto myself, so that I might finish my course with joy, and the ministry that I have received of the Lord Jesus, to testify the Gospel of the grace of God." (Acts 20:24.) Hear him again, when he writes to the Philippians: "This one thing I do; I press towards the mark for the prize of the high calling of God in Christ Jesus." (Philippians 3:13, 14.) See him from the day of his *conversion*, giving up his brilliant prospects — forsaking all for Christ's sake — and going forth to preach that very Jesus whom he had once despised. See him going to and fro throughout the world from that time — through persecution — through oppression — through opposition — through prisons — through bonds — through afflictions — through things next to death itself, up to the very day when he sealed his faith with his blood, and died at Rome — a *martyr* for that Gospel which he had so long proclaimed. This was true religious zeal.

(b) This again was the characteristic of the *early Christians*. They were men "everywhere spoken against." (Acts 28:22.) They were driven to worship God in dens and caves of the earth. They often lost everything in the world for their religion's sake. They generally gained nothing — but the cross, persecution, shame, and reproach. But they seldom, very seldom, went back. If they could not dispute — at least they could *suffer*. If they could not convince their adversaries by argument — at any rate they could *die*, and prove that they themselves were in earnest. Look at Ignatius cheerfully traveling to the place where he was to be devoured by lions, and saying as he went, "Now I *begin* to be a disciple of my Master, Christ!" Hear old *Polycarp* before the Roman Governor, saying boldly, when called upon to deny Christ, "Four-score and six years have I served Christ, neither has He ever offended me in anything — how then can I revile my King?" This was true zeal.

(c) This again was the characteristic of *Martin Luther*. He boldly defied the most powerful hierarchy that the world has ever seen. He unveiled its corruptions with an unflinching hand. He preached the long-neglected truth of *justification by faith* — in spite of *anathemas* and excommunications, fast and thickly poured upon him.

See him going to the Diet at Worms, and pleading his cause before the Emperor and the Legate, and a host of the men of this world. Hear him saying — when men were dissuading him from going, and reminding him of the dire fate of John Huss, "Though there were a devil under every the on the roofs of Worms, in the name of the Lord I shall go forward!" This was true zeal.

(d) This again was the characteristic of our own *English Reformers*. You have it in our first Reformer, *Wickliffe*, when he rose up on his sick bed, and said to the Friars, who wanted him to retract all he had said against the Pope, "I shall not die — but live to declare the villainies of the Friars." You have it in *Cranmer*, dying at the stake, rather than deny Christ's Gospel, holding forth that hand to be first burned which, in a moment of weakness, had signed a recantation, and saying, as he held it in the flames, *"This unworthy hand!"* You have it in old father *Latimer*, standing boldly on his faggot, at the age of seventy years, and saying to Ridley, "Courage, brother Ridley! We shall light such a candle this day as, by God's grace, shall never be put out!" This was zeal.

(e) This again has been the characteristic of all the greatest *missionaries*. You see it in Dr. Judson, in Carey, in Morrison, in Schwartz, in Williams, in Brainerd, in Elliott. You see it in none more brightly than in *Henry Martyn*. Here was a man who had reached the highest academic honors that Cambridge could bestow. Whatever profession he chose to follow, he had the most dazzling prospects of success. He turned his back upon it all. He chose to preach the Gospel to poor benighted heathen! He went forth to an early grave, in a foreign land. He said when he got there and saw the condition of the people, "I could bear to be torn in pieces, if I could but hear the sobs of *penitence* — if I could but see the eyes of *faith* directed to the Redeemer!" This was zeal.

(f) But let us look away from all earthly examples — and remember that zeal was pre-eminently the characteristic of our Lord and Savior *Jesus Christ* Himself. Of Him it was written hundreds of years before He came upon earth, that He was "clad with zeal as with a cloak," and "the zeal for your house has devoured me." And His own words were "My food is to do my Father's will, and to finish His work." (Psalm 69:9; Isaiah 59:17; John 4:34.)

Where shall we *begin*, if we try to give examples of His zeal? Where should we *end*, if we once began? Trace all the narratives of His life in the four Gospels. Read all the history of what He was from the beginning of His ministry to the end. Surely if there ever was one who was *all zeal*, it was our great Example — our Head — our High Priest — the great Shepherd of our profession, the Lord Jesus Christ.

If these things are so, we should not only beware of running down zeal — but we should also beware of allowing zeal to be run down in our presence. It may be badly directed, and then it becomes a curse — but it may be turned to the highest and best ends, and then it is a mighty blessing. Like fire, it is one of the *best of servants* — but, like fire also, if not well directed, it may be the *worst of masters*. Listen not to those people who talk of zeal as weakness and enthusiasm. Listen not to those who see no beauty in missions, who laugh at all attempts at the conversion of souls — who call Societies for sending the Gospel to the world useless — and who look upon City Missions, and District Visiting, and Ragged Schools and Open Air Preaching — as nothing but foolishness and fanaticism. Beware, lest in joining a cry of that kind, you condemn the Lord Jesus Christ Himself. Beware lest you speak against Him who has "left us an example, that we should follow His steps." (1 Peter 2:21.)

Alas I fear there are many *professing* Christians who if they had lived in the days when our Lord and His Apostles walked upon earth — would have called Him and all His followers *enthusiasts* and *fanatics*. There are many, I fear, who have more in common with Annas and Caiaphas — with Pilate and Herod — with Festus and Agrippa — with Felix and Gallio — than with Paul and the Lord Jesus Christ!

II. I pass on now to the second thing I proposed to speak of. **WHEN is a man truly zealous in religion?** There never was a *grace,* of which Satan has not made a *counterfeit*. There never was a good coin issued from the mint, but *forgers* at once have coined something very like it. It was one of Nero's cruel practices first to sew up Christians in the skins of wild beasts, and then bait them with dogs. It is one of Satan's devices to place *distorted copies* of the believer's graces before the eyes of men — and so to bring the true graces into contempt. No grace has suffered so much in this way, as zeal. Of none perhaps are there so many *shams* and *counterfeits* abroad. We must therefore clear the ground of all *rubbish* on this question. We must find out when zeal in religion is really good, and true, and of God.

(a) If zeal is true, it will be a zeal **according to knowledge**. It must not be a blind, ignorant zeal. It must be a calm, reasonable, intelligent principle, which can show the warrant of Scripture for every step it takes. The unconverted *Jews* had zeal. Paul says, "I bear them record that they have a zeal of God — but *not according to knowledge*."

(Romans 10:2.) *Saul* had zeal when he was a persecuting Pharisee. He says himself, in one of his addresses to the Jews, "I was zealous toward God as you all are this day." (Acts 22:3.) *Manasseh* had zeal in the days when he was an idolater. The man who made his own children pass through the fire — who gave up the fruit of his body to Moloch, to atone for the sin of his soul — that man had zeal. *James* and *John* had zeal when they would have called down fire on a Samaritan village. But our Lord rebuked them. *Peter* had zeal when he drew his sword and cut off the ear of Malchus. But he was quite wrong. *Bonner* and *Gardiner* had zeal when they burned Latimer and Cranmer. Were they not in earnest? Let us do them justice. They were zealous, though it was for an unscriptural religion. The members of the Catholic *Inquisition* in Spain had zeal when they tortured men, and put them to horrible deaths, because they would not forsake the Gospel. Yes! they marched men and women to the stake in solemn procession, and called it "An act of faith," and believed they were doing God service. The *Hindus*, who used to lie down before the car of Juggernaut and allow their bodies to be crushed under its wheels — had not they zeal? The *Indian widows*, who used to burn themselves on the funeral pile of their deceased husbands — had not they zeal? The Roman Catholics, who persecuted Christians to death, and cast down men and women from rocks and precipices, because they were heretics — had not they zeal? The *Crusaders* — the *Jesuits* — had they not all zeal? Yes! Yes! I do not deny it. All these had zeal beyond question. They were all zealous. They were all in earnest. But their zeal was not such zeal as God approves — it was not a "zeal according to knowledge."

(b) Furthermore, if zeal be true, it will be a zeal from **true motives**. Such is the subtlety of the heart, that *men will often do right things from wrong motives*. Amaziah and Joash, kings of Judah, are striking proofs of this. Just so a man may have zeal about things that are good and right — but from second-rate motives, and not from a desire to please God. And such zeal is worth nothing! It is reprobate silver. It is utterly lacking when placed in the balance of God. Man looks only at the *action* — God looks at the *motive*. Man only thinks of the *quantity* of work done — God considers the doer's *heart*.

There is such a thing as zeal from ***party spirit***. It is quite possible for a man to be unwearied in promoting the interests of his own Church or denomination — and yet to have no grace in his own heart — to be ready to die for the peculiar opinions of his own section of Christians — and yet to have no real love to Christ. Such was the zeal of the Pharisees. They "compassed sea and land to make one proselyte, and when he was made, they made him two-fold more the child of Hell than themselves!" (Matthew 23:15.) This zeal is not true.

There is such a thing as zeal from ***mere selfishness***. There are times when it is men's interest to be zealous in religion. Power and patronage are sometimes given to religious men. The good things of the world are sometimes to be attained by wearing a *cloak of religion*. And whenever this is the case — there is no lack of false zeal. Such was the zeal of *Joab*, when he served David. Such was the zeal of only too many Englishmen in the days of the Commonwealth, when the Puritans were in power.

There is such a thing as zeal from the ***love of praise***. Such was the zeal of *Jehu*, when he was putting down the worship of Baal. Remember how he met Jonadab the son of Rechab, and said, "Come with me, and *see my zeal* for the Lord." (2 Kings 10:16.) Such is the zeal that Bunyan refers to in "Pilgrim's Progress," when he speaks of some who went "for praise" to mount Zion. Some people *feed* on the praise of their fellow-creatures. They would rather have it from Christians, than have none at all.

It is a sad and humbling proof of man's corruption, that there is no degree of self-denial and self-sacrifice to which men may not go, from *false motives*. It does not follow that a man's religion is true, because he "gives his body to be burned," or because he "gives his goods to feed the poor." The Apostle Paul tells us that a man may do all this — and yet not have true love. (1 Corinthians 13:1-3.) It does not follow, because men go into a wilderness, and become hermits — that therefore they know what true self-denial is. It does not follow, because people immure themselves in monasteries and nunneries, or become "sisters of charity," and "sisters of mercy" — that therefore they know what true crucifixion of the flesh and self-sacrifice is in the sight of God. All these things people may do on *wrong principles*. They may do them from *wrong motives* — to satisfy a secret pride and love of notoriety — but not from the true motive of zeal for the glory of God. All such zeal, let us understand, is false. It is earthly, and not of Heaven.

(c) Furthermore, if zeal is true, it will be a zeal **about things according to God's mind**, and sanctioned by plain examples in God's Word.

Take, for one instance, that highest and best kind of zeal — I mean zeal for our own *growth in personal holiness*. Such zeal will make a man feel incessantly that *sin* is the mightiest of all evils — and *conformity to Christ* the greatest of all blessings. It will make him feel that there is nothing which ought not to be done, in order to keep up a close walk with God. It will make him willing to cut off the right hand, or pluck out the right eye, or make any sacrifice — if only he can attain a closer communion with Jesus.

Is not this just what you see in the Apostle Paul? He says, "No, I beat my body and make it my slave so that after I have preached to others, I myself will not be disqualified for the prize." "I do not consider myself yet to have taken hold of it. But one thing I do: Forgetting what is behind and straining toward what is ahead, I press on toward the goal to win the prize for which God has called me heavenward in Christ Jesus!" (1 Corinthians 9:27; Philippians 3:13, 14.)

Take, for another instance, zeal for the *salvation of souls*. Such zeal will make a man burn with desire to enlighten the darkness which covers the souls of multitudes, and to bring every man, woman, and child he sees to the knowledge of the Gospel. Is not this what you see in the Lord Jesus? It is said that He neither gave Himself nor His disciples leisure so much as to eat. (Mark 6:31.) Is not this what you see in the Apostle Paul? He says, "I am made all things to all men, that I might by all means save some." (1 Corinthians 9:22.)

Take, for another instance, zeal against *evil practices*. Such zeal will make a man hate everything which God hates — such as drunkenness, slavery, or infanticide — and long to sweep it from the face of the earth. It will make him jealous of God's honor and glory, and look on everything which robs him of it as an offence. Is not this what you see in Phinehas, the son of Eleazar? or in Hezekiah and Josiah, when they put down idolatry?

Take, for another instance, zeal for maintaining the *doctrines of the Gospel*. Such zeal will make a man hate unscriptural teaching, just as he hates sin. It will make him regard *religious error* as a pestilence which must be checked, whatever may be the cost. It will make him scrupulously careful about every jot and tittle of the counsel of God, lest by some omission the whole Gospel should be spoiled. Is not this what you see in Paul at Antioch, when he withstood Peter to the face, and said he was to be blamed? (Galatians 2:11.)

These are the kind of things about which true zeal is employed. Such zeal, let us understand, is honorable before God.

(d) Furthermore, if zeal is true, it will be a zeal **tempered with charity and love**. It will not be a *bitter* zeal. It will not be a fierce enmity against people. It will not be a zeal ready to take the sword, and to smite with carnal weapons. The weapons of true zeal are not carnal — but spiritual. True zeal will hate sin — and yet love the sinner. True zeal will hate heresy — and yet love the heretic. True zeal will long to break the idol — but deeply pity the idolater. True zeal will abhor every kind of wickedness — but labor to do good even to the vilest of transgressors.

True zeal will warn as Paul warned the Galatians — and yet feel **tenderly**, as a nurse or a mother over erring children. It will expose false teachers, as Jesus did the Scribes and Pharisees — and yet **weep** tenderly, as Jesus did over Jerusalem when He came near to it for the last time.

True zeal will be decided, as a surgeon dealing with a diseased limb; but true zeal will be **gentle**, as one who is dressing the wounds of a brother. True zeal will speak truth boldly, like Athanasius, against the world, and not care who is offended; but true zeal will endeavor, in all its speaking, to "speak the truth *in love*."

(e) Furthermore, if zeal is true, it will be joined to a **deep humility**. A truly zealous man will be the last to discover the greatness of his own attainments. All that he is and does will come so immensely short of his own desires, that he will be filled with a sense of his own unprofitableness, and amazed to think that God should work by him at all. Like Moses, when he came down from the Mount — he will not know that his face shines. Like the righteous, in the twenty-fifth chapter of Matthew — he will not be aware of his own good works.

Buchanan is one whose praise is in all the churches. He was one of the first to take up the cause of the perishing heathen. He literally spent himself, body and mind, in laboring to arouse sleeping Christians to see the importance of *missions*. Yet he says in one of his letters, "I do not know that I ever had what Christians call zeal." *Whitefield* was one of the most zealous preachers of the Gospel the world has ever seen. Fervent in spirit, instant in season and out of season, he was a burning and shining light, and turned thousands to God. Yet he says after preaching for thirty years, "Lord help me to *begin* to begin." *M'Cheyne* was one of the greatest blessings that God ever gave to the Church of Scotland. He was a minister insatiably desirous of the salvation of souls. Few men ever did so much good as he did, though he died at the age of twenty-nine. Yet he says in one of his letters, "None but God knows what an *abyss of corruption* is in my heart. It is astonishing that ever God could bless such a ministry." We may be very sure where there is self-conceit — there is little true zeal.

I ask the readers of this paper particularly to remember the description of true zeal which I have just given:
zeal according to *knowledge*,
zeal from *true motives*,
zeal warranted by *Scriptural examples*,
zeal tempered with *charity*,
zeal accompanied by deep *humility*
— this is true genuine zeal — this is the kind of zeal which God approves. Of such zeal you and I never need fear having too much.

I ask you to remember the description, because of the times in which you live. Beware of supposing that *sincerity alone* can ever make up true zeal — that *earnestness*, however ignorant, makes a man a really zealous Christian in the sight of God. There is a generation in these days which makes an *idol* of what it is pleased to call "earnestness" in religion. These men will allow no fault to be found with an "earnest man." Whatever his theological opinions may be — if he is but an earnest man — that is enough for these people, and we are to ask no more. They tell you we have nothing to do with minute points of doctrine, and with questions of "words and names," about which

Christians are not agreed. Is the man an earnest man? If he is — we ought to be satisfied. "Earnestness" in their eyes covers over a multitude of sins. I warn you solemnly to beware of this spurious doctrine. In the name of the Gospel, and in the name of the Bible, I enter my protest against the theory that *mere earnestness* can make a man a truly zealous and pious man in the sight of God.

These *idolaters of earnestness* would make out that God has given us no standard of truth and error; or that the true standard, the Bible, is so obscure, that no man can find out what truth is by simply going to it. They pour contempt upon the written Word — and therefore they must be wrong.

These *idolaters of earnestness* would make us condemn every witness for the truth, and every opponent of false teaching, from the time of the Lord Jesus down to this day. The Scribes and Pharisees were "in earnest," and yet our Lord opposed them. And shall we dare even to hint a suspicion that they ought to have been let alone? Queen Mary, and Bonner, and Gardiner were "in earnest" in restoring Popery, and trying to put down Protestantism — and yet Ridley and Latimer opposed them to the death. And shall we dare to say that as both parties were "in earnest," both were in the right? Devil-worshipers and idolaters at this day are in earnest — and yet our missionaries labor to expose their errors. And shall we dare to say that "earnestness" would take them to Heaven, and that missionaries to heathen and Roman Catholics had better stay at home? Are we really going to admit that the Bible does not show us what is truth? Are we really going to put a mere vague thing called "earnestness," in the place of Christ, and to maintain that no "earnest" man can be wrong? God forbid that we should give place to such doctrine! I shrink with horror from such theology.

I warn men solemnly to beware of being carried away by it, for it is *common* and most *seductive* in this day. Beware of it, for it is only a *new form of an old error* — that old error which says that a man, "Can't be wrong — whose life is in the right." Admire zeal. Seek after zeal. Encourage zeal. But see that your own zeal is *true*. See that the zeal which you admire in others is a zeal "according to knowledge" — a zeal from *right motives* — a zeal that can bring chapter and verse out of the Bible for its foundation. Any zeal but this is but a false fire. It is not lighted by the Holy Spirit.

III. I pass on now to the third thing I proposed to speak of. Let me show, **WHY it is good for a man to be zealous**.

It is certain that God never gave man a commandment which it was not man's *interest*, as well as *duty* to obey. He never set a grace before His believing people, which His people will not find it their highest happiness to follow after. This is true of all the graces of the Christian character. Perhaps it is preeminently true in the case of zeal.

(a) Zeal is good for a Christian's own soul. We all know that exercise is good for the health — and that regular employment of our muscles and limbs promotes our bodily comfort, and increases our bodily vigor. Now that which exercise does for our bodies — zeal will do for our souls. It will help mightily to promote inward feelings of joy, peace, comfort, and happiness. None have so much enjoyment of Christ, as those who are . . .
ever zealous for His glory,
jealous over their own walk,
tender over their own consciences,
full of concern about the souls of others, and
ever watching, working, laboring, striving, and toiling to extend the knowledge of Jesus Christ upon earth.

Such men live in the full light of the sun, and therefore their hearts are always warm. Such men water others, and therefore they are watered themselves. Their hearts are like a garden daily refreshed by the dew of the Holy Spirit. They honor God, and so God honors them.

I would not be mistaken in saying this. I would not appear to speak slightingly of any believer. I know that "the Lord takes pleasure in *all* His people." (Psalm 119:4.) There is not one, from the least to the greatest — from the smallest child in the kingdom of God, to the oldest warrior in the battle against Satan — there is not one in whom the Lord Jesus Christ does not take great pleasure. We are all His children — and however weak and feeble some of us may be, "as a father pities his children — so does the Lord pity those who love and fear Him." (Psalm 103:13.) We are all the *plants* of His own planting — and though many of us are poor, weakly exotics, scarcely keeping life together in a foreign soil — yet as the gardener loves that which his hands have reared — so does the Lord Jesus love every poor sinners who trusts in Him.

But while I say this, I do also believe that the Lord takes *special pleasure* in those who are zealous for Him — in those who give themselves body, soul, and spirit, to extend His glory in this world. To them He reveals Himself, as he does not to others. To them He shows things that other men never see. He blesses the work of their hands. He cheers them with spiritual consolations, which others only know by the hearing of the ear. They are men after His own heart, for they are men more like Himself than others. None have such joy and peace in believing — none have such sensible comfort in their religion — none have so much of "Heaven upon earth" Deuteronomy 11:21) — none see and feel so much of the consolations of the Gospel — as those who are zealous, earnest, thorough-going, devoted Christians! For the sake of our own souls, if there were no other reason, it is good to be zealous — to be very zealous in our religion.

(b) As zeal is good for ourselves individually — so it is also good for the professing CHURCH of Christ generally. Nothing so much keeps alive true religion — as a leaven of zealous Christians scattered to and fro throughout a Church. Like *salt*, they prevent the whole body falling into a state of corruption. None but men of this kind can revive Churches, when ready to die. It is impossible to over-estimate the *debt* that all Christians owe to zeal. The greatest mistake the rulers of a Church can make, is to drive zealous men out of its pale. By so doing they drain out the life-blood of the system, and hasten on ecclesiastical decline and death.

Zeal is that grace which God seems to delight to honor. Look through the list of Christians who have been eminent for usefulness. Who are the men that have left the deepest and most indelible marks on the Church of their day? Who are the men that God has generally honored to build up the walls of His Zion, and turn the battle from the gate? Not so much men of learning and literary talents — as men of zeal.

Latimer was not such a deeply-read scholar as Cranmer or Ridley. He could not quote *Fathers* from memory, as they did. He stuck to his Bible. Yet it is not too much to say that no English reformer made such a lasting impression on the nation as old Latimer did. And what was the reason? His simple zeal.

Richard Baxter, the Puritan, was not equal to some of his contemporaries in intellectual gifts. It is no disparagement to say that he does not stand on a level with Manton or Owen. Yet few men probably exercised so wide an influence on the generation in which he lived. And what was the reason? His burning zeal.

Whitefield, and Wesley, and Berridge, and Venn were inferior in mental attainments to Bishops Butler and Watson. But they produced effects on the people of this country which fifty Butlers and Watsons would probably never have produced. They saved the Church of England from ruin. And what was one secret of their power? Their zeal.

These men stood forward at turning points in the history of the Church. They bore unmoved, storms of opposition and persecution. They were not afraid to *stand alone*. They cared not, though their motives were misinterpreted. They counted all things but loss for the truth's sake. They were each and all and every one, eminently men of one thing — and that one thing was to advance the glory of God, and to maintain His truth in the world. They were *all fire*, and so they lighted others. They were *wide awake*, and so they awakened others. They were *all alive*, and so they quickened others. They were *always working*, and so they shamed others into working too. They came down upon men, like Moses from the mount. They shone as if they had been in the presence of God. They carried to and fro with them, as they walked their course through the world, something of the atmosphere and savor of Heaven itself.

There is a sense in which it may be said that *zeal is contagious.* Nothing is more useful to the professors of Christianity, than to see a real live Christian — a thoroughly zealous man of God.
They may rail at him,
they may carp at him,
they may pick holes in his conduct,
they may despise him,
they may not understand him at all —
but insensibly a zealous man does them good.

He opens their eyes.
He makes them feel their own sleepiness.
He makes their own great darkness visible.
He obliges them to see their own barrenness.
He compels them to *think*, whether they like it or not, "What are we doing? Are we not no better than mere cumberers of the ground?"

It may be sadly true that "one sinner destroys much good;" but it is also a blessed truth, that one zealous Christian can do much good. Yes, one single zealous man in a town — one zealous man in a congregation — one zealous man in a society — one zealous man in a family, may be a great, a most extensive blessing. How many machines of usefulness such a man sets a going! How much Christian activity he often calls into being, which would otherwise have slept! How many fountains he opens, which would otherwise have been sealed! Truly there is a deep mine of truth in those words of the Apostle Paul to the Corinthians: "Your zeal has stirred up most of them!" (2 Corinthians 9:2.)

(c) But, as zeal is good for the Church and for individuals, so zeal is good for the WORLD. Where would the Missionary work be, if it were not for zeal? Where would our City Missions and Ragged Schools be, if it were not for zeal? Where would our District-Visiting and Pastoral Aid Societies be, if it were not for zeal? Where would our Societies for rooting out sin and ignorance, for finding out the dark places of the earth, and recovering poor lost souls be? Where would all these glorious instruments for good be — if it were not for Christian zeal? Zeal called these institutions into being, and zeal keeps them at work when they have begun. Zeal gathers a few despised men, and makes them the nucleus of many a powerful Society. Zeal keeps up the collections of a Society when it is formed. Zeal prevents men from becoming lazy and sleepy when the machine is large and begins to get favor from the world. Zeal raises up men to go forth, putting their lives in their hands, like Moffatt and Williams in our own day. Zeal supplies their place when they are gathered into the garner, and taken *home.*

What would become of the ignorant masses who crowd the lanes

and alleys of our overgrown cities, if it were not for Christian zeal? Governments can do nothing with them — they cannot make laws that will meet the evil. The vast majority of professing Christians have no eyes to see it — like the priest and Levite, they pass by on the other side. But zeal has . . .
eyes to see,
and a heart to feel,
and a head to devise,
and a tongue to plead,
and hands to work,
and feet to travel —
in order to rescue poor souls, and raise them from their low estate.

Zeal does not stand poring over difficulties — but simply says, "Here are souls perishing — and something *shall* be done!" Zeal does not shrink back because there are *Anakim* (giants) in the way — it looks over their heads, like Moses on Pisgah, and says, "The land *shall* be possessed." Zeal does not wait for company, and tarry until good works are fashionable — it goes forward like a forlorn hope, and trusts that others will follow by and bye.

Ah! the world little knows what a debt it owes to Christian zeal. How much *crime* it has checked! How much *sedition* it has prevented! How much *public discontent* it has calmed! How much *obedience* to law and love of order it has produced! How many *souls* it has saved! Yes! and I believe we little know what might be done — if every Christian was a zealous man! How much if *ministers* were more like Bickersteth, and Whitefield, and M'Cheyne! How much if *laymen* were more like Howard, and Wilberforce, and Thornton, and Nasmith, and George Moore! Oh, for the world's sake, as well as your own — resolve, labor, strive to be a zealous Christian!

Let every one who professes to be a Christian, beware of checking zeal. Seek it. Cultivate it. Try to blow up the fire in your own heart, and the hearts of others — but never, never check it. Beware of throwing cold water on zealous souls, whenever you meet with them. Beware of nipping in the bud, this precious grace when first it shoots. If you are a *parent*, beware of checking it in your children — if you are a *husband*, beware of checking it in your wife — if you are a brother, beware of checking it in your sisters — and if you are a *minister*, beware of checking it in the members of your congregation. It is a *shoot* of Heaven's own planting. Beware of crushing it, for Christ's sake.

Zeal may make *mistakes*. Zeal may need *directing*. Zeal may need guiding, controlling, and advising. Like the elephants on ancient fields of battle — it may sometimes do injury to its own side. But zeal does not need *damping* in a wretched, cold, corrupt, miserable world like this! Zeal, like John Knox pulling down the Scotch monasteries, may hurt the feelings of narrow-minded and sleepy Christians. It may offend the prejudices of those *old-fashioned religionists* who hate everything new, and (like those who wanted soldiers and sailors to go on wearing pigtails) abhor all change. But zeal in the end will be justified by its results. Zeal, like John Knox, in the long run of life – will do infinitely more good than harm.

There is little danger of there ever being too much zeal for the glory of God. God forgive those who think there is!! You know little of human nature. You forget that *sickness* is far more contagious than health – and that it is much easier to catch a cold than impart a glow. Depend upon it, the Church seldom needs a *bridle* – but often needs a *spur*. It seldom needs to be *checked* – it often needs to be *urged on*.

And now, in conclusion, let me try to **APPLY** this subject to the conscience of every person who reads this paper. It is a *warning* subject, an *arousing* subject, an *encouraging* subject – according to the various spiritual states of my readers. I wish, by God's help, to give every reader his portion.

(1) First of all, let me offer a warning to all who make *no decided profession of true religion*. There are thousands and tens of thousands, I fear, in this condition. If you are one, the subject before you is full of solemn warning. Oh, that the Lord in mercy may incline your heart to receive it! I ask you, then, in all affection: *Where is your zeal in religion?* With the Bible before me, I may well be bold in asking. But with your life before me, I may well tremble as to the answer. I ask again: Where is your zeal for the glory of God? Where is your zeal for extending Christ's Gospel through an evil world? Zeal, which was the characteristic of the Lord Jesus; zeal, which is the characteristic of the angels; zeal, which shines forth in all the brightest Christians – where is your zeal, unconverted reader?

Where is your zeal indeed! You know well it is nowhere at all; you know well you see no beauty in it; you know well it is scorned and cast out as evil by you and your companions; you know well it has no place, no portion, no standing ground, in the religion of your soul. It is not perhaps that you know not what it is to be zealous in a certain way. You have zeal – but it is all *misapplied*. It is all earthly – it is all about the things of time. It is not zeal for the glory of God – it is not zeal for the salvation of souls. Yes, many a man has zeal for the newspaper – but not for the Bible; zeal for the daily reading of the Times – but no zeal for the daily reading of God's blessed Word. Many a man has zeal for the account book and the business book – but no zeal about the *Book of Life* and the last great account; zeal about silver and gold – but no zeal about the unsearchable riches of Christ. Many a man has zeal about his earthly concerns, his family, his pleasures, his daily pursuits – but no zeal about God, and Heaven, and eternity!

If this is the state of anyone who is reading this paper – awake, I do beseech you, to see your gross folly! You cannot live forever. You are not ready to die. You are utterly unfit for the company of saints and God. Awake! Be zealous and repent! Awake to see the harm you are doing! You are putting arguments in the hands of infidels by your shameful coldness. You are pulling down — as fast as ministers build. You are helping the devil! Awake! Be zealous, and repent! Awake to see your childish inconsistency! What can be more worthy of zeal — than eternal things, than the glory of God, than the salvation of souls? Surely if it is good to labor for rewards that are temporal — it is a thousand times better to labor for those that are eternal.

Awake! Ne zealous and repent! Go and read that long-neglected Bible. Take up that *blessed Book* which you have, and perhaps never use. Read that New Testament through. Do you find nothing there to make you zealous — to make you earnest about your soul? Go and look at the *cross of Christ*. Go and see how the Son of God there shed His precious blood — how He suffered and groaned, and died — how He poured out His soul as an offering for sin, in order that sinners might not perish — but have eternal life. Go and look at the cross of Christ, and never rest until you feel some zeal for your own soul — some zeal for the glory of God — some zeal for extension of the Gospel throughout the world. Once more I say, awake! Be zealous, and repent!

(2) Let me, in the next place, say something to arouse those who make a *profession* of being decided Christians, and are yet *lukewarm in their practice*. There are only too many, I regret to say, in this state of soul. If you are one, there is much in this subject which ought to lead you to searchings of heart.

Let me speak to your conscience. To you also I desire to put the question in all brotherly affection, Where is your zeal? Where is your zeal for the glory of God, and for extending the gospel throughout the world? You well know it is very low. You well know that your zeal is a little feeble glimmering spark, that just lives, and no more — it is like a thin "ready to die." (Rev. 3:2.) Surely, there is a fault somewhere, if this is the case. This state of things ought not to be. You, the child of God; you, redeemed at so glorious a price; you, ransomed with such precious blood; you, who are an heir of glory such as no tongue ever yet told, or eye saw — surely you ought to be a man of another kind. Surely your zeal ought not to be so small.

I deeply feel that this is a painful subject to touch upon. I do it with reluctance, and with a constant remembrance of my own unprofitableness. Nevertheless, truth ought to be spoken. The plain truth is, that many believers in the present day seem so dreadfully afraid of doing harm — that they hardly ever dare to do good. There are many who are fruitful in objections — but barren in actions. Truly, in looking around the Church of Christ, a man might sometimes think that God's kingdom had come, and God's will was being done upon earth — so small is the zeal that some believers show. It is vain to deny it. I need not go far for evidence. I point to Societies for doing good to the heathen, the colonies, and the dark places of our own land, languishing and standing still for lack of active support. I ask, Is this zeal? I point to thousands of pitiful donations which are never missed by the givers — and yet make up the sum of their Christian liberality. I ask, Is this zeal? I point to false doctrine allowed to grow up in churches and families without an effort being made to check it, while so-called believers look on, and content themselves with wishing it was not so. I ask, Is this zeal? Would the apostles have been satisfied with such a state of things? We know they would not.

If the conscience of anyone who reads this paper pleads guilty to any participation in the short-comings I have spoken of, I call upon him, in the name of the Lord — to awake, be zealous, and repent. Let not zeal be confined to banks, and shops, and counting houses. Let us see the same zeal in the Church of Christ. Let not zeal be abundant to lead forlorn hopes, or get gold from Australia, or travel over thick ribbed ice in voyages of discovery — but defective to send the Gospel to the heathen, or to pluck *Roman Catholics* like brands from the fire, or to enlighten the dark places of the colonies of this great land. Never were there such doors of usefulness opened — never were there so many opportunities for doing good.

I loathe that *squeamishness* which refuses to help Christian ministries — if there is a *blemish* about the *instrument* by which the work is carried on. At this rate we might never do anything at all! Let us resist the feeling, if we are tempted by it. It is one of Satan's devices. It is better to work with *feeble* instruments — than not to work at all.

At all events, try to do something for God and Christ — something against ignorance and sin. Give, collect, teach, exhort, visit, pray — according as God enables you. Only make up your mind that all can do something, and resolve that *by you*, at any rate, something *shall* be done. If you have only one talent — do not bury it in the ground. Try to live — so as to be missed. There is far more to be done in twelve hours — than most of us have ever yet done on any day in our lives.

Think of the precious souls which are perishing — while you are sleeping. Be taken up with your inward conflicts, if you will. Go on anatomizing your own feelings and poring over your own corruptions, if you are so determined. But remember all this time, that souls are going to Hell, and you might do something to save them by working, by giving, by writing, by begging, and by prayer. Oh, awake! be zealous, and repent!

Think of the *shortness of time*. You will soon be gone. You will have no opportunity for *works of mercy* in the eternal world. In Heaven there will be no ignorant people to instruct, and no unconverted to reclaim. Whatever you do — must be done now. Oh, when are you going to begin? Awake! be zealous, and repent.

Think of the devil, and his zeal to do harm. It was a solemn saying of old Bernard when he said that "Satan would rise up in judgment against some people at the last day, because he had shown more zeal to ruin souls than they had to save them." Awake! be zealous, and repent!

Think of your Savior, and all His zeal for you. Think of Him in Gethsemane and on Calvary, shedding His blood for sinners. Think of His life and death — His sufferings and His doings. This He has done for you. What are you doing for Him? Oh, resolve that for the time to come you will spend and be spent for Christ! Awake! be zealous and repent!

(3) Last of all, let me *encourage* all readers of this paper who are *truly zealous* Christians.

I have but one request to make, and that is that you will *persevere.* I beseech you to hold fast your zeal, and never let it go. I beseech you never to go back from your first works, never to leave you first love, never to let it be said of you that your first things were better than your last. Beware of *cooling down.* You have only to be lazy, and to sit still — and you will soon lose all your warmth! You will soon become another man from what you are now.

Oh, do not think this a needless exhortation! It may be very true that wise young believers are very rare. But it is no less true that *zealous old believers* are very rare also. Never allow yourself to think that you can *do* too much, that you can *spend* and *be spent* too much for Christ's cause. For one man that does too much — I will show you a thousand who do not do enough! Rather, think that "the night comes, when no man can work "(John 9:4) — and give, collect, teach, visit, work, pray — as if you were doing it for the last time. Lay to heart the words of that noble-minded man, who said, when told that he ought to rest a little, "What should we rest for? have we not all eternity to rest in?"

Fear not the reproach of men. *Faint* not because you are sometimes abused. *Heed* it not if you are sometimes called bigot, enthusiast, fanatic, madman, and fool. There is nothing disgraceful in these titles. They have often been given to the best and wisest of men. If you are only to be zealous when you are *praised* for it, if the wheels of your zeal must be *oiled by the world's commendation* — then your zeal will be but short-lived. Care nothing for the *praise* or *frown* of man. There is but one thing worth caring for — and that is the praise of God. There is but one question worth asking about our actions, "How will they look in the day of judgment?"

FREEDOM!

"If the Son makes you *free* — you shall be free indeed!" John 8:86

The subject before our eyes deserves a thousand thoughts. It should ring in the ears of Englishmen and Scotchmen like the voice of a trumpet. We live in a land which is the very *cradle of freedom*. But are we *ourselves* free?

The question is one which demands special attention at the present state of public opinion in Great Britain. The minds of many are wholly absorbed in politics. Yet there is a freedom, within the reach of all, which few, I am afraid, ever think of — a freedom independent of all political changes, a freedom which neither Queen, Lords and Commons, nor the cleverest popular leaders can bestow. This is the freedom about which I write this day. Do we know anything of it? Are we free?

In opening this subject, there are three points which I wish to bring forward.

I. I will show, in the first place, the *general excellence* of freedom.

II. I will show, in the second place, the *best and truest kind* of freedom.

III. I will show, in the last place, the *way* in which the best kind of freedom may become your own.

Let no reader think for a moment that this is going to be a political paper. I am no politician; I have no politics but those of the Bible. The only *party* I care for is the Lord's side; show me where that is, and it shall have my support. The only *election* I am very anxious about is the election of grace. My one desire is, that sinners should make their own calling and election sure. The *liberty* I desire above all things to make known, and further — is the glorious liberty of the children of God. The *Government* I care to support is the government which is on the shoulder of my Lord and Savior Jesus Christ. Before Christ I want every knee to bow, and every tongue to confess that He is Lord. I ask attention while I canvass these subjects. If you are not free, I want to guide you into true liberty. If you are free, I want you to know the full value of your freedom.

I. The first thing I have to show is the *general excellence* of freedom.

On this point some readers may think it needless to say anything; they imagine that all men know the value of freedom, and that to dwell on it is mere waste of time. I do not agree with such people at all. I believe that myriads of Englishmen know nothing of the blessings which they enjoy in their own land; they have grown up from infancy to manhood in the midst of free institutions. They have not the least idea of the state of things in other countries; they are ignorant alike of those two worst forms of tyranny, the crushing tyranny of a cruel military despot, and the intolerant tyranny of an unreasoning mob. In short, many Englishmen know nothing of the *value of liberty*, just because they have been born in the middle of it, and have never been for a moment without it.

I call then on everyone who reads this paper, to remember that liberty is one of the greatest temporal blessings that man can have on this side the grave.

We live in a land where our *bodies* are free. So long as we hurt nobody's person, or property, or character — no one can touch us; the poorest man's house is his castle.

We live in a land where our *actions* are free. So long as we support ourselves, we are free to choose what we will do, where we will go, and how we will spend our time.

We live in a land where our *consciences* are free. So long as we hold quietly on our own way, and do not interfere with others, we are free to worship God as we please, and no man can compel us to take his way to Heaven. We live in a land where no foreigner rules over us. Our laws are made and altered by Englishmen like ourselves, and our Governors dwell by our side, bone of our bone and flesh of our flesh.

In short, we have every kind of freedom to an extent which no other nation on earth can equal. We have personal freedom, civil freedom, religious freedom, and national freedom. We have free bodies, free consciences, free speech, free thought, free action, free Bibles, a free press, and free homes. How vast is this list of privileges! How endless the comforts which it contains! The full value of them can never perhaps be known. Well said the Jewish Rabbis in ancient days: "If the sea were ink and the world parchment — it would never serve to describe the praises of liberty."

The lack of this freedom has been the most fertile cause of misery to nations in every age of the world. What reader of the Bible can fail to remember the sorrows of the children of Israel, when they were slaves under Pharaoh in Egypt, or under Philistines in Canaan? What student of history needs to be reminded of the woes inflicted on the Netherlands, Poland, Spain, and Italy by the hand of foreign oppressors, or the Inquisition? Who, even in our own time, has not heard of that enormous fountain of wretchedness, the slavery of the Negro race? No misery is so great as the *misery of slavery*.

To win and preserve freedom has been the aim of many national struggles which have deluged the earth with blood. Liberty has been the cause in which myriads of Greeks, and Romans, and Germans, and Poles, and Swiss, and Englishmen, and Americans have willingly laid down their lives. No price has been thought too great to pay in order that nations might be free.

The champions of freedom in every age have been justly esteemed among the greatest benefactors of mankind. Such names as Moses and Gideon in Jewish history, the German Martin Luther, the Swiss William Tell, the Scotch Robert Bruce and John Knox, the English Alfred and Hampden and the Puritans, the American George Washington, are deservedly embalmed in history, and will never be forgotten. To be the mother of many patriots is the highest praise of a nation.

The enemies of freedom in every age have been rightly regarded as the pests and nuisances of their times. Such names as Pharaoh in Egypt, Dionysius at Syracuse, Nero at Rome, Charles IX in France, bloody Mary in England — are names which will never be rescued from disgrace. The public opinion of mankind will never cease to condemn them, on the one ground that they would not let people be free.

But why should I dwell on these things? Time and space would fail me if I were to attempt to say a tenth part of what might be said in *praise of freedom*. What are the annals of history — but a long record of conflicts between the friends and foes of liberty? Where is the nation upon earth which has ever attained greatness, and left its mark on the world, without freedom? Which are the countries on the face of the globe at this very moment which are making the most progress in trade, in arts, in sciences, in civilization, in philosophy, in morals, in social happiness? Precisely those countries in which there is the greatest amount of true freedom. Which are the countries at this very day where is the greatest amount of internal misery, where we hear continually of secret plots, and murmuring, and discontent, and attempts on life and property? Precisely those countries where freedom does not exist, or exists only in name, where men are treated as serfs and slaves, and are not allowed to think and act for themselves.

No wonder that a mighty American Statesman declared on a great occasion to his assembled countrymen: "Give me liberty, or give me death!" (Patrick Henry)

Let us beware of undervaluing the liberty we enjoy in this country of ours, as Englishmen. I am sure there is need of this warning. There is, perhaps, no country on earth where there is so much grumbling and fault-finding, as there is in England. Men look at the *imagined* evils which they see around them, and exaggerate both their number and their intensity. They refuse to look at the countless *blessings* and *privileges* which surround us, or underrate the *advantages* of them. They forget that comparison should be applied to everything. With all our faults and defects, there is at this hour no country on earth where there is so much liberty and happiness for all classes, as there is in England. They forget that as long as human nature is corrupt, it is vain to expect *perfection* here below. No laws or government whatever can possibly prevent a certain quantity of abuses and corruptions.

Once more then, I say, let us beware of undervaluing English liberty, and running eagerly after everyone who proposes sweeping changes. *Changes* are not always *improvements*. The old shoes may have some holes and defects — but the new shoes may pinch so much that we cannot walk at all. No doubt we might have better laws and government than we have — but I am quite sure we might easily have worse. At this very day, there is no country on the face of the globe where there is so much care taken of the life, and health, and property, and character, and personal liberty of the poorest inhabitant, as there is in England. Those who want to have more liberty, would soon find, if they crossed the seas, that there is no country on earth where there is so much real liberty as our own!

But while I bid men not *undervalue* English liberty, so also on the other hand I charge them not to *overvalue* it. Never forget that temporal slavery is not the only slavery, and temporal freedom not the only freedom. What will it profit you to be a citizen of a free country — so long as your soul is not free?

What is the good of living in a free land like ours, with free thought, free speech, free action, free conscience — so long as you are a slave to sin, and a captive to the devil? Yes, there are *tyrants* whom no eye can see, as real and destructive as Pharaoh or Nero! There are*chains* which no hands can touch, as true and heavy and soul-withering as ever crushed the limbs of a slave! It is these tyrants whom I want you to remember today. It is these chains from which I want you to be free. By all means *value* your earthly liberty — but do not *overvalue* it. Look higher, further than any earthly freedom. In the highest sense let us ensure that "we are free indeed."

II. The second thing I have to show, is the truest and best kind of freedom.

The freedom I speak of, is a freedom that is within the reach of every child of Adam who is willing to have it. No power on earth can prevent a man or woman having it, if they have but the will to receive it. Tyrants may threaten and cast in prison — but nothing they can do can stop a person having this liberty. And, once our own, nothing can take it away. Men may torture us, banish us, hang us, behead us, burn us — but they can never tear from us true freedom! The poorest may have it no less than the richest; the most unlearned may have it as well as the most learned, and the weakest as well as the strongest. Laws cannot deprive us of it; Pope's bulls cannot rob us of it. Once our own, it is an everlasting possession.

Now, *what* is this glorious freedom? Where is it to be found? What is it like? Who has obtained it for man? Who has got it at this moment to bestow? I ask my readers to give me their attention, and I will supply a plain answer to these questions.

The true freedom I speak of is spiritual freedom, freedom of soul. It is the freedom which Christ bestows, without money and without price, on all true Christians. Those whom the Son makes free, are free indeed: "Where the Spirit of the Lord is, there is liberty." (2 Corinthians 3:17.) Let men talk what they please of the comparative freedom of monarchies and republics; let them struggle, if they will, for universal liberty, fraternity, and equality: we never know the highest style of liberty — until we are enrolled citizens of the kingdom of God. We are ignorant of the best kind of freedom — if we are not Christ's freemen.

Christ's freemen are free from the **guilt of sin**. That heavy burden of unforgiven transgressions, which lies so heavy on many consciences, no longer presses them down. Christ's blood has cleansed it all away. They feel pardoned, reconciled, justified, and accepted in God's sight. They can look back to their old sins, however black and many, and say, "You cannot condemn me!" They can look back on long years of carelessness and worldliness and say, "Who shall lay anything to my charge?" This is true liberty. This is to be free.

Christ's freemen are free from the **power of sin**. It no longer rules and reigns in their hearts, and carries them before it like a flood. Through the power of Christ's Spirit, they mortify the deeds of their bodies, and crucify their flesh with its affections and lusts. Through His grace working in them, they get the victory over their evil inclinations. The *flesh* may fight — but it does not conquer them; the *devil* may tempt and vex — but does not overcome them; they are no longer the slaves of lusts and appetites, and passions, and tempers. Over all these things, they are more than conquerors, through Him who loved them. This is true liberty. This is to be free.

Christ's freemen are free from the **slavish fear of God**. They no longer look at Him with dread and alarm, as an offended Maker; they no longer hate Him, and get away from Him, like Adam among the trees of the garden; they no longer tremble at the thought of His judgment. Through the Spirit of adoption which Christ has given them, they look on God as a *reconciled Father*, and rejoice in the thought of His love. They feel that anger is passed away. They feel that when God the Father looks down upon them — He sees them in Christ, and unworthy as they are in themselves, is well-pleased. This is true liberty. This is to be free.

Christ's freemen are free from the **fear of man**. They are no longer afraid of man's opinions, or care much what man thinks of them; they are alike indifferent to his favor or his enmity, his smile or his frown. They look away from man who can be seen — to Christ who is not seen, and having the favor of Christ, they care little for the blame of man. "The fear of man" was once a snare to them. They trembled at the thought of what man would say, or think, or do; they dared not run counter to the *fashions* and *customs* of those around them; they shrank from the idea of standing alone. But the snare is now broken and they are delivered. This is true liberty/ This is to be free.

Christ's freemen are free from the **fear of death**. They no longer look forward to it with silent dismay, as a horrible thing which they do not care to think of. Through Christ, they can look this *last enemy* calmly in the face, and say, "You can not harm me!" They can look forward to all that comes after death, decay, resurrection, judgment, and eternity — and yet not feel cast down. They can stand by the side of an open grave, and say, "O death, where is your sting? O grave, where is your victory?" They can lay them down on their death-beds, and say, "Though I walk through the valley of the shadow of death, I will fear no evil." (Psalm 23:4.) "Not a hair of my head shall perish." This is true liberty. This is to be free.

Best of all, Christ's freemen are **free forever**. Once enrolled in the list of Heavenly citizens, their names shall never be struck off. Once presented with the freedom of Christ's kingdom, they shall possess it for evermore. The highest privileges of this world's freedom, can only endure for a life-time; the freest citizen on earth must submit at length to die — but the freedom of Christ's people is eternal. They carry it down to the grave, and it lives still; they will rise again with it at the last day, and enjoy the privileges of it for evermore. This is true liberty. This is to be free.

Does anyone ask *how* and in what *way* Christ has obtained these mighty privileges for His people? You have a right to ask the question, and it is one that can never be answered too clearly. Give me your attention, and I will show you by what *means* Christ has made His people free.

The freedom of Christ's people has been procured, like all other freedom, at a mighty *cost* and by a mighty *sacrifice*. Great was the bondage in which they were naturally held, and great was the price necessary to be paid to set them free. Mighty was the enemy who claimed them as his captives, and it needed mighty power to release them out of his hands. But, blessed be God, there was grace enough, and power enough in Jesus Christ. He provided to the uttermost, everything that was required to set His people free. The *price* that Christ paid for His people was nothing less than His own life-blood. He became their Substitute, and suffered for their sins on the cross. He redeemed them from the curse of the law, by being made a curse for them. (Galatians 3:13.) He paid all their debt in His own person, by allowing the chastisement of their peace to be laid on Him. (Isaiah 53:5.) He satisfied every possible demand of the law against them, by fulfilling its righteousness to the uttermost. He cleared them from every imputation of sin, by becoming sin for them. (2 Corinthians 5:21.) He fought their battle with the devil, and triumphed over him on the cross. As their Champion, He spoiled principalities and powers, and made a show of them openly on Calvary.

In a word, Christ having given Himself for us, has purchased the full right of redemption for us. Nothing can touch those to whom He gives freedom: their debts are paid, and paid a thousand times over; their sins are atoned for by a full, perfect, and sufficient atonement. A Divine Substitute's death completely meets the justice of God, and completely provides redemption for man.

Let us look well at this *glorious plan of redemption*, and take heed that we understand it. Ignorance on this point is one great secret of faint hopes, little comfort, and ceaseless doubts in the minds of Christians. Too many are content with a vague idea that Christ will somehow save sinners — but *how* or *why* they cannot tell. I protest against this ignorance. Let us set fully before our eyes, the doctrine of Christ's vicarious death and substitution, and rest our souls upon it. Let us grasp firmly the mighty truth — that Christ on the cross . . .

stood in the place of His people,
died for His people,
suffered for His people,
was counted a curse and sin for His people,
paid the debts of His people,
made satisfaction for His people,
became the surety and representative of His people,
and in this way procured His people's freedom.

Let us understand this clearly, and then we shall see what a mighty privilege it is to be made free by Christ.

This is the freedom which, above all other, is worth having. We can never value it too highly — there is no danger of overvaluing it. All other freedom is an *unsatisfying* thing at the best, and a poor *uncertain* possession at any time. Christ's freedom alone can never be overthrown. It is secured by a covenant ordered in all things and sure — its foundations are laid in the eternal councils of God, and no foreign enemy can overthrow them. They are cemented and secured by the blood of the Son of God Himself, and can never be cast down. The freedom of nations often lasts no longer than a few centuries — but the freedom which Christ gives to His people, is a freedom that shall outlive the solid world.

This is the truest, highest kind of freedom. This is the freedom which in a changing, dying world, I want men to possess.

III. I have now to show, in the last place — the way in which the best kind of freedom is made our own.

This is a point of vast importance, on account of the many mistakes which prevail about it. Thousands, perhaps, will allow that there is such a thing as spiritual freedom, and that Christ alone has purchased it for us — but when they come to the application of redemption, they go astray. They cannot answer the question, "Who are those whom Christ effectually makes free?" And for lack of knowledge of the answer, they sit still in their chains. I ask every reader to give me his attention once more, and I will try to throw a little light on the subject. Useless indeed, is the redemption which Christ has obtained, unless you know how the fruit of that redemption can become your own. In vain have you read of the freedom with which Christ makes people free — unless you understand how you yourself may have an interest in it.

We are not born Christ's freemen. The inhabitants of many a city enjoy privileges by virtue of their birth-place. Paul, who drew life-breath first at Tarsus in Cilicia, could say to the Roman Commander, "I was free-born." But this is not the case with Adam's children, in *spiritual* things. We are born slaves and servants of sin — we are by nature "children of wrath," and destitute of any title to Heaven.

We are not made Christ's freemen by *baptism*. Myriads are every year brought to the font, and solemnly baptized in the name of the Trinity, who serve sin like slaves, and neglect Christ all their days. Wretched indeed is that man's state of soul who can give no better evidence of his citizenship of Heaven, than the mere naked fact of his baptism!

We are not made Christ's freemen by mere *membership* of Christ's Church. There are Companies and Corporations whose members are entitled to vast privileges, without any respect to their personal character, if their names are only on the list of members. The kingdom of Christ is not a corporation of this kind. The grand test of belonging to it, is personal character.

Let these things sink down into our minds. Far be it from me to narrow the *extent* of Christ's redemption — the price He paid on the cross is sufficient for the whole world. Far be it from me to undervalue baptism or church membership — the ordinance which Christ appointed, and the Church which He maintains in the midst of a dark world — ought neither of them to be lightly esteemed. All I contend for is the absolute necessity of not being content either with baptism or church membership. If our religion stops short here, it is unprofitable and unsatisfying. It needs something more than this to give us a saving interest in the redemption which Christ has purchased.

There is no other way to become Christ's freemen, than that of simply *believing*. It is by faith, simple faith in Him as our Savior and

Redeemer, that men's souls are made free. It is by receiving Christ, trusting Christ, committing ourselves to Christ, reposing our whole weight on Christ — it is by this, and by no other plan, that spiritual liberty is made our own. As mighty as are the privileges which Christ's freemen possess — they all become a man's property in the day that he first *believes.* He may not yet know their full value — but they are all his own. He who believes in Christ is not condemned, is justified, is born again, is an heir of God, and has everlasting life!

The truth before us is one of priceless importance. Let as cling to it firmly, and never let it go. If you desire peace of conscience, if you want inward rest and consolation — stir not an inch off the ground that *faith is the grand secret of a saving interest in Christ's redemption.* Take the simplest view of faith: beware of confusing your mind by complicated ideas about it. Follow holiness as closely as you can — seek the fullest and clearest evidence of the inward work of the Spirit. But in the matter of an interest in Christ's redemption, remember that *faith stands alone.* It is by believing, simply believing, that souls become free.

No doctrine like this, to suit the *ignorant and unlearned!* Visit the poorest and humblest cottager, who knows nothing of theology, and cannot even repeat the creed. Tell him the story of the cross, and the good news about Jesus Christ, and His love to sinners; show him that there is freedom provided for him, as well as for the most learned in the land, freedom from guilt, freedom from the devil, freedom from condemnation, freedom from Hell. And then tell him plainly, boldly, broadly, unreservedly, that this freedom may be all his own, if he will but trust in Christ and believe.

No doctrine like this, to suit the *sick and dying!* Go to the bedside of the vilest sinner, when death is coming near, and tell him lovingly that there is a hope even for him, if he can receive it. Tell him that Christ came into the world to save sinners, even the chief of them; tell him that Christ has done all, paid all, performed all, purchased all that the soul of man can possibly need for salvation. And then assure him that he, even he, may be freed at once from all his guilt — if he will only believe. Yes, say to him, in the words of Scripture, "If you shall confess with your mouth the Lord Jesus, and believe in your heart that God has raised Him from the dead — you shall be saved." (Romans 10:9.)

Let us never forget that this is the point to which we must turn our own eyes, if we would know whether we have a saving interest in Christ's redemption. Waste not your time in speculations whether you are elect, and converted, and a vessel of grace. Stand not poring over the unprofitable question whether Christ died for you or not. That is a point of which no one ever made any question in the Bible. Settle your thoughts on this one simple inquiry, "Do I really trust in Christ, as a humble sinner? Do I cast myself on Him? Do I believe?" Look not to anything else. Look at this alone. Fear not to rest your soul on plain texts and promises of Scripture. If you believe, you are free.

(1) And now as I bring this paper to a conclusion, let me affectionately press upon every reader the inquiry which grows naturally out of the whole subject. Let me ask every one a plain question: *"Are you free?"*

I know not who or what you are, into whose hands this paper has fallen. But this I do know, there never was an age when the inquiry I press upon you was more thoroughly needed. Political liberty, civil liberty, commercial liberty, liberty of speech, liberty of the press — all these, and a hundred other kindred subjects, are swallowing up men's attention. Few, very few, find time to think of spiritual liberty. Many, too many, forget that no man is so thoroughly a slave, whatever his position, as the man who serves sin.

Yes! there are thousands in this country who are slaves of beer and alcohol, slaves of lust, slaves of ambition, slaves of political party, slaves of money, slaves of gambling, slaves of fashion, or slaves of temper! You may not see their *chains* with the naked eye, and they themselves may boast of their liberty: but for all that, they are thoroughly slaves! Whether men like to hear it or not, the gambler and the drunkard, the covetous and the passionate, the glutton and the sensualist, are not free — but slaves. They are bound hand and foot by the devil. "He who commits sin — is the slave of sin" (Romans 8:34.) He who boasts of liberty, while he is enslaved by lusts and passions — is *going down to Hell with a lie in his right hand!*

Awake to see these things, while health, and time, and life are granted to you. Let not political struggles and party strife make you forget your precious soul. Take any side in politics you please, and follow honestly your conscientious convictions; but never, never forget that there is a liberty far higher and more lasting than any that politics can give you. Rest not until that liberty is your own. Rest not until your soul is free!

(2) Do you feel any desire to be free? Do you find any longing within you for a higher, better liberty than this world can give a liberty that will not die at your death — but will go with you beyond the grave? Then take the advice I give you this day. Seek Christ, repent, believe, and be free. Christ has a glorious liberty to bestow on all who humbly cry to Him for freedom. Christ can take burdens off your heart, and strike chains off your inward man. "If the Son makes you free — you shall be free indeed." (John 8:36.)

Freedom like this is the secret of true happiness. None go through the world with such ease and content — as those who are citizens of a Heavenly country. Earth's *burdens* press lightly upon their shoulders; earth's *disappointments* do not crush them down as they do others; earth's *duties* and *concerns* do not drink up their spirit. In their darkest hours they have always this sustaining thought to fall back on, "I have something which makes me independent of this world — I am spiritually free."

Freedom like this is the secret of being a good politician. In every age, Christ's freemen have been the truest friends to law and order, and to measures for the benefit of all classes of mankind. Never, never let it be forgotten that the despised Puritans, two hundred years ago, did more for the cause of real liberty in England, than all the Governments which ever ruled this land. No man ever made this country so feared and respected as Oliver Cromwell. The root of the most genuine patriotism, is to be one of those whom Christ has made free.

(3) Are you spiritually free? Then rejoice, and be thankful for your freedom. Care nothing for the scorn and contempt of man — you have no cause to be ashamed of your religion or your Master. He whose citizenship is in Heaven (Philippians 3:20), who has God for his Father, and Christ for his Elder Brother, angels for his daily guards, and Heaven itself for his home — is one that is well provided for. No change of laws can add to his greatness — no extension of privileges can raise him higher than he stands in God's sight. "The lines are fallen to him in pleasant places, and he has a goodly heritage." (Psalm 16:6.) *Grace* now, and the hope of *glory* hereafter — are more lasting privileges than the power of voting for twenty boroughs or counties.

Are you free? Then **stand fast** in your liberty, and be not entangled again in the yoke of bondage. Listen not to those who by good words and fair speeches would draw you back to the Church of Rome. Beware of those who would persuade you that there is . . .
any *mediator,* but the one Mediator, Christ Jesus;
any *sacrifice,* but the one Sacrifice offered on Calvary;
any *priest,* but the great High Priest Emmanuel;
any *incense* needed in worship, but the savor of His name who was crucified;
any *rule of faith and practice,* but God's Word;
any *confessional,* but the throne of grace;
any effectual *absolution,* but that which Christ bestows on the hearts of His believing people;
any *purgatory,* but the one fountain open for all sins, the blood of Christ, to be only used while we are alive.

On all these points stand fast, and be on your guard. Scores of misguided teachers are trying to rob Christians of Gospel liberty, and to bring back among us exploded superstitions. Resist them manfully, and do not give way for a moment. Remember what *Romanism* was in this country before the blessed Reformation. Remember at what mighty cost our martyred Reformers brought spiritual freedom to light by the Gospel. Stand fast for this freedom like a man, and labor to hand it down to your children, whole and unimpaired.

Are you free? Then think every day you live of the millions of your fellow-creatures who are yet bound hand and foot in spiritual darkness! Think of six hundred millions of *heathen* who never yet heard of Christ and salvation. Think of the poor homeless *Jews*, scattered and wandering over the face of the earth, because they have not yet received their Messiah. Think of the millions of *Roman Catholics* who are yet in captivity under the Pope, and know nothing of true liberty, light, and peace. Think of the myriads of your own fellow-countrymen in our great cities, who, without means of grace, are practically heathens, and whom the devil is continually leading captive at his will. Think of them all, and feel for them. Think of them all, and often say to yourself, "What can I do for them? How can I help to set them free?"

What! Shall it be proclaimed at the last day, that Pharisees and Jesuits have compassed sea and land to make proselytes, that politicians have leagued and labored night and day to obtain free trade, that philanthropists have travailed in soul for years to procure the suppression of negro slavery — and shall it appear at the same time that Christ's freemen have done little to rescue men and women from Hell? Forbid it, faith! Forbid it, love! Surely if the children of this world are zealous to promote temporal freedom — the children of God ought to be much more zealous to promote spiritual freedom. Let the time past suffice us to have been selfish and indolent in this matter. For the rest of our days, let us use every effort to promote spiritual emancipation. If we have tasted the blessings of freedom, let us spare no pains to make others free.

Are you free? Then look forward in faith and hope for good things yet to come. As free as we are, if we believe on Christ, from the guilt and power of sin — we must surely feel every day that we are not free from its presence and the temptations of the devil. Redeemed as we are from the eternal consequences of the fall — we must often feel that we are not yet redeemed from sickness and infirmity, from sorrow and from pain. No, indeed! Where is the freeman of Christ on earth who is not often painfully reminded that we are not yet in Heaven? We are yet in the body; we are yet traveling through the *wilderness* of this world — we are not at *home*. We have shed many tears already, and probably we shall have to shed many more; we have got yet within us a poor weak heart; we are yet liable to be assaulted by the devil. Our redemption is *begun* indeed — but it is not yet *completed*. We have redemption now in the *root* — but we have it not in the *flower*.

But let us take courage — there are better days yet to come. Our great Redeemer and Liberator has gone before us to prepare a place for His people, and when He comes again — our redemption will be complete. The great *jubilee year* is yet to come.

A few more returns of Christmas and New Year's Days,
a few more meetings and partings,

a few more births and deaths,
a few more weddings and funerals,
a few more tears and struggles,
a few more sicknesses and pains,
a few more preachings and prayings,
a few more — and the end will come!

Our Master will come back again. The dead saints shall be raised. The living saints shall be changed. Then, and not until then, we shall be completely free. The liberty which we enjoyed by *faith* — shall be changed into the liberty of *sight*; and the freedom of hope — into the freedom of certainty.

Come, then, and let us resolve to *wait*, and *watch*, and *hope*, and *pray*, and live like men who have something laid up for them in Heaven. The night is far spent, and the day is at hand. Our King is not far off — our full redemption draws near. Our full salvation is nearer than when we believed. The kingdoms of this world are in confusion — the powers of this world, both temporal and ecclesiastical, are everywhere reeling and shaken to their foundations. Happy, thrice happy, are those who are citizens of Christ's eternal kingdom, and ready for anything that may come. Blessed indeed are those men and women who know and feel that they are free!

HAPPINESS

"Happy is that people whose God is the Lord." Psalm 144:15

An *infidel* was once addressing a crowd of people in the open air. He was trying to persuade them that there was no God and no devil no Heaven, and no Hell, no resurrection, no judgment, and no life to come. He advised them to throw away their Bibles, and not to mind what preachers said. He recommended them to think as he did, and to be like him. He talked boldly. The crowd listened eagerly. It was "the blind leading the blind." Both were falling into the ditch! (Matthew 15:14.)

In the middle of his address, a poor old woman suddenly pushed her way through the crowd, to the place where he was standing. She stood before him. She looked him fully in the face. *"Sir,"* she said, in a loud voice, *"Are you happy?"* The infidel looked scornfully at her, and gave her no answer. "Sir," she said again, "I ask you to answer my question. Are you happy? You want us to throw away our Bibles. You tell us not to believe what preachers say about the gospel. You advise us to think as you do, and be like you. Now before we take your advice — we have a right to know what good we shall get by it. Do your fine new notions give you much comfort? Do you yourself to be really feel happy?"

The infidel stopped, and attempted to answer the old woman's question. He stammered, and shuffled, and fidgeted, and endeavored to explain his meaning. He tried hard to turn the subject. He said, he "had not come there to preach about happiness." But it was of no use. The old woman stuck to her point. She insisted on her question being answered, and the crowd took her part. She pressed him hard with her inquiry, and would take no excuse. And at last the infidel was obliged to leave the ground, and sneak off in confusion. He could not reply to the question. His conscience would not let him — he dared not say that he was happy.

The old woman showed great wisdom in asking the question that she did. The argument she used may seem very simple — but in reality it is one of the most powerful that can be employed. It is a weapon that has more effect on some minds, than the most elaborate reasoning of Butler, or Paley, or Chalmers. Whenever a man begins to take up new views of religion, and pretends to despise old Bible Christianity — thrust home at his conscience the old woman's question. Ask him whether his new views make him feel *comfortable* within. Ask him whether he can say, with honesty and sincerity, that he is *happy*. The grand test of a man's faith and religion is, *"Does it make him happy?"*

Let me now affectionately invite every reader to consider the subject of this paper. Let me warn you to remember that the salvation of your soul, and nothing less, is closely bound up with the subject. The heart cannot be right in the sight of God, which knows nothing of happiness. That man or woman cannot be in a safe state of soul, who feels nothing of peace within.

There are three things which I purpose to do, in order to clear up the subject of happiness. I ask special attention to each one of them. And I pray the Spirit of God to *apply* all to the souls of all who read this paper.

I. Let me point out some things which are *absolutely essential* to all happiness.

II. Let me expose some *common mistakes* about the way to be happy.

III. Let me show *the way to be truly happy*.

I. First of all I have to point out some things which are *absolutely essential* to all true happiness.

Happiness is what all mankind want to obtain — the desire for it is deeply planted in the human heart. All men naturally dislike pain, sorrow, and discomfort. All men naturally like ease, comfort, and gladness. All men naturally hunger and thirst after happiness. Just as the sick man longs for health, and the prisoner of war longs for liberty; just as the parched traveler in hot countries longs to see the cooling fountain, or the ice-bound polar voyager longs to see the sun rising above the horizon — just in the same way does poor mortal man long to be happy. But, alas, how few consider what they really mean, when they talk of happiness! How vague and indistinct and undefined the ideas of most men are upon the subject! They think some are happy — who in reality are miserable; they think some are gloomy and sad — who in reality are truly happy. They *dream* of a happiness which in reality would never satisfy their nature's needs. Let me try this day to throw a little light on the subject.

True happiness is not perfect freedom from sorrow and discomfort. Let that never be forgotten. If it were so, there would be no such thing as happiness in the world. Such happiness is for angels who have never fallen, and not for man. The happiness I am inquiring about, is such as a poor, dying, sinful creature may hope to attain. Our whole nature is defiled by sin. Evil abounds in the world. Sickness, and death, and change — are daily doing their sad work on every side. In such a state of things — the highest happiness man can attain to on earth must necessarily be a *mixed* thing. If we expect to find any literally perfect happiness on this side of the grave — we expect what we shall not find!

True happiness does not consist in laughter and smiles. The face is very often a *poor index* of the inward man. There are thousands who laugh loud and are merry as a grasshopper in company — but are wretched and miserable in private, and almost afraid to be alone. On the other hand, there are hundreds who are grave and serious in their demeanor — whose hearts are full of solid peace. A poet of our own has truly told us that smiles are worth but little: "A man may smile and smile — and be a villain!"

And the eternal Word of God teaches us that "even in laughter, the heart may be sorrowful." (Proverbs 14:13.) Tell me not merely of smiling and laughing faces! I want to hear of something more than that, when I ask whether a man is happy. A truly happy man no doubt will often show his happiness in his countenance; but a man may have a very merry face — and yet not be happy at all.

Of all deceptive things on earth — nothing is so deceptive as mere worldly *gaiety* and *merriment.* It is a hollow empty show, utterly devoid of substance and reality! Listen to the brilliant talker in society, and mark the applause which he receives from an admiring company; follow him to his own private room, and you will very likely find him plunged in melancholy despondency. Colonel Gardiner confessed that even when he was thought most happy — he often wished he was a dog. Look at the smiling beauty in the ball-room, and you might suppose that she knew not what it was to be unhappy; see her next day at her own home, and you may probably find her out of temper with herself and everybody else besides!

Oh, no! *Worldly merriment is not real happiness!* There is a certain pleasure about it, I do not deny. There is an animal excitement about it, I make no question. There is a temporary elevation of spirits about it, I freely concede. But do not call it by the sacred name of 'happiness'. The most beautiful cut flowers stuck into the ground, do not make a garden. When glass is called diamond, and tinsel is called gold — then, and not until then, those people who can laugh and revel will deserve to be called happy people.

Cervantes, author of Don Quixote, at a time when all Spain was laughing at his humorous work, was overwhelmed with a deep cloud of melancholy.

Moliere, the first of French *comic writers,* carried into his domestic circle a sadness which the greatest worldly prosperity could never dispel.

Samuel Foote, the noted *wit* of the last century, died of a broken heart.

Theodore Hooke, the facetious novel writer, who could set everybody laughing, says of himself in his diary, "I am suffering under a constant depression of spirits, which no one who sees me in society dreams of."

A woebegone stranger consulted a physician about his health. The physician advised him to keep up his spirits by going to hear the great comic actor of the day: "You should go and hear Matthews. He would make you well." "Alas, sir," was the reply, "I am Matthews himself!"

1. To be truly happy — *the highest needs of a man's nature must be met and satisfied.* The *requirements* of his wondrously wrought constitution must all be filled up. There must be nothing about him that cries, "Give, give," but cries in vain and gets no answer. The horse and the ox are happy — as long as they are warmed and filled. And why? It is because they are satisfied. The little infant looks happy when it is clothed, and fed, and well, and in its mother's arms. And why? Because it is satisfied. And just so it is with man. His highest needs must be met and satisfied — before he can be truly happy. All must be filled up. There must be no void, no empty places, no unsupplied cravings. Until then he is never truly happy.

And WHAT are man's principal needs? Has he a body only? No! He has something more! He has a *soul*. Has he *sensual* faculties only? Can he do nothing but hear, and see, and smell, and taste, and feel? No! He has a thinking mind and a conscience! Has he no consciousness of any world, but that in which he lives and moves? He has. There is a still small voice within him which often makes itself heard: "This life is not all! There is an unseen world! There is a life beyond the grave!" Yes! it is true. We are fearfully and wonderfully made. All men *know* it — all men *feel* it, if they would only speak the truth. It is utter nonsense to pretend that food and clothing and earthly things alone — can make men happy. There are *soul*-needs. There are *conscience*-needs. There can be no true happiness — until *these* needs are satisfied.

2. To be truly happy — *a man must have sources of gladness which are not dependent on anything in this world.* There is nothing upon earth which is not stamped with the mark of *instability* and *uncertainty*. All the good things which money can buy, are but momentary: they either leave us — or we are obliged to leave them! All the sweetest relationships in life are liable to come to an end — death may come any day and cut them off. The man whose happiness depends entirely on things here below, is like him who builds his house on sand, or leans his weight on a reed.

Tell me not of your happiness, if it daily hangs on the *uncertainties* of earth. Your home may be rich in comforts; your wife and children may be all you could desire; your means may be amply sufficient to meet all your needs. But oh, remember, if you have nothing more than this to look to — that you stand on the brink of a precipice! Your *rivers of pleasure* may any day be dried up. Your joy may be deep and earnest — but it is fearfully *short-lived!* It has no *root*. It is not true happiness.

3. To be really happy — *a man must be able to look on every side without uncomfortable feelings.* He must be able to look back to the *past* without guilty fears; he must be able to look *around* him without discontent; he must be able to look *forward* without anxious dread. He must be able to sit down and think calmly about things past, present, and to come — and feel prepared. The man who has a weak side in his condition — a side that he does not like looking at or considering — that man is not really happy.

Do not talk to me of your happiness — if you are unable to look steadily either before or behind you. Your *present* position may be easy and pleasant. You may find many sources of joy and gladness in your profession, your dwelling-place, your family, and your friends. Your health may be good, your spirits may be cheerful. But stop and think quietly over your **past** life! Can you reflect calmly on all the sins of *omission* and *commission* of by-gone years? How will they bear God's inspection? How will you answer for them at the last day?

And then look **forward**, and think on the years yet to come. Think of the *certain end* towards which you are hastening: think of death; think of judgment; think of the hour when you will meet God face to face! Are you ready for it? Are you prepared? Can you look forward to these things without alarm? Oh, be very sure if you cannot look comfortably at any season but the present — then your *boasted happiness* is a poor unreal thing! It is but a white-washed sepulcher, fair and beautiful on the outside — but bones and corruption within! It is a mere thing of a day, like Jonah's gourd. It is not real happiness.

I ask my readers to fix in their minds the account of things essential to happiness, which I have attempted to give. Dismiss from your thoughts the many *mistaken notions* which pass current on this subject, like counterfeit coin. To be truly happy — the needs of your *soul* and *conscience* must be satisfied. To be truly happy — your joy must be founded on something more than this world can give you. To be truly happy — you must be able to look on every side — above, below, behind, before — and feel that all is right. This is real, sterling, genuine happiness — this is the happiness I have in view, when I urge on your notice the subject of this paper.

II. In the next place, let me expose some *common mistakes* about the way to be happy.

There are several roads which are thought by many, to lead to happiness. In each of these roads, thousands and tens of thousands of men and women are continually traveling. Each imagines that if he could only attain all that he wants — that he would be happy. Each imagines, if he does not succeed — that the fault is in his lack of *luck* and *good fortune*. And all alike seem ignorant that they are *hunting shadows*. They have started in a wrong direction! They are seeking that which can never be found in the place where they seek it.

I will mention by name *some of the principal delusions about happiness*. I do it in love, and charity, and compassion to men's souls. I believe it to be a public duty to warn people against *cheats, quacks, and impostors!* Oh, how much trouble and sorrow it might save my readers, if they would only believe what I am going to say!

It is an utter mistake to suppose that **RANK** and **GREATNESS** alone can give happiness. The kings and rulers of this world are not *necessarily* happy men. They have troubles and crosses, which none know but themselves! They see a thousand evils, which they are unable to remedy! They are *slaves working in golden chains*, and have less real liberty than any in the world! They have burdens and responsibilities laid upon them, which are a *daily weight* on their hearts. The Roman Emperor Antonine often said, that "the imperial power was *an ocean of miseries."* Queen Elizabeth, when she heard a milk-maid singing — wished that she had been born to a lot like her's. Never did our great Poet write a truer word than when he said, *"Uneasy lies the head that wears a crown!"*

It is an utter mistake to suppose that **RICHES** alone can give happiness. They can enable a man to command and possess everything — but inward peace! They cannot buy a *cheerful spirit* and *a light heart*. There is . . .

care in the *getting* of them,
care in the *keeping* of them,
care in the *using* of them,
care in the *disposing* of them,
care in the *gathering* of them,
and care in the *scattering* of them!

He was a wise man who said that "money" was only another name for "trouble," and that the same English letters which spelled "acres" would also spell "cares."

It is an utter mistake to suppose that **LEARNING** and **SCIENCE** alone can give happiness. They may occupy a man's time and attention — but they cannot really make him happy. Those who increase knowledge — often "increase sorrow;" the more they learn — the more they discover their own ignorance. (Eccles. 1:18.) It is not in the power of earthly things — to minister to a diseased heart. The *heart* needs something — as well as the head; the *conscience* needs food — as well as the intellect. All the secular knowledge in the world will not give a man joy and gladness — when he thinks on sickness, and death, and the grave. Those who have climbed the highest — have often found themselves solitary, dissatisfied, and empty of peace The learned *Selden*, at the close of his life, confessed that all his learning did not give him such comfort as these four verses of the apostle Paul — Titus 2:11-14.)

It is an utter mistake to suppose that **IDLENESS** alone can give happiness. The laborer who gets up at five in the morning, and goes out to work all day in a cold clay ditch, often thinks, as he walks past the rich man's door, *"What a fine thing it must be to have no work to do!"* Poor fellow! he little knows what he thinks. The most miserable creature on earth — is the man who has *nothing to do*. Work for the hands or work for the head — is absolutely essential to human happiness. Without it, the *mind feeds upon itself*, and the whole inward man becomes diseased. The machinery within *will* work — and without something to work upon, will often wear itself to pieces. There was no idleness in Eden. Adam and Eve had to "dress the garden and keep it." There will be no idleness in Heaven. God's "servants shall serve Him." Oh, be very sure, that the idlest man — is the man most truly unhappy! (Genesis 2:15; Rev. 22:3.)

It is an utter mistake to suppose that **PLEASURE-SEEKING** and **AMUSEMENTS** alone can give happiness. Of all roads that men can take in order to be happy, this is the one that is most completely wrong! Of all weary, flat, dull and unprofitable ways of spending life — this exceeds all. To think of a sinful, dying creature, with an immortal soul, expecting happiness . . .
in feasting and reveling,
in dancing and singing,
in dressing and visiting,
in ball-going and card-playing,
in races and fairs,
in hunting and shooting,
in crowds, in laughter, in noise, in music, in wine!

Surely it is a sight that is enough to make the devil laugh and the angels weep! Even a *child* will not play with its toys all day long! But when grown up men and women think to find happiness in a *constant round of amusement* — they sink far below a child!

I place before every reader of this paper, these *common mistakes about the way to be happy*. I ask you to mark them well. I warn you plainly against these *pretended short cuts to happiness*, however crowded they may be. I tell you that if you imagine any one of them can lead you to true peace, that you are entirely deceived. Your *conscience* will never feel satisfied; your immortal *soul* will never feel easy; your whole inward man will feel uncomfortable and out of health. Take any one of these roads, or take all of them, and if you have nothing besides to look to — you will never find happiness. You may travel on and on and on, and the *wished-for object* will seem as far away at the end of each stage of life as when you started. You are like one *pouring water into a sieve*, or putting money into a bag with holes. *You might as well try to make an elephant happy, by feeding him with a grain of sand a day — as try to satisfy that heart of your's with rank, riches, learning, idleness, or pleasure!*

Do you doubt the truth of all I am saying? I dare say you do. Then let us turn to the *great Book of human experience*, and read over a few lines out of its solemn pages. You shall have the testimony of a few competent witnesses on the great subject I am urging on your attention.

A *King* shall be our first witness — I mean *Solomon*, King of Israel. We know that he had power, and wisdom, and wealth, far exceeding that of any ruler of his time. We know from his own confession, that he tried the *great experiment* how far the things of this world can make man happy. We know, from the record of his own hand — the result of this curious experiment. He writes it by the inspiration of the Holy Spirit, for the benefit of the whole world, in the book of Ecclesiastes. Never, surely, was the experiment tried under such favorable circumstances: never was any one so likely to succeed as the Jewish King. Yet what is Solomon's testimony? You have it in his melancholy words: "All is vanity and vexation of spirit!" (Eccles. 1:14.)

A famous French lady shall be our next witness — I mean *Madam De Pompadour*. She was the friend and favorite of Louis the Fifteenth. She had unbounded influence at the Court of France. She lacked nothing that money could procure. Yet what does she say herself? "What a situation is that of the great! They only live in the future, and are only happy in hope. There is no peace in ambition. I am always gloomy, and often unreasonably so. The kindness of the King, the regard of courtiers, the attachment of my servants, and the fidelity of a large number of friends — motives like these, which ought to make me happy, affect me no longer. I have no longer inclinations for all which once pleased me. I have caused my house at Paris to be magnificently furnished — well; it pleased for two days! My residence at Bellevue is charming — but I cannot endure it. Kind people relate to me all the news and adventures of Paris; they think I listen — but when they are done, I ask them what they said. In a word, I do not live! I am dead before my time. I have no interest in the world. Everything conspires to embitter my life. *My life is a continual death!"* To such testimony I need not add a single word. (Sinclair's Anecdotes and Aphorisms, p. 33.)

A famous German writer shall be our next witness — I mean *Goethe*. It is well known that he was almost idolized by many during his life. His works were read and admired by thousands. His name was known and honored, wherever German was read, all over the world. And yet the *praise of man*, of which he reaped such an abundant harvest, was utterly unable to make Goethe happy. "He confessed, when about eighty years old, that he could not remember being in a really happy state of mind even for a few weeks together." (See Sinclair's Anecdotes and Aphorisms, p. 280.)

An English peer and poet shall be our next witness — I mean *Lord Byron*. If ever there was one who ought to have been happy according to the standard of the world — Lord Byron was the man! He began life with all the advantages of English rank and position. He had splendid abilities and powers of mind, which the world soon discovered and was ready to honor. He had a sufficiency of means to gratify every wish, and never knew anything of real poverty. Humanly speaking, there seemed nothing to prevent him enjoying life and being happy. Yet it is a notorious fact that Byron was a miserable man. Misery stands out in his poems — misery creeps out in his letters. Weariness, satiety, disgust, and discontent appear in all his ways. He is an solemn warning that *rank, and title, and literary fame,* alone — are not sufficient to make a man happy.

A man of science shall be our next witness — I mean *Sir Humphrey Davy*. He was a man eminently successful in the line of life which he chose, and deservedly so. A distinguished philosopher — the inventor of the famous safety-lamp which bears his name, and has preserved so many poor miners from death — a Baron of the United Kingdom, and President of the Royal Society — his whole life seemed a continual career of prosperity. If *learning* alone were the road to happiness, this man at least ought to have been happy. Yet what was the true record of Davy's feelings? We have it in his own melancholy journal at the latter part of his life. He describes himself in two painful words: *"Very miserable!"*

A man of wit and pleasure shall be our next witness — I mean *Lord Chesterfield*. He shall speak for himself — his own words in a letter shall be his testimony. "I have seen the silly round of business and pleasure, and am done with it all. I have experienced all the pleasures of the world — and consequently know their *futility*, and do not regret their loss. I appraise them at their real value — which in truth is very low; whereas those who have not experience them — always overrate them. They only see their mirthful *outside*, and are dazzled with their *glare* — but I have been behind the scenes. I have seen all the coarse pulleys and dirty ropes which exhibit and move the *gaudy machine*, and I have seen and smelled the candles which illuminate the whole decoration — to the astonishment and admiration of the ignorant audience! When I reflect on what I have seen, what I have heard, and what I have done — I cannot persuade myself that all that frivolous *hurry of bustle* and *pleasure* of the world had any reality. I look on all that is past, as one of those romantic dreams which opium occasions, and I do by no means wish to repeat the *nauseous dose* for the sake of the fleeting dream!" These sentences speak for themselves. I need not add to them one single word.

The *Statesmen* and *Politicians* who have swayed the destinies of the world, ought by good right to be our last witnesses. But I forbear, in Christian charity, to bring them forward. It makes my heart ache when I run my eye over the list of names famous in English history — and think how many have worn out their lives in a breathless struggle after place and distinction! How many of our greatest men have died of broken hearts — disappointed, disgusted, and tried with constant failure! How many have left on record some humbling confession that in the plenitude of their power they were pining for rest, as the caged eagle for liberty! How many whom the world is applauding as "masters of the situation" — are in reality little better than galley-slaves, chained to the oar and unable to get free! Alas, there are many sad proofs, both among the living and the dead — that to be *great* and *powerful* is not necessarily to be happy!

I think it very likely that people do not believe what I am saying. I know something of the *deceitfulness of the heart* on the subject of happiness. There are few things which man is so slow to believe as the truths I am now putting forth about the way to be happy. Bear with me then while I say something more.

Come and stand with me some afternoon in the heart of the city of London. Let us watch the faces of most of the wealthy men whom we shall see leaving their houses of business at the close of the day. Some of them are worth hundreds of thousands — some of them are worth millions of pounds. But what is written in the countenances of these grave men whom we see swarming out from Lombard Street and Cornhill, from the Bank of England and the Stock Exchange? What do those deep lines which furrow so many a cheek and so many a brow mean? What does that air of *anxious thoughtfulness* which is worn by five out of every six we meet mean? Ah, these things tell a serious tale. They tell us that it needs something more than gold and bank notes to make men happy!

Come next and stand with me near the Houses of Parliament, in the middle of a busy session. Let us scan the faces of Nobles whose names are familiar and well-known all over the civilized world. There you may see on some fine May evening, the mightiest Statesmen in England hurrying to a debate — like eagles to the carcass. Each has a power of good or evil in his tongue, which it is fearful to contemplate. Each may say things before tomorrow's sun dawns, which may affect the peace and prosperity of nations, and convulse the world! There you may see the men who hold the *reins of power and government* already; there you may see the men who are daily watching for an opportunity of snatching those reins out of their hands, and governing in their stead. But what do their faces tell us, as they hasten to their posts? What may be learned from their care-worn countenances? What may be read in many of their wrinkled foreheads — so absent-looking and sunk in thought? They teach us a solemn lesson. They teach us that it needs something more than *political greatness* to make men happy.

Come next and stand with me in the most fashionable part of London, in the height of the season. Let us visit *Regent Street* or *Pall Mall*, *Hyde Park* or *May Fair*. How many fair faces and splendid equipages we shall see! How many we shall count up in an hour's time who seem to possess the choicest gifts of this world — beauty, wealth, rank, fashion, and troops of friends! But, alas, how few we shall see who appear happy! In how many countenances we shall read weariness, dissatisfaction, discontent, sorrow, or unhappiness — as clearly as if it was written with a pen! Yes, it is a humbling lesson to learn — but a very wholesome one. It needs something more than rank, and fashion, and beauty, to make people happy!

Come next and walk with me through some *quiet country village* in merry England. Let us visit some *secluded corner* in our beautiful old father-land, far away from great towns, and fashionable dissipation and political strife. There are not a few such to be found in the land. There are rural villages where there is neither street, nor public-house, nor beer shop — where there is work for all the laborers, and a church for all the population, and a school for all the children, and a minister of the Gospel to look after the people. Surely, you will say — we shall find happiness here! Surely such parishes must be the very abodes of peace and joy!

Go into those quiet-looking cottages, one by one, and you will soon be undeceived. Learn the inner history of each family, and you will soon alter your mind. You will soon discover that backbiting, and lying, and slandering, and envy, and jealousy, and pride, and laziness, and drinking, and extravagance, and lust, and petty quarrels — can *murder happiness* in the country, quite as much as in the city! No doubt a *rural village* sounds pretty in poetry, and looks beautiful in pictures; but in sober reality, human nature is the same evil thing everywhere! Alas, it needs something more than a residence in a quiet country village to make any child of Adam a happy man!

I know these are ancient things. They have been said a thousand times before without effect, and I suppose they will be said without effect again. I want no greater proof of the corruption of human nature, than the pertinacity with which we seek happiness where happiness cannot be found! Century after century, wise men have left on record their experience about the way to be happy. Century after century, people will have it that they know the way perfectly well, and need no teaching. They cast our warnings to the winds; they rush, every one, on his own favorite path. They walk in a vain shadow, and disquiet themselves in vain, and wake up when too late — to find that their whole life has been a grand mistake. Their eyes are blinded — they will not see that their *visions* are as *baseless* and *disappointing* as the mirage of the African desert. Like the tired traveler in those deserts, they think they are approaching a lake of cooling waters; like the same traveler, they find to their dismay that this imagined lake was a splendid *optical delusion* — and that they are still helpless in the midst of burning sands!

Are you a **young** person? I entreat you to accept the affectionate warning of a minister of the Gospel — and not to seek happiness where happiness cannot be found.

Seek it not in riches;
seek it not in power and rank;
seek it not in pleasure;
seek it not in learning.

All these are bright and splendid fountains — their waters taste sweet. A crowd is standing round them, who will not leave them; but, oh, remember that God has written over each of these fountains, "He who drinks of this water — shall thirst again!" (John 4:13.) Remember this, and be wise.

Are you **poor**? Are you tempted to imagine that if you had the rich man's place — that you would be quite happy? Resist the temptation, and cast it behind you. Do not envy your wealthy neighbors — be content with such things as you have. Happiness does not depend on houses or lands! Silks and satins cannot shut out sorrow from the heart! Castles and fine halls cannot prevent anxiety and care coming in at their doors. There is as much misery riding and driving about in splendid carriages — as there is walking about on foot! There is as much unhappiness in large mansions — as in poor cottages. Oh, remember the mistakes which are common about happiness, and be wise!

III. Let me now, in the last place — point out *the way to be really happy*.

There is a sure path which leads to happiness, if men will only take it. There never lived the person who traveled in that path, and missed the object that he sought to attain.

It is a path **open to all**. It needs neither wealth, nor rank, nor learning in order to walk in it. It is for the servant as well as for the master: it is for the poor as well as for the rich. None are excluded but those who exclude themselves.

It is the **one and only path**. All who have ever been happy, since the days of Adam, have journeyed on it. There is no *royal road* to happiness. Kings must be content to go side by side with their humblest subjects, if they would be happy.

WHERE is this path? Where is this road? Listen, and you shall hear.

The way to be happy — is to be a real, thorough-going, true-

hearted Christian! Scripture declares it — experience proves it. The converted man, the believer in Christ, the child of God — he, and he alone, is the happy man.

It sounds too simple to be true — it seems at first sight so plain a receipt that it is not believed. But the *greatest* truths are often the *simplest*. The secret which many of the wisest on earth have utterly failed to discover — is revealed to the humblest believer in Christ. I repeat it deliberately, and defy the world to disprove it — the true Christian is the *only* happy man.

What do I mean when I speak of a true Christian? Do I mean everybody who goes to church or chapel? Do I mean everybody who professes an orthodox creed, and bows his head at the belief? Do I mean everybody who *professes* to love the Gospel? *No indeed!* I mean something very different. All are not Christians — who are *called* Christians. The man I have in view — is the Christian in *heart* and *life*. He who has been taught by the Spirit really to feel his sins — he who really rests all his hopes on the Lord Jesus Christ, and His atonement — he who has been born again and really lives a spiritual, holy life — he whose religion is not a mere *Sunday coat* — but a mighty constraining principle governing every day of his life — he is the man I mean, when I speak of a true Christian.

What do I mean when I say the true Christian is happy? Has he no *doubts* and no *fears?* Has he no *anxieties* and no *troubles?* Has he no *sorrows* and no *cares?* Does he never feel *pain*, and shed no *tears?* Far be it from me to say anything of the kind! He has a body weak and is frail like other men; he has affections and passions like everyone born of woman; he lives in a changeful world. But deep down in his heart, he has a mine of solid peace and substantial joy which is never exhausted! This is true happiness.

Do I say that all true Christians are *equally* happy? No, not for a moment! There are *babes* in Christ's family — as well as old men; there are *weak* members of the mystical body — as well as strong ones; there are tender lambs — as well as sheep. There are not only the cedars of Lebanon — but the *hyssop* that grows on the wall. There are *degrees* of grace and degrees of faith. Those who have most faith and grace — will have most happiness. But all, more or less, compared to the people of the world — are happy men.

Do I say that real true Christians are *equally happy at all times*? No, not for a moment! All have their *ebbs and flows* of comfort — some, like the Mediterranean sea, almost insensibly; some, like the tide at Chepstow, fifty or sixty feet at a time.

Their *bodily health* is not always the same;
their *earthly circumstances* are not always the same;
those they love fill them at seasons with special anxiety;

they themselves are sometimes overtaken by a fault, and walk in darkness.
They sometimes give way to inconsistencies and besetting sins, and lose their sense of pardon. But, as a general rule, the true Christian has a deep pool of peace within him, which even at the lowest is never entirely dry.

I use the words, "as a general rule," advisedly. When a believer falls into such a horrible sin as that of David, it would be monstrous to talk of his feeling inward peace.

The true Christian is the only happy man — because *his conscience is at peace.* That *mysterious witness for God*, which is so mercifully placed within us — is fully satisfied and at rest. It sees in the blood of Christ — a complete cleansing away of all its guilt. It sees in the priesthood and mediation of Christ — a complete answer to all its fears. It sees that through the sacrifice and death of Christ, God can now be just — and yet be the justifier of the ungodly. It no longer bites and stings, and makes its possessor afraid of himself. The Lord Jesus Christ has amply met all its requirements. *Conscience* is no longer the enemy of the true Christian — but his friend and adviser. Therefore he is happy.

The true Christian is the only happy man — because *he can sit down quietly and think about his soul.* He can look behind him and before him, he can look within him and around him, and feel, "All is well."

He can think calmly on his *past life*, and however many and great his sins, take comfort in the thought that they are all forgiven. The righteousness of Christ covers all, as Noah's flood overtopped the highest hills.

He can think calmly about *things to come* — and yet not be afraid. Sickness is painful; death is solemn; the judgment day is a solemn thing — but having Christ for him, he has nothing to fear. He can think calmly about the Holy God, whose eyes are on all his ways, and feel, "He is my Father, my reconciled Father in Christ Jesus. I am weak; I am unprofitable — yet in Christ He regards me as His dear child, and is well-pleased." Oh, what a blessed privilege it is to be able to *think* — and not be afraid! I can well understand the mournful complaint of the prisoner in solitary confinement. He had warmth, and food, and clothing, and work — but he was not happy. And why? He said, "He was obliged to *think.*"

The true Christian is the only happy man, because he has *sources of happiness entirely independent of this world.* He has something which cannot be affected by sickness and by deaths, by private losses and by public calamities — the "*peace of God,* which passes all understanding." He has a *hope* laid up for him in Heaven; he has a *treasure* which moth and rust cannot corrupt; he has a *house* which can never be taken down.

His loving wife may die — and his heart feel torn in two;
his darling children may be taken from him;
he may be left alone in this cold world;
his earthly plans may be crossed;
his health may fail —
but all this time he has . . .
a *portion* which nothing can harm,
one *Friend* who never dies,
eternal *possessions* beyond the grave —
of which nothing can deprive him! His lower springs may fail — but his upper springs are never dry. This is real happiness.

The true Christian is happy, because *he is in his right position.*

His abilities are being directed to right ends.

His *affections* are not set on things below — but on things above.

His *will* is not bent on self-indulgence — but is submissive to the will of God.

His *mind* is not absorbed in wretched perishable trifles.

He *desires* useful employment — he enjoys the *luxury of doing good.*

Who does not know the *misery of disorder?* Who has not tasted the discomfort of a house where everything and everybody are in their wrong places, the last things first — and the first things last? The heart of an unconverted man is just such a house! Saving grace puts everything in that heart in its right position. The things of the *soul* come first — and the things of the world come second. Anarchy and confusion cease — unruly passions no longer run loose. Christ reigns over the whole man — and each part of him does his proper work.

The heart of the Christian is the only heart that is in *order*. He has laid aside his pride and self-will; he sits at the feet of Jesus, and is in his right mind. He loves God and loves man — and so he is happy. In Heaven all are happy — because all do God's will perfectly. The nearer a man gets to this standard — the happier he will be.

The plain truth is, that without Christ there is no happiness in this world! He alone can give the *Comforter* who abides forever.

He is the sun — without Him, men never feel warm.

He is the light — without Him, men are always in the dark.

He is the bread — without Him, men are always starving.

He is the living water — without Him, people are always athirst.

Give them what you like — place them where you please — surround them with all the comforts you can imagine — it makes no difference. Separate from Christ, the Prince of Peace — a man cannot be happy.

Give a man a sensible interest in Christ — and he will be happy in spite of **poverty**. He will tell you that he lacks nothing that is really good. He is provided for, he has all that he needs now — and riches in eternity. He has *food* to eat which the world knows nothing of. He has *friends* who never leave him nor forsake him. The Father and the Son come to him, and make their abode with him; the Lord Jesus Christ sups with him, and he with Christ. (Rev. 3:20.)

Give a man a sensible interest in Christ, and he will be happy in spite of **sickness**. His *flesh* may groan, and his *body* be worn out with pain — but his *heart* will rest and be at peace. One of the happiest people I ever saw, was a young woman who had been hopelessly ill for many years with disease of the spine. She lay in a poor garret without a fire; the straw thatch was not two feet above her face. She had not the slightest hope of recovery. But she was always rejoicing in the Lord Jesus. The spirit triumphed mightily over the flesh. She was happy, because Christ was with her.

Give a man a sensible interest in Christ, and he will be happy in spite of abounding public **calamities**.
The government of his country may be thrown into confusion;
rebellion and disorder may turn everything upside down;
laws may be trampled under foot;
justice and equity may be outraged;
liberty may be cast down to the ground;
might may prevail over *right*
— but still his heart will not fail. He will remember that the kingdom of Christ will one day be set up. He will say, like the old Scotch minister who lived unmoved throughout the turmoil of the French revolution: "It is all right! It shall be well with the righteous!"

I know well that Satan hates the doctrine which I am endeavoring to press upon you. I have no doubt he is filling your mind with objections and reasonings, and persuading you that I am wrong. I am not afraid to meet these objections face to face. Let us bring them forward and see what they are.

You may tell me that "you know many very religious people who are not happy at all." You see them diligent in attending public worship. You know that they are never missing at church. But you see in them no marks of the peace which I have been describing.

But are you sure that these people you speak of are *true* believers in Christ? Are you sure that, with all their appearance of religion, they are born again and converted to God? Is it not very likely that they have nothing — but the *name* of Christianity, without the reality; and a *form* of godliness, without the power? Alas! you have yet to learn that people may do many *religious acts* — and yet possess no saving religion! It is not a *mere formal, ceremonial Christianity* which will ever make people happy. We need something more than *going to*

Church — to give us peace. There must be real, vital union with Christ. It is not the *formal* Christian — but the *true* Christian, who is the happy man.

You may tell me that "you know really spiritually-minded and converted people who do not seem happy." You have heard them frequently complaining of their own hearts, and groaning over their own corruption. They seem to you to be all doubts, and anxieties, and fears; and you want to know *where* is the happiness in these people of which I have been saying so much.

I do not deny that there *are* many saints of God such as these whom you describe, and I am sorry for it. I allow that there are many believers who *live far below their privileges*, and seem to know nothing of joy and peace in believing. But did you ever ask any of these people whether they would give up their Christianity, and go back to the world? Did you ever ask them, after all their groanings, and doubtings, and fearings, whether they think they would be happier if they ceased to follow Christ? Did you ever ask those questions? I am certain if you did, that the weakest and lowest believers would all give you one answer, I am certain they would tell you that they would rather cling to their *little scrap of hope* in Christ — than possess the world! I am sure they would all answer, "Our faith is weak, if we have any; our grace is small, if we have any; our joy in Christ is next to nothing at all — but we cannot give up what we have gotten. Though the Lord slays us — we must cling to Him."

The *root* of happiness lies deep in many a poor weak believer's heart — when neither *leaves* nor *blossoms* are to be seen!

But you will tell me, in the last place, that "you cannot think that most believers are happy, because they are so grave and serious." You think that they do not really possess this happiness I have been describing — because their *countenances* do not show it. You doubt the reality of their joy — because it is so little *seen*.

I might easily repeat what I told you at the beginning of this paper — that *a merry face is no sure proof of a happy heart*. But I will not do so. I will rather ask you whether *you yourself* may not be the cause why believers look grave and serious when you meet them? If you are not converted yourself — you surely cannot expect them to look at you without sorrow! They see you on the high road to destruction, and that alone is enough to give them pain! They see thousands like you, hurrying on to weeping and wailing and endless woe! Now, is it possible that such a daily sight, should not give them grief? *Your company*, very likely, is one cause why they are grave. Wait until you are a converted man yourself, before you pass judgment on the gravity of converted people. See them in companies where all are of one heart, and all love Christ, and so far as my own experience goes — you will find no people so truly happy, as true Christians.

When the infidel Hume asked Bishop Horne why religious people always looked melancholy, the learned prelate replied, "The sight of you, Mr. Hume, would make any Christian melancholy!"

I repeat my assertion in this part of my subject. I repeat it boldly, confidently, deliberately. I say that there is no happiness among worldly people, which will at all compare with that of the true Christian. All other happiness compared with his — is moonlight compared to sunshine, and brass compared to gold. Boast, if you will, of the laughter and merriment of irreligious men; sneer, if you will, at the gravity and seriousness, which appear in the demeanor of many Christians. I have looked the whole subject in the face, and am not moved. I say that the true Christian alone is the truly happy man — and the way to be happy is to be a true Christian.

And now I am going to close this paper by a few words of plain ***APPLICATION***. I have endeavored to show what is *essential to true happiness*. I have endeavored to expose the *fallacy* of many views which prevail upon the subject. I have endeavored to point out, in plain and unmistakable words, *where* true happiness alone can be found. Allow me to wind up all by *an affectionate appeal to the consciences* of all into whose hands this volume may fall.

(1) In the first place, let me entreat every reader of this paper to apply to his own heart the solemn inquiry: *Are you happy?* High or low, rich or poor, master or servant, farmer or laborer, young or old — here is a question that deserves an answer: Are you *really* happy?

Man of the world, who is caring for nothing but the things of time, neglecting the Bible, making a god of business or money, providing for everything but the day of judgment, scheming and planning about everything but eternity: Are you happy? You know you are not!

Foolish woman, who is trifling life away in levity and frivolity, spending hours after hours on that poor frail body which must soon feed the worms, making an idol of dress and fashion, and excitement, and human praise — as if this world was all: Are you happy? You know you are not!

Young man, who is bent on pleasure and self-indulgence, fluttering from one idle pastime to another, like the *moth* about the candle flame — imagining yourself clever and knowing, and too wise to be led by pastors, and ignorant that the devil is leading you captive, like the ox that is led to the slaughter: Are you happy? You know you are not!

Yes — each and all of you — you are not happy! And in your own consciences, you know it well. You may not allow it — but it is sadly true. There is a *great empty place* in each of your hearts — and nothing will fill it. Pour into it money, learning, rank, and pleasure — and it will be empty still. There is a *sore place* in each of your consciences — and nothing will heal it. Infidelity cannot; free-thinking cannot; Romanism cannot — they are all *quack medicines*. Nothing can heal it — but that which at present you have not used — the simple Gospel of Christ. Yes, you are indeed a miserable person! Take warning this day — that you never will be happy until you are converted. You might as well expect to feel the sun shine on your face when you turn your back to it, as to feel happy when you turn your back on God and on Christ.

(2) In the next place, let me warn all who are not true Christians — of the folly of living a life which cannot make them happy.

I pity you from the bottom of my heart, and would gladly persuade you to open your eyes and be wise. I stand as a watchman on the tower of the everlasting Gospel. I see you *sowing eternal misery* for yourselves, and I call upon you to stop and think, before it is too late. Oh, that God may show you your folly! You are hewing out cisterns, broken cisterns for yourselves — which can hold no water. You are spending your time, and strength, and affections on that which will give you no return for your labor, "spending your money on that which is not bread, and your labor for that which satisfies not." (Isaiah 55:2.) You are building up a *Babel* of your own contriving, and ignorant that God will pour contempt on *your schemes for procuring happiness* — because you attempt to be happy without Him.

Awake from your *dreams*, I entreat you, and show yourselves men! Think of the *uselessness* of living a life which you will be ashamed of when you die; and of having a *mere nominal religion* — which will utterly fail you when it is most needed.

Open your eyes and look round the world. Tell me who was ever really happy, without God and Christ and the Holy Spirit. Look at the road in which you are traveling. Mark the footsteps of those who have gone before you — see how many have turned away from it, and confessed they were wrong.

I warn you plainly, that if you are not a true Christian — you will miss happiness in the present world, as well as in the world to come. Oh, believe me, the way of *happiness*, and the way of *salvation* — are one and the same! He who will have his own way, and refuses to serve Christ — will never be really happy. But he who serves Christ has the promise of both lives. He is happy on earth, and will be happier still in Heaven!

If you are neither happy in this world nor the next, it will be all your own fault. Oh, think of this! Do not be guilty of such *enormous folly!* Who does not mourn over the folly of the drunkard, the opium eater, and the suicide? But there is no folly like that of the impenitent child of the world.

(3) In the next place, let me entreat all readers of this book, who are not yet happy — to seek happiness where alone it can be found.

The *keys* of the way to happiness are in the hands of the Lord

Jesus Christ. He is sealed and appointed by God the Father, to give the *bread of life* to those who hunger, and to give the *water of life* to those who thirst. The *door* which riches and rank and learning have so often tried to open, and tried in vain — is now ready to open to every humble, praying believer. Oh, if you want to be happy — come to Christ! Come to Him, confessing that you are weary of your own ways, and want rest; that you find you have no power and might to make yourself holy or happy or fit for Heaven; and have no hope but in Him. Tell Him this unreservedly. This is coming to Christ.

Come to Him, imploring Him to show you His mercy, and grant you His salvation — to wash you in His own blood, and take your sins away — to speak peace to your conscience, and heal your troubled soul. Tell Him all this unreservedly. This is coming to Christ.

You have everything to *encourage* you. The Lord Jesus *Himself* invites you. He proclaims to you as well as to others, "Come unto Me, all you who labor and are heavy laden, and I will give you rest. Take my yoke upon you, and learn of Me; for I am meek and lowly in heart: and you shall find rest unto your souls. For my yoke is easy, and my burden is light." (Matthew 11. 28-30.) Wait for nothing. You may feel unworthy. You may feel as if you did not repent enough. But wait no longer. Come to Christ.

You have everything to encourage you. Thousands have walked in the way you are invited to enter, and have found it good. Once, like yourself — they served the world, and plunged deeply into folly and sin. Once, like yourself — they became weary of their wickedness, and longed for deliverance and rest. They heard of Christ, and His willingness to help and save; they came to Him by faith and prayer, after many a doubt and hesitation; they found Him a thousand times more gracious than they had expected! They rested on Him and were happy — they carried His cross and tasted peace. Oh, walk in their steps.

I beseech you, by the mercies of God, to come to Christ. As ever you would be happy, I entreat you to come to Christ. Cast off delays. Awake from your past slumber — arise, and be free! This day come to Christ.

(4) In the last place, let me offer a few hints to all true Christians for the *increase* and *promotion* of their happiness.

I offer these hints with diffidence. I desire to apply them to my own conscience as well as to your's. You have found Christ's service happy. I have no doubt that you feel such sweetness in Christ's peace that you would gladly know more of it. I am sure that these hints deserve attention.

Believers, if you would have an increase of happiness in Christ's service, labor every year to **grow in grace**. Beware of standing still. The *holiest* men are always the *happiest*. Let your aim be every year to be more holy — to know more, to feel more, to see more of the fullness of Christ !do not rest upon *old* grace — do not be content with the degree of grace whereunto you have attained.

Search the Scriptures more earnestly;
pray more fervently;
hate sin more;
mortify self-will more;
become more humble;
seek more direct personal communion with the Lord Jesus;
strive to be more like Enoch — daily walking with God;
keep your conscience clear of little sins;
do not grieve the Spirit;
avoid wranglings and disputes about the lesser matters of religion; lay more firm hold upon those great truths, without which no man can be saved. Remember and practice these things — and you will be more happy!

Believers, if you would have an increase of happiness in Christ's service — labor every year to be more **thankful**. Pray that you may know more and more what it is to "rejoice in the Lord." (Philippians 3:1.) Learn to have a deeper sense of your own wretched sinfulness and corruption, and to be more deeply grateful, that by the grace of God you are what you are. Alas, there is too much complaining — and too little thanksgiving among the people of God! There is too much *murmuring,* and *coveting* things that we have not. There is too little praising and blessing for the many *undeserved mercies* that we have. Oh, that God would pour out upon us a great spirit of thankfulness and praise!

Believers, if you would have an increase of happiness in Christ's service, labor every year to **do more good**. Look around the circle in which your lot is cast — and lay yourself out to be useful. Strive to be of the same character with God: He is not only good — but "does good." (Psalm 119:68.) Alas, there is far too much *selfishness* among believers in the present day! There is far too much lazy sitting by the fire *nursing* our own spiritual diseases, and croaking over the state of our own hearts! Up, and be useful in your day and generation! Is there no one that you can *speak* to? Is there no one that you can *write* to? Is there literally nothing that you can *do* for the glory of God, and the benefit of your fellow-men? Oh I cannot think it! I cannot think it. There is much that you might do, if you had only the desire. For your own happiness' sake — arise and do it, without delay. The bold, outspoken, working Christians — are always the happiest!

The compromising, lingering Christian must never expect to taste perfect peace. The most decided Christian — will always be the happiest man.

FORMAL RELIGION

"Having a form of godliness — but denying the power thereof." 2 Timothy 3:5

"A man is not a Jew if he is only one outwardly, nor is circumcision merely outward and physical. No, a man is a Jew if he is one inwardly; and circumcision is circumcision of the heart, by the Spirit, not by the written code. Such a man's praise is not from men, but from God." Romans 2:28-29

READER,

The texts which head this page deserves your serious attention at any time. I take it for granted that you have *some religion*. You are not an infidel. You profess and call yourself a Christian. Well, is your Christianity *formal* — or *spiritual?* Is religion with you a matter of form — or a matter of the heart? Is it form — or heart?

The question deserves especial notice in this age of the church and world. Never since the Lord Jesus Christ left the earth, was there so much formality and false profession, as there is at the present day. Now, if ever, we ought to examine ourselves, and search our religion, that we may know of what sort it is. Reader, let us find out whether our Christianity is a thing of form — or a thing of heart.

I know no better way of unfolding the subject than by turning to a plain passage of the Word of God. Let us hear what the apostle Paul says about it. He lays down the following great principles in his Epistle to the Romans: "A man is not a Jew if he is only one outwardly, nor is circumcision merely outward and physical. No, a man is a Jew if he is one inwardly; and circumcision is circumcision of the heart, by the Spirit, not by the written code. Such a man's praise is not from men, but from God." Three most instructive lessons appear to me to stand out on the face of that passage. Let us see what they are.

I. We learn, firstly, that *formal religion is not true religion;* and a formal Christian is not a true Christian in God's sight.

II. We learn, secondly, that *the heart is the seat of true religion,* and that the true Christian is the Christian in heart.

III. We learn, thirdly, that true religion must never expect to be *popular*. It will not have the "praise of man — but of God."

Let us thoroughly consider these great principles. Two hundred years have passed away since a mighty Puritan divine said, "Formality, formality, formality, is the great sin of England at this day, under which the land groans. There is more *light* than there was — but less life; more *shadow* — but less substance; more *profession* — but less holiness." (Thomas Hall, 1658). What would this good man have said if he had lived in our times?

I. We learn, first, that formal religion is not true religion, and a formal Christian is not a true Christian in God's sight.

What do I mean when I speak of formal religion? This is a point that must be made clear. Thousands, I suspect, know nothing about it. Without a distinct understanding of this point, my whole paper will be useless. My first step shall be to paint, describe, and define. When a man is a Christian in *name only* — and not in reality; in *outward* things only — and not in his inward feelings; in profession only — and not in practice; when his Christianity, in short, is a mere matter of form, or fashion, or custom, without any influence on his heart or life — in such a case as this, the man has what I call a "formal religion." He possesses indeed the *form*, or *husk*, or *skin* of religion — but he does not possess its *substance* or its *power*.

Look, for example, at those thousands of people whose whole religion seems to consist in keeping religious ceremonies and ordinances. They attend regularly on public worship. They go regularly to the Lord's table. But they never get any further. They know nothing of *experimental* Christianity. They are not familiar with the Scriptures — and take no delight in reading them. They do not separate themselves from the ways of the world. They draw no distinction between godliness and ungodliness in their friendships, or matrimonial alliances. They care little or nothing about the distinctive doctrines of the Gospel. They appear utterly indifferent as to what they hear preached. You may be in their company for weeks, and for anything you may hear or see — you might suppose they were infidels! What can be said about these people? They are Christians undoubted, by *profession*; and yet there is neither heart nor life in their Christianity. There is but one thing to be said about them: They are formal Christians — their religion is a *mere form!*

Look in another direction, at those hundreds of people whose whole religion seems to consist in *talk* and *high profession*. They know the *theory* of the Gospel with their heads, and profess to delight in Evangelical doctrine. They can say much about the "soundness" of their own views, and the "darkness" of all who disagree with them; but they never get any further! When you examine their inner *lives* — you find that they know nothing of *practical godliness*. They are neither truthful, nor charitable, nor humble, nor honest, nor kind-tempered, nor unselfish, nor honorable. What shall we say of these people? They are Christians, no doubt, in *name* — and yet there is neither *substance* nor *fruit* in their Christianity. There is but one thing to be said: They are *formal Christians* — their religion is an *empty form!*

Such, reader, is the formal religion against which I wish to warn you this day. Here is the point about which I offer you a question. Here is a *rock* on which myriads on every side are making miserable shipwreck of their souls. One of the wickedest things that Machiavel ever said was this, "Religion itself should not be cared for — but only the *appearance* of it." Such notions, reader, are of the earth, earthy. Nay, rather, they are from beneath; they smell of the pit. Beware of them, and stand upon your guard. *If there is anything about which the Scripture speaks expressly — it is the sin and uselessness of formality!*

Hear what Paul tells the Romans: "A man is not a Jew if he is only one *outwardly*, nor is circumcision merely outward and physical. No, a man is a Jew if he is one inwardly; and circumcision is circumcision of the heart, by the Spirit, not by the written code." These are strong words indeed! A man might be a son of Abraham according to the flesh, a member of one of the twelve tribes, circumcised the eighth day, a keeper of all the feasts, a regular worshiper in the temple — and yet in God's sight, not be a Jew!

Just so, a man may be a Christian by outward profession — a member of a Christian Church — baptized with Christian baptism — an attendant on Christian ordinances — and yet, in God's sight, not a Christian at all!

Hear what the prophet Isaiah says: "The multitude of your sacrifices — what are they to me?" says the LORD. "I have more than enough of burnt offerings, of rams and the fat of fattened animals; I have no pleasure in the blood of bulls and lambs and goats. When you come to appear before me, who has asked this of you, this trampling of my courts? Stop bringing meaningless offerings! Your incense is detestable to me. New Moons, Sabbaths and convocations — I cannot bear your evil assemblies. Your New Moon festivals and your appointed feasts — my soul hates. They have become a burden to me; I am weary of bearing them. When you spread out your hands in prayer, I will hide my eyes from you; even if you offer many prayers, I will not listen. Your hands are full of blood. Take your evil deeds out of my sight!" (Isaiah 1:11-15)

These words, when duly weighed, are very extraordinary. The sacrifices which are here declared to be useless were appointed by God Himself. The feasts and ordinances which God says He "hates," had been prescribed by Himself! God Himself pronounces His own institutions to be useless — when they are used formally and without heart in the worshiper. In fact they are worse than useless; they are even offensive and hurtful. Words cannot be imagined more distinct and unmistakable. They show that *formal religion is worthless* in God's sight. It is not worth calling religion!

Hear, lastly, what our Lord Jesus Christ says. We find Him saying of the Jews of His day, "This people draws near unto Me with their mouth, and honors Me with their lips; but their heart is far from Me. In vain do they worship Me!" (Matthew 15:8, 9). We see Him repeatedly denouncing the formalism and hypocrisy of the Scribes and Pharisees, and warning His disciples against it. Eight times in one chapter (Matthew 23) He says to them, "Woe unto you, Scribes and Pharisees, *hypocrites!"*

For sinners of the worst description He always had a word of kindness, and held out to them an open door. But formalism, He would have us know, is a desperate disease, and must be exposed in the severest language. To the eye of the ignorant man, a formalist may seem to have a very decent quantity of religion, though not perhaps of the best quality. In the eye of Christ, however, the case is very different. In His sight, formality is no religion at all.

Reader, what shall we say to these testimonies of Scripture? It would be easy to add to them. They do not stand alone. If words mean anything, they are a clear warning to all who *profess* and *call* themselves Christians. They teach you plainly that as you dread *sin* and avoid sin — so you ought to dread *formality* and avoid formality. *Formalism* may take your hand with a smile, and look like a brother — while *sin* comes against you with sword drawn, and strikes at you like an open enemy. But both have one end in view. Both want to ruin your soul; and, of the two, formalism is far the most likely to do it! Reader, if you love life, beware of *formality* in religion.

Nothing is so **common**. It is one of the great *family diseases* of the whole race of mankind. It is *born* with us, *grows* with us, and is never completely cast out of us until we die. It meets us in church — and it meets us in chapel. It meets us among rich — and it meets us among poor. It meets us among learned people — and it meets us among unlearned. It meets us among Romanists — and it meets us among Protestants. It meets us among High Churchmen — and it meets us among Low Churchmen. It meets us among Evangelicals — and it meets us among Tractarians. Go wherever we will, and join whatever Church we may — we are never beyond the risk of its infection! We shall find it among Quakers and Plymouth Brethren, as well as at Rome. The man who thinks that there is no formal religion in his own camp, at any rate, is a very blind and ignorant person! Reader, if you love life, *beware of formality!*

Nothing is so **dangerous** to a man's own soul. Familiarity with the form of religion, while we neglect its reality — has a fearfully deadening effect on the conscience. It brings up by degrees a thick crust of *insensibility* over the whole inner man. None seem to become so desperately hard, as those who are continually repeating holy words and handling holy things, while their hearts are running after sin and the world. Landlords who only go to church formally, to set an example to their tenants; masters who have family prayers formally, to keep up a good appearance in their households; unconverted clergymen, who are every week reading prayers and lessons of Scripture in which they feel no real interest; unconverted clerks, who are constantly reading responses and saying "Amen," without feeling what they say; unconverted singers, who sing the most spiritual hymns every Sunday, merely because they have good voices, while their affections are entirely on things below — all, all, all are in solemn danger! They are gradually *hardening* their hearts, and *searing* the skin of their consciences. Reader, if you love your own soul, *beware of formality!*

Nothing, finally, is so **foolish**, **senseless**, and **unreasonable**. Can a formal Christian really suppose that the mere *outward* Christianity he professes, will comfort him in the day of sickness and the hour of death? The thing is impossible. A *painted fire* cannot warm, and a *painted banquet* cannot satisfy hunger — and a *formal religion* cannot bring peace to the soul.

Can he suppose that *God* does not see the heartlessness and deadness of his Christianity? Though he may deceive neighbors, acquaintances, fellow-worshipers, and ministers with a *form of godliness*, does he think that he can deceive God? The very idea is absurd. He who formed the eye — shall He not see? He knows the very secrets of the heart. He will judge the secrets of men at the last day. He who said to each angel of the seven churches, "I know your works," is not changed. He who said to the man without the wedding garment, "Friend, how did you get in here?" will not be deceived by a *little cloak of outward religion*. Reader, if you would not be put to shame at the last day, once more I say, *beware of formality!*

II. I pass on to the second thing which I proposed to consider. The heart is the seat of true religion — and the true Christian is the Christian in heart.

The heart is the real test of a man's **character**. It is not what he *says* or what he *does*, by which the man may be always known. He may say and do things that are right from false and unworthy motives — while his heart is altogether wrong. The *heart* is the man! "As he thinks in his heart — so is he" (Proverbs 23:7).

The heart is the right test of a man's **religion**. It is not enough that a man holds a correct creed of doctrine, and maintains a proper outward form of godliness. What is his heart? That is the grand question. This is what God looks at. "Man looks on the outward appearance — but the Lord looks on the heart!" (1 Samuel 16:7). This is what Paul lays down distinctly as the standard measure of the soul: "A man is not a Jew if he is only one outwardly, nor is circumcision merely outward and physical. No, a man is a Jew if he is one inwardly; and circumcision is circumcision of the heart, by the Spirit, not by the written code." (Romans 2:28). Who can doubt that this mighty sentence was written for *Christians* as well as for Jews? He is a Christian, the apostle would have us know — who is one inwardly, and baptism is that of the heart.

The heart is the place where **saving religion must begin**. It is naturally *irreligious*, and must be renewed by the Holy Spirit. "A new heart will I give unto you." It is naturally *hard*, and must be made tender and broken. "I will take away the heart of stone, and I will give you a heart of flesh." "The sacrifices of God are a broken spirit — a broken and a contrite heart, O God, You will not despise." It is naturally *closed* and shut against God, and must be opened. The Lord "opened the heart" of Lydia (Ezekiel 36:26; Psalm 51:7; Acts 16:14).

The heart is the **seat of true saving faith**. "With the heart man believes unto righteousness" (Romans 10:10). A man may believe that Jesus is the Christ, as the devils do — and yet remain in his sins. He may believe that he is a sinner, and that Christ is the only Savior, and feel occasional, lazy wishes that he was a better man. But no one ever lays hold on Christ, and receives pardon and peace, until he believes with the heart. It is *heart-faith* which justifies.

The heart is the **spring of true holiness** and steady continuance in well doing. True Christians are holy, because their hearts are renewed. They obey from the heart. They do the will of God from the heart. Weak, and feeble, and imperfect as all their doings are — they please God, because they are *done from a loving heart*. He who commended the widow's mite more than all the offerings of the wealthy Jews — regards *quality* far more than *quantity*. What He likes to see is, a thing done from an honest and good heart. There is no real holiness without a right heart.

Reader, the things I am saying may sound strange. Perhaps they run counter to all your notions. Perhaps you have thought that if a man's religion is correct *outwardly* — he must be one with whom God is well pleased. You are completely mistaken! You are rejecting the whole tenor of Bible teaching. Outward correctness, without a right heart — is neither more nor less than Phariseeism! The outward things of Christianity — baptism, the Lord's Supper, Church-membership, alms-giving, and the like — will never take any man's soul to Heaven, unless his heart is right. There must be inward things, as well as outward — and it is on the inward things, that God's eyes are chiefly fixed.

Hear how Paul teaches us about this matter, in three most striking texts. "In Jesus Christ neither circumcision avails anything, nor uncircumcision — but faith which works by love." "In Christ Jesus neither circumcision avails anything, nor uncircumcision, but a new creature." "Circumcision is nothing, and uncircumcision is nothing — but the keeping of the commandments of God" (Galatians 5:6; Galatians 6:5; 1 Corinthians 7:9). Did the Apostle only mean in these texts, that circumcision was no longer needed under the Gospel? Was that all? No, indeed! I believe he meant much more. He meant that true religion did not consist of *forms*, and that its essence was something far greater than being circumcised or not circumcised. He meant that under Christ Jesus, everything depended on being born again — on having true saving faith — on being holy in life and conduct. He meant that these are the things we ought to look at chiefly, and not at outward forms. "Am I a new creature? Do I really believe on Christ? Am I a holy man?" These are the *grand questions* that I must seek to answer.

When the heart is wrong — all is wrong in God's sight! Many right things may be done. The forms and ordinances which God Himself has appointed may seem to be honored. But so long as the heart is at fault, God is not pleased. He will have man's heart — or nothing.

The *ark* was the most sacred thing in the Jewish tabernacle. On it was the mercy-seat. Within it were the tables of the law, written by God's own finger. The High Priest alone was allowed to go into the place where it was kept, within the veil, and that only once every year. The presence of the ark with the camp was thought to bring a special blessing. And yet this very ark could do the Israelites no more good than any common wooden box — when they trusted to it like an idol, with their hearts full of wickedness. They brought it over into the camp, on a special occasion, saying, "Let us fetch the ark, that it may save us out of the hand of our enemies" (1 Samuel 4:3). When it came into the camp, they showed it all reverence and honor. "They shouted with a great shout, so that the earth rang again." But it was all in vain! They were smitten before the Philistines and the ark itself was captured. And why was this? It was because their religion was a *mere form.* They honored the *ark* — but did not give the *God* of the ark their hearts.

There were kings of Judah and Israel who did many things that were right in God's sight — and yet were never written in the list of godly and righteous men. *Rehoboam* began well, and for three years walked in the way of David and Solomon" (2 Chronicles 11:17). But afterwards he did evil, because he prepared not his *heart* to seek the Lord" (2 Chronicles 12. 14). Abijah, in Chronicles, said many things that were right, and fought successfully against Jeroboam. Nevertheless the general verdict is against him. We read, in Kings, that "his *heart* was not perfect with the Lord His God" (1 Kings 15:3). *Amaziah,* we are expressly told, "did that which was right in the sight of the Lord — but not with a perfect *heart*" (2 Chronicles 25:2). *Jehu,* King of Israel, was raised up, by God's command, to put down idolatry. He was a man of special zeal in doing God's work. But unhappily it is written of him, "he took no heed to walk in the law of the Lord God of Israel with all his *heart* — for he departed not from the sins of Jeroboam, who made Israel to sin" (2 Kings 10:31). In short, one general remark applies to all these Kings. They were all *wrong inwardly.* They were *rotten at heart.*

There are places of worship at this very day, where all the outward things of religion are done to perfection. The *building* is beautiful. The *service* is beautiful. The *singing* is beautiful. The *forms of devotion* are beautiful. There is everything to gratify the senses. Eye, and ear, and natural sentimentality are all pleased. But all this time, God is not pleased. One thing is lacking, and the lack of that one thing spoils all. What is that one thing? It is heart! God sees, under all this fair outward show — the *form* of religion put in the place of the *substance*; and when He sees that, He is displeased. He sees nothing with an eye of favor in the building, the service, the pastor, or the people — if He does not see converted, renewed, broken, penitent hearts. Bowed heads, bended knees, loud *amens* — all, all are nothing in God's sight, without right hearts.

When the heart is right — God can look over many things that are defective. There may be faults in judgment, and infirmities in practice. There may be many deviations from the best course in the outward things of religion. But if the heart is sound in the main, God is not extreme to mark that which is amiss. He is merciful and gracious, and will pardon much that is imperfect — when He sees a true heart and a single eye.

Jehoshaphat and Asa were Kings of Judah, who were defective in many things. *Jehoshaphat* was a timid, irresolute man, who joined affinity with Ahab, the wickedest king that ever reigned over Israel. *Asa* was an unstable man, who at one time trusted in the King of Syria more than in God, and at another time was angry with God's prophet for rebuking him (2 Chronicles 16:10). Yet both of them had one great redeeming point in their characters. With all their faults — they had right hearts!

The Passover kept by *Hezekiah* was one at which there were many irregularities. The proper forms were not observed by many. They ate the Passover "otherwise than the commandment" ordered. But they did it with true and honest hearts. And we read that Hezekiah prayed for them, saying, "The good Lord pardon every one who prepares his heart to seek God, though he be not cleansed according to the purification of the sanctuary. And the Lord hearkened to Hezekiah, and healed the people" (2 Chronicles 30:18-20).

The Passover kept by *Josiah* must have been far smaller and worse attended than scores of Passovers in the days of David and Solomon, or even in the reign of Jehoshaphat and Hezekiah. How then can we account for the strong language used in Scripture about it? "There was no Passover like to that kept in Israel, from the days of Samuel the prophet; neither did all the Kings of Israel keep such a Passover as Josiah kept!" (2 Chronicles 35:18). There is but one explanation. There never was a Passover at which the *hearts* of the worshipers were so truly in the feast. The Lord does not look at the *quantity* of worshipers

— so much as the *quality*. The glory of Josiah's Passover, was the state of people's hearts.

There are many assemblies of Christian worshipers on earth, at this very day, in which there is literally nothing to attract the natural man. They meet in miserable dirty chapels — or in wretched upper rooms and cellars. They sing unmusically. They hear feeble prayers, and more feeble sermons. And yet the Holy Spirit is often in the midst of them! Sinners are often converted in them, and the kingdom of God prospers far more than in any grand Roman Catholic cathedral, or than many gorgeous Protestant churches. How is this? How can it be explained? The cause is simply thus: that in these humble assemblies, heart-religion is taught and held. Heart-work is aimed at. Heart-work is honored. And the consequence is, that God is pleased and grants His blessing.

Reader, I leave this part of my subject here. I ask you to weigh well the things that I have been saying. I believe that they will bear examination, and are all true. Resolve this day, whatever Church you belong to — to be a Christian in heart. Whether Episcopalian or Presbyterian, Baptist or Independent — be not content with a mere *form of godliness*, without the power. Settle it down firmly in your minds, that *formal* religion is not saving religion, and that *heart* religion is the only religion that leads to Heaven.

I only give you one word of *caution*. Do not suppose because formal religion will not save, that forms of religion are of no use at all. Beware of any such senseless extreme. The *misuse* of a thing is no argument against the *right use* of it. The *blind idolatry of forms* which prevails in some quarters, is no reason why you should throw all forms aside. The ark, when made an idol of by Israel and put in the place of God, was unable to save them from the Philistines. And yet the same ark, when irreverently and profanely handled, brought death on Uzza; and when honored and reverenced, brought a blessing on the house of Obed-Edom. These words are strong, but true: "He who has but a form — is a hypocrite; but he who has not a form — is an Atheist" (Hall's sermons, No. 28). Forms cannot *save* us — but they are not therefore to be *despised*. A lantern is not a man's home — and yet it is a *help* to a man if he travels towards his home in a dark night. Use the forms of Christianity diligently — and you will find them a blessing. Only remember, in all your use of forms, the great principle, that *the first thing in religion is the state of the heart.*

I come now to the last thing which I proposed to consider.

III. I said that true religion must never expect to be *popular*. It will not have the praise of *man* — but of *God*.

Reader, I dare not turn away from this part of my subject, however painful it may be. As anxious as I am to commend heart-religion to every one who reads this tract — I will not try to conceal what heart-religion entails. I will not gain a recruit for my Master's army under false pretenses. I will not promise anything which the Scripture does not warrant. The words of Paul are clear and unmistakable. Heart-religion is a religion "whose praise is not of men — but of God" (Romans 2:29).

God's truth and Scriptural Christianity are never really *popular*. They never have been. They never will be, as long as the world stands. No one can calmly consider what *human nature* is, as described in the Bible — and reasonably expect anything else. As long as man is what man is — the majority of mankind will always like a *religion of form,* far better than a religion of heart.

Formal religion just suits an unenlightened conscience. Some religion a man will have. Atheism and downright infidelity, as a general rule, are never very popular. But a man must have a religion which does not *require* much — nor *trouble* his heart much — nor interfere with his *sins* much. Formal Christianity satisfies him. It seems the very thing that he needs.

Formal religion *gratifies the secret self-righteousness* of man. We are, all of us, more or less Pharisees. We all naturally cling to the idea that the way to be saved is to *do* so many religious things, and *go* through so many religious observances — and that at last we shall get to Heaven. Formalism meets us here. It seems to show us a way by which we can make our own peace with God.

Formal religion *pleases the natural indolence of man.* It attaches an excessive importance to that which is the *easiest* part of Christianity — the *shell* and the *form.*

Man likes this. He hates trouble in religion. He wants something which will not meddle with his conscience and inner life. Only leave conscience alone, and, like Herod, he will "do many things." Formalism seems to open a *wider gate*, and a *more easy way* to Heaven (Mark 6:20). Facts speak louder than assertions. *Facts are stubborn things.* Look over the history of religion in every age of the world, and observe what has always been popular.

Look at the history of *Israel* from the beginning of Exodus to the end of the Acts of the Apostles — and see what has always found favor. Formalism was one main sin against which the Old Testament prophets were continually protesting. Formalism was the great plague which had overspread the Jews, when our Lord Jesus Christ came into the world.

Look at the history of the *Christian Church* after the days of the Apostles. How soon formalism ate out the life and vitality of the primitive Christians!

Look at the *middle ages*, as they are called. Formalism so

completely covered the face of Christendom that the Gospel lay as one dead.

Look, lastly, at the history of *Protestant Churches* in the three last centuries. How few are the places where religion is a living thing! How many are the countries where Protestantism is nothing more than a mere form!

There is no getting over these things. They speak with a voice of thunder. They all show that formal religion is a *popular* thing. It has the praise of man.

But why should we look at facts in history! Why should we not look at facts under our own eyes, and by our own doors? Can anyone deny that a mere outward religion, a religion of downright formality — is the religion which is popular in England at the present day? Only say your prayers — and go to church with tolerable regularity — and receive the sacrament occasionally — and the vast majority of Englishmen will set you down as *an excellent Christian*. "What more would you have?" they say: "If this is not Christianity — then what is?" To require more of anyone is thought bigotry, intolerance, fanaticism, and enthusiasm! To insinuate a doubt whether such a man as this will go to Heaven, is called the height of uncharitableness! Reader, when these things are so, it is vain to deny that formal religion is *popular*. It is popular. It always was popular. It always will be popular, until Christ comes again. It always has had, and always will have the praise of man.

Turn now to the religion of the heart, and you will hear a very different report. As a general rule, it has never had the good word of mankind. It has entailed on its professors laughter, mockery, ridicule, scorn, contempt, enmity, hatred, slander, persecution, imprisonment, and even death. Its lovers have been faithful and ardent — but they have always been few. It has never had, comparatively, the praise of man.

Heart-religion is too **humbling** to be popular. It leaves natural man no room to boast. It tells him that he is a guilty, lost, hell-deserving sinner, and that he must flee to Christ for salvation. It tells him that he is dead, and must be made alive again, and born of the Spirit. The pride of man rebels against such tidings as these. He hates to be told that his case is so bad.

Heart-religion is too **holy** to be popular. It will not leave natural man alone. It interferes with his *worldliness* and his *sins*. It requires of him things that he loathes and abominates — conversion, faith, repentance, spiritual-mindedness, Bible reading, prayer. It bids him give up many things that he loves and clings to, and cannot make up his mind to lay aside. It would be strange indeed if he *liked* it. It crosses his path as a *kill-joy* — and it is absurd to expect that he will be pleased.

Was heart-religion popular in *Old Testament* times? We find David complaining, "Those who sit in the gate speak against me; and I was the song of the drunkards" (Psalm 69:12). We find the prophets persecuted and ill-treated, because they preached against sin, and required men to give their hearts to God. Elijah, Micaiah, Jeremiah, Amos, are all cases in point. To formalism and ceremonialism, the Jews never seem to have made objection. What they did dislike, was serving God with their hearts.

Was heart-religion popular in *New Testament* times? The whole history of our Lord Jesus Christ's ministry, and the lives of His apostles, are a sufficient answer. The Scribes and Pharisees would have willingly received a Messiah who encouraged *formalism*, and a Gospel which exalted *ceremonialism*. But they could not tolerate a religion of which the first principles were *humiliation* and *holiness* of heart.

Has heart-religion ever been popular in the professing Church of Christ during the last eighteen centuries? Never hardly, except in the early centuries, when the primitive Church had not left her first love. Soon, very soon, the men who protested against *formalism* and *sacramentalism* were fiercely denounced as "troublers of Israel." Long before the Reformation, things came to this pass, that anyone who cried up heart-holiness and cried down formality, was treated as a common enemy! He was either silenced, excommunicated, imprisoned, or put to death, like John Huss. In the time of the Reformation itself, the work of Luther and his companions was carried on under an incessant storm of calumny and slander. And what was the cause? It was because they protested against formalism, ceremonialism, monkery, and priestcraft — and taught the necessity of heart-religion.

Has heart-religion ever been popular in our own land in days gone by? Never, excepting for a little season. It was not popular in the days of Queen Mary, when Latimer and his brother-martyrs were burned. It was not popular in the days of the Stuarts, when to be a *Puritan* was worse for a man than to get drunk or swear. It was not popular in the middle of last century, when Wesley and Whitfield were shut out of the Established Church. The cause of our martyred Reformers, of the early Puritans, and of the Methodists, was essentially one and the same. They were all hated because they preached the *uselessness of formalism*, and the impossibility of salvation without repentance, faith, regeneration, and holiness of heart.

Is heart-religion popular in England at this very day? I answer sorrowfully that I do not believe it! Look at the followers of it among the *laity*. They are always comparatively few in number. They stand alone in their respective congregations and parishes. They have to put up with many hard things, hard words, hard imputations, hard treatment, laughter, ridicule, slander, and petty persecution. This is not popularity!

Look at the teachers of heart-religion in the *pulpit*. They are loved and liked, no doubt, by the few hearers who agree with them. They are sometimes admired for their talents and eloquence by the many who do not agree with them. They are even called popular preachers, because of the crowds who listen to their preaching. But none know so well as the faithful teachers of heart-religion, that few really *like* them. Few really *help* them. Few *sympathize* with them. Few stand by them in any time of need. They find, like their Divine Master, that they must work almost alone. I write these things with sorrow — but I believe they are true. Real heart-religion at this day, no less than in days gone by, has not "the praise of man."

But after all, it signifies little what *man* thinks, and what man praises. He who judges us is the Lord. *Man* will not judge us at the last day. Man will not sit on the great white throne, examine our religion, and pronounce our eternal sentence. Those only whom God commends, will be commended at the bar of Christ. Here lies the value and glory of heart-religion. It may not have the praise of man — but it has "the praise of God."

God approves and honors heart-religion in the present life. He looks down from Heaven, and reads the hearts of all men. Wherever He sees . . .
heart-repentance for sin,
heart-faith in Christ,
heart-holiness of life,
heart-love to His Son, His law, His will, and His word
— wherever God sees these things, He is well pleased. He writes a book of remembrance for that man, however poor and unlearned he may be. He gives His angels special charge over him. He maintains in him the work of grace, and gives him daily supplies of peace, hope, and strength. He regards him as a member of His own dear Son, as one who is witnessing for the truth, as His Son did. As weak as the man's heart may seem to himself, it is the *living sacrifice* which God loves, and the heart which He has solemnly declared He will not despise. Reader, such praise is worth more than the praise of man!

God will proclaim His approval of heart religion before the assembled world at the *last day*. He will command His angels to gather together His saints, from every part of the globe, into one glorious company. He will raise the dead and change the living — and place them at the right hand of His beloved Son's throne. Then all who have served Christ with the *heart* shall hear Him say, "Come, you who are blessed of My Father — receive the kingdom prepared for you from the foundation of the world! You were faithful over few things — and I will make you rulers over many things; enter into the joy of your Lord. You confessed Me before men, and I will confess you before My Father and His holy angels. I appoint unto you a kingdom!"

Reader, these words will be addressed to none but those who have given Christ their hearts! They will not be addressed to the formalist, the hypocrite, the wicked, and the ungodly. They will, indeed, stand by, and see the *fruits* of heart-religion — but they will not eat of them. We shall never know the full value of heart-religion until the last day. Then, and only then, we shall fully understand how much better it is to have the praise of God, than the praise of man.

Reader, if you take up heart-religion, I cannot promise you the praise of man. Pardon, peace, hope, guidance, comfort consolation, grace according to your need, strength according to your day, joy which the world can neither give nor take away — all this I can boldly promise to the man who comes to Christ, and serves Him with his heart. But I cannot promise him that his religion will be *popular* with man. I would rather warn him to expect mockery and ridicule, slander and unkindness, opposition and persecution. There is a *cross* belonging to heart-religion, and we must be content to *carry* it. "Through much tribulation, we must enter the kingdom." "All who will live godly in Christ Jesus shall suffer persecution" (Acts 14:22; 2 Tim. 3:12). But if the world hates you — God will love you. If the world forsakes you — Christ has promised that He will never forsake and never fail. Reader, whatever you may lose by heart-religion, be sure that the praise of God will make up for all.

And now I close this tract with three plain words of ***APPLICATION***. I want it to strike and stick to the conscience of every one into whose hands it falls. May God make it a blessing to many a soul, both in time and eternity!

1. Reader, is your religion a matter of form and not of heart? Answer this question honestly, and as in the sight of God. If it is, consider solemnly the *immense danger* in which you stand.

You have got nothing to *comfort* your soul in the day of trial, nothing to give you *hope* on your death-bed, nothing to *save* you at the last day. *Formal religion never took any man to Heaven.* Like base metal, it will not stand the fire. Continuing in your present state, you are in imminent peril of being lost forever.

Reader, I earnestly beseech you this day to know your danger, to open your eyes and repent. Churchman or Dissenter, high church or low church, if you have only a *name to live*, and a *form of godliness* without the power — awake and repent. Awake, above all, if you are an *Evangelical formalist*. "There is no devil," said the quaint old Puritans, "like a *white* devil." There is no formalism so dangerous — as Evangelical formalism.

I can only warn you. I do so with all affection. God alone can apply the warning to your soul. Oh, that you would see the *folly* as well as the *danger* of a *heartless Christianity!* It was sound advice which a dying man once gave to his son: "Son," he said, "whatever religion you have, never be content with wearing a *cloak*."

2. Reader, if your heart condemns you, and you wish to know what to do, consider seriously the only course that you can safely take.

Apply to the Lord Jesus Christ without delay, and spread before Him the state of your soul. Confess before Him your formality in time past, and ask Him to forgive it. Seek from Him the promised grace of the Holy Spirit, and entreat Him to quicken and renew your inward man.

The Lord Jesus is appointed and commissioned to be the *Physician of man's soul.* There is no case too hard for Him. There is no condition of soul which He cannot cure. Seared and hardened as the heart of a formalist may be — there is balm in Gilead which can heal him, and a Physician who is mighty to save. Reader, go and call on the Lord Jesus Christ this very day. "Ask, and it shall be given you; seek, and you shall find; knock, and it shall be opened unto you" (Luke 11:9).

3. Reader, if your heart condemns you not, and you have real well-grounded confidence towards God, consider seriously the many *responsibilities* of your position.

Praise Him daily who has called you out of darkness into light, and made you to differ. Praise Him daily, and ask Him never to forsake the work of His own hands.

Watch with a jealous watchfulness every part of your inward man. Formality is ever ready to come in upon us, like the Egyptian plague of frogs, even into the king's chamber. Watch, and be on your guard. Watch over your Bible-reading, your praying — your temper and your tongue, your family life and your Sunday religion. There is nothing so good and spiritual, that we may not fall into *formal habits* about it. There is none so spiritual, but that he may have a heavy fall. Watch, therefore, and be on your guard.

Look forward, finally, and hope for the coming of the Lord. *Your best things are yet to come!* The second coming of Christ will soon be here. The time of temptation will soon be past and gone. The judgment and reward of the saints shall soon make amends for all. Rest in the hope of that day. Work, watch, and look forward. One thing, at any rate, that day will make abundantly clear. It will show that there was never an hour in our lives in which we gave our hearts too thoroughly to Christ!

THE WORLD

"Therefore **come out from among them and be separate**, says the Lord. Touch no unclean thing, and I will receive you. I will be a Father to you, and you will be my sons and daughters, says the Lord Almighty." 2 Corinthians 6:17-18

The text which heads this page touches a subject of vast importance in religion. That subject is the great duty of *separation from the world.* This is the point which Paul had in view when he wrote to the Corinthians, "Come out — be separate."

The subject is one which demands the best attention of all who profess and call themselves Christians. In every age of the Church, *separation from the world* has always been one of the grand evidences of a work of grace in the heart. He who has been really born of the Spirit, and made a new creature in Christ Jesus, has always endeavored to "come out from the world," and live a separate life. They who have only had the *name* of Christian, without the *reality*, have always refused to "come out and be separate" from the world.

The subject perhaps was never more important than it is at the present day. There is a widely-spread desire to make things *pleasant* in religion — to *saw off the corners and edges of the cross*, and to avoid, as far as possible, self-denial. On every side we hear professing Christians declaring loudly that we must not be "narrow and exclusive," and that there is no harm in many things which the holiest saints of old thought bad for their souls. That we may . . .

go anywhere,
and *do* anything,
and spend our *time* in anything,
and *read* anything,
and keep any *company*,
and plunge into anything —
and all the while may be very good Christians! This, this is the maxim of thousands. In a day like this, I think it good to raise a warning voice, and invite attention to the teaching of God's Word. It is written in that Word, "Come out — and be separate."

There are *four points* which I shall try to show my readers, in examining this mighty subject.

I. First, I shall try to show that the world is a source of great danger to the soul.

II. Secondly, I shall try to show what is *not* meant by separation from the world.

III. Thirdly, I shall try to show in what *real* separation from the world consists.

IV. Fourthly, I shall try to show the *secret of victory* over the world.

And now, before I go a single step further, let me warn every reader of this paper that he will never understand this subject, unless he first understands what a true Christian is. If you are one of those unhappy people who think everybody is a Christian who goes to a place of worship, no matter how he lives, or what he believes — I fear you will care little about *separation from the world.* But if you read your Bible, and are in earnest about your soul — you will know that there are two classes of *professing Christians* — converted and unconverted. You will know that what the Jews were among the nations under the Old Testament — this the true Christian is meant to be under the New. You will understand what I mean when I say that true Christians are meant, in like manner, to be a "peculiar people" under the Gospel, and that there must be a *difference* between believers and unbelievers. To you, therefore, I make a special appeal this day. While many avoid the subject of *separation from the world,* and many positively hate it; and many are puzzled by it — give me your attention while I try to show you "the thing as it is."

I. First of all, let me show that the world is a source of great DANGER to the soul.

By "the world," be it remembered, I do not mean the *material* world on the face of which we are living and moving. He who pretends to say that anything which God has created in the Heavens above, or the earth beneath, is in itself harmful to man's soul — says that which is unreasonable and absurd. On the contrary, the sun, moon, and stars — the mountains, the valleys, and the plains — the seas, lakes, and rivers — the animal and vegetable creation — all are in themselves "very good." (Genesis 1:31.) All are full of lessons of God's wisdom and power, and all proclaim daily, "The hand that made us is Divine!" The idea that "matter" is in itself sinful and evil — is a foolish heresy.

When I speak of "the world" in this paper, I mean those people who think only, or chiefly, of this world's things, and neglect the world to come — the people who are always thinking . . .
more of *earth* than of Heaven,
more of *time* than of eternity,
more of the *body* than of the soul,
more of pleasing *man* than of pleasing God.

It is of them and their ways, habits, customs, opinions, practices, tastes, aims, spirit, and tone — that I am speaking when I speak of "the world." This is the world from which Paul tells us to "Come out — and be separate."

Now that "the world," in this sense, is an enemy to the soul, the well-known Church Catechism teaches us at its very beginning. It tells us that there are three things which a Christian is bound to renounce and give up, and three enemies which he ought to fight with and resist. These three are the flesh, the devil, and "the world." All three are terrible foes, and all three must be overcome if we would be saved.

But, whatever men please to think about the Catechism, we shall do well to turn to the testimony of Holy Scripture. If the texts I am about to quote do not prove that the world is a source of danger to the soul, there is no meaning in words.

(a) Let us hear what the apostle *Paul* says: "Be not conformed to this world: but be you transformed by the renewing of your mind." (Romans 12:2.)

"We have received, not the spirit of the world — but the Spirit which is of God." (1 Corinthians 2:12.)

"Christ gave Himself for us, that He might deliver us from this present evil world." (Galatians 1:4.)

"In time past you walked according to the course of this world." (Ephesians 2:2.)

"Demas has forsaken me, having loved this present world." (2 Tim. 4:10.)

(b) Let us hear what the apostle *James* says: "Pure and undefiled religion before God and the Father is this: To visit the fatherless and widows in their affliction, and to keep himself unspotted from the world." (James 1:27.)

"Don't you know that the friendship of the world is enmity with God? Whoever therefore will be a friend of the world is the enemy of God." (James 4:4.)

(c) Let us hear what the apostle *John* says: "Love not the world, neither the things that are in the world. If any man loves the world — the love of the Father is not in him. For all that is in the world, the lust of the flesh, and the lust of the eyes, and the pride of life, is not of the Father — but is of the world. And the world passes away, and the lust thereof; but he who does the will of God abides forever." (1 John 2:15-17.)

"The world knows us not, because it knew Him not." (1 John 3:1.)

"They are of the world: therefore speak they of the world, and the world hears them." (1 John 4:5.)

"Whatever is born of God *overcomes* the world." (1 John 5:4.)

"We know that we are of God — and the whole world lies in wickedness." (1 John 5:19.)

(d) Let us hear, lastly, what the *Lord Jesus Christ* says: "The cares of this world choke the Word, and it becomes unfruitful." (Matthew 13:22.)

"You are of this world — I am not of this world." (John 8:23.)

"The Spirit of truth; whom the world cannot receive, because it sees Him not, neither knows Him." (John 14:17.)

"If the world hates you, you know that it hated Me before it hated you." (John 15:18.)

"If you were of the world, the world would love his own: but because you are not of the world — but I have chosen you out of the world, therefore the world hates you." (John 15:19.)

"In the world you shall have tribulation: but be of good cheer; I have overcome the world." (John 16:33.)

"They are not of the world, even as I am not of the world." (John 17:16.)

I make no comment on these twenty-one texts. They speak for themselves. If anyone can read them carefully, and fail to see that "the world" is an *enemy* to the Christian's soul, and that there is an utter *opposition* between the friendship of the world and the friendship of Christ — he is past the reach of argument, and it is a waste of time to reason with him. To my eyes they contain a lesson as clear as the sun at noon day.

I turn from *Scripture* to matters of *fact* and *experience*. I appeal to any old Christian who keeps his eyes open, and knows what is going on in the Churches. I ask him whether it be not true that nothing damages the cause of religion so much as "the world"? It is not *open sin*, or open unbelief, which robs Christ of His professing servants — so much as . . .
the *love* of the world,
the *fear* of the world,
the *cares* of the world,
the *business* of the world,
the *money* of the world,
the *pleasures* of the world, and
the desire to *keep in* with the world.

The world is the *great rock* on which thousands of young people are continually making shipwreck. They do not object to any article of the Christian faith. They do not deliberately choose evil, and openly rebel against God. They hope somehow to get to Heaven at last; and they think it proper to have *some* religion. But they cannot give up their idol — they must have the world. And so after running well and bidding fair for Heaven, while boys and girls — they turn aside when they become men and women, and go down the *broad way* which leads to destruction. They begin with Abraham and Moses — -and end with *Demas* and *Lot's wife*.

The last day alone will prove how many souls "the world" has slain. Hundreds will be found to have been trained in religious families, and to have known the Gospel from their very childhood — and yet missed Heaven. They left the harbor of home with bright prospects, and launched forth on the *ocean of life* with a father's blessing and a mother's prayers, and then got out of the right course through the seductions of the world, and ended their voyage in shallows and in misery! It is a sorrowful story to tell; but, alas, it is only too common. I cannot wonder that Paul says, "Come out — and be separate."

II. Let me now try to show what does NOT constitute separation from the world.

The point is one which requires clearing up. There are many mistakes made about it. You will sometimes see sincere and well-meaning Christians doing things which God never intended them to do, in the matter of separation from the world, and honestly believing that they are in the *path of duty*. Their mistakes often do great harm. They give occasion to the wicked to ridicule all religion, and supply them with an excuse for having none. They cause the way of truth to be evil spoken of, and add to the *offence* of the cross. I think it a plain duty to make a few remarks on the subject. We must never forget that it is possible to be very much in earnest, and to think we are "doing God service" — when in reality, we are making some great mistake. There is such a thing as "zeal not according to knowledge." (John 16:2, Romans 10:2.) There are few things about which it is so important to pray for a right judgment and sanctified common sense, as about separation from the world.

(a) When Paul said, "Come out — and be separate," he did not mean that Christians ought to give up all worldly callings, trades, professions, and business. He did not forbid men to be soldiers, sailors, lawyers, doctors, merchants, bankers, shop-keepers, or tradesmen. There is not a word in the New Testament to justify such a line of conduct. Cornelius the centurion, Luke the physician, Zenas the lawyer, are examples to the contrary. Idleness is in itself a sin. A solemn calling is a remedy against temptation. "If any man will not work — neither shall he eat." (2 Thessalonians 3:10.) To give up any business of life, which is not necessarily sinful, to the wicked and the devil, from fear of getting harm from it — is lazy, cowardly conduct. The right plan is to *carry our religion into our business*, and not to give up business under the specious pretense that it interferes with our religion.

(b) When Paul said, "Come out — and be separate," he did not mean that Christians ought to decline all fellowship with unconverted people, and refuse to go into their society. There is no warrant for such conduct in the New Testament. Our Lord and His disciples did not refuse to go to a marriage feast, or to sit at a Pharisee's table. Paul does not say, "If any of those who believe not bid you to a feast," you must not go — but only tells us how to behave if we do go. (1 Corinthians

10:27.) Moreover, it is a dangerous thing to begin judging people too closely, and settling who are converted and who are not, and what society is godly and what ungodly. We are sure to make mistakes. Above all, such a course of life would cut us off from many opportunities of doing good. If we carry our Master with us wherever we go — who can tell but we may "save some," and get no harm? (1 Corinthians 9:22.)

(c) When Paul says, "Come out — and be separate," he did not mean that Christians ought to take no interest in anything on earth except religion. To neglect science, art, literature, and politics, to read nothing which is not directly spiritual — to know nothing about what is going on among mankind, and never to look at a newspaper — to care nothing about the government of one's country, and to be utterly indifferent as to the people who guide its counsels and make its laws — all this may seem very right and proper in the eyes of some people. But I think that it is an idle, selfish neglect of duty.

Paul knew the value of good government, as one of the main helps to our "living a quiet and peaceable life in godliness and honesty." (1 Tim. 2:2.) Paul was not ashamed to read heathen writers, and to quote their words in his speeches and writings. Paul did not think it beneath him to show an acquaintance with the laws and customs and callings of the world, in the illustrations he gave from them. Christians who plume themselves on their *ignorance of secular things* are precisely the Christians who bring religion into contempt! I knew the case of a blacksmith who would not come to hear his clergyman preach the Gospel, until he found out that he knew the properties of iron. Then he came.

(d) When Paul said, "Come out — and be separate," he did not mean that Christians should be singular, eccentric, and peculiar in their dress, manners, demeanor, and voice. Anything which *attracts notice* in these matters is most objectionable, and ought to be carefully avoided. To wear clothes of such a color, or made in such a fashion, that when you go into company — every eye is fixed on you, and you are the object of general observation — is an enormous mistake. It gives occasion to the wicked to ridicule religion, and looks *self-righteous* and *affected*. There is not the slightest proof that our Lord and His apostles, and Priscilla, and Persis, and their companions, did not dress and behave just like others in their own ranks of life.

On the other hand, one of the many charges our Lord brings against the Pharisees was that of "making broad their phylacteries, and enlarging the borders of their garments," so as to be "seen by men." (Matthew 23:5.) True sanctity and *sanctimoniousness* — are entirely different things. Those who try to show their unworldliness by wearing conspicuously ugly clothes, or by speaking in a whining, snuffling voice, or by affecting an unnatural slavishness, humility, and gravity of manner — miss their mark altogether, and only give occasion to the enemies of the Lord to blaspheme.

(e) When Paul said, "Come out — and be separate," he did not mean that Christians ought to retire from the company of mankind, and shut themselves up in *solitude*. It is one of the crying errors of the Church of Rome, to suppose that eminent holiness is to be attained by such monkish practices. It is the unhappy delusion of the whole army of monks, nuns, and hermits. Separation of this kind is not according to the mind of Christ. He says distinctly in His last prayer, "I pray not that You should take them *out* of the world — but that You should keep them from the evil." (John 17:15.) There is not a word in the Acts or Epistles to recommend *such* a separation.

True believers are always represented as mixing in the world, doing their duty in it, and glorifying God by patience, meekness, purity, and courage in their several positions — and not by cowardly desertion of them. Moreover, it is foolish to suppose that we can keep the world and the devil out of our hearts by going into holes and corners! True religion and unworldliness are best seen, not in timidly *forsaking* the post which God has allotted to us — but in manfully standing our ground, and showing the power of grace to *overcome* evil.

(f) Last — but not least, when Paul said, "Come out — and be separate," he did not mean that Christians ought to withdraw from every Church in which there are unconverted members, or to refuse to worship in company with any who are not believers, or to keep away from the Lord's table if any ungodly people go up to it. This is a very common but a very grievous mistake. There is not a text in the New Testament to justify it, and it ought to be condemned as a pure invention of man. Our Lord Jesus Christ Himself deliberately allowed *Judas Iscariot* to be an apostle for three years, and gave him the Lord's Supper. He has taught us, in the parable of the wheat and tares, that converted and unconverted will be "together until the harvest," and cannot be divided. (Matthew 13:30.) In His Epistles to the Seven Churches, and in all Paul's Epistles, we often see faults and corruptions mentioned and reproved; but we are never told that they justify *desertion* of the assembly, or neglect of ordinances. In short, we must not look for a perfect Church, a perfect congregation, and a perfect company of communicants, until the marriage supper of the Lamb.

If others are unworthy Churchmen, or unworthy partakers of the Lord's Supper — the sin is theirs and not ours: we are not their judges. But to separate ourselves from Church assemblies, and deprive ourselves of Christian ordinances, because others use them unworthily — is to take up a foolish, unreasonable, and unscriptural position. It is not the mind of Christ, and it certainly is not Paul's idea of separation from the world.

I commend these six points to the calm consideration of all who wish to understand the subject of separation from the world. About each and all of them, far more might be said than I have space to say in this paper. About each and all of them, I have seen so many mistakes made, and so much misery and unhappiness caused by those mistakes — that I want to put Christians on their guard. I want them not to take up positions hastily, in the zeal of their first love, which they will afterwards be obliged to give up.

I leave this part of my subject with *two pieces of advice*, which I offer especially to **young** Christians.

I advise them, for one thing, if they really desire to come out from the world, to remember that the *shortest* path is not always the path of duty. To quarrel with all our unconverted relatives, to "cut" all our old friends, to withdraw entirely from mixed society, to live an exclusive life, to give up every act of courtesy and civility in order that we may devote ourselves to the direct work of Christ — all this may seem very right, and may satisfy our consciences and save us trouble. But I think that it is often a selfish, lazy, self-pleasing line of conduct — and that the *true cross* and true line of duty, may be to adopt a very different course of action.

I advise them, for another thing, if they want to come out from the world, to watch against a sour, morose, uncongenial, gloomy, unpleasant, bearish demeanor — and never to forget that there is such a thing as "winning without the Word." (1 Peter 3:1.) Let them strive to show unconverted people that their principles, whatever may be thought of them — make them cheerful, amiable, good-tempered, unselfish, considerate for others, and ready to take an interest in everything that is innocent and of good report. In short, let there be no *needless separation* between us and the world. In many things, as I shall soon show, we must be separate; but let us take care that it is separation of the right sort. If the world is offended by such separation, we cannot help it. But let us never give the world occasion to say that our separation is foolish, senseless, ridiculous, unreasonable, uncharitable, and unscriptural.

III. In the third place, I shall try to show what true separation from the world really is.

I take up this branch of my subject with a very deep sense of its *difficulty*. That there is a certain line of conduct which all true Christians ought to pursue with respect to "the world, and the things of the world," is very evident. The texts already quoted make that plain. The key to the solution of that question lies in the word "separation." But in what separation consists, it is not easy to show. On some points it is not hard to lay down *particular rules;* on others it is impossible to do more than state *general principles,* and leave everyone to apply them according to his position in life. This is what I shall now attempt to do.

(a) First and foremost, he who desires to "come out from the world, and be separate," must steadily and habitually refuse to be *guided by the world's standard of right and wrong*.

The rule of the bulk of mankind is . . .
to *go with the stream*,
to do as others,
to follow the fashions of the times,
to keep in with the common opinion,
and to set your watch by the town-clock.

The true Christian will never be content with such a rule as that. He will simply ask: What do the Scriptures say? What is written in the Word of God? He will maintain firmly that nothing can be right — which God says is wrong; and that the customs and opinions of his neighbors, can never make that to be a trifle — which God calls serious; or that to be no sin — which God calls sin. He will never think lightly of such sins as drinking, swearing, gambling, lying, cheating, swindling, or breach of the seventh commandment, because they are *common*, and many say, "Where is the mighty harm?" That miserable argument, "Everybody *thinks* so, everybody *says* so, everybody *does* it, everybody will be there" — goes for nothing with him. Is it *condemned* or *approved* by the Bible? That is his only question. If he stands *alone* in the parish, or town, or congregation — he will not go against the Bible. If he has to come out from the crowd, and take a position by himself — he will not flinch from it, rather than disobey the Bible. This is genuine Scriptural separation.

(b) He who desires to "come out from the world and be separate," must be *very careful how he spends his leisure time.*

This is a point which at first sight appears of little importance. But the longer I live, the more I am persuaded that it deserves most serious attention. Honorable occupation and honest business are a great safeguard to the soul, and the time that is spent upon them is comparatively the time of our least danger. The devil finds it hard to get a hearing from a *busy man*. But when the day's work is over, and the time of *leisure* arrives — then comes the hour of temptation.

I do not hesitate to warn every man who wants to live a Christian life, to be very careful how he spends his *evenings*. Evening is the time when we are naturally disposed to *unbend* after the labors of the day; and evening is the time when the Christian is too often tempted to lay aside his armor, and consequently brings trouble on his soul. "Then comes the devil," and with the devil — the world. Evening is the time when the poor man is tempted to go to the ale-house, and fall into sin.

Evening is the time when the tradesman too often goes to the Inn parlor, and sits for hours hearing and seeing things which do him no good. Evening is the time which the higher classes choose for dancing, card playing, and the like; and consequently never get to bed until late at night. If we love our souls, and would not become worldly — let us mind how we spend our evenings! Tell me how a man spends his evenings — and I can generally tell what his character is.

The true Christian will do well to make it a settled rule never to waste his evenings. Whatever others may do, let him resolve always to make time for quiet, calm thought, for Bible-reading, and prayer. The rule will prove a hard one to keep. It may bring on him the charge of being unsocial and over strict. Let him not mind this. Anything of this kind is better than habitual late hours in company, hurried prayers, slovenly Bible reading, and a bad conscience. Even if he stands alone in his parish or town, let him not depart from his rule. He will find himself in a minority, and be thought a peculiar man. But this is *genuine Scriptural separation.*

(c) He who desires to "come out from the world and be separate," must steadily and habitually determine not to be swallowed up and absorbed in the business of the world.

A true Christian will strive to do his duty in whatever station or position he finds himself, and to do it well. Whether statesman, or merchant, or banker, or lawyer, or doctor, or tradesman, or farmer — he will try to do his work so that no one can find occasion for fault in him. But he will not allow it to get *between him and Christ.* If he finds his business beginning to eat up his Sundays, his Bible-reading, his private prayer, and to bring *clouds* between him and Heaven — he will say, "Stand back! There is a limit. Hitherto you may go — but no further. I cannot sell my soul for place, fame, or gold!"

Like Daniel, he will make time for his communion with God, whatever the cost may be. Like Havelock, he will deny himself anything rather than lose his Bible-reading and his prayers. In all this, he will find he stands almost alone. Many will laugh at him, and tell him they get on well enough without being so strict and particular. He will heed it not. He will resolutely hold the world at arm's length, whatever present loss or sacrifice it may seem to entail. He will choose rather to be less rich and prosperous in this world, than not to prosper about his soul. To stand alone in this way, to run counter to the ways of others, requires immense self-denial. But this is genuine Scriptural separation.

(d) He who desires to "come out from the world and be separate" must steadily abstain from all *amusements* and *recreations* which are inseparably connected with sin.

This is a hard subject to handle, and I approach it with pain. But I do not think I would be faithful to Christ, and faithful to my office as a minister — if I did not speak very plainly about it, in considering such a matter as separation from the world.

Let me, then, say honestly, that I cannot understand how anyone who makes any pretense to real vital religion, can allow himself to attend *races* and *theaters*. Conscience, no doubt, is a strange thing, and every man must judge for himself and use his liberty. One man sees no harm in things which another regards with abhorrence as evil. I can only give my own opinion for what it is worth, and entreat my readers to consider seriously what I say.

That to look at *horses running at full speed* is in itself perfectly harmless, no sensible man will pretend to deny. That many plays, such as Shakespeare's, are among the finest productions of the human intellect, is equally undeniable. But all this is beside the question. The question is whether horse-racing and theaters, as they are now conducted in England, are not inseparably bound up with things that are downright wicked. I assert without hesitation, that they are so bound up. I assert that the breach of God's commandments so invariably accompanies the race and the play, that you cannot go to the amusement without *helping sin*.

I entreat all professing Christians to remember this, and to take heed what they do. I warn them plainly that they have no right to shut their eyes to facts which every intelligent person knows, for the mere pleasure of seeing a horse-race, or listening to good actors or actresses. I warn them that they must not talk of separation from the world, if they can lend their sanction to amusements which are invariably connected with gambling, betting, drunkenness, and immorality. These are the things "which God will judge." "The end of these things is death." (Hebrews 13:4; Romans 6:21.)

Hard words these, no doubt! But are they not true? It may seem to your relatives and friends very narrow-laced, strict, and narrow — if you tell them you cannot go to the races or the theater with them. But we must fall back on first principles. Is the world a danger to the soul — or is it not? Are we to come out from the world — or are we not? These are questions which can only be answered in one way.

If we love our souls — we must have nothing to do with amusements which are bound up with sin. Nothing short of this can be called genuine scriptural separation from the world.

(e) He who desires to "come out from the world, and be separate," must be *moderate in the use of solemn and innocent recreations.*

No sensible Christian will ever think of condemning *all* recreations. In a world of wear and tear like that we live in, occasional *unbending* and *relaxation* are good for all. Body and mind alike require seasons of lighter occupation, and opportunities of letting off high spirits, and especially when they are young. Exercise itself is a positive necessity for the preservation of mental and bodily health. I see no harm in cricket, rowing, running, and other manly athletic recreations. I find no fault with those who play at chess and such-like games of skill. We are all fearfully and wonderfully made. No wonder the poet says,

"Strange that a harp of thousand strings, should keep in tune so long!"

Anything which strengthens nerves, and brain, and digestion, and lungs, and muscles, and makes us more fit for Christ's work, so long as it is not in itself sinful — is a blessing, and ought to be thankfully used. Anything which will occasionally divert our *thoughts* from their *usual grinding channel,* in a healthy manner — is a good and not an evil.

But it is the *excess* of these innocent things which a true Christian must watch against, if he wants to be separate from the world. He must not devote his whole heart, and soul, and mind, and strength, and time to them, as many do, if he wishes to serve Christ. There are hundreds of lawful things which are good in moderation — but bad when taken in excess; healthful medicine in small quantities — but downright poison when swallowed down in huge doses. In nothing is this so true as it is in the matter of recreations. The *use* of them is one thing, and the *abuse* of them is another. The Christian who uses them must know when to stop, and how to say "Stop! Enough!"

Do they interfere with his private religion? Do they take up too much of his thoughts and attention? Have they a *secularizing effect* on his soul? Have they a tendency to pull him down to earth? Then let him hold hard and take care. All this will require courage, self-denial, and firmness. It is a line of conduct which will often bring on us the ridicule and contempt of those who know not what *moderation* is, and who spend their lives in making trifles, serious things; and serious things, trifles. But if we mean to come out from the world, we must not mind this. We must be "temperate" even in lawful things, whatever others may think of us. This is genuine Scriptural separation.

(f) Last — but not least, he who desires to "come out from the world and be separate" must be careful how he allows himself in friendships, intimacies, and close relationships with worldly people.

We cannot help meeting many unconverted people as long as we live. We cannot avoid having fellowship with them, and doing business with them, unless "we go out of the world." (1 Corinthians 5:10.) To treat them with the utmost courtesy, kindness, and charity, whenever we do meet them, is a positive duty. But *acquaintance* is one thing, and *intimate friendship* is quite another. To seek their society without cause, to choose their company, to cultivate *intimacy* with them — is very dangerous to the soul.

Human nature is so constituted that we cannot be much with other people, without effect on our own character. The old proverb will never fail to prove true: "Tell me with whom a man chooses to live — and I will tell you what he is." The Scripture says expressly, "He who walks with wise men — shall be wise; but a *companion of fools* shall be destroyed." (Proverbs 13:20.) If then a Christian, who desires to live consistently, chooses for his friends those who either do not care for their souls, or the Bible, or God, or Christ, or holiness, or regard them as of secondary importance — it seems to me impossible for him to prosper in his religion. He will soon find that their *ways* are not his ways, nor their *thoughts* his thoughts, nor their *tastes* his tastes; and that, unless they change, he must give up intimacy with them.

In short, there must be separation. Of course such separation will be painful. But if we have to choose between the loss of a friend, and the injury of our souls — there ought to be no doubt in our minds. If friends will not walk in the *narrow* way with us — we must not walk in the *broad* way to please them. But let us distinctly understand, that to attempt to keep up close intimacy between a converted and an unconverted person, if both are consistent with their natures — is to attempt an *impossibility*.

The principle here laid down ought to be carefully remembered by all unmarried Christians in the choice of a husband or wife. I fear it is too often entirely forgotten. Too many seem to think of everything except religion in choosing a partner for life, or to suppose that it will come somehow as a matter of course. Yet when a praying, Bible-reading, God-fearing, Christ-loving Christian marries a person who takes no interest whatever in serious religion — what can the result be but injury to the Christian, or immense unhappiness?

Health is not *infectious* — but *disease* is. As a general rule, in such cases, the good go down to the level of the bad — and the bad do not come up to the level of the good. The subject is a delicate one, and I do not care to dwell upon it. But this I say confidently to every unmarried Christian man or woman — if you love your soul, if you do not want to fall away and backslide, if you do not want to destroy your own peace and comfort for life — resolve never to marry any person who is not a thorough Christian, whatever the resolution may cost you. You had better die — than marry an unbeliever. Stand to this resolution, and let no one ever persuade you out of it. Depart from this resolution, and you will find it almost impossible to "come out and be separate." You will find you have *tied a mill-stone around your own neck* in running the race towards Heaven; and, if saved at last, it will be "so as by fire." (1 Corinthians 3:15.)

I offer these *six general hints* to all who wish to follow Paul's advice, and to come out from the world and be separate. In giving them, I lay no claim to infallibility; but I believe they deserve consideration and attention. I do not forget that the subject is full of difficulties, and that scores of doubtful cases are continually arising in a

Christian's course, in which it is very hard to say what the *path of duty* is, and how to behave.

Perhaps the following *bits of advice* may be found useful.

In all doubtful cases, we should first pray for wisdom and sound judgment. If prayer is worth anything, it must be specially valuable when we desire to do right — but do not see our way.

In all doubtful cases, let us often try ourselves by recollecting the eye of God. Should I go to such and such a place, or do such and such a thing, if I really thought God was looking at me?

In all doubtful cases, let us never forget the second advent of Christ and the day of judgment. Would I like to be found in such and such company, or employed in such and such ways?

Finally, in all doubtful cases, let us find out what the conduct of the holiest and best Christians has been under similar circumstances. If we do not clearly see our own way, we need not be ashamed to follow *good examples.*

I throw out these suggestions for the use of all who are in difficulties about disputable points in the matter of separation from the world. I cannot help thinking that they may help to *untie many knots*, and solve many problems.

IV. I shall now conclude the whole subject by trying to show *the secrets of real victory over the world.*

To come out from the world of course is not an easy thing. It cannot be easy — so long as *human nature* is what it is, and a *busy devil* is always near us. It requires a constant struggle and exertion; it entails incessant conflict and self-denial; it often places us in exact opposition to members of our own families, to relations and neighbors; it sometimes obliges us to do things which give great offence, and bring on us ridicule and petty persecution.

It is precisely this which makes many hang back and shrink from decided religion. They know they are not right; they know that they are not so "thorough" in Christ's service as they ought to be, and they feel uncomfortable and ill at ease. But the *fear of man* keeps them back. And so they linger on through life with aching, dissatisfied hearts — with too much *religion* to be happy in the world, and too much of the *world* to be happy in their religion. I fear this is a very common case, if the truth were known.

Yet there are some in every age who seem to get the victory over the world. They come out decidedly from its ways, and are unmistakably separate. They are independent of its *opinions*, and unshaken by its *opposition*. They move on like planets in an orbit of their own, and seem to rise equally above the world's *smiles* and *frowns*. And what are the secrets of their victory? I will set them down.

(a) The first secret of victory over the world, is a *right heart*. By that I mean a heart renewed, changed and sanctified by the Holy Spirit — a heart in which Christ dwells, a heart in which old things have passed away, and all things become new. The grand mark of such a heart, is the *bias* of its tastes and affections. The owner of such a heart no longer likes the world, and the things of the world — and therefore finds it no trial or sacrifice to give them up. He has no longer any appetite for the company, the conversation, the amusements, the occupations, the books which he once loved — and to "come out" from them seems natural to him.

Great indeed is *the expulsive power of a new principle!* Just as the new spring-buds in a beech hedge push off the old leaves and make them quietly fall to the ground — so does the new heart of a believer invariably affect his tastes and likings, and make him drop many things which he once loved and lived in, because he now likes them no more.

Let him who wants to "come out from the world and be separate," make sure first and foremost that he has got a new heart. If the heart is really right — everything else will be right in time. "If your eye is single — your whole body shall be full of light." (Matthew 6:22.) If the *affections* are not right — there never will be right *action*.

(b) The second secret of victory over the world, is a lively practical *faith* in unseen things. What says the Scripture? "This is the victory that overcomes the world, even our *faith*." (1 John 5:4.) To attain and keep up the habit of looking steadily at invisible things, as if they were visible — to set before our minds every day, as grand realities, our souls, God, Christ, Heaven, Hell, judgment, eternity — to nourish an abiding conviction that spiritual realities are just as real as what we do see, and ten thousand times more important — this, this is one way to be conquerors over the world. This was the faith which made the noble army of saints, described in the eleventh chapter of Hebrews, obtain such a glorious testimony from the Holy Spirit. They all acted under a firm persuasion that they had a real *God*, a real *Savior*, and a real home in *Heaven* — though unseen by mortal eyes.

Armed with this faith, a man regards this world as a shadow, compared to the world to come, and cares little for its praise or blame, its enmity or its rewards. Let him who wants to come out from the world and be separate — but shrinks and hangs back for fear of the things seen, pray and strive to have this faith. "All things are possible to him that believes." (Mark 9:23.) Like Moses, he will find it possible to forsake Egypt, seeing Him who is invisible. Like Moses, he will not care what he loses and who is displeased — because he sees afar off, like one looking through a telescope, a substantial recompense of reward. (Hebrews 11:26.)

(c) The third and last secret of victory over the world, is to attain and cultivate the habit of boldly confessing Christ on all proper occasions. In saying this I would not be mistaken. I want no one to *blow a trumpet* before him, and thrust his religion on others at all seasons. But I do wish to encourage all who strive to come out from the world to show their colors, and to act and speak out like men who are not ashamed to serve Christ. A steady, quiet assertion of our own principles, as Christians — a habitual readiness to let the people of the world see that we are guided by other rules than they are, and do not mean to swerve from them — a calm, firm, courteous maintenance of our own standard of things in every company — all this will insensibly form a *habit* within us, and make it comparatively easy to be a *separate* man.

It will be hard at first, no doubt, and cost us many a struggle; but the longer we go on, the easier will it be. Repeated acts of confessing Christ will produce *habits.* Habits once formed will produce a *settled character*. Our characters once known, we shall be saved much trouble. Men will know what to expect from us, and will count it no strange thing if they see us living the lives of separate peculiar people. He who grasps the nettle most firmly will always be less hurt than the man who touches it with a trembling hand. It is a great thing to be able to say "No!" decidedly — but courteously, when asked to do anything which conscience says is wrong. He who shows his colors boldly from the first, and is never ashamed to let men see "whose he is and whom he serves" — will soon find that he has overcome the world, and will be let alone. Bold confession is a long step towards victory.

It only remains for me now to CONCLUDE the whole subject with a few short words of ***APPLICATION***.

The danger of the world ruining the soul,
the nature of true separation from the world,
the secrets of victory over the world —
are all before the reader of this paper. I now ask him to give me his attention for the last time, while I try to say something directly for his personal benefit.

(1) My first word shall be a QUESTION. Are you overcoming the world — or are you overcome by it? Do you know what it is to come out from the world and be separate, or are you yet entangled by it, and conformed to it? If you have any desire to be saved, I entreat you to answer this question.

If you know *nothing* of "separation," I warn you affectionately that your soul is in great danger. The world passes away; and those who cling to the world, and think only of the world — will pass away with it to everlasting ruin! Awake to know your peril before it be too late. Awake and flee from the wrath to come. The *time* is short. The *end* of all things is at hand. The shadow are lengthening. The sun is going down. The night comes, when no man can work. The great white throne will soon be set. The judgment will begin. The books will be opened. Awake, and come out from the world while it is called today!

Yet a little while, and there will be no more worldly occupations and worldly amusements — no more getting money and spending money — no more eating, and drinking, and feasting, and dressing, and ball-going, and theaters, and races, and cards, and gambling. What will you do when all these things have passed away forever? How can you possibly be happy in an eternal Heaven — where holiness is all in all, and worldliness has no place? Oh consider these things, and be wise! Awake, and break the *chains* which the world has thrown around you! Awake, and flee from the wrath to come!

(2) My second word shall be a COUNSEL. If you want to come out from the world — but know not what to do, take the advice which I give you this day. Begin by applying direct, as a penitent sinner, to our Lord Jesus Christ, and put your case in His hands. Pour out your heart before Him. Tell Him your whole story, and keep nothing back. Tell Him that you are a sinner wanting to be saved from the world, the flesh, and the devil, and entreat Him to save you.

That blessed Savior "*gave* Himself for us that He might *deliver* us from this present evil world." (Galatians 1:2.) He knows what the world is, for He lived in it thirty and three years. He knows what the difficulties of a man are, for He was made man for our sakes, and dwelt among men. High in Heaven, at the right hand of God, He is able to save to the uttermost all who come to God by Him — able to keep us from the evil of the world while we are still living in it — able to give us power to become the sons of God — able to keep us from falling — able to make us more than conquerors. Once more I say, Go directly to Christ with the prayer of faith, and put yourself wholly and unreservedly in His hands. As hard as it may seem to you now to come out from the world and be separate — you shall find that with Jesus nothing is impossible. You, even you, shall overcome the world.

(3) My third and last word shall be ENCOURAGEMENT. If you have learned by experience what it is to come out from the world, I can only say to you: Take comfort, and persevere. You are in the right road; you have no cause to be afraid. The everlasting hills are in sight. Your salvation is nearer than when you believed. Take comfort and press on.

No doubt you have had many a battle, and made many a false step. You have sometimes felt ready to faint, and been half disposed to go back to Egypt. But your Master has never entirely left you, and He will never allow you to be tempted above that you are able to bear. Then persevere steadily in your separation from the world, and never be ashamed of standing alone. Settle it firmly in your mind that the most decided Christians are always the *happiest*; and remember that no one ever said at the end of his course — that he had been too holy, and lived too near to God.

Hear, last of all, what is written in the Scriptures of truth: "I tell you the truth, no one who has left home or brothers or sisters or mother or father or children or fields for me and the gospel will fail to receive a hundred times as much in this present age (homes, brothers, sisters, mothers, children and fields — and with them, persecutions) and in the age to come, eternal life!" (Mark 10:29, 30.)

"So do not throw away your confidence; it will be richly rewarded. You need to persevere so that when you have done the will of God, you will receive what he has promised. For in just a very little while, He who is coming will come and will not delay. But my righteous one will live by faith!" (Hebrews 10:35-38.)

Those words were written and spoken for our sakes. Let us lay hold on them, and never forget them. Let us *persevere* to the end, and never be ashamed of coming out from the world, and being separate. We may be sure it brings its own reward.

N.B. Readers will observe that, under the head of *worldly amusements* — I have said nothing about ball-going, card-playing, and field-sports. They are delicate and difficult subjects, and many classes of society are not touched by them. But I am quite willing to give *my opinion*, and the more so because I do not speak of them without experience in the days of my youth.

(a) Concerning **ball-going**, I only ask Christians to judge the amusement by its *tendencies* and *accompaniments*. To say there is anything morally wrong in the mere bodily act of dancing would be absurd. David danced before the ark. Solomon said, "There is a time to dance." (Ecclesiastes 3:4.) Just as it is natural to lambs and kittens to frisk about, so it seems natural to young people, all over the world, to jump about to a lively tune of music. If dancing were taken up for mere exercise, if dancing took place at morning hours, and men only danced with men, and women with women — it would be needless and absurd to object to it. But everybody knows that this is not what is meant by *modern* ball-going. This is an amusement which involves very late hours, extravagant dressing, and an immense amount of frivolity, vanity, jealousy, unhealthy excitement, and vain conversation. Who would like to be found in a modern ball-room when the Lord Jesus Christ comes the second time? Who that has taken much part in balls, as I myself once did, before I knew better — can deny that they have a most dissipating effect on the mind, like opium-eating and alcohol-drinking on the body? I cannot withhold my opinion that ball-going is one of those worldly amusements which "war against the soul," and which it is wisest and best to give up. And as for those parents who urge their sons and daughters, against their wills and inclinations, to go to balls — I can only say that they are taking on themselves a most dangerous responsibility, and risking great injury to their children's souls.

(b) Concerning **card-playing**, my judgment is much the same. I ask Christian people to try it by its *tendencies* and *consequences*. Of course it would be nonsense to say there is positive wickedness in an innocent game of cards, for diversion, and not for money. I have known instances of old people of lethargic and infirm habit of body, unable to work or read, to whom cards in an evening were really useful, to keep them from drowsiness, and preserve their health. But it is vain to shut our eyes to facts. If masters and mistresses once begin to play cards in the parlor, servants are likely to play cards in the kitchen; and then comes in a whole train of evils. Moreover, from simple card-playing to desperate *gambling* — there is but a chain of steps. If parents teach young people that there is no harm in the first step, they must never be surprised if they go on to the last.

I give this opinion with much diffidence. I lay no claim to infallibility. Let every one be persuaded in his own mind. But, considering all things, it is my deliberate judgment that the Christian who wishes to keep his soul right, and to "come out from the world," will do wisely to have nothing to do with card-playing. It is a habit which seems to grow on some people so much that it becomes at last a necessity, and they cannot live without it. "Madam," said Romaine to an old lady at Bath, who declared she could not do without her cards, "Madam, if this is the case — then cards are your god, and your god is a very poor one." Surely in doubtful matters like these, it is well to give our souls the benefit of the doubt, and to refrain.

(c) Concerning **field-sports**, I admit that it is not easy to lay down a strict rule. I cannot go the length of some, and say that galloping across country, or shooting grouse, partridges, or pheasants, or catching salmon or trout — are in themselves positively sinful occupations, and distinct marks of an unconverted heart. There are many people, I know, to whom rigorous out-door exercise and complete diversion of mind are absolute necessities, for the preservation of their bodily and mental health. But in all these matters the chief question is one of *degree*. Much depends on the company men are thrown into, and the extent to which the thing is carried. The great danger lies in *excess*. It is possible to be *intemperate* about hunting and shooting — as well as about eating and drinking. We are commanded in Scripture to be "temperate in all things," if we would so run as to obtain; and those who are addicted to field-sports should not forget this rule.

The question, however, is one about which Christians must be careful in expressing an opinion, and moderate in their judgments. The man who can neither ride, nor shoot, nor throw a fly — is hardly qualified to speak dispassionately about such matters. It is cheap and easy work to condemn others for doing things which you cannot do yourself, and are utterly unable to enjoy! One thing only is perfectly certain — all *intemperance* or *excess* is sin. The man who is wholly absorbed in sports, and spends all his years in such a manner that he seems to think God only created him to be a "hunting, shooting, and fishing animal," is a man who at present knows very little of Scriptural Christianity. It is written, "Where your treasure is — there will your heart be also." (Matthew 6:21.)

RICHES AND POVERTY

"There was a *rich man* who was dressed in purple and fine linen and lived in luxury every day. At his gate was laid a *beggar* named Lazarus, covered with sores and longing to eat the crumbs which fell from the rich man's table. Even the dogs came and licked his sores.

The time came when the beggar died and the angels carried him to Abraham's bosom. The rich man also died and was buried. In Hell, where he was in torment, he looked up and saw Abraham far away, with Lazarus by his side. So he called to him, 'Father Abraham, have pity on me and send Lazarus to dip the tip of his finger in water and cool my tongue, because I am in agony in this fire.'

But Abraham replied, 'Son, remember that in your lifetime you received your good things, while Lazarus received bad things, but now he is comforted here and you are in agony!" Luke 16:19-25

There are probably few readers of the Bible who are not familiar with the *parable of the Rich Man and Lazarus*. It is one of those passages of Scripture which leave an indelible impression on the mind. Like the parable of the Prodigal Son — once read it is never forgotten.

The reason of this is clear and simple. The whole parable is a most *vividly painted picture*. The story, as it goes on, carries our senses with it with irresistible power. Instead of *readers*, we become *lookers*. We are witnesses of all the events described. We see. We hear. We imagine we could almost touch. The rich man's banquet — the purple — the fine linen — the gate — the beggar lying by it — the sores — the dogs — the crumbs — the two deaths — the rich man's burial — the ministering angels — the bosom of Abraham — the rich man's fearful waking up — the fire — the gulf — the hopeless remorse — all, all stand out before our eyes in bold relief, and stamp themselves upon our minds. This is the perfection of language. This is the attainment of the famous Arabian standard, "He speaks the best — who turns the ear into an eye!"

But after all, it is one thing to admire the *masterly composition* of this parable, and quite another to receive the *spiritual lesson* it contains. The eye of the *intellect* can often see beauties while the *heart* remains asleep, and sees nothing at all. Hundreds read "Pilgrim's Progress" with deep interest, to whom the struggle for the celestial city is foolishness. Thousands are familiar with every word of the parable before us this day, who never consider how it comes home to their own case. Their conscience is deaf to the cry which ought to ring in their ears as they read, "You are the man!" Their heart never turns to God with the solemn inquiry, "Lord, is this *my* picture? Lord, is it I?"

Reader, I invite you this day to consider the *leading truth* which this parable is meant to teach us. I purposely omit to notice any part of it but that which stands at the head of this paper. May the Holy Spirit give you a *teachable spirit*, and an *understanding heart*, and so produce *lasting impressions* on your soul!

I. Observe, first of all — how different are the *conditions* which God allots to different men.

The Lord Jesus begins the parable by telling us of a rich man and a beggar. He says not a word in praise either of poverty or of riches. He describes the circumstances of a wealthy man and the circumstances of a poor man; but neither condemns the temporal position of one, nor praises that of the other.

The contrast between the two men is painfully striking. Look on this picture, and on that.

Here is one who possessed *abundance of this world's good things*. "He was clothed in purple and fine linen, and fared sumptuously every day."

Here is another who *has literally nothing*. He is a friendless, diseased, half-starved pauper. "He lies at the rich man's gate full of sores," and begs for crumbs.

Both are children of Adam. Both came from the same dust, and belong to one family. Both are living in the same land and subjects of the same government. And yet how different is their condition!

We must take heed that we do not draw lessons from the parable which it was never meant to teach. The *rich* are not always evil men, and do not always go to Hell. The *poor* are not always holy men, and do not always go to Heaven. We must not rush into the *extreme* of *supposing that it is sinful to be rich*. We must not run away with the idea that there is anything wicked in the difference of condition here described, and that *God intended all men to be equal*. There is nothing in our Lord Jesus Christ's words to warrant any such conclusion. He simply describes things as they are often seen in the world, and as we must expect to see them.

Many in every age have disturbed society by *stirring up the poor* against the rich. But so long as the world is under the present order of things, *universal equality* cannot be attained.

So long as . . .
  some are wise, and some are foolish;
  some are strong, and some are weak;
  some are healthy, and some are diseased;
so long as children reap the fruit of their parent's misconduct;
so long as sun, and rain, and heat, and cold, and wind, and waves, and

drought, and blight, and storm, and tempest are beyond man's control—so long will there be *inequality* in this world.

Take all the property in England by force this day, and divide it equally among the inhabitants. Give every man over twenty years old an *equal portion*. Let all share alike, and begin the world over again.

Do this, and see where you would be at the end of fifty years. You would just have come round to the point where you began! You would just find things as *unequal* as before!

Some would have worked—and some would have been idle;
some would have been always careless—and some always scheming;
some would have sold—and others would have bought;
some would have wasted—and others would have saved.

And the end would be, that some would be *rich*—and others *poor*.

We might as well say . . .

that all men ought to be of the same height, weight, strength, and cleverness;
or that all oak trees ought to be of the same shape and size;
or that all blades of grass ought to be of the same length
—as that all men were meant to be equal.

Settle it in your mind that the main cause of all the suffering you see around you, is sin. Sin is the grand cause . . .

of the enormous luxury of the rich—and the painful degradation of the poor;
of the heartless selfishness of the highest classes—and the helpless poverty of the lowest.

Sin must be first cast out of the world;
the hearts of all men must be renewed and sanctified;
the devil must be bound;
the Prince of Peace must come down and take His great power and reign
—all this must be before there ever can be universal happiness, or the gulf be filled up which now divides the rich and poor.

Beware of expecting a millennium to be brought about . . .

by any method of government,
by any system of education,
or by any political party.

Labor to do good to all men; pity your poorer brethren, and help every reasonable endeavor to raise them from their low estate; do not slacken your hand from any endeavor to increase knowledge—to promote morality—to improve the temporal condition of the poor.

But never, never forget that you live in a fallen world—that sin is all around you—and that the devil is abroad.

And be very sure that the rich man and Lazarus are *emblems of two classes of people which will always be in the world until the Lord comes!*

II. Observe, in the next place — that a man's temporal condition is no test to the state of his soul.

"There was a rich man who was dressed in purple and fine linen and lived in luxury every day." The **rich man** in the parable appears to have been the world's pattern of a prosperous man. If the *present* life were all — he seems to have had everything that heart could wish. We know that he was clothed in purple and fine linen, and fared sumptuously every day — we need not doubt that he had everything else which money could procure. The wisest of men had good cause for saying, "Money answers all things;" "The rich has many friends" (Eccles. 10:19; Proverbs 14:20).

But who that reads the story through to the end, can fail to see that in the highest and best sense — the rich man was pitiably poor? Take away the good things of *this* life, and he had nothing left — nothing after death, nothing beyond the grave, nothing in the world to come. With all his riches — he had no *treasure laid up in Heaven.* With all his purple and fine linen — he had no 'garment of righteousness'. With all his admiring companions — he had no Friend and Advocate at God's right hand. With all his sumptuous fare — he had never tasted the bread of life. With all his splendid palace — he had no home in the eternal world. Without God, without Christ, without faith, without grace, without pardon, without holiness — he lives to himself for a few short years, and then goes down hopelessly into the pit of Hell! How hollow and unreal was all his prosperity! Reader, judge what I say — *The rich man was very poor!*

"At his gate was laid a beggar named Lazarus, covered with sores and longing to eat the crumbs which fell from the rich man's table. Even the dogs came and licked his sores." **Lazarus** appears to have been one who had literally nothing in this world. It is hard to conceive a case of greater misery and destitution than his. He had neither house, nor money, nor food, nor health, nor, in all probability, even clothes. His picture is one that can never be forgotten. He lay at the rich man's gate, covered with sores; he desired to be fed with the crumbs which fell from the rich man's table; moreover, the dogs came and licked his sores. Truly the wise man might well say, "The poor is hated even of his neighbor." "The destruction of the poor is their poverty." (Proverbs 14:20; 10:15).

But who that reads the parable to the end, can fail to see that in the highest sense Lazarus was not poor — but rich? He was a child of God. He was an heir of glory. He possessed durable riches and righteousness. His name was in the book of life. His place was prepared for him in Heaven. He had the best of clothing — the righteousness of a Savior. He had the best of friends — God Himself was his portion. He had the best of food — he had food to eat which the world knew nothing of. And, best of all, he had these things *forever!* They supported him in life — they did not leave him in the hour of death. They went with him beyond the grave — they were his to eternity. Surely in this point of view, we may well say, not "poor Lazarus," but "rich Lazarus!"

Reader, you would do well to measure all men by God's standard — to measure them not by the amount of their income — but by the condition of their souls. When the Lord God looks down from Heaven upon men, He takes no account of many things which are highly esteemed by the world. He looks not at men's money, or lands, or titles. He looks only at the state of their souls — and reckons them accordingly. Oh, that you would strive to do likewise! Oh, that you would value *grace* above titles, or intellect, or gold! Often, far too often, the only question asked about a man is, "How much is he worth?" It would be well for us all to remember that every man is pitiably poor — until he is rich in faith, and rich toward God.

As astonishing as it may seem to some — all the money in the world is worthless in God's balances, compared to grace! As hard as the saying may sound — I believe that a converted beggar is far more important and honorable in the sight of God — than an unconverted king. The king may glitter like the butterfly in the sun for a little season, and be admired by an ignorant world — but his latter end is darkness, and misery forever! The beggar may crawl through the world like a crushed worm, and be despised by every one who sees him — but his latter end is a glorious resurrection and a blessed eternity with Christ! Of him the Lord says, "I know your poverty — but you are rich!" (Rev. 2:9).

King Ahab was *ruler* over the ten tribes of Israel. Obadiah was nothing more than a *servant* in his household. Yet who can doubt which was most precious in God's sight — the servant or the king?

Ridley and Latimer were deposed from all their dignities, cast into prison as malefactors, and at length burned at the stake. Bonner and Gardiner, their persecutors, were raised to the highest pitch of ecclesiastical greatness, enjoyed large incomes, and died unmolested in their beds. Yet who can doubt which of the two parties was on the Lord's side?

Richard Baxter, the famous divine, was persecuted with savage malignity, and condemned to a long imprisonment by a most unjust judgment. Jeffreys, the Lord Chief Justice, was a man of infamous character, without either morality or religion. Baxter was sent to jail — and Jeffreys was loaded with honors. Yet who can doubt who was the good man of the two, the Lord Chief Justice — or the author of "The Saint's Everlasting Rest?"

Reader, be very sure that riches and worldly greatness are no certain marks of God's favor. They are often, on the contrary — a snare and hindrance to a man's soul. They make him love the world and forget God. What says Solomon? "Labor not to be rich!" (Proverbs

23:4). What says Paul? "Those who will be rich, fall into temptation, and a snare, and into many foolish and hurtful lusts, which drown men in destruction and perdition" (1 Tim. 6:9).

Reader, be no less sure that *poverty* and *afflictions* are no certain proof of God's displeasure. They are *blessings in disguise!* They are always sent in divine *love* and *wisdom*. They often serve to wean man from the world; they teach him to set his affections on things above. They often show the sinner his own heart: they often make the saint fruitful in good works. What says the book of Job? "Happy is the man whom God corrects; therefore despise not the chastening of the Almighty" (Job 5:17). What says Paul? "Whom the Lord loves — He chastens" (Hebrews 12:6).

One great secret of happiness in this life is to be of a patient, contented spirit. Strive daily to realize the truth that this present life is not the place of reward. The time of retribution and recompense is yet to come! Do not judge anything hastily before that time. Remember the words of the wise man: "If you see the poor oppressed in a district, and justice and rights denied — do not be surprised at such things." (Eccles. 5:8). Yes, there is a day of judgment yet to come! That day shall put all in their right places. At last, a *mighty difference* there shall be seen between him who fears God — and him who does not fear God. The children of Lazarus and the children of the rich man, shall at length be seen in their true colors — and everyone shall receive according to his works.

III. Observe, in the next place — how all classes alike come to the *grave*.

"The time came when the *beggar* died and the angels carried him to Abraham's side. The *rich man* also died and was buried." Luke 16:22

Lazarus died — and the rich man also died. As different and divided as they were in their lives — they had both to *drink of the same cup* at the last. Both went to the house appointed for all living. Both went to that place where rich and poor meet together. Dust they were — and unto dust they returned.

This is the lot of all men. It will be our own, unless the Lord shall first return in glory. After all our scheming, and contriving, and planning, and studying — after all our inventions, and discoveries, and scientific attainments — there remains one *enemy* we cannot conquer and disarm — and that is Death! The chapter in Genesis, which records the long lives of Methuselah, and the rest who lived before the flood, winds up the simple story of each by two expressive words,"He died." And now, after thousands of years, what more can be said of the greatest among ourselves? The histories of Marlborough, and Washington, and Napoleon, and Wellington arrive at the same humbling conclusion. The end of each, after all his greatness, is just this, "He died."

Death is a mighty leveler! He spares none, he waits for none! He will not tarry until you are ready. He will not be kept out by doors, and bars, and bolts. The Englishman boasts that his home is his castle — but, with all his boasting, he cannot exclude death. An Austrian nobleman forbade death and the smallpox to be named in his presence. But named or not named, it matters little — in God's appointed hour, death will come!

One man rolls lazily along the road in the smoothest and handsomest carriage which money can procure; another toils wearily along the path on foot — yet both are sure to meet at last in the same home!

One man, like Absalom, has fifty servants to wait upon him and do his bidding; another has none to lift a finger to do him a service — but both are traveling to a place where they must lie down alone.

One man is the owner of millions; another has scarcely a dollar that he can call his own property — yet neither one nor the other can carry one penny with him into the unseen world.

One man is the possessor of half a county; another has not so much as an inch of land — and yet 'six feet' of dirt will be amply sufficient for either of them at the last.

One man pampers his body with every possible delicacy, and clothes it in the richest and softest apparel; another has scarcely enough to eat, and seldom enough to put on — yet both alike are hurrying on to a day when "ashes to ashes, and dust to dust," shall be proclaimed over them! Fifty years hence, none shall be able to say, "This was the *rich* man's bone — and this the bone of the *poor* man."

Reader, I know that these are ancient things. I do not deny it for a moment. I am writing stale old things that all men *know* — but I am also writing things that all men do not *feel.* Oh, no! if they did feel them, they would not speak and live as they do.

You wonder sometimes at the tone and language of ministers of the Gospel. You marvel that we press upon you immediate decision. You think us extreme and extravagant in our views, because we urge upon you to close with Christ — to leave nothing uncertain — to make sure that you are born again and ready for Heaven. You hear — but do not approve. You go away, and say to one another, "The man means well — but he goes too far."

But do you not see, that the reality of death is continually forbidding us to use other language? We see him gradually thinning our congregations; we miss face after face in our assemblies; we know not whose turn may come next! We only know as the tree falls — there it will lie, and that "after death comes the judgment!" We must be bold and decided, and uncompromising in our language. We would rather run the risk of offending some than of losing any. We would aim at the standard set up by old Baxter "I'll preach as though I never would preach again! I preach as a *dying man* to dying men!"

We would realize the character given by Charles II of one of his preachers: "That man preaches as though death was behind his back! When I hear him, I cannot go to sleep."

Oh, that men would learn to live — as those who must one day die! Truly it is poor work to set our affections on a dying world and its short-lived comforts, and for the sake of an inch of time to lose a glorious immortality! Here we are toiling, and laboring, and wearying ourselves about *trifles*, and running to and fro like ants upon a heap — and yet after a few years we shall all be gone, and another generation will fill our place. Live for eternity, reader! Seek a portion which can never be taken from you; and never forget John Bunyan's golden rule: "He who would live well — let him make his dying day his company-keeper."

IV. Observe, in the next place — how precious a believer's soul is in the sight of God.

The rich man, in the parable, dies and is buried. Perhaps he had a splendid funeral — a funeral proportioned to his expenditure while he was yet alive. But we hear nothing further of the moment when soul and body were divided. The next thing we hear of, is that he is in Hell.

The poor man, in the parable, dies also. What kind of burial he had, we know not. A *pauper's funeral* is a melancholy business! But this we do know, that the moment Lazarus dies — he is carried by the angels into Abraham's bosom — carried to a place of rest, where all the *faithful* are waiting for the 'resurrection of the just'.

Reader, there is something to my mind very striking, very touching, and very comforting in this expression of the parable. I ask your especial attention to it. It throws great light on the relation of all sinners who *believe* in Christ to their God and Father. It shows a little of the care bestowed on the least and lowest of Christ's disciples by the King of kings.

No man has such friends and attendants as the believer, however little he may think it. *Angels* rejoice over him in the day that he is born again of the Spirit; angels minister to him all through life; angels encamp around him in the wilderness of this world; angels take charge of his soul in death, and bear it safely home. Yes, as vile as he may be in his own eyes, and lowly in his own sight — the very poorest and humblest believer in Jesus is cared for by his Father in Heaven with a care that surpasses knowledge! The Lord has become his Shepherd — and he can lack nothing really good. Only let a man come sincerely to Christ — and he shall have all the benefits of a covenant ordered in all things and sure.

Is he laden with many sins? Though they be as scarlet — they shall be as white as snow!

Is his heart hard and prone to evil? A new heart shall be given to him, and a new spirit put in him!

Is he weak and cowardly? He who enabled Peter to confess Christ before his enemies, shall make him bold!

Is he ignorant? He who bore with Thomas' slowness, shall bear with him, and guide him into all truth!

Is he alone in his position? He who stood by Paul when all men forsook him, shall also stand by his side!

Is he in circumstances of special trial? He who enabled men to be saints in Nero's household, shall also enable him to persevere!

The very hairs of his head are all numbered. Nothing can harm him without God's permission. He who hurts him — hurts the apple of God's eye, and injures a brother and member of Christ Himself!

His *trials* are all wisely ordered. Satan can only vex him as he did Job — when God permits him. No temptation can happen to him, above what he is able to bear. All things are working together for his good!

His steps are all ordered — from *grace* to *glory*. He is kept on earth until he is ripe for Heaven — and not one moment longer. The *harvest* of the Lord must have its appointed proportion of sun and wind, of cold and heat, of rain and storm — and then, when the believer's work is done, the angels of God shall come for him as they did for Lazarus, and carry him safely home!

Ah, reader, the men of the world little think whom they are *despising*, when they mock Christ's people! They are mocking those whom angels are not ashamed to attend upon. They are mocking the brethren and sisters of Christ Himself! Little do they consider that these are those for whose sakes the days of tribulation are shortened: these are those by whose intercession kings reign peacefully. Little do they reckon that the prayers of men like Lazarus have more weight in the affairs of nations, than hosts of armed men.

Believers in Christ who read these pages, you little know the full extent of your privileges and possessions. Like *children* at school — you know not half of what your Father is doing for your welfare. Learn to live by *faith* more than you have done. Acquaint yourself with the fullness of the treasure laid up for you in Christ even now. This world, no doubt, must always be a place of *trial* while we are in the body; but still there are *comforts* provided for the *brethren of Lazarus* which many never enjoy.

V. Observe, in the last place — what a dangerous and soul-ruining sin is the sin of *selfishness*.

You have the *rich* man in the parable, in a *hopeless* state. If there was no other picture of a lost soul in Hell in all the Bible — you have it here. You meet him in the *beginning* — clothed in purple and fine linen; you part with him at the *last* — tormented in the everlasting fire!

And yet there is nothing to show that this man was a murderer, or a thief, or an adulterer, or a liar. There is no reason to say that he was an atheist, or an infidel, or a blasphemer. For anything we know — he faithfully attended to all the ordinances of the Jewish religion. But we do know that he was lost forever.

There is something to my mind very solemn in this thought. Here is a man whose outward life in all probability was correct — at all events, we know nothing against him. He dresses richly — but then he had money to spend on his apparel. He gives splendid feasts and entertainments — but then he was wealthy, and could well afford it. We read nothing recorded against him that might not be recorded of hundreds and thousands in the present day — who are counted respectable and good sort of people. And yet the *end* of this man, is that he goes to Hell. Surely this deserves serious attention!

I believe it is meant to teach us to ***beware of living only for ourselves***. It is not enough that we are able to say, "I live correctly. I pay every one his due. I discharge all the relations of life with propriety. I attend to all the outward requirements of Christianity." There remains behind another question, to which the Bible requires an answer: "To whom do you live — to yourself or to Christ? What is the great end, aim, object, and ruling motive in your life?" Let men call the question extreme if they please. For myself, I can find nothing short of this in Paul's words, "He died for all, that they which live should not henceforth live unto themselves — but unto Him who died for them, and rose again" (2 Corinthians 5:15). And I draw the conclusion that if, like the rich man, we live only to ourselves — we shall ruin our souls forever!

I believe further that this passage is meant to teach us ***the damnable nature of sins of omission***. It does not seem that it was so much the things the rich man *did* — but the things he left *undone*, which made him miss Heaven. Lazarus was at his gate — and he merely let him alone. But is not this exactly in keeping with the history of the judgment in the twenty-fifth chapter of Matthew? Nothing is said there of the sins of *commission* of which the lost are guilty. How does the *charge* run?

"For I was *hungry* — and you gave Me nothing to eat;
I was *thirsty* — and you gave Me nothing to drink;
I was a *stranger* — and you did not take Me in;
I was *naked* — and you did not clothe Me,
I was *sick* and in *prison* — and you did not take care of Me!"
(Matthew 25:42, 43).

The charge against them is simply that they *did not do* certain things. On this their *sentence* turns. And I draw the conclusion again, that except we take heed, *sins of omission* may ruin our souls! Truly it was a solemn saying of good old Usher, on his death-bed: "Lord, forgive me all my sins — but specially my sins of *omission*."

I believe further, that the passage is meant to teach us that ***riches bring special danger with them***. Yes! riches, which the vast majority of men are always seeking after — riches for which they spend their lives, and of which they make an idol — riches entail on their possessor immense spiritual peril! The possession of them has a very *hardening effect* on the soul — they chill; they freeze; they petrify the inward man! They close the eye to the things of faith. They insensibly produce a tendency to *forget God*.

And does not this stand in perfect harmony with all the language of Scripture on the same subject?

What does *our Lord* say? "How hard it is for the rich to enter the kingdom of God! It is easier for a camel to go through the eye of a needle — than for a rich man to enter the kingdom of God!" Mark 10:23-25 !" (Mark 10:23, 25).

What does *Paul* say? "For the love of money is a root of all kinds of evil. Some people, eager for money, have wandered from the faith and pierced themselves with many griefs!" (1 Tim. 6:10).

What can be more striking than the fact that the Bible has frequently spoken of *money* as a most fruitful cause of sin and evil?
For money, *Achan* brought defeat on the armies of Israel, and death on himself.
For money, *Balaam* sinned against light, and tried to curse God's people.
For money, *Delilah* betrayed Samson to the Philistines.
For money, *Gehazi* lied to Naaman and Elisha, and became a leper.
For money, *Ananias* and *Sapphira* became the first hypocrites in the early Church, and lost their lives.
For money, *Judas Iscariot* sold Christ, and was ruined eternally.
Surely these facts speak loudly!

Money, in truth is one of the most unsatisfying of possessions. It takes away some cares, no doubt — but it brings with it quite as many cares as it takes away!
There is trouble in the getting of it;
there is anxiety in the keeping of it;
there are temptations in the use of it;
there is guilt in the abuse of it;
there is sorrow in the losing of it;
there is perplexity in the disposing of it.

Two-thirds of all the strifes, quarrels, and lawsuits in the world, arise from one simple cause — money!

Money most certainly is one of the most heart-ensnaring of possessions. It seems *desirable* at a distance — yet it often proves a *poison* when in our hand! No man can possibly tell the effect of money on his soul, if it suddenly falls to his lot to possess it. Many a one *did* run well — as a *poor man* who forgets God when he becomes rich.

Reader, I draw the conclusion that those who have money, like the rich man in the parable, ought to take double pains about their souls. They live in a most unhealthy atmosphere — they have double need to be on their guard!

I believe, not least, that the passage is meant to stir up ***special carefulness about selfishness*** in these last days. You have a special warning in 2 Timothy 3:1-2; "In the last days perilous times shall come: for men shall be *lovers of their own selves*, covetous." I believe we have come to the last days, and that we ought to beware of the sins here mentioned, if we love our souls.

Perhaps we are poor judges of our own times: we are apt to exaggerate and magnify their evils, just because we see and feel them; but after every allowance, I doubt whether there ever was more need of warnings against *selfishness* than in the present day. I am sure there never was a time when all classes in England had so many *comforts* and so many *temporal* good things; and yet I believe there is an utter disproportion between men's expenditure on *themselves* — and their outlay on works of *charity* and works of *mercy*. I see this in the miserable donations to which many rich men confine their charity. I see it in the languishing condition of many of our best Christian societies, and the painfully slow growth of their annual incomes. I see it in the small number of names which appear in the list of contributions to any good work. There are, I believe, thousands of rich people in this country, who literally give away nothing at all. I see it in the notorious fact that few, even of those who give — give anything *proportioned* to their means. I see all this, and mourn over it! I regard it as the *selfishness* and *covetousness* predicted as likely to arise in the last days.

Readers, I know that this is a *painful* and *delicate* subject. But it must not on that account, be avoided by the minister of Christ. It is a subject for the times, and it needs pressing home. I desire to speak to myself, and to all who make any profession of religion. Of course I cannot expect worldly and utterly ungodly people to view this subject in Bible light — to them the Bible is no rule of faith and practice; to quote texts to them would be of little use.

But I do ask all *professing Christians* to consider well what Scripture says against *covetousness* and *selfishness*, and on behalf of *liberality* in giving money.

Is it for nothing that the *Lord Jesus* spoke the parable of *the Rich*

Fool, and blamed him because he was not "rich towards God?" (Luke 12:21). Is it for nothing that in the parable of the *Sower,* He mentions the deceitfulness of riches as one reason why the seed of the Word bears no fruit? (Matthew 13:22.) Is it for nothing that He says, "I tell you, use worldly wealth to gain friends for yourselves, so that when it is gone, you will be welcomed into eternal dwellings." (Luke 16:9.) Is it for nothing that He says, "When you give a luncheon or dinner, do not invite your friends, your brothers or relatives, or your rich neighbors; if you do, they may invite you back and so you will be repaid. But when you give a banquet, invite the poor, the crippled, the lame, the blind, and you will be blessed. Although they cannot repay you, you will be repaid at the resurrection of the righteous." (Luke 14:12-14.) Is it for nothing that He says, "Sell your possessions and give to the poor. Provide purses for yourselves that will not wear out, a treasure in Heaven that will not be exhausted, where no thief comes near and no moth destroys." (Luke 12:33.) Is it for nothing that He says, "It is more blessed to give than to receive?" (Acts 20:35). Is it for nothing that He warns us against the example of the priest and Levite, who saw the wounded traveler — but passed by on the other side? Is it for nothing that He praises the *good Samaritan,* who denied himself to show kindness to a stranger? (Luke 10:34.)

Is it for nothing that *Paul* classes covetousness with sins of the grossest description, and denounces it as idolatry? (Coloss. 3:5.) And is there not a striking and painful difference between this language and the habits and feeling of society about money? I appeal to any one who knows the world. Let him judge what I say.

Reader, I only ask you to consider calmly the passages of Scripture to which I have referred. I cannot think they were meant to teach nothing at all. That the habits of the East and our own are different, I freely allow; that some of the expressions I have quoted are *figurative* I freely admit; but still, after all, *a principle lies at the bottom of all these expressions.* Let us take heed that this principle is not neglected. I wish that many a professing Christian in this day, who perhaps dislikes what I am saying, would try to write a *commentary* on these expressions, and try to explain to himself what they mean!

To know that alms-giving cannot atone for sin, is well. To know that our good works cannot justify us, is excellent. To know that we may give all our goods to feed the poor, and build hospitals and cathedrals, without any real charity, is most important. But let us beware lest we go into the other extreme, and because our money cannot *save* us — give away no money at all.

Has anyone who reads these pages **money**? Then take heed and beware of covetousness! Remember you carry *weight* in the *race towards Heaven.* All men are naturally in danger of being lost forever; but you are doubly so, because of your possessions. Nothing is said to put out fire so soon — as *earth* thrown upon it; and nothing, I am sure, has such a tendency to quench the fire of religion — as the possession of money. It was a solemn message which Buchanan, on his death-bed, sent to his old pupil: "He was going to a place where *few* kings and great men would come."

It is possible, no doubt, for you to be saved as well as others. With God, nothing is impossible. Abraham, Job, and David were all rich — and yet saved. But oh, take heed to yourself! Money is a *good servant* — but a *bad master*. Let that saying of our Lord's sink down into your heart: "I tell you the truth, it is hard for a rich man to enter the kingdom of Heaven!"

Well said an old divine: "The surface above gold mines is generally very barren." Well might old Latimer begin one of his sermons before Edward VI by quoting three times over our Lord's words: "Take heed and beware of covetousness!" And then saying, "What if I should say nothing else these three or four hours?" There are few prayers more wise and more necessary than that petition: "In all time of our wealth, good Lord deliver us!"

Has anyone who reads these pages **little** or no money? Then do not *envy* those who are richer than yourself? *Pray* for them. *Pity* them. Be charitable to their faults. Remember that *high* places are *giddy* places, and be not too hasty in your condemnation of their conduct. Perhaps if you had *their difficulties* — you would do no better yourself. Beware of the *love* of money! A man may love money overmuch, without having any at all. Beware of the love of *self* — it may be found in a poor cottage as well as in a palace. And beware of thinking that poverty alone will save you! If you would sit with Lazarus in glory — you must not only have fellowship with him in suffering — but in *grace*.

Does any reader desire to know the **remedy** against that *love of self*, which ruined the rich man's soul, and cleaves to us all by nature, like our skin! I tell him plainly there is *only one* remedy, and I ask him to mark well what that remedy is. It is not the fear of Hell. It is not the hope of Heaven. It is not any sense of duty. Oh, no! The *disease of selfishness* is far too deeply rooted to yield to such secondary motives as these. Nothing will ever cure it, but an experimental knowledge of Christ's redeeming love! You must know the misery and guilt of your own estate by nature; you must experience the power of Christ's atoning blood sprinkled upon your conscience, and making you whole; you must taste the sweetness of peace with God through the mediation of Jesus, and feel the love of a reconciled Father shed abroad in your heart by the Holy Spirit.

Then, and not until then, the *mainspring of selfishness* will be broken! Then, knowing the immensity of your debt to Christ, you will feel that nothing is too great and too costly to give to Him. Feeling that you have been loved much, when you deserved nothing — you will heartily love in return, and cry, "What shall I render unto the Lord for all His benefits?" Feeling that you have freely received countless mercies, you will think it a privilege to do anything to please Him to Whom you owe all. Feeling that you have been bought with a price, and are no longer your own — you will labor to glorify God with body and spirit, which are His.

Yes, reader, I repeat it this day! I know no *effectual remedy for the love of self* — but a believing apprehension of the love of Christ. Other remedies may *palliate* the disease — this alone will heal it. Other antidotes may hide its deformity — this alone will work a perfect cure.

An easy, good-natured temper may cover over selfishness in one man; a love of praise may conceal it in a second; a self-righteous asceticism and an affected spirit of self-denial, may keep it out of sight in a third; but nothing will ever cut up selfishness by the roots — but the love of Christ revealed in the mind by the Holy Spirit, and felt in the heart by simple faith. Once let a man see the full meaning of the words, "Christ *loved* me and *gave* Himself for me!" and then he will delight to give himself to Christ, and all that he has to His service. He will live to Him, not in order that he may *be* saved — but because he *is* saved already. He will work for Him, not that he may have life and peace — but because life and peace are his already.

Go to the *cross of Christ* — all you who want to be delivered from the *power of selfishness*. Go and see what a *price* was paid there to provide a ransom for *your* soul. Go and see what an astounding *sacrifice* was there made that a *door to eternal life* might be provided for poor sinners like you. Go and see how the Son of God gave Himself for you — and learn to think it a small thing to give yourself to Him.

Reader, the *disease* which ruined the rich man in the parable, may be cured. But oh, remember, there is only one real remedy! If you would not live to yourself — you must live to Christ. See to it that this remedy is not only *known* — but *applied*; not only *heard* of — but *used*.

1. And now let me conclude, all by urging on every reader of these pages the great duty of self-examination.

A passage of Scripture like this parable ought surely to raise in many an one great searchings of heart. "What am I? Where am I going? What am I doing? What is likely to be my condition after death? Am I prepared to leave the world? Have I any *home* to look forward to in the world to come. Have I put off the old man and put on the new? Am I really one with Christ, and a pardoned soul?" Surely such questions as these, may well be asked when the story of the rich man and Lazarus has been heard. Oh, that the Holy Spirit may incline many a reader's heart to ask them!

2. In the next place, I invite all readers who desire to have their souls saved, and have no good account to give of themselves at present — to seek salvation while it can be found. I do entreat you to apply to Him, by Whom alone man can enter Heaven and be saved, even Jesus Christ the Lord. He has the *keys* of Heaven. He is sealed and appointed by God the Father to be the Savior of all who will come to Him. Go to Him in earnest and hearty prayer, and tell Him your case. Tell Him that you have heard that He receives sinners — and that you come to Him as such. Tell Him that you desire to be saved by Him in His Own way — and ask Him to save you. Oh that you may take this course without delay! Remember the hopeless end of the rich man. Once dead — there is no more opportunity to be saved.

3. Last of all, I entreat all professing Christians to encourage themselves in habits of liberality towards causes of charity and mercy. Remember that you are *God's stewards* — and give money liberally, freely, and without grudging, whenever you have an opportunity. You cannot keep your money forever. You must give account one day of the manner in which it has been expended. Oh, lay it out with an *eye to eternity*, while you can!

I do not ask rich men to leave their situations in life and go into the workhouse. I ask no man to neglect his worldly calling, and to omit to provide for his family. *Diligence in business* is a positive Christian duty; provision for those dependent on us, is proper Christian prudence. But I ask all to look around continually as they journey on, and to remember the poor — the poor in *body* and the poor in *soul.*

We are here for a few short years. How can we do most good with our money while we are here? How can we so spend it as to leave the world somewhat *happier* and somewhat *holier* when we are gone? Might we not abridge some of our *luxuries?* Might we not lay out less upon *ourselves* — and give more to Christ's cause and Christ's poor? Is there none we can do good to? Are there no sick, no poor, no needy — whose sorrows we might lessen, and whose comforts we might increase? Such questions will never fail to elicit an answer from some quarter. I am thoroughly persuaded that the income of every Christian and charitable society in England might easily be multiplied tenfold, if English Christians would give in *proportion* to their means.

There are none, surely, to whom such appeals ought to come home with such power — as professing believers in the Lord Jesus. The parable of the text is a striking illustration of our *position* by nature, and our *debt* to Christ. We all lay, like Lazarus at Heaven's gate, sick unto the death, helpless, and starving. Blessed be God, we were not *neglected* as he was! Jesus came forth to relieve us. Jesus gave Himself for us — that we might have hope and live. For a *poor Lazarus-like world* — He came down from Heaven, and humbled

Himself to become a man. For a poor Lazarus-like world — He went up and down doing good, caring for men's bodies as well as souls, until He died for us on the cross!

I believe that in giving to support works of charity and mercy, we are doing that which is according to Christ's mind — and I ask readers of these pages to *begin* the habit of giving, if they never began it before; and to go on with it increasingly, if they have begun.

I believe that in offering a *warning against covetousness*, I have done no more than bring forward a warning specially called for by the times, and I ask God to bless the consideration of these pages to many souls!

THE BEST FRIEND!

"This is my Friend!" Song of Solomon 4:16

A *friend* is one of the greatest blessings on earth. Tell me not of money — love is better than gold; sympathy is better than lands. He is the poor man — who has no friends!

This world is full of *sorrow* — because it is full of *sin*. It is a *dark* place. It is a *lonely* place. It is a *disappointing* place. The brightest sunbeam in it, is a friend. Friendship halves our troubles — and doubles our joys!

A real friend is *scarce* and *rare*. There are many who will eat, and drink, and laugh with us in the *sunshine of prosperity*. There are few who will stand by us in the *days of darkness* — few who will love us when we are sick, helpless, and poor — few, above all, who will care for our souls!

Does any reader of this paper want a real friend? I write to recommend one to your notice this day. I know of One "who sticks closer than a brother!" (Proverbs 18:24.) I know of One who is ready to be your friend *for time and for eternity*, if you will receive Him. Hear me, while I try to tell you something about Him.

The friend I want you to know is *Jesus Christ*. Happy is that family in which Christ has the foremost place! Happy is that person whose chief friend is Christ!

I. Do we want a friend in NEED? Such a friend is the Lord Jesus Christ!

Man is the *neediest* creature on God's earth, because he is a *sinner*. There is no need as great as that of sinners: poverty, hunger, thirst, cold, sickness — all are nothing in comparison. Sinners need *pardon* — and they are utterly unable to provide it for themselves; they need deliverance from a *guilty conscience* and the *fear of death* — and they have no power of their own to obtain it. This need, the Lord Jesus Christ came into the world to relieve. "He came into the world to save sinners!" (1 Tim. 1:15.)

We are all by nature, **poor dying creatures**. From the king on his throne, to the pauper in the workhouse — we are all sick of a *mortal disease of soul*. Whether we *know* it or not, whether we *feel* it or not — we are all *dying daily*. The *plague of sin* is in our blood. We cannot *cure ourselves* — we are hourly getting worse and worse! All this, the Lord Jesus undertook to remedy. He came into the world to bring in health and cure; He came to deliver us "from the second death;" He came "to abolish death, and bring life and immortality to light through the Gospel." (Jeremiah 33:6; Rev. 2:11; 2 Tim. 1:10.)

We are all by nature **imprisoned debtors**. We owed our God millions — and had nothing to pay. We were wretched bankrupts, without hope of freeing ourselves. We could never have freed ourselves from our load of liabilities, and were daily getting more deeply indebted. All this the Lord Jesus saw, and undertook to remedy. He engaged to "ransom and redeem us." He came to "proclaim liberty to the captives, and the opening of the prison to those who are bound." "He came to redeem us from the curse of the law." (Hos. 13:14; Isaiah 41:1; Galatians 3:13.)

We were all by nature **shipwrecked and cast away**. We could never have reached the *harbor of everlasting life*. We were sinking in the midst of the waves — hopeless, helpless, and powerless; tied and bound by the *chain of our sins*, foundering under the burden of our own guilt, and likely to become a prey to the devil. All this the Lord Jesus saw and undertook to remedy. He came down from Heaven to be our "mighty helper." He came to "seek and to save those who are lost;" and to "deliver us from going down into the pit." (Psalm 89:19; Luke 19:10; Job 33:24.)

Could we have been saved without the Lord Jesus Christ coming down from Heaven? It would have been utterly impossible. The wisest men of Egypt, and Greece, and Rome never found out the way to *peace with God*. Without the friendship of Christ — we would all have been lost for evermore in Hell.

Was the Lord Jesus Christ *obliged* to come down to save us? Oh, no! no! It was His own free love, mercy, and pity — which brought Him down. He came unsought and unasked — because He was gracious.

Let us think on these things. Search all history from the beginning of the world — look around the whole circle of those you know and love — you never heard of such friendship among men. There never was such a real friend in *need* as Jesus Christ!

II. Do you want a friend in DEED? Such a friend is the Lord Jesus Christ.

The true extent of a man's friendship must be measured by his *deeds*. Tell me not what he *says*, and *feels*, and *wishes*; tell me not of his *words* and *letters* — tell me rather what he *does*. *"A friend is measured by what he does."*

The *doings* of the Lord Jesus Christ for man are the grand proof of His friendly feeling towards him. Never were there such acts of *kindness* and *self-denial* — as those which He has performed on our behalf. He has not loved us in *word* only — but in *deed*.

For our sakes, He took our nature upon Him, and was born of a woman. He who was very God, and equal with the Father, laid aside

His glory for a season, and took upon Him flesh and blood like our own. The *almighty Creator* of all things — became a little babe like any of us, and experienced all our bodily weaknesses and infirmities, sin only excepted. "Though He was rich — He became poor; that we through His poverty — might be rich." (2 Corinthians 8:9.)

For our sakes, He lived thirty-three years in this evil world, despised and rejected by men, a man of sorrows, and acquainted with grief. Though He was King of kings — He had nowhere to lay His head; though He was Lord of lords — He was often weary, and hungry, and thirsty, and poor. "He took on Him the form of a servant, and humbled Himself." (Philippians 3:7, 8.)

For our sakes, He suffered the most painful of all deaths, even the death of the cross! Though innocent, and without fault, He allowed Himself to be condemned, and found guilty. He who was the *Prince of Life* — was led as a lamb to the slaughter, and poured out His soul unto death. He "died for us." (1 Thessalonians 5:10.)

Was He *obliged* to do this? Oh, no! He might have summoned to His help, more than twelve legions of angels, and scattered His enemies with a word. He suffered *voluntarily* and of His own free will, to make atonement for our sins. He knew that nothing but the sacrifice of His body and blood — could ever make peace between sinful man and a holy God. He laid down His life — to pay the price of our redemption. He died — that we might live. He suffered — that we might reign. He bore shame — that we might receive glory. "He suffered for sins, the just for the unjust, that He might bring us to God." "God made him who had no sin to be sin for us — so that in him we might become the righteousness of God." (1 Peter 3:18; 2 Corinthians 5:21.)

Such friendship as this surpasses man's understanding. Friends who would die for those who *love* them — we may have *heard* of sometimes. But who can find a man who would lay down his life for those that *hate* him? Yet this is what Jesus has done for us. "Christ died for the *ungodly*. God commends His love towards us, in that while we were yet *sinners* — Christ died for us. When we were God's *enemies* — we were reconciled to him through the death of his Son!" (Romans 5:6, 8, 10.)

Ask all the tribes of mankind, from one end of the world to the other — and you will nowhere hear of a deed like this! None was ever so *high* and stooped down so *low* — as Jesus the Son of God! None ever gave so costly a proof of his friendship! None ever paid so much and endured so much to do good to others. Never was there such a friend in *deed* as Jesus Christ!

III. Do we want a MIGHTY and POWERFUL friend? Such a friend is Jesus Christ.

Power to help, is that which few possess in this world. Many have *desire* enough to do good to others — but no *power*. They feel for the sorrows of others, and would gladly relieve them if they could; they can weep with their friends in affliction — but are unable to take their grief away. But though *man* is weak — *Christ* is strong; though the best of our earthly friends is feeble — Christ is almighty! "All power is given unto Him in Heaven and earth." (Matthew 28:18.) No one can do so much for those whom He befriends, as Jesus Christ. Others can befriend their bodies a little — He can befriend both body and soul. Others can do a little for them in time — He can be a friend both for time and eternity!

(a) He is able to *pardon* and *save* the very chief of sinners. He can deliver the *most guilty conscience* from all its burdens, and give it perfect peace with God. He can wash away the *vilest stains of wickedness*, and make a man whiter than snow in the sight of God. He can *clothe* a poor weak child of Adam in everlasting righteousness, and give him a *title* to Heaven that can never be overthrown. In a word, He can give any one of us peace, hope, forgiveness, and reconciliation with God — if we will only trust in Him. "The blood of Jesus Christ cleanses from all sin!" (1 John 1:7.)

(b) He is able to *convert* the hardest of hearts, and create in man a new spirit. He can take the most thoughtless and ungodly people, and give them another mind by the Holy Spirit whom He puts in them. He can cause old things to pass away, and all things to become new. He can make them *love* the things which they once hated — and *hate* the things which they once loved. "He can give them power to become the sons of God." "If any man is in Christ — he is a new creature." (John 1:12; 2 Corinthians 5:17.)

(c) He is able to *preserve* to the end all who believe in Him, and become His disciples. He can give them grace to overcome the world, the flesh and the devil, and fight a good fight until the last. He can . . .
lead them on safely in spite of every temptation,
carry them home through a thousand dangers, and
keep them faithful, though they stand alone and have none to help them. "He is able to save them to the uttermost, all who come unto God by Him." (Hebrews 7:25.)

(d) He is able to give those who love Him the *best of gifts*. He can give them in *this life* — inward comforts, which money can never buy — peace in poverty, joy in sorrow, patience in suffering. He can give them *in death* — bright hopes, which enable them to walk through the dark valley without fear. He can give them *after death* — an unfading crown of glory, and a *reward* compared to which, the Queen of England has nothing to bestow.

This is power indeed! This is true greatness! This is real strength!

Go and look at the poor *Hindu idolater*, seeking peace in vain by afflicting his body; and, after fifty years of self-imposed suffering, unable to find it.

Go and look at the *benighted Romanist*, giving money to his priest to pray for his soul — and yet dying without comfort.

Go and look at *rich men*, spending thousands in search of happiness — and yet always discontented and unhappy.

Then turn to Jesus, and think what He can do, and is daily doing for all who trust Him. Think how He . . .
heals all the broken-hearted,
comforts all the sick,
cheers all the poor that trust in Him,
and supplies all their daily need.

The fear of *man* is strong,
the opposition of this *evil world* is mighty,
the lusts of the *flesh* rage horribly,
the fear of *death* is terrible,
the *devil* is a roaring lion seeking whom he may devour
— but Jesus is stronger than them all, Jesus can make us *conquerors* over all these *foes!*

And then say whether there was ever was so *mighty* a friend as Jesus Christ.

IV. Do we want a LOVING and affectionate friend? Such a friend is Jesus Christ.

Kindness is the very essence of true friendship. *Money* and *advice* and *help* lose half their grace, if not given in a loving manner. What kind of love is that of the Lord Jesus toward man? It is called, "A love that surpasses knowledge." (Ephesians 3:19.)

Love shines forth in His **reception** of sinners. He refuses none who come to Him for salvation, however *unworthy* they may be. Though their *lives* may have been most wicked, though their *sins* may be more in number than the stars of Heaven — the Lord Jesus is ready to receive them, and give them pardon and peace! There is no end to His *compassion!* There are no bounds to His *pity!* He is not ashamed to befriend those whom the world casts off as hopeless. There are none too bad, too filthy, and too much diseased with sin — to be admitted into His home! He is willing to be the friend of any sinner. He has kindness and mercy and healing medicine for all. He has long proclaimed this to be His rule: "Whoever comes unto Me — I will never cast out." (John 6:37.)

Love shines forth in His **dealings** with sinners, *after* they have believed in Him and become His friends. He is very patient with them, though their conduct is often very trying and provoking. He is never tired of hearing their complaints — however often they may come to

Him. He sympathizes deeply in all their sorrows. He knows what pain is — He is "acquainted with grief" (Is. 53:3.) In all their afflictions, He is afflicted. He never allows them to be tempted above what they are able to bear. He supplies them with daily grace for their daily conflict. Their poor services are acceptable to Him. He is as well pleased with them as a parent is with his child's endeavors to speak and walk. He has caused it to be written in His book, that "He takes pleasure in His people," and that "He takes pleasure in those who fear Him." (Psalm 147:11; 119:4.)

There is no love on earth that can even be named together with this! We love those in whom we see something that deserves our affection, or those who are our relatives — but the Lord Jesus loves sinners in whom there is *no good thing*. We love those from whom we get some return for our affection — but the Lord Jesus loves those who can do little or nothing for Him, compared to what He does for them. We love where we can give some *reason* for loving — but the great *Friend of sinners* draws His reasons out of His own everlasting compassion. His love is purely unselfish — purely free. Never, never was there so truly *loving* a friend as Jesus Christ.

V. Do we want a WISE prudent friend? Such a friend is the Lord Jesus Christ.

Man's friendship is sadly blind. He often *injures* those he loves by injudicious kindness. He often errs in the counsel he gives — he often leads his friends into trouble by bad advice, even when he means to help them. He sometimes keeps them back from the way of life, and entangles them in the vanities of the world, when they have well near escaped. The friendship of the Lord Jesus is not so — it always does us good, and never evil.

The Lord Jesus never *spoils* His friends by extravagant indulgence. He gives them everything that is really for their benefit. He withholds nothing from them that is really good. He requires them to take up their cross daily and follow Him. He bids them endure hardships as good soldiers. He calls on them to fight the good fight against the world, the flesh, and the devil. His people often dislike it at the time, and think it hard — but when they reach Heaven, they will see it was all *well done*.

The Lord Jesus makes no *mistakes* in managing His friends' affairs. He orders all their concerns with perfect wisdom — all things happen to them at the right *time*, and in the right *way*. He gives them . . .
as much of sickness — and as much of health,
as much of poverty — and as much of riches,
as much of sorrow — and as much of joy —
as He sees their souls require.

He leads them by the *right way* to bring them to the city of habitation. He mixes their *bitterest cups* like a wise physician, and takes care that they have not a drop too little — or too much.

His people often misunderstand His dealings — they are silly enough to imagine their course of life might have been better ordered. But in the resurrection-day, they will thank God that not their will — but Christ's will was done.

Look round the world and see the *harm* which people are continually getting from their friends. Mark how much more ready men are to encourage one another in worldliness and levity — than to provoke to love and good works. Think how often they meet together, not for the better — but for the worse; not to quicken one another's souls in the way to Heaven — but to confirm one another in the love of this present world. Alas, there are thousands who are *wounded* unexpectedly in the house of their friends!

And then turn to the great Friend of sinners, and see how different a thing is His friendship from that of man. Listen to Him as He walks by the way with His disciples — mark how He comforts, reproves, and exhorts with perfect wisdom. Observe how He *times* His visits to those He loves — as to Mary and Martha at Bethany. Hear how He converses, as He dines on the shore of the sea of Galilee: "Simon, son of Jonah, do you love Me?" (John 21:16.)

His *company* is always sanctifying.
His *gifts* are always for our soul's good.
His *kindness* is always wise.
His *fellowship* is always to edification.

One day with the Son of Man — is better than a thousand in the society of earthly friends! One hour spent in private communion with Him — is better than a year in kings' palaces. Never, never was there such a *wise* friend as Jesus Christ.

VI. Do we want a TRIED and PROVED friend? Such a friend is Jesus Christ.

Six thousand years have passed away since the Lord Jesus began His work of befriending mankind. During that long period of time, He has had many friends in this world. Millions on millions, unhappily, have refused His offers, and been miserably lost forever; but thousands on thousands have enjoyed the mighty privilege of His friendship and been saved. He has had great experience.

(a) He has had friends of every *rank* and *station* in life. Some of them were kings and rich men, like David, and Solomon, and Hezekiah, and Job. Some of them were very poor in this world, like the shepherds of Bethlehem, and James, and John, and Andrew. But they were all alike Christ's friends.

(b) He has had friends of every *age* that man can pass through. Some of them never knew Him until they were advanced in years, like Manasseh, and Zacchaeus, and probably the Ethiopian Eunuch. Some of them were His friends even from their earliest childhood, like Joseph, and Samuel, and Josiah, and Timothy. But they were all alike Christ's friends.

(c) He has had friends of every possible *temperament* and *disposition*. Some of them were *simple plain* men, like Isaac. Some of them were *mighty* in word and deed, like Moses. Some of them were fervent and *warm-hearted*, like Peter. Some of them were *gentle* and retiring spirits, like John. Some of them were *active* and *stirring*, like Martha. Some of them loved to sit *quietly* at His feet, like Mary. Some dwelt unknown among their own people, like the Shunamite. Some have gone everywhere and turned the world upside down, like Paul. But they were all alike Christ's friends.

(d) He has had friends of every *condition* in life. Some of them were *married*, and had sons and daughters, like Enoch. Some of them lived and died *unmarried*, like Daniel and John the Baptist. Some of them were often *sick*, like Lazarus and Epaphroditus. Some of them were *strong* to labor, like Persis, and Tryphena, and Tryphosa. Some of them were *masters*, like Abraham and Cornelius. Some of them were *servants*, like the saints in Nero's household. Some of them had *bad servants*, like Elisha. Some of them had *bad masters*like Obadiah. Some of them had *bad* wives and children, like David. But they were all alike Christ's friends.

(e) He has had friends of almost every *nation*, and people, and tongue. He has had friends in hot countries and in cold; friends among nations highly civilized, and friends among the simplest and rudest tribes. His *book of life* contains the names of Greeks and Romans, of Jews and Egyptians, of bond and of free. There are to be found on its lists . . .
reserved Englishmen and cautious Scotsmen,
impulsive Irishmen and fiery Welshmen,
volatile Frenchmen and dignified Spaniards,
refined Italians and solid Germans,
crude Africans and refined Hindus,
cultivated Chinese and half-savage New Zealanders.
But they were all alike Christ's friends!

All these have made *trial* of Christ's friendship, and *proved* it to be good. They all found nothing lacking when they began — they all found nothing lacking as they went on. No lack, no defect, no deficiency was ever found by any one of them, in Jesus Christ. Each found his own soul's needs fully supplied; each found every day, that in Christ there was enough and to spare. Never, never was there a friend so fully tried and proved as Jesus Christ.

VII. Last — but not least, do we want an UNFAILING friend? Such a friend is the Lord Jesus Christ.

The saddest part of all the good things of earth is their *instability*.
Riches make themselves wings and flee away;
youth and *beauty* are but for a few years;
strength of body soon decays;
mind and *intellect* are soon exhausted.
All is perishing.
All is fading.
All is passing away.
But there is one splendid exception to this general rule, and that is the *friendship of Jesus Christ*.

The Lord Jesus is a friend who never changes. There is no fickleness about Him. Those whom He loves — He loves unto the end. Husbands have been known to forsake their wives; parents have been known to cast off their children; human vows and promises of faithfulness have often been forgotten. Thousands have been neglected in their poverty and old age — who were honored by all when they were rich and young. But Christ never changed His feelings towards one of His friends. He is "the same yesterday, today, and forever." (Hebrews 13:8.)

The Lord Jesus never goes away from His friends. There is never a *parting* and *good-bye* between Him and His people. From the time that He makes His abode in the sinner's heart — He abides in it forever. The world is full of leave-takings and departures; death and the lapse of time break up the most united family; sons go forth to make their way in life; daughters are married, and leave their father's house forever. *Scattering, scattering, scattering* — is the yearly history of the happiest home. How many we have tearfully watched as they drove away from our doors, whose pleasant faces we have never seen again! How many we have sorrowfully followed to the grave — and then come back to a cold, silent, lonely, and blank fireside! But, thanks be to God, there is One who never leaves His friends! The Lord Jesus is He who has said, "I will never leave you, nor forsake you." (Hebrews 13:5.)

The Lord Jesus goes with His friends wherever they go. There is no possible *separation* between Him and those whom He loves. There is no place or position on earth that can divide them from the great Friend of their souls. When the path of duty calls them far away from home — He is their companion. When they pass through the fire and water of fierce tribulation — He is with them. When they lie down on the bed of sickness — He stands by them and makes all their trouble work for good. When they go down the valley of the shadow of death, and friends and relatives stand still and can go no further — He goes down by their side. When they wake up in the unknown world of Paradise — they are still with Him. When they rise with a new body at the judgment day — they will not be alone. He will own them for His friends, and say, "They are mine! Deliver them and let them go free." He will make good His own words: "I am with you always, even unto the end of the world." (Matthew 28:20.)

Look around the world, and see how *failure* is written on all men's schemes. Count up the partings, and separations, and disappointments, and bereavements which have happened under your own knowledge. Think what a privilege it is that there is One at least who never fails, and in whom no one was ever disappointed! Never, never was there so *unfailing* a friend as Jesus Christ!

And now, allow me to *conclude* this paper with a few plain words of **APPLICATION**. I know not who you are or in what state your soul may be; but I am sure that the words I am about to say deserve your serious attention. Oh, that this paper may not find you heedless of spiritual things! Oh, that you may be able to give a few thoughts to Christ!

(1) Know then, for one thing, that I call upon you to seriously consider whether Christ is your Friend, and you are His.

There are thousands on thousands, I grieve to say, who are not Christ's friends. Baptized in His name, members of a Christian Church, attendants on His means of grace — all this they are, no doubt. But they are not Christ's friends.

Do they *hate the sins* which Jesus died to put away? No.

Do they *love the Savior* who came into the world to save them? No.

Do they *care for the souls* which were so precious in His sight? No.

Do they *delight in the His Word*? No.

Do they try to *speak* with the Friend of sinners in prayer? No.

Do they seek close *fellowship* with Him? No.

Oh, reader, is this your case? How is it with you? Are you or are you not, one of Christ's friends?

(2) Know, in the next place, that if you are not one of Christ's friends — then you are a poor miserable being.

I write this down deliberately. I do not say it without thought. I say that if Christ is not your friend — then you are a poor, miserable being.

You are in the midst of a failing, sorrowful world — and you have no real source of comfort, or refuge for a time of need. You are a dying creature — and you are not ready to die. You have sins — and they are not forgiven. You are going to be judged — and you are not prepared to meet God: you might be — but you refuse to use the one only Mediator and Advocate. You love the world better than Christ. You refuse the great Friend of sinners, and you have no friend in Heaven to plead your cause. Yes, it is sadly true! You are a poor, miserable being! It matters nothing what your income is — without Christ's friendship, you are very poor.

(3) Know, in the third place, that if you really want a friend — then Christ is willing to become your friend.

He has long wanted you to join His people, and He now invites you by my hand. He is ready to receive you, all unworthy as you may feel, and to write your name down in the list of His friends. He is ready to pardon all the past, to clothe you with righteousness, to give you His Spirit, to make you His own dear child. All He asks you to do, is to come to Him.

He bids you to *come with all your sins;* only acknowledging your vileness, and confessing that you are ashamed. Just as you are — waiting for nothing — unworthy of anything in yourself — Jesus bids you come and be His friend.

Oh, come and be wise! Come and be safe. Come and be happy. Come and be Christ's friend.

(4) Know, in the last place, that if Christ is your friend — then you have great *privileges*, and ought to walk worthy of them.

Seek every day to have closer communion with Him who is your Friend, and to know more of His grace and power. True Christianity is not merely the *believing a certain set of dry theological propositions* — it is to live in daily personal communication with an actual living person — Jesus the Son of God. "To me," said Paul, "to live is Christ." (Philippians 1:21.)

Seek every day to *glorify* your Lord and Savior in all your ways. "He who has a friend, should show himself friendly" (Proverbs 18:24), and no man surely is under such mighty *obligations* as the friend of Christ. Avoid everything which would grieve your Lord. Fight hard against besetting sins, against inconsistency, against backwardness to confess Him before men. Say to your soul, whenever you are tempted to that which is wrong, "Soul, soul — is this your kindness to your Friend?"

Think, above all, of the *mercy* which has been shown you, and learn to rejoice daily in your Friend! What though your body is bowed down with disease? What though your poverty and trials are very great? What though your earthly friends forsake you, and you are alone in the world? All this may be true; but if you are in Christ, then you have a *Friend*, a *mighty* Friend, a *loving* Friend, a *wise* Friend, a Friend that *never fails*. Oh, think, think much upon your friend! Yet in a little while, your Friend shall come to take you home, and you shall dwell with Him forever. Yet in a little while, you shall see as you have been seen, and know as you have been known. And then you shall hear assembled worlds confess, that *he is the rich and happy man, who has had Christ for his friend!*

SICKNESS

"Lord, he whom You love is sick!" John 11:3

The chapter from which this text is taken, is well known to all Bible readers. In life-like description, in touching interest, in sublime simplicity — there is no writing in existence that will bear comparison with that chapter. A narrative like this is to my own mind, one of the great proofs of the inspiration of Scripture. When I read the *story of Bethany,* I feel "There is something here which the infidel can never account for. This is nothing else but the finger of God!"

The words which I specially dwell upon in this chapter are singularly affecting and instructive. They record the message which Martha and Mary sent to Jesus when their brother Lazarus was sick: *"Lord, he whom You love is sick!"* That message was short and simple. Yet almost every word is deeply suggestive.

Mark the ***child-like faith*** of these holy women. They turned to the Lord Jesus in their hour of need, as the frightened infant turns to its mother, or the compass-needle turns to the North Pole. They turned to Him as their Shepherd, their almighty Friend, their Brother born for adversity. As different as they were in natural temperament, the two sisters were entirely agreed in this matter. Christ's help was their first thought in the *day of trouble.* Christ was the *refuge* to which they fled in the hour of need. Blessed are all those who do likewise!

Mark the ***simple humility*** of their language about Lazarus. They call him "He whom You love. They do not say, "He who *loves* You, *believes* in You, *serves* You" — but "He whom You love." Martha and Mary were deeply taught of God. They had learned that *Christ's love* towards us, and not *our love* towards Christ — is the true ground of expectation, and true foundation of hope! Blessed, again, are all those who are taught likewise! To look inward to *our* love towards Christ — is painfully unsatisfying. To look outward to *Christ's*love towards us — is peace.

Mark, lastly, the ***touching circumstance*** which the message of Martha and Mary reveals: "He whom You love is sick." Lazarus was a godly man, converted, believing, renewed, sanctified, a friend of Christ, and an heir of glory. And yet Lazarus was *sick!* Then *sickness is no sign that God is displeased.* Sickness is intended to be a blessing to us — and not a curse. "All things work together for good to those who love God, and are called according to His purpose." "All things are yours — life, death, things present, or things to come; for you are Christ's; and Christ is God's." (Romans 8:28; 1 Corinthians 3:22-23. Blessed, I say again, are those who have learned this! Happy are they who can say, when they are ill, "This is *my Father's* doing. It must be well!"

I invite the attention of my readers to the subject of sickness. The subject is one which we ought frequently to look in the face. We cannot avoid it. It needs no prophet's eye to see *sickness* coming to each of us in turn one day. "In the midst of life — we are in death." Let us turn aside for a few moments, and consider *sickness as Christians*. The consideration of the topic of sickness, will not hasten its coming; and by God's blessing, may teach us wisdom.

In considering the subject of sickness, three points appear to me to demand attention. On each I shall say a few words.

I. The *universal prevalence* of sickness and disease.

II. The *general benefits* which sickness confers on mankind.

III. The *special duties* to which sickness calls us.

I. The UNIVERSAL PREVALENCE of sickness.

I need not dwell long on this point. To elaborate the proof of it would only be *multiplying truisms*, and heaping up self-evident truths which all allow.

Sickness is **everywhere**. In Europe, in Asia, in Africa, in America; in hot countries and in cold, in civilized nations and in savage tribes — men, women, and children sicken and die!

Sickness is among **all classes**.

Grace does not lift a believer above the reach of it.

Riches will not buy exemption from it.

Rank cannot prevent its assaults.

Kings and their subjects,
masters and servants,
rich men and poor,
learned and unlearned,
teachers and scholars,
doctors and patients,
ministers and hearers —
all alike go down before this great foe!

The Englishman's house is called his *castle*; but there are no *doors* and *bars* which can keep out disease and death!

Sickness is of **every sort and description**. From the crown of our head, to the sole of our foot — we are liable to disease! Our *capacity of suffering* is something fearful to contemplate. Who can count up the *ailments* by which our bodily frame may be assailed? Who ever visited a museum of anatomy without a shudder? "Strange that *a harp of thousand strings* should keep in tune so long." It is not, to my mind, so astonishing that men should *die so soon* — as it is that they should *live so long!*

Sickness is often one of the most **humbling** and **distressing** trials that can come upon man. It can turn the strongest into a little child, and make him feel "the grasshopper a burden." (Eccles. 12:5.) It can unnerve the boldest, and make him tremble at the fall of a pin! We are "fearfully and wonderfully made." (Psalm 139:14.) The connection between body and mind is amazingly close. The influence that some diseases can exercise upon the temper and spirits is immensely great. There are ailments of brain, and liver, and nerves, which can bring down a *Solomon in mind* to a state little better than that of a babe! He who would know to what depths of humiliation poor man can fall, has only to attend for a short time on sick-beds.

Sickness is **not preventable** by anything that man can do. The average *duration* of life may doubtless be somewhat lengthened. The skill of doctors may continually discover new remedies, and effect surprising cures. The enforcement of wise sanitary regulations may greatly lower the death rate in a land. But, after all — whether in healthy, or unhealthy localities — whether in mild climates, or in cold — whether treated by homeopathy, or allopathy — men will sicken and die! "The length of our days is seventy years — or eighty, if we have the strength; yet their span is but trouble and sorrow, for they quickly pass, and we fly away!" (Psalm 90:10.) That witness is indeed true. It was true thousands of years ago. It is true still.

Now what can we make of this great fact — the *universal prevalence* of sickness? How shall we account for it? What explanation can we give of it? What answer shall we give to our inquiring children when they ask us, "Father, why do people get ill and die?" These are grave questions. A few words upon them will not be out of place.

Can we suppose for a moment that God created sickness and disease at the beginning? Can we imagine that He who formed our world in such *perfect* order was the Former of needless suffering and pain? Can we think that He who made all things "very good," made Adam's race to sicken and to die? The idea is, to my mind, revolting! It introduces a *grand imperfection* into the midst of God's perfect works. I must find another solution to satisfy my mind.

The only explanation that satisfies me is that which the Bible gives. *Something* has come into the world which has dethroned man from his original position, and stripped him of his original privileges. Something has come in, which, like a handful of gravel thrown into the midst of machinery — has marred the perfect order of God's creation. And what is that *something?* I answer, in one word, It is SIN. "Sin has entered into the world, and death by sin." (Romans 5:12.) Sin is the cause of all the sickness, and disease, and pain, and suffering which prevail on the earth. They are all a part of that curse which came into the world when Adam and Eve ate the forbidden fruit and fell. There would have been no sickness — if there had been no *fall.* There would have been no disease — if there had been no *sin.*

I pause for a moment at this point — and yet in pausing I do not depart from my subject. I pause to remind my readers that there is no ground so untenable as that which is occupied by the Atheist, the Deist, or the unbeliever in the Bible. I advise every young reader of this paper, who is puzzled by the bold and specious arguments of the infidel, to study well that most important subject — *the Difficulties of Infidelity*. I say boldly that it requires far more credulity to be a infidel — than to be a Christian. I say boldly that there are great broad patent facts in the condition of mankind, which nothing but the Bible can explain, and that one of the most striking of these facts is the *universal prevalence* of pain, sickness, and disease. In short, one of the mightiest difficulties in the way of Atheists and Deists, is the *body of man*.

You have doubtless heard of **Atheists**. An Atheist is one who professes to believe that there is no God, no Creator, no First Cause — and that all things came together in this world by *mere chance*. Now shall we listen to such a doctrine as this? Go, take an Atheist to one of the excellent surgical schools of our land, and ask him to study the wonderful structure of the human body. Show him the matchless skill with which every joint, and vein, and valve, and muscle, and sinew, and nerve, and bone, and limb, has been formed. Show him the *perfect adaptation* of every part of the human frame to the purpose which it serves. Show him the thousand delicate contrivances for meeting wear and tear, and supplying daily waste of vigor. And then ask this man who denies the being of a God, and a great First Cause — if all this wonderful mechanism is the result of *chance?* Ask him if it came together at first by *luck* and *accident?* Ask him if he so thinks about the *watch* he looks at, the *bread* he eats, or the *coat* he wears? Oh, no! *Design* is an insuperable difficulty in the Atheist's way. There is a God.

You have doubtless heard of **Deists**. A Deist is one who professes to believe that there is a God, who made the world and all things therein. But He does not believe the Bible. "A God — but no Bible! A Creator — but no Christianity!" This is the Deist's creed. Now, shall we listen to this doctrine? Go again, I say, and take a Deist to an hospital, and show him some of the solemn handiwork of disease. Take him to the bed where lies some tender child, with an incurable cancer. Send him to the ward where there is a loving mother of a large family in the last state of some excruciating disease. Show him some of the racking pains and agonies to which flesh is heir, and ask him to account for them. Ask this man, who believes there is a great and Wise God who made the world — but cannot believe the Bible — ask him how he accounts for these *traces of disorder and imperfection* in his God's creation. Ask this man, who sneers at Christian theology and is too wise to believe the fall of Adam — ask him upon his theory, to explain the *universal prevalence of pain and disease* in the world. You may ask in vain! You will get no satisfactory answer. Sickness and suffering are insuperable difficulties in the Deist's way. Man has sinned — and therefore man suffers. Adam fell from his first estate — and therefore Adam's children sicken and die!

The universal prevalence of sickness is one of the indirect evidences that the Bible is true. The Bible *explains* it. The Bible answers the questions about it which will arise in every inquiring mind. No other systems of religion can do this. They all fail here. They are silent. They are confounded. The Bible alone looks the subject in the face. It boldly proclaims the fact that man is a fallen creature, and with equal boldness proclaims a vast remedial system to meet his needs. I feel shut up to the conclusion that the Bible is from God. Christianity is a revelation from Heaven. "Your word is truth." (John 17:17.)

Let us stand fast on the old ground — that the Bible, and the Bible alone, is God's revelation of Himself to man. Do not be moved by the many new assaults which modern skepticism is making on the inspired volume. Heed not the hard questions which the enemies of the faith are fond of putting about Bible difficulties, and to which perhaps you often feel unable to give an answer. Anchor your soul firmly on this safe principle — that the whole book is God's truth. Tell the enemies of the Bible that, in spite of all their arguments, there is no book in the world which will bear comparison with the Bible — none that so thoroughly meets man's needs — none that explains so much of the state of mankind. As to the *hard things* in the Bible, tell them you are content to *wait*. You find enough *plain truth* in the book to satisfy your conscience and save your soul. The hard things will be cleared up one day. What you do not understand now — you will know hereafter.

II. The second point I propose to consider, is the GENERAL BENEFITS which sickness confers on mankind.

I use that word "benefits" advisedly. I feel it of deep importance to see this part of our subject clearly. I well know that sickness is one of the supposed *weak points* in God's government of the world, on which skeptical minds love to dwell. "Can God be a God of love, when He allows pain? Can God be a God of mercy, when He permits disease? He might prevent pain and disease — but He does not. How can these things be?" Such is the reasoning which often comes across the heart of man.

I reply to all such *reasoners*, that their doubts and questionings are most unreasonable. They might as well doubt the existence of a Creator, because the order of the universe is disturbed by earthquakes, hurricanes, and storms. They might as well doubt the providence of God, because of the horrible massacres of Delhi and Cawnpore. All this would be just as reasonable as to doubt the mercy of God, because of the presence of sickness in the world.

I ask all who find it hard to reconcile the prevalence of disease and pain with the love of God, to cast their eyes on the world around them,

and to mark what is going on. I ask them to observe the extent to which men constantly submit to . . .
present loss for the sake of *future gain*;
present sorrow for the sake of future joy;
present pain for the sake of future health.

The *seed* is thrown into the ground, and rots — but we sow in the hope of a future harvest. The *boy* is sent to school amid many tears — but we send him in the hope of his getting future wisdom. The father of a family undergoes some fearful surgical *operation* — but he bears it, in the hope of future health. I ask men to apply this great principle to God's government of the world. I ask them to believe that God allows pain, sickness, and disease, not because He loves to vex man — but because He desires to benefit man's heart, and mind, and conscience, and soul, to all eternity.

Once more I repeat, that I speak of the "benefits" of sickness on purpose and advisedly. I know the suffering and pain which sickness entails. I admit the misery and wretchedness which it often brings in its train. But I cannot regard it as an *unmixed* evil. I see in it a *wise permission* of God. I see in it a *useful provision* to check the ravages of sin and the devil among men's souls. If man had never sinned — I would have been at a loss to discern the benefit of sickness. But since sin is in the world, I can see that sickness is a good. It is a blessing quite as much as a curse. It is a *rough schoolmaster*, I grant — but it is a *real friend* to man's soul.

(a) Sickness helps to remind men of *death*. Most people live as if they were never going to die. They follow business, or pleasure, or politics, or science — as if earth was their *eternal home*. They plan and scheme for the future, like the rich fool in the parable, as if they had a long lease of life, and were not *tenants* whose length of stay is brief. A heavy illness sometimes goes far to dispel these delusions. It awakens men from their day-dreams, and reminds them that they have to *die*, as well as to live. Now this I say emphatically is a mighty good.

(b) Sickness helps to make men think seriously of *God*, and their *souls*, and the *world to come*. Most people, in their days of health, can find no time for such thoughts. They dislike them. They put them away. They count them troublesome and disagreeable. Now a severe disease has sometimes a wonderful power of mustering and rallying these thoughts, and bringing them up before the eyes of a man's soul. Even a wicked king like Benhadad, when sick, could think of Elisha (2 Kings 8:8.) Even heathen sailors, when death was in sight, were afraid, and "cried every man to his god." (Jonah 1:5.) Surely anything that helps to make men *think*, is a good.

(c) Sickness helps to soften men's hearts, and teach them wisdom. The natural heart is as hard as a stone! It can see no good in anything which is not of this life, and no happiness excepting in this world. A long illness sometimes goes far to correct these ideas. It exposes the emptiness and hollowness of what the world calls "good" things, and teaches us to hold them with a loose hand. The man of business finds that money alone, is not everything which the heart requires. The woman of the world finds that costly apparel, and novel reading, and the reports of balls and operas — are miserable comforters in a sick room. Surely anything that obliges us to alter our *weights and measures* of earthly things, is a real good.

(d) Sickness helps to humble us. We are all naturally proud and high-minded. Few, even of the poorest, are free from the infection. Few are to be found who do not look down on somebody else, and secretly flatter themselves that they are "not as other men." A sick bed is a *mighty tamer* of such thoughts as these. It forces on us the mighty truth that we are all poor worms, that we "dwell in houses of clay," and are "crushed before the moth." (Job 4:19), and that kings and subjects, masters and servants, rich and poor — are all dying creatures, and will soon stand side by side at the judgment bar of God. In the sight of the *coffin* and the *grave* — it is not easy to be proud. Surely anything that teaches that lesson, is good.

(e) Finally, sickness helps to try men's religion, of what sort it is. There are not many on earth who have no religion at all. Yet few have a religion which will bear inspection. Most are content with *traditions* received from their fathers, and can render no reason of the hope that is in them. Now disease is sometimes most useful to a man in exposing the utter worthlessness of his *soul's foundation.* It often shows him that he has nothing solid under his feet, and nothing firm under his hand. It makes him find out that, although he may have had a *form of religion,* he has been all his life worshiping "an unknown god." Many a creed looks well on the *smooth waters of health* — which turns out utterly unsound and useless on the *rough waves of the sick bed.* The *storms of winter* often bring out the defects in a man's dwelling — and sickness often exposes the gracelessness of a man's soul. Surely anything that makes us find out the real character of our faith, is a good.

I do not say that sickness confers these benefits on *all* to whom it comes. Alas, I can say nothing of the kind! Myriads are yearly laid low by illness, and restored to health — who evidently learn no lesson from their sick beds, and return again to the world. Myriads are yearly passing through sickness to the grave — and yet receiving no more spiritual impressions from it than the beasts which perish! While they live, they have no feeling; and when they die, there are "no bands in their death." (Psalm 73:4.) These are solemn things to say. But they are true. The degree of deadness to which man's heart and conscience may attain, is a *depth* which I cannot pretend to fathom!

But does sickness confer the benefits of which I have been

speaking on only a few? I will allow nothing of the kind. I believe that in very many cases, sickness produces impressions more or less akin to those of which I have just been speaking. I believe that in many minds sickness is God's "day of visitation," and that feelings are continually aroused on a sick bed which, if improved, might, by God's grace, result in salvation. I believe that in heathen lands, sickness often paves the way for the missionary, and makes the poor idolater lend a willing ear to the glad tidings of the Gospel. I believe that in our own land, sickness is one of the greatest aids to the minister of the Gospel, and that *sermons* and *counsels* are often brought home in the day of disease, which we have neglected in the day of health. I believe that sickness is one of God's most important subordinate instruments in the saving of men, and that though the feelings it calls forth are often temporary — it is also often a means whereby the Spirit works effectually on the heart. In short, I believe firmly that the sickness of men's bodies has often led, in God's wonderful providence, to the salvation of men's souls!

I leave this branch of my subject here. It needs no further remark. If sickness can do the things of which I have been speaking (and who will dispute it?), if sickness in a wicked world can help to make men think of God and their souls — then sickness confers *benefits* on mankind.

We have no right to *murmur* at sickness, and *repine* at its presence in the world. We ought rather to thank God for it. It is *God's witness*. It is the *soul's adviser*. It is an *awakener* to the conscience. It is a *purifier* to the heart. Surely I have a right to tell you that sickness is a *blessing,* and not a curse — a *help,* and not an injury — a *gain,* and not a loss — a *friend,* and not a foe to mankind. So long as we have a world wherein there is sin, it is a mercy that it is a world where there is sickness.

III. The third and last point which I propose to consider, is the *special duties* which the prevalence of sickness entails on each one of ourselves.

I would be sorry to leave the subject of sickness without saying something on this point. I hold it to be of cardinal importance, not to be content with *generalities* in delivering God's message to souls. I am anxious to impress on each one into whose hands this paper may fall, his own personal responsibility in connection with the subject. I would sincerely have no one lay down this paper unable to answer the questions, "What *practical lesson* have I learned? What, in a world of disease and death — what ought I to do?"

(a) One paramount duty which the prevalence of sickness entails on man, is that of *living habitually prepared to meet God.* Sickness is a remembrancer of *death.* Death is the *door* through which we must all pass to *judgment*. Judgment is the time when we must at last see *God* face to face. Surely the first lesson which the inhabitant of a sick and dying world should learn — should be to *prepare to meet his God*.

When are you prepared to meet God? Never until your iniquities are forgiven, and your sin covered! Never until your heart is renewed, and your will taught to delight in the will of God! You have many sins. If you go to church, your own mouth is taught to confess this every Sunday. The blood of Jesus Christ, can alone cleanse those sins away. The righteousness of Christ, can alone make you acceptable in the sight of God. Faith, simple childlike faith, can alone give you a saving interest in Christ and His benefits.

Would you know whether you are prepared to meet God? Then where is your *faith*? Your heart is naturally unfit for God's company. You have no real pleasure in doing His will. The Holy Spirit must transform you after the image of Christ. Old things must pass away. All things must become new.

Would you know whether you are prepared to meet God? Then, where is your *grace*? Where are the evidences of your conversion and sanctification?

I believe that this, and nothing less than this, is preparedness to meet God. Forgiveness of sin; justification by faith; sanctification of the heart; the blood of Christ sprinkled on us; and the Spirit of Christ living in us — these are the grand essentials of the Christian faith. These are not mere words and names to furnish bones of contention for disputing theologians. These are sober, solid, substantial realities. To live in the actual possession of these things, in a world full of sickness and death, is the first duty which I press home to your soul.

(b) Another paramount duty which the prevalence of sickness entails on you, is that of *living habitually ready to bear it patiently*. Sickness is no doubt a trying thing to flesh and blood. To feel our nerves unstrung, and our natural force abated — to be obliged to sit still and be cut off from all our usual avocations — to see our plans broken off and our purposes disappointed — to endure long hours, and days, and nights of weariness and pain — all this is a severe strain on poor sinful human nature! What wonder if peevishness and impatience are brought out by disease! Surely in such a dying world as this, we should study patience.

How will we learn to bear sickness patiently, when it is our turn to suffer sickness? We must lay up *stores of grace* in the time of health. We must seek for the sanctifying influence of the Holy Spirit over our unruly tempers and dispositions. We must make a real business of our prayers, and regularly ask for strength to *endure* God's will — as well as to *do* it. Such strength is to be had for the asking: "If you shall ask anything in my name — I will do it for you." (John 14:14.)

I cannot think it needless to dwell on this point. I believe the *passive graces* of Christianity receive far less notice than they deserve. Meekness, gentleness, patience, faith, patience, are all mentioned in the Word of God as *fruits of the Spirit.* They are passive graces which specially glorify God. They often make men think, who despise the active side of the Christian character. Never do these graces shine so brightly, as they do in the sick room. They enable many a sick person to *preach a silent sermon,* which those around him never forget. Would you adorn the doctrine you profess? Would you make your Christianity beautiful in the eyes of others? Then take the hint I give you this day. Lay up a store of patience against the time of illness. Then, though your sickness is not unto death, it shall be for the "glory of God." (John 11:4.)

(c) One more paramount duty which the prevalence of sickness entails on you, is that of habitual readiness to *feel* with and *help* your fellow-man. Sickness is never very far from us. Few are the families who have not some sick relative. Few are the churches where you will not find someone ill. But wherever there is sickness, there is a call to duty. A little timely *assistance* in some cases — a kindly *visit* in others — a friendly *inquiry* — a mere expression of *sympathy* — may do a vast good. These are the sort of things which soften grudges, and bring men together, and promote good feeling. These are ways by which you may ultimately lead men to Christ and save their souls. These are good works to which every professing Christian should be ready. In a world full of sickness and disease, we ought to "bear one another's burdens," and be "kind one to another." (Galatians 6:2; Ephesians 4:32.)

These things, I dare say, may appear to some, as little and trifling. They must needs be doing something great, and grand, and striking, and heroic! I say that conscientious attention to these *little acts of brotherly-kindness* is one of the clearest evidences of having "the mind of Christ." They are acts in which our blessed Master Himself was abundant. He was ever "going about doing good" to the sick and sorrowful. (Acts 10:38.) They are acts to which He attaches great importance in that most solemn passage of Scripture, the description of the last judgment. He says there: "I was sick — and you visited Me." (Matthew 25:36.)

Have you any desire to prove the *reality of your love* — that blessed grace which so many *talk* of, and so few practice? If you have, beware of unfeeling selfishness and neglect of your sick brethren. Search them out. Assist them if they need aid. Show your sympathy with them. Try to lighten their burdens. Above all, strive to do good to their souls. It will do *you* good, if it does no good to them. It will keep your heart from murmuring. It may prove a blessing to your own soul. I firmly believe that God is testing and proving us by every case of sickness within our reach. By permitting suffering, He tries whether

Christians have any feeling. Beware, lest you are weighed in the balances, and found lacking. If you can live in a sick and dying world and not feel for others — you have yet much to learn.

I leave this branch of my subject here. I throw out the points I have named as suggestions, and I pray God that they may work in many minds. I repeat, that habitual preparedness to meet God — habitual readiness to suffer patiently — habitual willingness to sympathize heartily — are plain duties which sickness entails on all. They are duties within the reach of every one. In naming them, I ask nothing extravagant or unreasonable. I bid no man retire into a monastery and ignore the duties of his station. I only want men to realize that they live in a sick and dying world — and to live accordingly. And I say boldly, that the man who lives the life of faith, and holiness, and patience, and love — is not only the most true Christian — but the most wise and reasonable man!

And now I conclude all with four words of **PRACTICAL APPLICATION**. I want the subject of this paper to be turned to some spiritual use. My heart's desire and prayer to God in placing it in this volume, is to do good to souls.

(1) In the first place, I offer a QUESTION to all who read this paper, to which, as God's ambassador, I entreat their serious attention. It is a question which grows naturally out of the subject on which I have been writing. It is a question which concerns all, of every rank, and class, and condition. I ask you: *What will you do when you are ill?* The time must come when you, as well as others, must go down the dark valley of the shadow of death. The hour must come when you, like all your forefathers, must sicken and die. The time may be near or far off. God only knows. But whenever the time may be, I ask again:

What are you going to do?

Where do you mean to turn for comfort?

On what do you mean to rest your soul?

On what do you mean to build your hope?

From where will you fetch your consolations?

I entreat you not to put these questions away. Allow them to work on your conscience, and rest not until you can give them a satisfactory answer. Trifle not with that precious gift — your immortal soul. Defer not the consideration of the matter to a more convenient season. *Presume* not on a death-bed repentance. The greatest business ought surely not to be left to the last. One *dying thief* was saved that men might not despair — but *only one* that none might presume! I repeat the question. I am sure it deserves an answer. *"What will you do when you are ill?"*

If you were going to live forever in this world, I would not address you as I do. But it cannot be. There is no escaping the common lot of all mankind. Nobody can die in our stead. The day must come when we must each go to our *long home*. Against that day I want you to be prepared. The body which now takes up so much of your attention — the body which you now clothe, and feed, and warm with so much care — that body must return again to the dust! Oh, think what a solemn thing it would prove at last to have provided for everything, except the one thing needful — to have provided for the body — but to have neglected the soul! Once more I press my question on your conscience: "What will you do when you are ill?"

(2) In the next place, I offer COUNSEL to all who feel they need it and are willing to take it, to all who feel they are not yet prepared to meet God. That counsel is short and simple. Acquaint yourself with the Lord Jesus Christ without delay. Repent, be converted, flee to Christ, and be saved.

Either you have a *soul* — or you have not. You will surely never deny that you have. Then if you have a soul, seek that soul's salvation. Of all *gambling* in the world, there is none so reckless as that of the man who lives unprepared to meet God — and yet puts off repentance.

Either you have *sins* — or you have not. If you have (and who will dare to deny it?), break off from those sins, cast away your transgressions, and turn away from them without delay.

Either you need a *Savior* — or you do not. If you do, flee to the only Savior this very day, and cry mightily to Him to save your soul. Apply to Christ at once. Seek Him by faith. Commit your soul into His keeping. Cry mightily to Him for pardon and peace with God. Ask Him to pour down the Holy Spirit upon you, and make you a thorough Christian. He will hear you. No matter what you have been, He will not refuse your prayer. He has said, "Him that comes to Me — I will never cast out." (John 6:37.)

Beware, I beseech you, of a vague and indefinite Christianity. Do not be content with a *general hope that all is right,* because you belong to the old Church of England; and that all will be well at last, because God is merciful. Rest not, rest not without personal union with Christ Himself. Rest not, rest not until you have the witness of the Spirit in your heart, that you are washed, and sanctified, and justified, and one with Christ, and Christ in you. Rest not until you can say with the apostle, "I know *whom* I have believed, and am persuaded that He is able to keep that which I have committed to Him against that day!" (2 Tim. 1:12.)

Vague, and indefinite, and indistinct religion may do very well in time of *health*. It will never do in the day of *sickness*. A mere formal, perfunctory Church membership may carry a man through the *sunshine of youth and prosperity*. It will break down entirely when *death* is in sight. Nothing will do then but real heart-union with Christ. Christ interceding for us at God's right hand, Christ known and believed as our Priest, our Physician, our Friend. Christ alone can rob death of its sting, and enable us to face sickness without fear. He alone can deliver those who through fear of death are in bondage. I say to every one who needs advice: Be acquainted with Christ. As ever you would have hope and comfort on the bed of sickness — be acquainted with Christ. Seek Christ. Apply to Christ.

Take every care and trouble to Him when you are acquainted with Him. He will keep you and carry you through all. Pour out your heart before Him, when your conscience is burdened. He is the true Confessor. He alone can absolve you and take the burden away. Turn to Him first in the day of sickness, like Martha and Mary. Keep on looking to Him to the last breath of your life. Christ is worth knowing. The more you know Him — the better you will love Him. Then be acquainted with Jesus Christ.

(3) In the third place, I exhort all true Christians who read this paper to remember how much they may *glorify God* in the time of sickness, and to lie quite in God's hand when they are ill. I feel it very important to touch on this point. I know how ready the heart of a believer is to faint, and how busy Satan is in suggesting doubts and questionings, when the body of a Christian is weak. I have seen something of the *depression* and *melancholy* which sometimes comes upon the children of God when they are suddenly laid aside by disease, and obliged to sit still. I have marked how prone some good people are to torment themselves with morbid thoughts at such seasons, and to say in their hearts, "God has forsaken me — I am cast out of His sight."

I earnestly entreat all sick believers to remember that they may honor God as much by *patient suffering* — as they can by *active work*. It often shows more grace to *sit still* — than it does to go to and fro, and perform great exploits. I entreat them to remember that Christ cares for them as much when they are *sick* — as He does when they are well; and that the very chastisement they feel so acutely — is sent in love, and not in anger.

Above all, I entreat them to recollect the *sympathy of Jesus for all His weak members*. They are always tenderly cared for by Him — but never so much as in their time of need. Christ has had great experience of sickness. He knows the heart of a sick man. He used to see "all manner of sickness, and all manner of disease" when He was upon earth. He felt specially for the sick in the days of His flesh. He feels for them specially still. Sickness and suffering, I often think, make believers more like their Lord in experience, than health. "Himself took our infirmities, and bore our sicknesses." (Isaiah 53:3; Matthew 8:17.) The Lord Jesus was a "Man of sorrows, and acquainted with grief." None have such an opportunity of learning the mind of a suffering Savior — as suffering disciples.

(4) I conclude with a word of exhortation to all believers, which I heartily pray God to impress upon their souls. I exhort you to keep up a habit of close communion with Christ, and never to be afraid of "going too far" in your religion. Remember this, if you wish to have "great peace" in your times of sickness.

I observe with regret, a tendency in some quarters to lower the standard of practical Christianity, and to denounce what are called "extreme views" about a Christian's daily walk in life. I remark with pain, that even religious people will sometimes look coldly on those who withdraw from worldly society, and will censure them as "exclusive, narrow-minded, illiberal, uncharitable, sour-spirited," and the like. I warn every believer in Christ who reads this paper to beware of being influenced by such *censures*. I entreat him, if he needs light in the valley of death, to "keep himself unspotted from the world," to "follow the Lord fully," and to walk very closely with God. (James 1:27; Num. 14:24.)

I believe that the lack of "thoroughness" about many people's Christianity is one secret of their little comfort, both in health and sickness. I believe that the "half-and-half, keep-in-with everybody" religion, which satisfies many in the present day, is offensive to God, and sows thorns in dying pillows, which hundreds never discover until too late. I believe that the weakness and feebleness of such a religion never comes out so much, as it does upon a sick bed.

If you and I want "strong consolation" in our time of need, we must not be content with a bare *union* with Christ. (Hebrews 6:18.) We must seek to know something of heart-felt, *experimental communion* with Him. Never, never let us forget, that "union" is one thing, and "communion" another. Thousands, I fear, who know what "union" with Christ is, know little of "communion."

The day may come when after a long fight with disease, we shall feel that medicine can do no more, and that nothing remains but to die. Friends will be standing by, unable to help us. Hearing, eyesight, even the power of praying, will be fast failing us. The world and its shadows will be melting beneath our feet. Eternity, with its realities, will be looming large before our minds. What shall *support* us in that trying hour? What shall enable us to feel, "I fear no evil"? (Psalm 23:4.) Nothing, nothing can do it but *close communion* with Christ. Christ dwelling in our hearts by faith — Christ putting His right arm under our heads — Christ felt to be sitting by our side — Christ can alone give us the complete victory in the last struggle.

Let us . . .
cleave to Christ more closely,
love Him more heartily,
live to Him more thoroughly,
copy Him more exactly,

confess Him more boldly,
and *follow* Him more fully.

Religion like this will always bring its own reward. Worldly people may laugh at it. Weak brethren may think it extreme. But it will *wear well.* At evening time, it will bring us light. In sickness, it will bring us peace. In the world to come, it will give us an unfading crown of glory.

The time is short. The fashion of this world passes away. A few more sicknesses — and all will be over! A few more funerals — and our own funeral will take place! A few more storms and tossings — and we shall be safe in *harbor.* We travel towards a world where there is no more sickness — where parting, and pain, and crying, and mourning, are done with for evermore. Heaven is becoming every year more full — and earth more empty. The friends ahead are becoming more numerous than the friends astern. "Yet a little while, and He who shall come will come, and will not tarry." (Hebrews 10:37.) In His presence shall be fullness of joy. Christ shall wipe away all tears from His people's eyes. The *last enemy* that shall be destroyed is Death. But He shall be destroyed. Death himself shall one day die. (Rev. 20:14.) In the meantime, let us live a *life of faith* in the Son of God. Let us lean all our weight on Christ, and rejoice in the thought that He lives for evermore.

Yes, blessed be God! Christ lives — though we may die. Christ lives — though friends and families are carried to the grave. He lives, who abolished death, and brought life and immortality to light by the Gospel. He lives, who said, "O death, I will be your plague! O grave, I will be your destruction!" (Hos. 13:14.) He lives, who will one day change our vile body, and make it like unto His glorious body. In sickness and in health, in life and in death, let us lean confidently on Him. Surely we ought to say daily with one of old, "Blessed be God for Jesus Christ!"

THE FAMILY OF GOD

"The whole family in Heaven and earth." Ephesians 3:15

Reader, Look at the words which form the title of this tract, and ponder them well. They are words which ought to stir some feelings in our minds at any time, and especially at Christmas. There lives not the man or woman on earth, who is not a member of some "family." The poorest as well as the richest, has his *kith and kin*, and can tell you something of "his family."

Family gatherings at Christmas, we all know, are very common. Thousands of firesides are crowded then, if at no other time of the year. The young man in town snatches a few days from business, and takes a run down to "the old folks at home." The young woman gets a short holiday, and comes to visit her father and mother. Brothers and sisters meet for a few hours. Parents and children look one another in the face. How much there is to talk about! How many questions to be asked! How many interesting things to be told! Happy indeed is that fireside which sees gathered round it at Christmas, "the whole family!"

Family gatherings at Christmas are natural, and right, and good. I approve them with all my heart. It does me good to see them kept up. They are one of the very few pleasant things which have survived the fall of man. Next to the grace of God, I see no principle which unites people so much in this sinful world — as family feeling. Community of blood is a most powerful tie. I have often observed that people will stand up for their relations, merely because they are their relations — and refuse to hear a word against them — even when they have no sympathy with their tastes and ways. Anything which helps to keep up family feeling ought to be commended. It is a wise thing, when it can be done, to gather together at Christmas "the whole family."

Family gatherings, nevertheless, are often sorrowful things. It would be strange indeed, in such a world as this, if they were not. Few are the family circles which do not show *gaps* and vacant places as years pass away. Changes and deaths make sad havoc as time goes on. Thoughts will rise up within us, as we grow older, about faces and voices no longer with us, which no Christmas merriment can entirely keep down. When the younger members of the family have once begun to shift for themselves and launch forth into the world — the old heads may long survive the scattering of the nest. But after a certain time, it seldom happens that you see together "the whole family."

And now, reader, let me take occasion from Christmas to tell you of a great family to which I want you to belong. It is a family despised by many, and not even known by some; but it is a family of far more importance than any family on earth. To belong to it entitles a man to far greater privileges than to be the son of a king. It is the family of which Paul speaks to the Ephesians, when he tells them of the "whole family in Heaven and earth." It is *the family of God.*

Reader, give me your attention while I try to describe this family, and recommend it to your notice. I do not wish to mar your Christmas merriment, or to lessen the joy of your Christmas gathering, wherever it may be. I only want to remind you of a *better* family, even a *Heavenly* one, and of the great *benefits* which membership of that family conveys. I want you to be found one of that family, when its gathering shall come at last — a gathering without separation, or sorrow, or tears. Hear me while, as a minister of Christ and friend to your soul — I talk for a few minutes about "the whole family in Heaven and earth."

I. First of all — what is this family?

II. Secondly — what is its present position?

III. Thirdly — what are its future prospects?

I wish to unfold these three things before you, and I invite your serious consideration of them. Our Christmas gatherings on earth must have an end one day. Our last earthly Christmas must come. Happy indeed, is that Christmas which finds us prepared to meet God!

I. What is that family which the Bible calls "the whole family in Heaven and earth"? Of whom does it consist?

The family before us consists of *all real Christians* — of all who have the Spirit — of all true believers in Christ — of the saints of every age, and church, and nation, and tongue. It includes the blessed company of all faithful people. It is the same as the election of God — the household of faith — the mystical body of Christ — the bride — the living temple — the sheep that never perish — the Church of the first-born. All these expressions are only "the family of God" under other names.

Membership in the family of God, does not depend on any earthly connection. It comes not by natural birth — but by *new birth.* Ministers cannot impart it to their hearers. Parents cannot give it to their children. You may be born in the godliest family in the land, and enjoy the richest means of grace a church can supply — and yet never belong to the family of God. To belong to it, you must be born again. None but the Holy Spirit can make a living member of this family. It is His special office and prerogative, to bring into the Church such as shall be saved. Those who are born again, are "born not of blood, nor of the will of the flesh, nor of the will of man — but of God." (John 1:13.)

Reader, do you ask the reason of this name which the Bible gives to the company of all true Christians? Would you like to know why they are called "a family"? Listen, and I will tell you.

1. True Christians are called a "family" — because they have all *one Father*. They are all *children of God by faith* in Christ Jesus. They are all born of one Spirit. They are all sons and daughters of the Lord Almighty. They have received the Spirit of adoption, whereby they cry, 'Abba Father!' (Galatians 3:26; John 3:8; 2 Corinthians 4:18; Romans 8:15.) They do not regard God with slavish fear — as an austere Being, only ready to punish them. They look up to Him with tender confidence as a reconciled and loving parent — as One forgiving iniquity, transgression and sin, to all who believe on Jesus; and full of pity even to the least and feeblest. The words, "Our Father who is in Heaven," are no mere form in the mouth of true Christians. No wonder they are called God's "family."

2. True Christians are called "a family" — because they all rejoice in *one name*. That name is the name of their great Head and Elder Brother, even Jesus Christ the Lord. Just as a common family name is the uniting link to all the members of a human family, so does the name of Jesus tie all believers together in one vast family. As members of outward visible Churches, they have various names and distinguishing appellations. As living members of Christ, they all, with one heart and mind, rejoice in one Savior. Not a heart among them, but feels drawn to Jesus as the only object of hope. Not a tongue among them, but would tell you that "Christ is all." Sweet to them all, is the thought of Christ's death for them on the cross. Sweet is the thought of Christ's intercession for them at the right hand of God. Sweet is the thought of Christ's coming again to unite them to Himself in one glorified company forever. In fact, you might as well take away the sun out of Heaven — as take away the name of Christ from believers. To the world there may seem little in His name. To believers it is full of comfort, hope, joy, rest, and peace. No wonder they are called "a family."

3. True Christians, above all, are called "a family" — because there is so strong a *family likeness* among them. They are all led by one Spirit, and are marked by the same general features of life, heart, taste, and character. Just as there is a general *physical* resemblance among the brothers and sisters of a family, so there is a general *spiritual* resemblance among all the sons and daughters of the Lord Almighty. They all hate sin and love God. They all rest their hope of salvation on Christ, and have no confidence in themselves. They all endeavor to come out and be separate from the ways of the world, and to set their affections on things above. They all turn naturally to the same Bible as the only food of their souls, and the only sure guide in their pilgrimage toward Heaven. They find it a "lamp to their feet, and a light to their path." (Psalm. 119:105.) They all go to the same throne of grace in prayer, and find it as needful to speak to God as to breathe. They all live by the same rule, the Word of God, and strive to conform their daily life to its precepts. They have all the same inward experience. Repentance, faith, hope, charity, humility, inward conflict, are things with which they are all more or less acquainted. No wonder they are called "a family."

Reader, this family likeness among true believers is a thing that deserves special attention. To my own mind it is one of the strongest indirect evidences of the truth of Christianity. It is one of the greatest proofs of the reality of the work of the Holy Spirit. Some true Christians live in civilized countries — and some in the midst of heathen lands. Some are highly educated — and some are unable to read a letter. Some are rich — and some are poor. Some are Churchmen — and some are Dissenters. Some are old — and some are young. And yet, notwithstanding all this, there is a marvelous oneness of heart and character among them.

Their joys and their sorrows,
their love and their hatred,
their likes and their dislikes,
their tastes and their distastes,
their hopes and their fears —
are all most curiously alike! Let others think what they please, I see in all this the finger of God. His handiwork is always one and the same. No wonder that true Christians are compared to "a family."

Take an converted Englishman and a converted Hindu, and let them suddenly meet for the first time. I will engage, if they can understand one another's language, they will soon find common ground between them, and feel at home. The one may have been brought up at school and college, and enjoyed every privilege of English civilization. The other may have been trained in the midst of gross heathenism, and accustomed to habits, ways, and manners as unlike the Englishman's as darkness compared to light. And yet now in half an hour, they feel that they are friends! The Englishman finds that he has more in common with his Hindu brother — than he has with many an old college companion or school-fellow! Who can account for this? How can it be explained? Nothing can account for it but the unity of the Spirit's teaching. It is "one touch" of grace, not nature, "that makes the whole world kin." God's people are in the highest sense "a family."

Reader, this is the family to which I wish to direct your attention this Christmas. This is the family to which I want you to belong. I ask you this day to consider it well, if you never considered it before. I have shown you the *Father* of the family, the God and Father of our Lord Jesus Christ. I have shown you the *Head* and Elder Brother of the family, the Lord Jesus Himself. I have shown you the *features* and *characteristics* of the family. Its members have all great general marks of resemblance. Once more I say, consider it well.

Outside this family, remember, there is no salvation. None but those who belong to it, according to the Bible, are in the way that leads to Heaven. The salvation of our souls does not depend on union with one church or separation from another. They are miserably deceived, who think that it does, and will find it out to their cost one day, except they awake. No, reader, the life of our souls depends on something far more important! This is life eternal, to be a member of "the whole family in Heaven and earth." I will now pass on to the *second* thing which I promised to consider.

II. What is the *present position* of "the whole family in Heaven and earth"?

The family to which I am directing your attention this day is *divided into two great parts*. Each part has its own residence or dwelling-place. Part of the family is in Heaven, and part is on earth. For the present, the two parts are entirely *separated* from one another. But they form *one body* in the sight of God, though resident in two places: and their union is sure to come one day.

Two places, be it remembered, and two only, contain the family of God. The Bible tells us of no third habitation. There is no such thing as *Purgatory*, whatever some may think fit to say. There is no place of *purification* for those who are not true Christians when they die. Oh no! There are but two parts of the family — the part that is seen — and the part that is unseen, the part that is in "Heaven" — and the part that is on "earth." The members of the family that are not in Heaven are on earth, and those that are not on earth are in Heaven. Two parts, and two only! Two places, and two only! Let this never be forgotten.

Some of God's family are safe in **Heaven**. They are at rest in that place which the Lord Jesus expressly calls "Paradise." (Luke 23:43.) They have finished their course. They have fought their battle. They have done their appointed work. They have learned their lessons. They have carried their cross. They have passed through the ocean of this troublesome world and reached the *harbor*. As little as we know about them — we know that they are happy. They are no longer troubled by sin and temptation. They have said goodbye forever to poverty and anxiety, to pain and sickness, to sorrow and tears. They are with Christ Himself, who loved them and gave Himself for them, and in His company they must needs be happy. (Philippians 1:23.) They have nothing to fear in looking *back* to the past. They have nothing to dread in looking *forward* to things to come. Three things only are lacking to make their happiness complete. These three are:
the second advent of Christ in glory,
the resurrection of their own bodies, and
the gathering together of all believers.
And of these three things they are sure.

Some of God's family are still upon **earth**. They are scattered to

and fro in the midst of a wicked world, a few in one place and a few in another. All are more or less occupied in the same way, according to the measure of their grace. All are . . .
running a race,
doing a work,
warring a warfare,
carrying a cross,
striving against sin,
resisting the devil,
crucifying the flesh,
struggling against the world,
witnessing for Christ,
mourning over their own hearts,
hearing, reading, and praying, however feebly, for the life of their souls.

Each is often disposed to think no cross so heavy as his own, no work so difficult, no heart so hard. But each and all hold on their way — a wonder to the ignorant world around them, and often a wonder to themselves.

But, reader, however divided God's family may be at present in dwelling-place and local habitation — it is still one family. Both parts of it are still one in character, one in possessions, and one in relation to God. The part in *Heaven* has not so much superiority over the part on *earth* — as at first sight may appear. The difference between the two is only one of degree.

1. Both parts of the family love the same *Savior*, and delight in the same perfect will of God. But the part on *earth* loves with much imperfection and infirmity, and lives by faith, not by sight. The part in *Heaven* loves without weakness, or doubt, or distraction. It walks by sight, and not by faith, and sees what it once believed.

2. Both parts of the family are *saints*. But the saints on *earth* are often poor weary pilgrims, who find the "flesh lusting against the spirit and the spirit lusting against the flesh, so that they cannot do the things they would." (Galatians 5:17.) They live in the midst of an evil world, and are often sick of themselves and of the sin they see around them. The saints in *Heaven*, on the contrary, are delivered from the world, the flesh, and the devil, and enjoy a glorious liberty. They are called "the spirits of just men made perfect." (Hebrews 12:23.)

3. Both parts of the family are alike God's *children*. But the children in *Heaven* have learned all their lessons, have finished their appointed tasks, have begun an eternal holiday. The children on *earth* are still at school. They are daily learning wisdom, though slowly and with much trouble, and often needing to be reminded of their past lessons by chastisement and the rod. Their holidays are yet to come.

4. Both parts of the family are alike God's *soldiers*. But the soldiers on *earth* are yet militant. Their warfare is not accomplished. Their fight is not over. They need every day to put on the whole armor of God. The soldiers in *Heaven* are all triumphant. No enemy can hurt them now. No fiery dart can reach them. Helmet and shield may both be laid aside. They may at last say to the sword of the Spirit, "Rest and be still!" They may at length sit down, and need not to watch and stand on guard.

5. Last, but not least — both parts of the family are alike *safe* and *secure*. As wonderful as this may sound, it is true! Christ cares as much for His members on earth — as His members in Heaven. You might as well think to pluck the stars out of Heaven — as to pluck one saint, however feeble, out of Christ's hand. Both parts of the family are alike secured by "an everlasting covenant ordered in all things and sure." (2 Sam. 23:5.) The members on earth, through the burden of the flesh and the dimness of their faith — may neither see, nor know, nor feel their own safety. But they are safe, though they may not see it. The whole family is "kept by the power of God, through faith unto salvation." (1 Peter 1:5.) The members yet on the *road*, are as secure as the members who have got *home!* Not one shall he found missing at the last day. The words of the Christian poet shall be found strictly true: "More *happy* — but not more *secure* — are the glorified spirits in Heaven!"

Reader, before I leave this part of my subject, I ask you to understand thoroughly the present position of God's family, and to form a just estimate of it. Learn not to measure its numbers or its privileges — by what you see with your eyes. You see only a small body of believers in this present time. But you must not forget that a great company has gotten safe to Heaven already, and that when all are assembled at the last day, they will be "a multitude which no man can number." (Rev. 7:9.) You only see that part of the family which is *struggling* on earth. You must never forget that the greater part of the family has got home and is *resting* in Paradise. You see the *militant* part, but not the *triumphant*. You see the part that is carrying the cross — but not the part which is safe at the other side of the river. The family of God is far more rich and glorious than you suppose. Believe me, it is no small thing to belong to the "whole family in Heaven and earth." I will now pass on to the last thing which I promised to consider.

III. What are the *future prospects* of "the whole family" in Heaven and earth?

The future prospects of a family! What a vast amount of *uncertainty* these words open up when we look at any family now in the world! How little we can tell of the things coming on any of us!

What a mercy that we do not know the sorrows, and trials, and separations, through which our beloved children will have to pass, when we have left the world! It is a mercy that we do not know "what a day may bring forth," and a far greater mercy that we do not know what may happen in twenty years! (Proverbs 27:1.) Reader, foreknowledge of the future of our families, would spoil many a family gathering this Christmas, and fill the whole party with gloom!

Think how many a fine boy, who is now the delight of his parents — will by and by walk in the *prodigal's footsteps*, and never return home! Think how many a fair daughter, the joy of a mother's heart — will follow the bent of her self-will after a few years, and insist on some miserably mistaken marriage! Think how disease and pain will often lay low the loveliest of a family circle, and make her life a burden and weariness to herself and others! Think of the endless *breaches* and *divisions* arising out of money matters! Alas, there is many a lifelong quarrel about a few dollars, between those who once played together in the same nursery! Reader, think of these things! The "future prospects" of many a family which will meet together this Christmas are a solemn and serious subject. Hundreds, to say the least, are gathering together for the last time! When they part — they will never meet again.

But, thank God, there is one great family whose prospects are very different. It is the family of which I am speaking in this tract, and commending to your attention. The future prospects of the family of God are not *uncertain*. They are good, and only good — happy, and only happy. Listen to me, and I will try to set them in order before you.

1. The members of God's family shall all be *brought safely home* one day! Here upon earth they may be scattered, tried, tossed with tempests, and bowed down with afflictions. But not one of them shall perish! (John 10:28.) The *weakest lamb* shall not be left to perish in the wilderness. The *feeblest child* shall not be missing when the muster-roll is brought out at the last day. In spite of the world, the flesh, and the devil — the whole family shall get safely home! "If, when we were enemies, we were reconciled to God by the death of His Son, much more, being reconciled, we shall be saved by His life." (Romans 5:10.)

2. The members of God's family shall all have *glorious bodies* one day! When the Lord Jesus Christ comes the second time, the dead saints shall all be raised, and the living shall all be changed. They shall no longer have a vile mortal body, full of weaknesses and infirmities. They shall have a body like that of their risen Lord — without the slightest liability to sickness and pain. They shall no longer be clogged and hindered by an aching frame when they want to serve God. They shall be able to serve Him night and day without weariness, and to attend upon Him without distraction. The former things will have passed away. That word will be fulfilled, "I make all things new!" (Rev. 21:5.)

3. The members of God's family shall all be *gathered into one company* one day! It matters nothing where they have lived or where they have died. They may have been separated from one another both by *time* and *space*. One may have lived in tents, with Abraham, Isaac, and Jacob — and another traveled by railway in our own day. One may have laid his bones in an Australian desert — and another may have been buried in an English churchyard. It makes no difference. All shall be gathered together, from north and south, and east and west — and meet in one happy assembly, to part no more. The earthly partings of God's family are only for a few days. Their meeting is for *eternity*. It matters little where we *live*. It is a time of scattering now, and not of gathering. It matters little where we *die*. All graves are equally near to Paradise. But it does matter much, whether we belong to God's family. If we do — we are sure to meet again at last.

4. The members of God's family shall all be *united in mind and judgement* one day. They are not so now, about many little things. About the things needful to salvation, there is a marvelous unity among them. About many *speculative points* in religion — about forms of worship and Church government, they often sadly disagree. But there shall be no disagreement among them one day. Ephraim shall no longer vex Judah, nor Judah Ephraim. Churchmen shall no more quarrel with Dissenters, nor Dissenters with Churchmen. *Partial knowledge* and *dim vision* shall be at an end forever. Divisions and separations, misunderstandings and misconstructions — shall be buried and forgotten. As there shall only be one *language*, so there shall only be one *opinion*. At last, after six thousand years of strife and jangling — *perfect* unity and harmony shall be found! A family shall at length be gathered, in which *all* are of one mind.

5. The members of God's family shall all be *perfected in holiness* one day! They are not literally perfect now. Though born again, and renewed after the image of Christ — they offend and fall short in many things. (James 3:2.) None know it better than they do themselves. It is their grief and sorrow, that they do not love God more heartily and serve Him more faithfully. But they shall be *completely freed from all sinful corruption* one day. They shall rise again at Christ's second appearing without any of the *infirmities* which cleave to them in their lives. Not a single evil temper or corrupt inclination shall he found in them! They shall be presented by their Head to the Father — without spot, or wrinkle, or any such thing — perfectly holy and without blemish — as fair as the moon and as clear as the sun! (Ephesians 5:27; Canticles 5:10.) Grace, even now, is a beautiful thing, when it lives, and shines, and flourishes in the midst of imperfection. But how much more beautiful will *grace* appear — when it is seen pure, unmixed, disentangled, and alone. And it shall be seen so, when Christ comes to be glorified in His saints at the last day.

6. Last, but not least — the members of God's family shall all be *eternally provided for* one day! When the affairs of this sinful world are finally wound up and settled, there shall be an *everlasting portion* for all the sons and daughters of the Lord Almighty. Not even the weakest of them shall be overlooked and forgotten. There shall be something for everyone, according to his measure. The smallest *vessel* of grace, as well as the greatest — shall be *filled* to the brim with glory — the precise nature of that glory and reward it would be folly to pretend to describe. It is a thing which eye has not seen, nor mind of man conceived. Enough for us to know that each member of God's family, when he awakes up after His Master's likeness, shall be *satisfied*. (Psalm 17:15.) Enough, above all, to know that their *joy*, and *glory*, and *reward* shall be forever. What they receive in the day of the Lord — they will never lose. The *inheritance reserved* for them, when they come of age, is "incorruptible, undefiled, and unfading!" (1 Peter 1:4.)

Reader, these prospects of God's family are great realities. They are not vague shadowy talk of man's invention. They are real true things, and will be seen as such before long. They deserve your serious consideration. Examine them well.

Look around the families of earth with which you are acquainted, the richest, the greatest, the noblest, the happiest. Where will you find one among them all, which can show prospects to compare with those of which you have just heard? The earthly riches, in many a case, will be gone in a hundred years hence. The noble blood, in many a case, will not prevent some disgraceful deed *staining the family name*. The happiness in many a case, will be found hollow and surface. Few, indeed, are the homes which have not a *secret sorrow* or "a skeleton in the closet." Whether for *present possessions* or *future prospects*, there is no family so well off as "the whole family in Heaven and earth." Whether you look at what they have *now*, or will have *hereafter* — there is no family like the family of God.

Reader, my task is done. My tract is drawing to a close. It only remains to close it with a few words of **PRACTICAL APPLICATION**. Give me your attention for the last time. May God bless what I am going to say to the good of your soul!

(1) I ask you a plain question. Take it with you to the family gathering which you are going to join at Christmas. Take it with you, and amidst all your Christmas happiness make time for thinking about it. It is a simple question, but a solemn one: *Do you yet belong to the family of God?*

To the family of *God*, remember! This is the point of my question.

It is no answer to say that you are a Protestant, or a Churchman, or a Dissenter. I want to hear of something more and better than that. I want you to have some soul-satisfying and soul-saving religion — a religion which will give you peace while you live, and *hope* when you die. To have such peace and hope, you must be something more than a Protestant, or a Churchman, or a Dissenter. You must belong to "the family of God." Thousands around you do not belong to it. But that is no reason why you should not.

Reader, if you do not yet belong to God's family, I invite you this day to join it without delay. Open your eyes to see . . .
the value of your soul,
the sinfulness of sin,
the holiness of God,
the danger of your present condition,
the absolute necessity of a mighty change!

Open your eyes to see these things, and repent this very day! Open your eyes to see the great Head of God's family, even Christ Jesus, waiting to save your soul. See how He has loved you, lived for you, died for you, risen again for you, and obtained complete redemption for you. See how He offers you free, full, immediate pardon, if you will believe in Him. Open your eyes to see these things. Seek Christ at once. Come and believe on Him, and commit your soul to His keeping this very day.

I know nothing of your family or past history. I know not where you are going to spend your Christmas, or what company you are going to be in. But I am bold to say, that if you join the family of God this Christmas — it will be the best and happiest Christmas in your life.

(2) Reader, if you really belong to the whole family in Heaven and earth, count up your privileges, and learn to be more thankful! Think what a mercy it is to have something which the world can neither give nor take away — something which is independent of sickness or poverty — something which is your own for evermore. The old family *fireside* will soon be cold and tenantless. The old family *gatherings* will soon be past and gone forever. The loving faces we now delight to gaze on, are rapidly leaving us. The cheerful voices which now welcome us, will soon be silent in the grave. But, thank God, if we belong to Christ's family — there is a better gathering yet to come. Let us often think of it — and be thankful!

Those grey-haired old patriarchs, whose cheerfulness made their Christianity so beautiful, and who thought of everybody more than of themselves — those tender mothers, whose memory is still so fragrant to their children, and whose sun seemed to go down at noonday — we shall see them all again. They are not lost — but only gone before. All, all will meet us in the great home, when the last trumpet sounds and "the whole family" is gathered together. Reader, let us often think of this, and be thankful.

The family gathering of all God's people will *make amends* for all that their religion now costs them. A meeting where none are missing — a meeting where there are no gaps and empty places — a meeting where there are no tears — a meeting where there is no parting — such a meeting as this is worth a fight and a struggle! And such a meeting is yet to come to "the whole family in Heaven and earth."

In the meantime, let us strive to *live worthy* of the family to which we belong. Let us labor to do nothing that may cause our Father's house to be spoken against. Let us endeavor to make our Master's name beautiful by our temper, conduct and conversation. Let us love as brethren, and abhor all quarrels. Let us behave as if the honor of the family depended on our behavior.

So living, by the grace of God, we shall make our calling and election sure, both to ourselves and others. So living, we may hope to have an abundant entrance, and to enter harbor in full sail, whenever we change earth for Heaven. So living, we shall recommend our Father's family to others, and perhaps, by God's blessing incline them to say, "We will go with you!"

Reader, I commend these *Christmas thoughts* to your attention; and, wishing you a happy Christmas in the best and highest sense!

I remain, your affectionate friend,
J.C. Ryle

OUR HOME!

"Lord, you have been our dwelling place throughout all generations!" Psalm 90:1

There are two reasons why the text which heads this paper should ring in our hearts with special power. It is the first verse of a deeply solemn Psalm, the first bar of a wondrous piece of spiritual music. How others feel when they read the ninetieth Psalm, I cannot tell. It always makes me lean back in my chair and think.

For one thing, this ninetieth Psalm is the only Psalm composed by "*Moses*, the man of God." It expresses that holy man's feelings, as he saw the whole generation whom he had led forth from Egypt, dying in the wilderness. Year after year he saw that fearful judgment fulfilling, which Israel brought on itself by unbelief: "In this desert your bodies will fall — every one of you twenty years old or more who was counted in the census and who has grumbled against me." (Numbers 14:29.)

One after another he saw the heads of the families whom he had led forth from Egypt, laying their bones in the desert. For forty long years he saw the strong, the swift, the wise, the tender, the beautiful, who had crossed the Red Sea with him in triumph — cut down and withering like grass. For forty years he saw his companions continually changing, consuming, and passing away. Who can wonder that he should say, "Lord, you have been our dwelling place." We are all pilgrims and strangers upon earth, and there is none abiding. "Lord, You are our home."

For another thing, the ninetieth Psalm forms part of the *Burial Service* of the Church of England. Whatever fault men may find with the Prayer-book, I think no one can deny the singular beauty of the Burial Service. Beautiful are the texts which it puts into the minister's mouth as he meets the coffin at the churchyard gate, and leads the mourners into God's house. Beautiful is the chapter from the first Epistle to the Corinthians about the resurrection of the body. Beautiful are the sentences and prayers appointed to be read as the body is laid in its long home. But specially beautiful, to my mind, are the Psalms which are selected for reading when the mourners have just taken their places in church. I know nothing which sounds so soothing, solemnizing, heart-touching, and moving to man's spirit, at that trying moment — as the wondrous utterance of the old inspired law-giver: "Lord, you have been our dwelling place." "Lord, You are our home."

I want to draw from these words two thoughts that may do the readers of this paper some good. An English *home* is famous all over the world for its happiness and comfort. It is a little bit of Heaven left upon earth. But even an English home is not forever. The *family nest* is sure to be taken down, and its inhabitants are sure to be scattered. Bear with me for a few short minutes, while I try to set before you *the best, truest, and happiest home.*

I. The first thought that I will offer you is this: I will show you what the *world* is.

It is a *beautiful* world in many respects, I freely admit. Its seas and rivers, its sunrises and sunsets, its mountains and valleys, its harvests and its forests, its fruits and its flowers, its days and its nights — all, all are beautiful in their way. Cold and unfeeling must that heart be which never finds a day in the year when it can admire anything in nature! But as *beautiful* as the world is, there are many things in it to remind us that it is not *home.* It is an inn, a tent, a tabernacle, a lodging, a training school — but it is not *home.*

(a) It is a *changing* world. All around us is continually moving, altering, and passing away. Families, properties, landlords, tenants, farmers, laborers, tradesmen — all are continually on the move. To find the same name in the same dwelling for three generations running is so uncommon, that it is the exception and not the rule. A world so full of *change,* cannot be called *home.*

(b) It is a *trying* and *disappointing* world. Who ever lives to be fifty years old, and does not find to his cost that it is so? Trials in *married* life and trials in *single* life, trials in *children* and trials in *brothers* and *sisters,* trials in *money* matters and trials in *health* — how many they are! Their name is *legion.* And not the tenth part of them perhaps ever comes to light. Few indeed are the families which have not *"a skeleton in the closet."* A world so full of trial and disappointment, cannot be called *home.*

(c) It is a *dying* world. Death is continually about us and near us, and meets us at every turn. Few are the family gatherings, when Christmas comes round, in which there are not some *empty chairs* and *vacant places.* Few are the men and women, past thirty, who could not number a long list of names, deeply cut forever in their hearts, but names of beloved ones now dead and gone. Where are our fathers and mothers? Where are our ministers and teachers? Where are our brothers and sisters? Where are our husbands and wives? Where are our neighbors and friends? Where are the old grey-headed worshipers, whose reverent faces we remember so well, when we first went to God's house? Where are the boys and girls we played with when we went to school? How many must reply, *"Dead, dead, dead!* The daisies are growing over their graves, and we are left alone." Surely a world so full of death, can never be called a *home.*

(d) It is a *scattering* and *dividing* world. Families are continually breaking up, and going in different directions. How rarely do the members of a family ever meet together again, after the surviving parent is laid in the grave! The band of union seems snapped, and nothing welds it again. The cement seems withdrawn from the parts of the building, and the whole principle of cohesion is lost. How often some miserable squabble about trinkets, or some wretched wrangle about money — makes a breach that is never healed, and, like a crack in china, though riveted, can never be quite cured! Rarely indeed do those who played in the same *nursery* — lie down at length in the same churchyard, or keep peace with one another until they die. A world so full of division, can never be *home*.

These are ancient things. It is useless to be surprised at them. They are the bitter fruit of sin, and the sorrowful consequence of the fall. Change, trial, death, and division — all entered into the world when Adam and Eve transgressed. We must not murmur. We must not fret. We must not complain. We must accept the situation in which we find ourselves. We must each do our best to lighten the sorrows, and increase the comforts of our position. We must steadily resolve to make the best of everybody and everything around us. But we must never, never, never, forget that *the world is not home*.

Are you **young**? Does all around and before you seem bright, and cheerful, and happy? Do you secretly think in your own mind that I take too gloomy a view of the world? Take care. You will not say so by and by. Be wise early. Learn to moderate your expectations. Depend on it, the less you *expect* from people and things here below — the happier you will be.

Are you **prosperous** in the world? Have death, and sickness, and disappointment, and poverty, and family troubles, passed over your door up to this time, and not come in? Are you secretly saying to yourself, "Nothing can hurt me much. I shall die quietly in my bed, and see no sorrow." Take care. You are not yet in harbor. A sudden *storm* of unexpected trouble may make you change your note. Set not your affection on things below. Hold them with a very loose hand, and be ready to surrender them at a moment's notice. Use your prosperity well while you have it; but lean not all your weight on it, lest it break suddenly and pierce your hand!

Have you a **happy home**? Are you going to spend Christmas round a family hearth, where sickness, and death, and poverty, and partings, and quarrelings, have never yet been seen? Be thankful for it — oh, be thankful for it! A really happy Christian home is the nearest approach to Heaven on earth. But take care. This state of things will not last forever. It must have an end; and if you are wise, you will never forget that "The time is short. From now on those who have wives should live as if they had none; those who mourn, as if they did not; those who are happy, as if they were not; those who buy something, as if it were not theirs to keep; those who use the things of the world, as if not engrossed in them. For this world in its present form is passing away!" (1 Corinthians 7:29-31.)

II. The second thought that I will offer you is this: I will show you what Christ is, even in this life, to true Christians.

Heaven, beyond doubt, is the *final home* in which a true Christian will dwell at last. Towards that, he is daily traveling — nearer to that, he is daily coming. "We know that if our earthly house of this tabernacle were dissolved, we have a building of God, a house not made with hands, eternal in the Heavens." (2 Corinthians 5:1.) Body and soul united once more, renewed, beautified, and perfected, will live forever in the Father's great house in Heaven. To that home, we have not yet come. We are not yet in Heaven.

But is there meanwhile no home for our souls? Is there no spiritual dwelling-place to which we may continually repair in this desolate world, and, repairing to it, find rest and peace? Thank God, there is no difficulty in finding an answer to that question. There is a *home* provided for all laboring and heavy-laden souls, and that home is *Christ*.

To know Christ by faith,
to live the life of faith in Him,
to abide in Him daily by faith,
to flee to Him in every storm of conscience,
to use Him as our refuge in every day of trouble,
to employ Him as our Priest, Confessor, Absolver, and spiritual Director, every morning and evening in our lives —
this is to be at home spiritually, even before we die.

To all sinners who by faith use Christ in this fashion — Christ is in the highest sense a dwelling-place. They can say with truth, "We are pilgrims and strangers on earth — and yet we have a home."

Of all the emblems and figures under which Christ is set before man, I know few more cheering and comforting, than the one before us. *Home* is one of the sweetest, tenderest words in the English language. Home is the place with which our pleasantest thoughts are closely bound up. All that the best and happiest home is to its inhabitants — that Christ is to the soul that believes on Him. In the midst of a dying, changing, disappointing world — a true Christian has always something which no power on earth can take away. Morning, noon, and night, he has near him a living *Refuge*, a *living home* for his soul. You may rob him of life, and liberty, and money; you may take from him health, and lands, and house, and friends; but, do what you will, you cannot rob him of his *home*. Like those humblest of God's creatures which curry their shells on their backs, wherever they are — so the Christian, wherever he goes, carries his home.

(a) No home like Christ! In Him there is room for all — and room for all sorts. None are unwelcome guests and visitors, and none are refused admission. The door is always open, and never bolted. The best robe, the fatted calf, the ring, the shoes — are always ready for all comers. What though in time past you have been the vilest of the vile, a slave of sin, an enemy of all righteousness, a Pharisee of Pharisees, a Sadducee of Sadducees, a publican of publicans? It matters nothing! There is yet hope. All may be pardoned, forgiven, and forgotten. There is a home and refuge where your soul may be admitted this very day. That home is Christ. "Come unto Me," He cries. "Knock, and it shall be opened unto you." (Matthew 11:28; 7:7.)

(b) No home like Christ! In Him there is boundless and unwearied mercy for all, even after admission. None are rejected and cast forth again after probation, because they are too weak and bad to stay. Oh, no! Whom He receives — them He always keeps. Where He begins — there He makes a good end. Whom He admits — them He at once fully justifies. Whom He justifies — them He also sanctifies. Whom He sanctifies — them He also glorifies. No hopeless characters are ever sent away from His house. No men or women are ever found too bad to heal and renew. Nothing is too hard for Him to do, who made the world out of nothing. He who is Himself the Home, has said it, and will stand to it: "Him that comes unto Me, I will never cast out!" (John 6:37.)

(c) No home like Christ! In Him there is unvarying kindness, patience, and gentle dealing for all. He is not "an austere man," but "meek and lowly in heart." (Matthew 11. 29.) None who apply to Him are ever treated roughly, or made to feel that their company is not welcome. A feast of fat things is always provided for them. The Holy Spirit is placed in their hearts, and dwells in them as in a temple. Leading, guiding, and instruction are daily provided for them.

If they err — they are brought back into the right way;
if they fall — they are raised again;
if they transgress willfully — they are chastised to make them better.
But the rule of the whole house, is love.

(d) No home like Christ! In Him there is *no change.* From youth to old age — He loves all who come to Him, and is never tired of doing them good. Earthly homes, alas, are full of fickleness and uncertainty. Favor is deceitful. Courtesy and civility are often on men's lips, while inwardly they are weary of your company and wish you were gone. You seldom know how long your presence is welcome, or to what extent your friends really care to see you. But it is not so with Christ. "He is the same yesterday, and today, and forever." (Hebrews 13:8.)

(e) No home like Christ! Communion once begun with Him, shall never be broken off. Once joined to the Lord by faith, you are joined to Him for an endless eternity. Earthly homes always come to an end sooner or later — the dear old furniture is sold and dispersed; the dear old heads of the family are gathered to their fathers; the dear old *nest* is pulled to pieces. But it is not so with Christ. *Faith* will at length be swallowed up in *sight — hope* shall at last be changed into *certainty.* We shall *see* one day with our eyes, and no longer need to *believe.* We shall be moved from the lower chamber to the upper, and from the outer court to the Holy of Holies. But once in Christ — we shall never be out of Christ. Once let our name be placed in the Lamb's book of life, and we belong to a home which shall continue for evermore.

(1) And now, before I conclude, let me ask every reader of this paper a plain QUESTION. *Have you got a home for your soul?* Is it safe? Is it pardoned? Is it justified? Is it prepared to meet God? With all my heart, I wish you a happy home. But remember my question. Amidst the greetings and salutations of home, amidst the meetings and partings, amidst the laughter and merriment, amidst the joys and sympathies and affections — think, think of my question, *Have you got a home for your soul?*

Our earthly homes will soon be closed forever. Time hastens on with giant strides. Old age and death will be upon us before many years have passed away. Oh, seek an abiding home for the better part of you, the part that never dies! Before it be too late seek a home for your soul.

Seek Christ, that you may be safe. Woe to the man who is found *outside the ark* when the *flood of God's wrath* bursts at length on a sinful world! Seek Christ, that you may be happy. None have a real right to be cheerful, merry, light-hearted, and at ease — except those who have got a home for their souls. Once more I say — Seek Christ without delay.

(2) If Christ is the home of your soul, accept a friendly CAUTION. Beware of being ashamed of your home in any place or company.

The man who is ashamed of the home where he was born, the parents who brought him up when a baby, the brothers and sisters who played with him, that man, as a general rule, may be set down as a mean and despicable being. But what shall we say of the man who is ashamed of Him who died for him on the cross? What shall we say of the man who is ashamed of his religion, ashamed of his Master, ashamed of his home?

Take care that you are not that man. Whatever others around you please to think — never be ashamed of being a Christian. Let them laugh, and mock, and jest, and scoff, if they will. They will not scoff in the hour of death and in the day of judgment. Hoist your flag; show your colors; nail them to the mast. Of drinking, gambling, lying, swearing, idleness, pride — you may well be ashamed. Of Bible-reading, praying, and belonging to Christ — you have no cause to be ashamed at all. Let those laugh that win. A good soldier is never ashamed of his Queen's colors, and his uniform. Take care that you are never ashamed of your Master. Never be ashamed of your home.

(3) If Christ is the home of your soul, accept a piece of friendly ADVICE. Let nothing tempt you to stray away from home.

The world and the devil will often try hard to make you drop your religion for a little season, and walk with them. Your own flesh will whisper that there is no danger in going a little with them, and that it can do you no mighty harm. Take care, I say: take care when you are tempted in this fashion. Take care of looking back, like Lot's wife. Forsake not your home.

There are *pleasures in sin* no doubt — but they are not real and satisfactory. There is an excitement and short-lived enjoyment in the world's ways, beyond all question — but it is joy that leaves a bitter taste behind it. Oh, no! wisdom's ways alone are ways of pleasantness, and wisdom's paths alone are paths of peace. Cleave to them strictly, and turn not aside. Follow the Lamb wherever He goes. Stick to Christ and His rule, through evil report and good report. The longer you live the happier you will find His service — the more ready will you be to sing, in the highest sense, "There is no place like home!"

(4) If Christ is the home of your soul, accept a HINT about your duty. Mind that you take every opportunity of telling others about your happiness. Tell them that you have a happy home.

Tell them, if they will hear you, that you find Christ a good Master, and Christ's service a happy service. Tell them that His yoke is easy, and His burden is light. Tell them that, whatever the devil may say, the rules of your home are not grievous, and that your Master pays far better wages than the world does! Try to do a little good wherever you are. Try to enlist more inhabitants for your happy home. Say to your friends and relatives, if they will listen, as one did of old, "Come with us, and we will do you good; for the Lord has spoken good concerning Israel" (Numbers 10:29.)

HEIRS OF GOD!

"As many as are led by the Spirit of God, they are the sons of God. For you did not receive a spirit that makes you a slave again to fear, but you received the Spirit of sonship. And by him we cry, "Abba, Father." The Spirit himself testifies with our spirit that we are God's children. Now if we are children, then we are heirs—*heirs of God and joint-heirs with Christ*, if indeed we share in his sufferings in order that we may also share in his glory." Romans 8:14-17

The people of whom Paul speaks in the verses before our eyes, are the richest people upon earth. It must needs be so. They are called "heirs of God, and joint-heirs with Christ."

The *inheritance* of these people is the only inheritance **really worth having**. All others are unsatisfying and disappointing. They bring with them many cares. They cannot cure an aching heart, or lighten a heavy conscience. They cannot keep off family troubles. They cannot prevent sicknesses, bereavements, separations, and deaths. But there is no disappointment among the "heirs of God."

The inheritance I speak of is the only inheritance which can be **kept forever**. All others must be left in the hour of death, if they have not been taken away before. The owners of millions can carry nothing with them beyond the grave. But it is not so with the "heirs of God." Their inheritance is *eternal*.

The inheritance I speak of is the only inheritance which is **within everybody's reach**. Most men can never obtain riches and greatness, though they labor hard for them all their lives. But glory, honor, and eternal life, are offered to every man freely, who is willing to accept them on God's terms. "Whoever will," may be an "heir of God, and joint heir with Christ."

If any reader of this paper wishes to have a portion of this inheritance, let him know that he must be a member of that one family on earth to which it belongs, and that is the family of all true Christians. You must become one of God's children on earth—if you desire to have glory in Heaven. I write this paper in order to persuade you to become a child of God this day, if you are not one already. I write it to persuade you to make sure work that you are one, if at present you have only a vague hope, and nothing more. None but true Christians are the children of God! None but the children of God are heirs of God! Give me your attention, while I try to unfold to you these things, and to show the *lessons* contained in the verses which head this page.

I. Let me show the *relation* of all true Christians to God. They are "sons of God"

II. Let me show the special *evidences* of this relation. True Christians are "led by the Spirit." They have "the Spirit of adoption." They have the "witness of the Spirit." They "suffer with Christ".

III. Let me show the *privileges* of this relation. True Christians are "heirs of God, and joint heirs with Christ".

I. First let me show the *relation* of all true Christians to God. They are God's "SONS."

I know no higher and more comfortable word that could have been chosen. To be servants of God, to be subjects, soldiers, disciples, friends—all these are excellent titles; but to be the "sons" of God is a step higher still. What does the Scripture say? "The servant abides not in the house forever—but the Son abides ever." (John 8:35.)

To be son of the rich and noble in this world, to be son of the princes and kings of the earth—this is commonly reckoned a great advantage and privilege. But to be a son of the King of kings, and Lord of lords, to be a son of the High and Holy One, who inhabits eternity—this is something far higher. And yet this is the portion of every true Christian.

The son of an earthly parent looks naturally to his father for affection, maintenance, provision, and education. There is a *home* always open to him. There is a *love* which, generally speaking, no bad conduct can completely extinguish. All these are things belonging even to the sonship of this world. Think then how great is the privilege of that poor sinner who can say of God, "He is my Father."

But HOW can sinful men like ourselves become sons of God? When do we enter into this glorious relationship? We are not the sons of God by nature. We were not born so when we came into the world. No man has a natural right to look to God as his Father. It is a vile heresy to say that he has. Men are said to be *born* poets and painters—but men are never born sons of God. The Epistle to the Ephcsians tells us, "You were by nature *children of wrath*, even as others." (Ephesians 2:3.) The Epistle of John says, "The children of God are manifest, and the children of the devil: whoever does not righteousness is not of God." (1 John 3:10.) The Catechism of the Church of England wisely follows the doctrine of the Bible, and teaches us to say, "By nature we are born in sin, and children of wrath." Yes, we are all rather children of the *devil*—than children of God! *Sin* is indeed hereditary, and runs in the family of Adam. *Grace* is anything but hereditary, and holy men have not, as a matter of course, holy sons. How then and when does this mighty change and translation come upon men? When and in what manner do sinners become the "sons and daughters of the Lord Almighty? "(2 Corinthians 6. 18.)

Men become sons of God in the day that the Spirit leads them to believe on Jesus Christ for salvation, and not before. What says the

Epistle to the Galatians? "You are all the children of God by *faith* in Christ Jesus." (Galatians 3:26.) What says the first Epistle to the Corinthians? "Of Him are you in Christ Jesus." (1 Corinthians 1:30.) What says the Gospel of John? "As many as *received* Christ, to them He gave the privilege to become the sons of God, even to those who *believe* on His name." (John 1:12.)

Faith unites the sinner to the Son of God, and makes him one of His members. Faith makes him one of those in whom the Father sees no spot, and is well-pleased. Faith marries him to the beloved Son of God, and entitles him to be reckoned among the sons. Faith gives him "fellowship with the Father and the Son." (1 John 1:3.) Faith grafts him into the Father's family, and opens up to him a room in the Father's house. Faith gives him life instead of death, and makes him, instead of being a servant, a son. Show me a man who has this faith, and, whatever be his church or denomination, I say that he is a son of God.

This is one of those points we should never forget. You and I know nothing of a man's sonship—until he believes. No doubt the sons of God are foreknown and chosen from all eternity, and predestined to adoption. But, remember, it is not until they are *called* in due time, and *believe*—it is not until then, that you and I can be certain they are sons. It is not until they repent and believe, that the angels of God rejoice over them. The angels cannot read the book of God's election: they know not who are "His hidden ones" in the earth. They rejoice over no man, until he believes. But when they see some poor sinner repenting and believing, then there is joy among them, joy that one more brand is plucked from the burning, and one more son and heir born again to the Father in Heaven. (Luke 15:10.) But once more I say, you and I know nothing certain about a man's sonship to God—until he believes on Christ.

I warn you to beware of the delusive notion that *all* men and women are alike children of God, whether they have faith in Christ or not. It is a wild theory which many are clinging to in these days—but one which cannot be proved out of the Word of God. It is a perilous dream, with which many are trying to soothe themselves—but one from which there will be a fearful waking up at the last day.

That God in a certain sense is the *universal Father of all mankind*, I do not pretend to deny. He is the Great First Cause of all things. He is the *Creator* of all mankind, and in Him alone, all men, whether Christians or heathens, "live and move and have their being." All this is unquestionably true. In this sense Paul told the Athenians, a poet of their own had truly said, "we are His offspring." (Acts 16:28.) But this *sonship* gives no man a title to Heaven. The sonship which we have by creation is one which belongs to stones, trees, beasts, or even to the devils, as much as to us. (Job 1:6.)

That God loves all mankind with a love of *pity* and *compassion*, I do not deny. "His tender mercies are over all His works." "He is not willing that any should perish, but that all should come to repentance." "He has no pleasure in the death of him that dies." All this I admit to the full. In this sense our Lord Jesus tells us, "God so loved the world, that He gave His only begotten Son, that whoever believes in Him should not perish—but have eternal life." (2 Peter 3:9; Ezekiel 18:32; John 3:16.)

But that God is a reconciled and pardoning Father to any but the members of His Son Jesus Christ, and that any are members of Jesus Christ who do not believe on Him for salvation—this is a doctrine which I utterly deny! The holiness and justice of God are both against the doctrine. They make it impossible for sinful men to approach God, excepting through the Mediator. They tell us that *God out of Christ* is "a consuming fire." (Hebrews 12:29.) The whole system of the New Testament is against the doctrine. That system teaches that no man can claim interest in Christ—unless he will receive Him as his Mediator, and believe on Him as his Savior. Where there is no faith in Christ—it is a dangerous error to say that a man may take comfort in God as his Father. God is a reconciled Father to none but the members of Christ!

It is unreasonable to talk of the view I am now upholding as narrow-minded and harsh. The Gospel sets an open door before every man. Its *promises* are wide and full. Its *invitations* are earnest and tender. Its *requirements* are simple and clear. "Only believe on the Lord Jesus Christ, and, whoever you are, you shall be saved." But to say that *proud* men, who will not bow their necks to the easy yoke of Christ, and *worldly* men who are determined to have their own way and their sins—to say that such men have a right to claim an interest in Christ, and a right to call themselves sons of God—is to say what never can be proved from Scripture. God offers to be their Father; but He does it on certain distinct terms—they must draw near to Him through Christ. Christ offers to be their Savior; but in doing it He makes one simple requirement—they must commit their souls to Him, and give Him their hearts.

They refuse the terms—and yet dare to call God their Father! They scorn the requirement, and yet dare to hope that Christ will save them! God is to be their Father—but on their *own terms!* Christ is to be their Savior—but on their *own conditions!* What can be more unreasonable? What can be more proud? What can be more unholy than such a doctrine as this? Let us beware of it, for it is a common doctrine in these latter days. Let us beware of it, for it is often speciously put forward, and sounds beautiful and charitable in the mouth of poets, novelists, sentimentalists, and weak-hearted women. Let us beware of it, unless we mean to throw aside our Bible altogether, and set up ourselves to be wiser than God. Let us stand fast on the old Scriptural ground: No sonship to God without Christ! No saving interest in Christ without faith!

I wish there was not so much cause for giving *warnings* of this kind. I have reason to think they need to be given clearly and unmistakably. There is a school of theology rising up in this day, which appears to me most eminently calculated to promote infidelity, to help the devil, and to ruin souls! It comes to us like Joab to Amasa, with the highest professions of love, liberality, and love. "God is all mercy and love," according to this theology; His holiness and justice are completely left out of sight! Hell is never spoken of in this theology—its talk is all of Heaven! Damnation is never mentioned—it is treated as an impossible thing: all men and women are to be saved! Faith, and the work of the Spirit, are refined away into nothing at all! "Everybody who *believes* anything has faith! Everybody who *thinks* anything has the Spirit! Everybody is right! Nobody is wrong! Nobody is to blame for any action he may commit! It is the result of his position—it is the effect of circumstances! He is not accountable for his opinions, any more than for the color of his skin! He must be what he is! The Bible is a very imperfect book! It is old-fashioned! It is obsolete! We may believe just as much of it as we please, and no more!"

Of all this *theology* I warn men solemnly to beware. In spite of big swelling words about "liberality," and "love," and "broad views," and "new light," and "freedom from bigotry," and so forth—I do believe it to be *a theology that leads to Hell.*

(a) Facts are directly against the teachers of this theology. Let them visit Mesopotamia, and see what desolation reigns where Nineveh and Babylon once stood. Let them go to the shores of the Dead Sea, and look down into its mysterious bitter waters. Let them travel in Palestine, and ask what has turned that fertile country into a wilderness. Let them observe the wandering Jews, scattered over the face of the world, without a land of their own—and yet never absorbed among other nations. And then let them tell us, if they dare, that God is so entirely a *God of mercy and love*—that He never does and never will punish sin.

(b) The **conscience** of man is directly against these teachers. Let them go to the bedside of some dying child, and try to comfort him with their doctrines. Let them see if their vaunted theories will calm his gnawing, restless anxiety about the future, and enable him to depart in peace. Let them show us, if they can, a few well- authenticated cases of joy and happiness in death without Bible promises, without conversion, and without that faith in the blood of Christ, which old-fashioned theology enjoins. Alas! when men are leaving the world, conscience makes sad work of the *new systems* of these latter days. Conscience is not easily satisfied, in a dying hour, that there is no such thing as Hell.

(c) Every reasonable conception that we can form of a **future**

state is directly against these teachers. Imagine a Heaven which should contain all mankind! Imagine a Heaven in which holy and unholy, pure and impure, good and evil, would be all gathered together in one confused mass! What point of union would there be in such a company? What common bond of harmony and brotherhood? What common delight in a common service? What concord, what harmony, what peace, what oneness of spirit could exist? Surely the mind revolts from the idea of a Heaven in which there would be no distinction between the righteous and the wicked, between Pharaoh and Moses, between Abraham and the Sodomites, between Paul and Nero, between John and Judas Iscariot, between the man who dies in the act of murder or drunkenness, and men like Baxter, George Herbert, Wilberforce, and M'Cheyne! Surely an eternity in such a miserably confused crowd would be worse than annihilation itself! *Surely such a Heaven would be no better than Hell!*

(d) The interests of all **holiness** and **morality** are directly against these teachers. If all men and women alike are God's children, whatever is the difference between them in their lives, and all alike going to Heaven, however different they may be from one another here in the world—then where is the use of laboring after holiness at all? What motive remains for living soberly, righteously, and godly? What does it matter how men conduct themselves, if all go to Heaven, and nobody goes to Hell? Surely the heathen poets and philosophers of Greece and Rome could tell us something better and wiser than this! Surely a doctrine which is subversive of holiness and morality, and takes away all motives to exertion, carries on the face of it the stamp of its origin. It is of earth, and not of Heaven. It is of the devil, and not of God.

(e) The **Bible** is against these teachers from first to last. Hundreds of texts might be quoted which are diametrically opposed to their theories. These texts must be rejected summarily, if the Bible is to square with their views. There may be no reason why they should be rejected—but to suit the theology I speak of, they must be thrown away! At this rate, the authority of the whole Bible is soon at an end. And what do men give us in its place? Nothing, nothing at all! They rob us of the bread of life, and do not give us in its stead so much as a stone!

Once more I warn all into whose hands this volume may fall to beware of this theology. I charge you to hold fast the doctrine which I have been endeavoring to uphold in this paper. Remember what I have said, and never let it go. No inheritance of glory—without sonship to God! No sonship to God—without an interest in Christ! No interest in Christ—without your own personal faith! This is God's truth. Never forsake it.

Who now among the readers of this paper desires to know whether he is a son of God? Ask yourself this question, and ask it this day, and ask it as in God's sight, whether you have *repented* and *believed.* Ask yourself whether you are *experimentally acquainted* with Christ, and united to Him in heart. If not, you may be very sure you are no son of God. You are not yet born again. You are yet in your sins. God may be your Father in *creation*—but He is not your *reconciled* and *pardoning* Father. Yes! though Church and world may agree to tell you to the contrary, though clergy and laity unite in flattering you—your *sonship* is worth little or nothing in the sight of God. Let God be true and every man a liar. Without faith in Christ you are no son of God—you are not born again.

Who is there among the readers of this paper who desires to become a son of God? Let that person see and feel his sins, and flee to Christ for salvation, and this day he shall be placed among the children. Only acknowledge your iniquity, and lay hold on the hand that Jesus holds out to you this day, and sonship, with all it privileges, is your own! Only confess your sins, and bring them unto Christ, and God is "faithful and just to forgive you your sins, and cleanse you from all unrighteousness." (1 John 1:9.) This very day, old things shall pass away, and all things become new. This very day, you shall be forgiven, pardoned, "accepted in the Beloved." (Ephesians 1:7) This very day, you shall have a new name given to you in Heaven. You took up this book as a child of wrath—but you shall lie down tonight as a child of God! Mark this, if your professed desire after sonship is sincere, if you are truly weary of your sins, and have really something more than a lazy wish to be free, there is real comfort for you. It is all true. It is all written in Scripture, even as I have put it down. I dare not raise barriers between you and God. This day I say, Believe on the Lord Jesus Christ, and you shall be "a son," and be saved.

Who is there among the readers of this paper that is a son of God indeed? Rejoice, I say, and be exceeding glad of your privileges! Rejoice, for you have good cause to be thankful. Remember the words of the beloved apostle: "Behold what manner of love the Father has bestowed upon us, that we should be called the sons of God." (1 John 3:1.) How wonderful that Heaven should look down on earth, that the holy God should set His affections on *sinful man*, and admit him into His family! What though the world does not understand you! What though the men of this world laugh at you, and cast out your name as evil! Let them laugh if they will—God is your Father! You have no need to be ashamed. The Queen can create a nobleman. The Bishops can ordain clergymen. But Queen, Lords, and Commons, bishops, priests, and deacons—all together cannot, of their own power, make one son of God, or one of greater dignity than a son of God. The man that can call God his Father, and Christ his elder brother—that man may be poor and lowly, yet he never need be ashamed.

II. Let me show, in the second place, the special *evidences* of the true Christians relation to God.

How shall a man make sure work of his own sonship? How shall he find out whether he is one that has come to Christ by faith and been born again? What are the *marks* and *signs*, and *tokens*, by which the "sons of God" may be known? This is a question which all who love eternal life ought to ask. This is a question to which the verses of Scripture I am asking you to consider, like many others, supply an answer.

(a) The sons of God, for one thing, are all **led by His Spirit**. What says the Scripture which heads this paper? "As many as are led by the Spirit of God—they are the sons of God." (Romans 8:14.)

They are all under the leading and teaching of a power which is Almighty, though unseen—even the power of the Holy Spirit. They no longer turn every man to his own way, and walk every man in the light of his own eyes, and follow every man his own natural heart's desire. The Spirit *leads* them. The Spirit *guides* them. There is a movement in their hearts, lives, and affections, which they feel, though they may not be able to explain; and a movement which is always more or less in the same direction.

They are all led . . .
away from sin,
away from self-righteousness,
away from the world!
This is the *road* by which the Spirit leads God's children. Those whom God adopts as His children—He teaches and trains. He shows them their own *hearts*. He makes them weary of their own *ways*. He makes them long for inward peace.

They are all led to Christ.
They are all led to the Bible.
They are all led to prayer.
They are all led to holiness.
This is the *beaten path* along which the Spirit makes them to travel.

Those whom God adopts—He always sanctifies.

He makes *sin* very bitter to them.

He makes *holiness* very sweet.

It is the Spirit who leads them to *Sinai*, and first shows them the *law*—that their hearts may be broken. It is He who leads them to *Calvary*, and shows them the *cross*—that their hearts may be bound up and healed. It is He who leads them to *Pisgah*, and gives them distinct views of the promised land—that their hearts may be cheered. When they are taken into the *wilderness*, and taught to see their own emptiness—it is the leading of the Spirit. When they are carried up to *Tabor* or *Hermon*, and lifted up with glimpses of the glory to come, it is the leading of the Spirit. Each and all of God's sons is the subject of these leadings. Each and every one is "willing in the day of the Spirit's power," and yields himself to it. And each and all is led by the *right* way, to bring him to a city of habitation. (Psalm 110:3; 107:7.)

Settle this down in your heart, and do not let it go. The sons of God are a people "led by the Spirit of God," and always led more or less in the same way. Their experience will tally wonderfully when they compare notes in Heaven. This is one mark of sonship.

(b) Furthermore, all the sons of God have the **feelings of adopted children towards their Father in Heaven**. What says the Scripture which heads this paper? "For you did not receive a spirit that makes you a slave again to fear, but you received the Spirit of sonship. And by him we cry, *Abba, Father!"* (Romans 8:15.)

The sons of God are delivered from that *slavish fear of God* which sin begets in the natural heart. They are redeemed from that feeling of *guilt* which made Adam "hide himself in the trees of the garden," and Cain "go out from the presence of the Lord." (Genesis 3:8; 4:16.) They are no longer afraid of God's holiness, and justice, and majesty. They no longer feel as if there was a great gulf and barrier between themselves and God, and as if God was *angry* with them, and must be angry with them, because of their sins. From these *chains* and *fetters* of the soul—the sons of God are delivered.

Their feelings towards God are now those of peace and confidence. They see Him as a *reconciled Father* in Christ Jesus. They look on Him as a God whose attributes are all satisfied by their great Mediator and Peacemaker, the Lord Jesus, as a God who is "just—and yet the Justifier of every one that believes on Jesus." (Romans 3:26.) As a Father, they *draw near* to Him with boldness—as a Father, they can *speak* to Him with freedom. They have exchanged the spirit of *bondage*—for that of liberty, and the spirit of *fear*—for that of love. They know that God is holy—but they are not afraid; they know that they are sinners—but they are not afraid. Though holy—they believe that God is completely reconciled; though sinners—they believe they are clothed all over with Jesus Christ. Such is the feeling of the sons of God.

I allow that some of them have this feeling more vividly than others. Some of them carry about scraps and remnants of the old spirit of bondage to their dying day. Many of them have fits and paroxysms of the old man's complaint of fear, returning upon them at intervals. But very few of the sons of God could be found who would not say, if cross-examined, that since they knew Christ they have had very different feelings towards God from what they ever had before. They feel as if something like the old Roman form of adoption had taken place between themselves and their Father in Heaven. They feel as if He had said to each one of them, "Will you be my son?" and as if their hearts had replied, "I will."

Let us try to grasp this also, and hold it fast. The sons of God are a people who feel towards God, in a way that the children of the world do not. They feel no more slavish fear towards Him—they feel towards Him as a reconciled parent. This, then, is another mark of sonship.

(c) But, again, the sons of God have the **witness of the Spirit** in their consciences. What says the Scripture which heads this paper? "The Spirit Himself bears witness with our spirit, that we are the children of God." (Romans 8:16.)

The sons of God have got something within their hearts, which tells them there is a relationship between themselves and God. They feel something which tells them that old things are passed away, and all things become new; that guilt is gone, that peace is restored; that Heaven's door is open, and hell's door is shut. They have, in short, what the children of the world have not—a felt, positive, reasonable hope. They have what Paul calls the "seal" and "pledge" of the Spirit. (2 Corinthians 1:22; Ephesians 1:13.)

I do not for a moment deny that this *witness of the Spirit* is exceedingly various in the extent to which the sons of God possess it. With some it is a loud, clear, ringing, distinct testimony of conscience: "I am Christ's, and Christ is mine!" With others it is a little, feeble, stammering whisper, which the devil and the flesh often prevent being heard. Some of the children of God speed on their course towards Heaven, under the full sails of assurance. Others are tossed to and fro all their voyage, and will scarcely believe they have got any faith.

But take the least and lowest of the sons of God. Ask him if he will give up the little bit of hope which he has attained? Ask him if he will exchange his heart, with all its doubts and conflicts, its fightings and fears—ask him if he will exchange that heart for the heart of the downright worldly and careless man? Ask him if he would be content to turn round and throw down the things he has got hold of—and go back to the world? Who can doubt what the answer would be? "I cannot do that," he would reply. "I do not know whether I have faith, I do not feel sure I have got grace; but I have got something within me I would not like to part with!" And what is that "something"? I will tell you. It is the witness of the Spirit.

Let us try to understand this also. The sons of God have the witness of the Spirit in their consciences. This is another mark of sonship.

(d) One thing more let me add. All the sons of God take part in **suffering with Christ**. What says the Scripture which heads this paper? "If children, then heirs, heirs of God and joint heirs with Christ—if so be that we suffer with Him." (Romans 8:17.)

All the children of God have a *cross* to carry. They have trials, troubles, and afflictions to go through for the Gospel's sake. They have . . .

trials from the *world*,
trials from the flesh,
and trials from the devil.

They have sharp trials from *relations* and *friends*—hard words, hard treatment, and hard judgment.

They have trials in the matter of *character:* slander, misrepresentation, mockery, insinuation of false motives—all these often rain thick upon them.

They have trials in the matter of *worldly interests.* They have often to choose whether they will please man and lose glory—or gain glory and offend man.

They have trials from their own *hearts.* They have each generally their own *thorn* in the flesh, their own home-devil—who is their *worst foe!*

This is the experience of the sons of God.

Some of them suffer more, and some less. Some of them suffer in one way, and some in another. God *measures out their portions* like a wise physician, and cannot err. But never, I believe, was there one child of God who reached paradise *without a cross.*

Suffering is the *diet* of the Lord's family. "Whom the Lord loves—He chastens." "If you are without chastisement—then are you bastards, and not sons." "Through much tribulation we must enter the kingdom of God." "All who will live godly in Christ Jesus shall suffer persecution." (Hebrews 12:6, 8; Acts 14:22; 2 Timothy 3:12.)

Suffering is a part of the process by which the sons of God are *sanctified.* They are *chastened* to wean them from the world, and make them partakers of God's holiness. The Captain of their salvation was "made perfect through suffering," and so are they. (Hebrews 2:10; 12:10.) There never yet was a great saint who had not either great *afflictions*—or great *corruptions.* Well said Philip Melancthon: "Where there are no cares—there will generally be no prayers."

Let us try to settle this down into our hearts also. The sons of God have all to bear a *cross.* A suffering *Savior*—generally has suffering *disciples.* The Bridegroom was a *man of sorrows.* The Bride must not be a *woman of pleasures* and unacquainted with grief. Blessed are those who mourn! Let us not *murmur* at the cross. This also is a sign of sonship.

I warn men never to suppose that they are sons of God—unless they have the scriptural marks of sonship. Beware of a *sonship without evidences.* Again I say, Beware! When a man has . . .
no leading of the Spirit to show me,
no spirit of adoption to tell of,
no witness of the Spirit in his conscience,
no cross in his experience—
is this man a son of God? Whatever others may think, I dare not say so!

His spot is "not the spot of God's children." (Deuteronomy 32:5.) He is no heir of glory.

Tell me not that you have been *baptized* and taught the *catechism* of the Church of England—and therefore must be a child of God. I tell you that the *parish register* is not the *book of life!* I tell you that to be *called* a child of God, and regenerate in *infancy* is one thing; but to *be* a child of God indeed, another thing altogether. It is the "death unto sin and the new birth unto righteousness," which makes men children of grace. Except you know these by personal experience—you are no child of God.

Tell me not that you are a *member of a church*, and so must be a son. I answer that the sons of the church—are not necessarily the sons of God. Such sonship is not the sonship of the eighth of Romans. That is the sonship you must have if you are to be saved.

And now, I doubt not, that some reader of this paper will want to know if he may not be saved without the witness of the Spirit.

I answer, If you mean by the witness of the Spirit, the *full* assurance of hope—you may be so saved, without question. But if you want to know whether a man can be saved without *any* inward sense, or knowledge, or hope of salvation, I answer—that ordinarily He cannot. I warn you plainly to cast away all indecision as to your state before God, and to make your calling sure. Clear up your position and relationship. Do not think there is anything praiseworthy in always *doubting*. Leave that to the Papists. Do not imagine it wise and humble to be ever living like the *borderers* of old time, on the "debatable ground." "Assurance," said old Dod, the puritan, "may be attained: and what have we been doing all our lives, since we became Christians, if we have not attained it?"

I doubt not, that some true Christians who read this paper will think their *evidence of sonship* is too small to be good, and will write bitter things against themselves. Let me try to cheer them.

Who gave you the feelings you possess?

Who made you hate sin?

Who made you love Christ?

Who made you long and labor to be holy?

Whence did these feelings come?

Did they come from nature? There are no such products in a natural man's heart. Did they come from the devil? He would gladly stifle such feelings altogether. Cheer up, and take courage. Fear not, neither be cast down. Press forward, and go on. There is hope for you after all. Strive. Labor. Seek. Ask. Knock. Follow on. You shall yet see that you are "sons of God."

III. Let me show, in the last place, the PRIVILEGES of the true Christians relation to God.

Nothing can be conceived more glorious than the *prospects* of the sons of God. The words of Scripture which head this paper contain a rich mine of good and comfortable things. "If we are children," says Paul, "then we are heirs, heirs of God, and joint heirs with Christ, to be glorified together with Him." (Romans 8:17.)

True Christians then are "heirs." Something is prepared for them all which is yet to be revealed.

They are "heirs of God." To be heirs of the rich on earth, is something. How much more then is it to be son and heir of the *King of kings!*

They are "joint heirs with Christ." They shall share in His majesty, and take part of His glory. They shall be glorified together with Him.

And this, we must remember, is for *all* the children. Abraham took care to provide for all his children, and God takes care to provide for His. None of them are disinherited. None will be cast out. None will be cut off. Each shall stand in his lot, and have a portion, in the day when the Lord brings many sons to glory.

Who can tell the *full nature* of the inheritance of the saints in light? Who can describe the *glory* which is yet to be revealed and given to the children of God? Words fail us. Language falls short. Mind cannot conceive fully, and tongue cannot express perfectly—the things which are comprised in the glory yet to come upon the sons and daughters of the Lord Almighty! Oh, it is indeed a true saying of the Apostle John: "It does not yet appear what we shall be!" (1 John 3:2.)

The very Bible itself only *lifts a little of the veil* which hangs over this subject. How could it do more? We could not thoroughly understand more, if more had been told us. Our mental constitution is as yet too earthly, our understanding is as yet too carnal to appreciate more, if we had it. The Bible generally deals with the subject in *negative* terms, and not in positive assertions. It describes what there will *not* be in the glorious inheritance, that thus we may get some faint idea of what there *will* be. It paints the absence of certain things, in order that we may drink in a little the blessedness. It tells us that the inheritance is "incorruptible, undefiled, and fades not away." It tells us that "the crown of glory fades not away." It tells us that the devil is to be "bound," that there shall be "no more night and no more curse," that "death shall be cast into the lake of fire," that "all tears shall be wiped away," and that the inhabitant shall no more say, "I am sick."

And these are glorious things indeed.

No corruption!

No fading!

No withering!

No devil!

No curse of sin!
No sorrow!
No tears!
No sickness!
No death!
Surely the cup of the children of God will indeed run over!

But there are *positive* things told us about the glory yet to come upon the heirs of God, which ought not to be kept back. There are many sweet, pleasant, and unspeakable comforts in their future inheritance, which all true Christians would do well to consider. There are*cordials for fainting pilgrims* in many words and expressions of Scripture, which you and I ought to lay up against time of need.

(a) Is **knowledge** pleasant to us now? Is the little that we know of God and Christ, and the Bible precious to our souls, and do we long for more? We shall have it perfectly in glory. What says the Scripture? "Then shall I know—even as also I am known." (I Corinthians 13:12.) Blessed be God, there will be no more *disagreements* among believers! Episcopalians and Presbyterians, Calvinists and Arminians, Millennarians and Anti-millennarians, friends of Establishments and friends of the Voluntary system, advocates of infant baptism and advocates of adult baptism—all will at length see eye to eye. The former *ignorance* will have passed away. We shall marvel to find how childish and blind we have been!

(b) Is **holiness** pleasant to us now? Is **sin** the burden and bitterness of our lives? Do we long for entire conformity to the image of God? We shall have it perfectly in glory! What says the Scripture? "Christ gave Himself for the Church," not only that He might sanctify it on earth—but also "that He might present it to Himself a glorious Church, not having spot or wrinkle, or any such thing." (Ephesians 5:27.) Oh, the blessedness of *an eternal goodbye to sin!* Oh, how little the best of us do at present! Oh, what unutterable *corruption* sticks, like birdlime—to all our motives, all our thoughts, all our words, all our actions! Oh, how many of us, like Naphtali, are goodly in our words—but, like Reuben, unstable in our works! Thank God, all this shall be changed. (Genesis 49:4, 21.)

(c) Is **rest** pleasant to us now? Do we often feel "faint though pursuing?" (Judges 8:4.) Do we long for a world in which we need not to be always watching and warring? We shall have it perfectly in glory. What says the Scripture? "There remains a *rest* for the people of God." (Hebrews 4:9.) The daily, hourly *conflict* with the world, the flesh, and the devil—shall at length be at an end. The *enemy* shall be bound. The *warfare* shall be over. The wicked shall at last cease from troubling. The weary shall at length be at rest. There shall be a great calm.

(d) Is **service** pleasant to us now? Do we find it sweet to work for Christ—and yet groan being burdened by a feeble body? Is our spirit often willing—but hampered and clogged by the poor weak flesh? Have our hearts burned within us, when we have been allowed to give a cup of cold water for Christ's sake, and have we sighed to think what unprofitable servants we are? Let us take comfort. We shall be able to serve perfectly in glory, and without weariness. What says the Scripture? "They serve Him day and night in His temple." (Rev. 7:15.)

(e) Is **satisfaction** pleasant to us now? Do we find the world empty? Do we long for the filling up of every void place and gap in our hearts? We shall have it perfectly in glory. We shall no longer have to mourn over . . .
cracks in all our earthen vessels,
and *thorns* in all our roses,
and *bitter dregs* in all our sweet cups!

We shall no longer lament with Jonah over *withered gourds*. We shall no longer say with Solomon, "All is vanity and vexation of spirit!" We shall no longer cry with aged David, "I have seen an end of all perfection." What says the Scripture? "I shall be satisfied when I awake with Your likeness!" (Eccles. 1:14; Psalm 119:96; 17:15.)

(f) Is communion with the **saints** pleasant to us now? Do we feel that we are never so happy as when we are with the "excellent of the earth?" Are we never so much at home as in their company? (Psalm 16:3.) We shall have it perfectly in glory. What says the Scripture? "The Son of man shall send His angels, and they shall gather out of His kingdom all they that offend, and them which work iniquity." "He shall send His angels with a great sound of a trumpet, and they shall gather together His elect from the four winds." (Matthew 13:41; 24:31.) Praised be God! We shall see all the saints of whom we have read in the Bible, and in whose steps we have tried to walk. We shall see apostles, prophets, patriarchs, martyrs, reformers, missionaries, and ministers, of whom the world was not worthy. We shall see the faces of those we have known and loved in Christ on earth, and over whose departure we shed bitter tears. We shall see them more bright and glorious than they ever were before. And, best of all, we shall see them without hurry and anxiety, and without feeling that we only meet to part again. In the coming glory there is no *death*, no *parting*, no *farewell!*

(g) Is communion with **Christ** pleasant to us now? Do we find His name precious to us? Do we feel our hearts burn within us at the thought of His dying love? We shall have *perfect communion with Him* in glory. "We shall ever be with the Lord." (1 Thessalonians 4:17.) We shall be with Him in paradise. (Luke 23:43.) We shall see His face in the kingdom. These *eyes* of ours will behold those hands and feet which were pierced with nails, and that head which was crowned with thorns!

Where He is, there will the sons of God be. When He comes, they will come with Him. When He sits down in His glory, they shall sit down by His side. Blessed prospect indeed!

I am a dying man in a dying world. All before me is dark. The world to come is a harbor unknown. But Christ is there, and that is enough. Surely if there is rest and peace in following Him by faith on earth, there will be far more rest and peace when we see Him face to face. If we have found it good to follow the pillar of cloud and fire in the *wilderness*—we shall find it a thousand times better to sit down in our eternal inheritance, with our Joshua, in the promised land.

If anyone among the readers of this paper is not yet among the sons and heirs, I *pity* you with all my heart! How much you are missing! How little true comfort you are enjoying! There you are . . .
struggling on, and toiling in the fire,
and wearying yourself for mere earthly ends,
seeking rest and finding none,
chasing shadows and never catching them,
wondering why you are not happy,
and yet refusing to see the cause,
hungry, and thirsty, and empty—and yet blind to the plenty within your reach. Oh, that you were wise! Oh, that you would hear the voice of Jesus, and learn of Him!

If you are one of those who *are* sons and heirs, you may well rejoice and be happy. You may well wait, like the boy *Patience* in Pilgrim's Progress—your best things are yet to come! You may well bear crosses without murmuring—your light affliction is but for a moment. "The sufferings of this present time are not worthy to be compared to the glory which is to be revealed!" "When Christ our life appears, then you also shall appear with Him in glory!" (Romans 8:18; Colos. 3:4.)

You may well not *envy* the transgressor and his prosperity. You are the truly rich! Well said a dying believer in my own parish: "I am more rich than I ever was in my life!" You may say as Mephibosheth said to David: "Let the world take all—my king is coming again in peace." (2 Sam. 19:30.)

You may well not be cast down by *sickness*—the eternal part of you is safe and provided for, whatever happens to your body. You may well look calmly on *death*—it opens a door between you and your eternal inheritance. You may well not sorrow excessively over the things of the world, over partings and bereavements, over losses and crosses—the day of *gathering* is before you. Your *treasure* is beyond reach of harm. Heaven is becoming every year more full of those you love—and earth more empty. Glory in your inheritance. It is all yours, if you are a son of God: "If we are children—then we are heirs!"

(1) And now, in CONCLUDING this paper, let me ask every one who reads it **Whose child are you?** Are you the child of nature—or the child of grace? Are you the child of the devil—or the child of God? You cannot be *both* at once. Which are you?

Settle the question without delay, for you must die at last—either one or the other. Settle it, for it can be settled, and it is folly to leave it doubtful. Settle it, for time is short, the world is getting old, and you are fast drawing near to the judgment seat of Christ. Settle it, for death is near, the Lord is at hand—and who can tell what a day might bring forth? Oh, that you would never rest until the question is settled! Oh, that you may never feel satisfied until you can say, "I have been born again! I am a son of God!"

(2) If you are **not** a son and heir of God—let me entreat you to become one without delay. Would you be *rich?* There are unsearchable riches in Christ! Would you be *noble?* You shall be a king! Would you be *happy?* You shall have a peace which passes understanding, and which the world can never give and never take away. Oh, come out, and take up the cross, and follow Christ! Come out from among the thoughtless and worldly, and hear the word of the Lord: "I will receive you, and will be a Father unto you—and you shall be my sons and daughters, says the Lord Almighty." (2 Corinthians 6:18.)

(3) If you **are** a son of God, I beseech you to *walk worthy* of your Father's family. I charge you solemnly to honor Him in your life; and above all to honor Him by *implicit obedience* to all His commands, and *hearty love* to all His children. Labor to travel through the world like a child of God and heir to glory. Let men be able to trace a *family likeness* between you and Him who begat you. Live a *Heavenly life.* Seek things that are above. Do not seem to be building your *nest* below. Behave like a man who seeks a city out of sight, whose citizenship is in Heaven, and who would be content with many *hardships* until he gets home.

Labor to *feel* like a son of God in every condition in which you are placed. Never forget you are on your *Father's ground*, so long as you are here on earth. Never forget that *a Father's hand*, sends all your mercies and crosses. Cast every care on Him. Be happy and cheerful in Him. Why indeed are you ever sad—if you are the King's son? Why should men ever doubt, when they look at you—whether it is a pleasant thing to be one of God's children?

Labor to *behave towards others* like a son of God. Be blameless and harmless in your day and generation. Be a "peacemaker among all you know." (Matthew 5:9.) Seek for your children *sonship to God*, above everything else. Seek for them an inheritance in Heaven, whatever else you do for them. No man leaves his children so well provided for—as he who leaves them sons and heirs of God!

Persevere in your Christian calling, if you are a son of God, and press forward more and more. Be careful to lay aside every weight, and the sin which most easily besets you. Keep your eyes steadily fixed on

Jesus. Abide in Him. Remember that without Him you can do nothing—and with Him you can do all things. (John 15:5; Philip. 4:13.) *Watch* and *pray* daily. Be steadfast, unmoveable, and always abounding in the work of the Lord. Settle it down in your heart that not a cup of cold water given in the name of a disciple shall lose its reward, and that every year—you are so much *nearer home*.

"Yet a little time and He who shall come will come, and will not tarry." (Hebrews 10:37.) Then shall be the glorious liberty, and the full manifestation of the sons of God! (Romans 8:19, 21.) Then shall the world acknowledge that they were the truly wise. Then shall the sons of God at length come of age, and be no longer heirs in *expectancy*—but heirs in *possession*. Then shall they hear with exceeding joy those comfortable words: "Come, you who are blessed by my Father—inherit the *kingdom* prepared for you from the foundation of the world!" (Matthew 25:34.) *Surely, that day will make amends for all!*

THE GREAT GATHERING!

"Concerning the coming of our Lord Jesus Christ, and ***our gathering together*** unto Him" 2 Thessalonians 2:1

The text which heads this page contains an expression which deserves no common attention. That expression is, "Our gathering together."

"Our gathering together!" Those three words touch a note which ought to find a *response* in every part of the world. Man is by nature a social being — he does not like to be alone. Go where you will on earth, people generally like meeting together, and seeing one another's faces. It is the exception, and not the rule — to find children of Adam who do not like "gathering together."

For example, *Christmas* is peculiarly a time when English people "gather together." It is the season when family meetings have become almost a national institution. In town and in country, among rich and among poor, from the palace to the workhouse — Christmas cheer and Christmas gatherings are proverbial things. It is the one time in the year with many, for seeing their friends at all. Sons snatch a few days from London business to run down and see their parents; brothers get leave of absence from the desk to spend a week with their sisters; friends accept long-standing invitations, and contrive to pay a visit to their friends; boys rush home from school, and glory in the warmth and comfort of the old house. Business for a little space comes to a standstill — the weary wheels of incessant labor seem almost to cease revolving for a few hours. In short, there is a general spirit of "gathering together."

Happy is the land where such a state of things exists! Long may it last in England, and never may it end! Poor and shallow is that philosophy which sneers at Christmas gatherings. Cold and hard is that religion which pretends to frown at them, and denounces them as wicked. *Family affection* lies at the very roots of well-ordered society. It is one of the few good things which have survived the fall, and prevent men and women from being mere devils! It is the *secret oil* on the wheels of our social system which keeps the whole machine going, and without which neither steam nor fire would avail. Anything which helps to keep up *family affection* and *brotherly love* is a positive good to a country. May the Christmas day never arrive in England when there are no family meetings and no gatherings together!

But earthly gatherings after all have something about them that is sad and sorrowful. The happiest parties sometimes contain *uncongenial members* — the merriest meetings are only for a very *short time*. Moreover, as years roll on, the *hand of death* makes painful gaps in the family circle. Even in the midst of Christmas merriment, we cannot help remembering those who have passed away. The longer we live — the more we feel to stand alone. The old faces will rise before the eyes of our minds, and the old voices will sound in our ears, even in the midst of holiday mirth and laughter. People do not *talk* much on such things; but there are few that do not *feel* them. We need not intrude our inmost thoughts on others, and especially when all around us are bright and happy. But there are not many, I suspect, who reach middle age, who would not admit, if they spoke the truth — that there are *sorrowful things* inseparably mixed up with a Christmas party. In short, there is no *unmixed pleasure* about any earthly "gathering."

But is there no better "gathering" yet to come? Is there no bright prospect in our horizon, of an assembly which shall far outshine the assemblies of Christmas and New Year, an assembly in which there shall be joy without sorrow, and mirth without tears? I thank God that I can give a plain answer to these questions; and to give it is the simple object of this paper. I ask my readers to give me their attention for a few minutes, and I will soon show them what I mean.

I. There is a "gathering together" of true Christians which is to *come*. *What* is it, and *when* shall it be?

The gathering I speak of, shall take place at the end of the world, in the day when Christ returns to earth the second time. As surely as He came the first time — so surely shall He come the second time. In the clouds of Heaven He went away — and in the clouds of Heaven He shall return. Visibly, in the body, He went away — and visibly, in the body, He will return. And the very first thing that Christ will do, will be to "gather together" His people. "He shall send His angels with a great sound of a trumpet, and they shall *gather together His elect* from the four winds, from one end of Heaven to the other." (Matthew 24:31.)

The **MANNER** of this "gathering together" is plainly revealed in Scripture. The dead saints shall all be *raised*, and the living saints shall all be *changed*. It is written, "The sea gave up the dead that were in it, and death and Hades gave up the dead that were in them." "The dead in Christ shall rise first. Those who are alive and remain shall be caught up together with them in the clouds, to meet the Lord in the air." "We shall not all sleep — but we shall all be changed, in a moment, in the twinkling of an eye, at the last trumpet; for the trumpet shall sound, and the dead shall be raised incorruptible, and we shall be changed!" (Revelation 20:13; 1 Thessalonians 4:16, 17; 1 Corinthians 15:51, 52.) And then, when every member of Christ is found, and not one left behind, when *soul and body*, those old companions, are once more reunited — then shall be the grand "gathering together."

The **OBJECT** of this "gathering together" is as clearly revealed in Scripture as its manner.

It is partly for the *final reward* of Christ's people — that their complete justification from all guilt may be declared to all creation; that they may receive the "unfading crown of glory," and the "kingdom prepared before the foundation of the world;" that they may be admitted publicly into the joy of their Lord.

It is partly for the *safety* of Christ's people, that, like Noah in the ark and Lot in Zoar, they may be hid and covered before the *storm of God's judgment* comes down on the wicked; that when the last plagues are falling on the enemies of the Lord — they may be untouched, as Rahab's family in the fall of Jericho, and unscathed as the three Hebrew children in the midst of the fire. The saints have no cause to fear the day of gathering, however fearful the signs that may accompany it. Before the final crash of all things begins — they shall be hidden in the secret place of the Most High. The grand gathering is for their *safety* and their *reward.* "Come, my people," shall their Master say: "enter your rooms and shut the doors behind you; hide yourselves for a little while until his wrath has passed by!" (Isaiah 26:20.)

(a) This gathering will be a **great** one. ALL children of God who have ever lived, from Abel the first saint down to the last born in the day that our Lord comes — all of every age, and nation, and church, and people, and tongue — all shall be assembled together. Not one shall be overlooked or forgotten. The weakest and feeblest shall not be left behind. Now, when "scattered," true Christians seem a *little flock*; then, when "gathered," they shall be found *a multitude which no man can number.*

(b) This gathering will be a **wonderful** one. The saints from distant lands, who never saw each other in the flesh, and could not understand each other's speech if they met — shall all be brought together in one harmonious company. The dwellers in Australia shall find they are as near Heaven, and as soon there, as the dwellers in England. The believers who died five thousand years ago, and whose bones are mere dust — shall find their bodies raised and renewed as quickly as those who are alive when the trumpet sounds. Above all, *miracles of grace* will be revealed. We shall see some in Heaven, who we never expected would have been saved at all. The *confusion of tongues* shall at length be reversed, and done away. The assembled multitude will cry with one heart and in one language, "What has God wrought!" (Num. 23:23.)

(c) This gathering shall be a **humbling** one. It shall make an end of bigotry and narrow-mindedness forever. The Christians of one denomination shall find themselves side by side with those of another denomination. If they would not *tolerate* them on earth — they will be obliged to tolerate them in Heaven. Churchmen and Dissenters, who will neither pray together nor worship together now, will discover to their shame, that they must praise together hereafter to all eternity! The very people who will not receive us at their ordinances now, and keep us back from their Table – will be obliged to acknowledge us before our Master's face, and to let us sit down by their side. Never, will the world have seen such a complete overthrow of sectarianism, party-spirit, unbrotherliness, religious jealousy, and religious pride! At last ,we shall all be completely "clothed with humility." (1 Peter 5:5.)

This mighty, wonderful "gathering together," is the gathering which ought to be often in men's thoughts. It deserves consideration – it demands attention. Gatherings of other kinds are incessantly occupying our minds, political gatherings, scientific gatherings, gatherings for pleasure, gatherings for gain. But the hour comes, and will soon be here, when gatherings of this kind will be completely forgotten! One thought alone will swallow up men's minds – that thought will be, "Shall I be gathered with Christ's people into a place of safety and honor – or be left behind to everlasting woe?" Let us take care that we are not left behind!

II. WHY is this "gathering together" of true Christians a thing to be desired? Let us try to get an answer to that question.

Paul evidently thought that the gathering at the last day was a cheering object which Christians ought to keep before their eyes. He classes it with that second coming of our Lord, which he says elsewhere, believers love and long for. He exalts it in the distant horizon as one of those "good things to come," which should animate the faith of every pilgrim in the narrow way. Not only, he seems to say, will each servant of God have rest, and a kingdom, and a crown – he will also have besides a happy "gathering together." Now, where is the peculiar blessedness of this gathering? Why is it a thing that we ought to look forward to with joy, and expect with pleasure? Let us see.

(a) For one thing, the "gathering together" of all true Christians will be a state of things **totally *unlike* their present condition**. To be scattered, and not gathered, seems the rule of man's existence now. Of all the millions who are annually born into the world, how few continue together until they die! Children who draw their first breath under the same roof, and play by the same fireside – are sure to be separated as they grow up, and to draw their last breath far distant from one another.

The same law applies to the people of God. They are spread abroad like salt, one in one place and one in another, and never allowed to continue long side by side. It is doubtless good for the world, that it is so. A town would be a very dark place at night, if all the lighted candles were crowded together into one room. But, as good as it is for the world – it is no small trial to believers. Many a day they feel desolate and alone; many a day they long for a little more communion with their brethren, and a little more companionship with those who love the Lord! Well, they may look forward with hope and comfort. The hour is coming when they shall have no lack of companions. Let them lift up their heads and rejoice. There will be a "gathering together" by and by!

(b) For another thing, the gathering together of all true Christians will be an assembly **entirely of one mind**. There are no such assemblies now. Mixture, hypocrisy, and false profession — creep in everywhere. Wherever there is *wheat* — there are sure to be *tares*. Wherever there are good fish — there are sure to be bad. Wherever there are wise virgins — there are sure to be foolish. There is no such thing as a *perfect church* now. There is a *Judas Iscariot* at every communion table — and a *Demas* in every Apostolic company! And wherever the "sons of God" come together — Satan is sure to appear among them. (Job 1:6.)

But all this shall come to an end one day. Our Lord shall at length present to the Father a *perfect* church, "having neither spot nor wrinkle, nor any such thing." (Ephesians 5:27.) How glorious such a Church will be!

To meet with half-a-dozen believers together now is a rare event in a Christian's year, and one that cheers him like a sunshiny day in winter — it makes him feel his heart burn within him, as the disciples felt on the way to Emmaus. But how much more joyful will it be to meet a "multitude that no man can number!"

To find too, that all we meet are at last of one opinion and one judgment, and see eye to eye — to discover that all our miserable controversies are buried forever, and that Calvinists no longer hate Arminians, nor Arminians Calvinists; Churchmen no longer quarrel with Dissenters, nor Dissenters with Churchmen; to join a company of Christians in which there is neither jarring, squabbling, nor discord, every man's graces fully developed, and every man's besetting sins dropped off like *leaves in Autumn* — all this will be happiness indeed! No wonder that Paul bids us to look forward.

(c) For another thing, the gathering together of true Christians will be a meeting at which **none shall be absent**. The *weakest lamb* shall not be left behind in the wilderness. We shall once more see our beloved friends and relatives who fell asleep in Christ, and left us in sorrow and tears — better, brighter, more beautiful, more pleasant than ever we found them on earth! We shall hold communion with all the saints of God who have fought the good fight *before* us, from the beginning of the world to the end. Patriarchs and Prophets, Apostles and Fathers, Martyrs and Missionaries, Reformers and Puritans — all the host of *God's elect* shall be there. If to *read* their words and works has been pleasant — how much better shall it be to *see* them! If to *hear* of them, and be stirred by their example, has been useful —

how much more delightful to *talk* with them, and ask them questions! To sit down with Abraham, Isaac, and Jacob, and hear how they kept the faith without any Bible; to converse with Moses, and Samuel, and David, and Isaiah, and Daniel, and hear how they could believe in a Christ yet to come; to converse with Peter, and Paul, and Lazarus, and Mary, and Martha, and listen to their wondrous tale of what their Master did for them — all this will be sweet indeed! No wonder that Paul bids us to look forward.

(d) In the last place, the gathering of all true Christians shall be a **meeting without a parting**. There are no such meetings now. We seem to live in an endless hurry, and can hardly sit down and take breath — before we are off again. *"Good-bye!"* treads on the heels of *"Hello!"*

The cares of this world,
the necessary duties of life,
the demands of our families,
the work of our various stations and callings
— all these things appear to eat up our days, and to make it impossible to have long quiet times of communion with God's people. But, blessed be God — it shall not always be so. The hour comes, and shall soon be here, when "good-bye" and "farewell" shall be words that are laid aside and buried forever! When we meet in a world where the former things have passed away, where there is . . .
no more *sin,*
no more *sorrow,*
no more *poverty,*
no more *work* of body or work of brains,
no more need of *anxiety* for families,
no more *sickness,*
no more *pain,*
no more *old age,*
no more *death,*
no more *change* —
when we meet in that endless state of being, calm, and restful, and unhurried — who can tell what the bliss and blessedness will be? I cannot wonder that Paul bids us look up and look forward.

I lay these things before all who read this paper, and ask their serious attention to them. If I know anything of a Christian's experience, I am sure they contain *food for reflection.* This, at least, I say confidently: the man who sees nothing much in the second coming of Christ and the public "gathering" of Christ's people — nothing happy, nothing joyful, nothing pleasant, nothing desirable — such a man may well doubt whether he himself is a true Christian and has got any grace at all!

In closing, let me offer the following **APPLICATIONS**.

(1) I ask you a plain question. Do not turn away from it and refuse to look it in the face. Shall you be gathered by the angels into God's *home* when the Lord returns — or shall you be left behind?

One thing, at any rate, is very certain — there will only be *two groups* of mankind at the last great day:
those who are on the right hand of Christ — and those who are on the left;
those who are counted righteous — and those who are wicked;
those who are safe in the ark — and those who are outside;
those who are gathered like *wheat* into God's barn — and those who are left behind like *tares* to be burned.

Now, what will *your* portion be?

Perhaps you do not know yet. You cannot say. You are not sure. You *hope* the best. You *trust* it will be all right at last — but you won't undertake to give an opinion. Well! I only hope you will never rest until you do know. The *Bible* will tell you plainly who are they that will be gathered. Your own heart, if you deal honestly, will tell you whether you are one of the number. Rest not, rest not, until you know!

How men can stand the partings and separations of this life — if they have no hope of anything better? How they can bear to say "good-bye" to sons and daughters, and launch them on the *troublesome waves of this world* — if they have no expectation of a safe "gathering" in Christ at last? How they can part with beloved members of their families, and let them journey forth to the other side of the globe, not knowing if they shall ever meet happily in this life or a life to come? How all this can be, completely baffles my understanding! I can only suppose that the many never *think*, never consider, never look forward. Once let a man begin to think — and he will never be satisfied until he has found Christ and is safe.

(2) I offer you a plain means of testing your own soul's condition, if you want to know if you will be gathered into God's home. Ask yourself what kind of gatherings you like best here upon earth? Ask yourself whether you really love the assembling together of God's people?

How could that man enjoy the meeting of true Christians in Heaven — who takes no pleasure in meeting true Christians on earth? How can that heart which is wholly set on balls, and races, and feasts, and amusements, and worldly parties — and thinks Christian worship a weariness — how can such a heart be in tune for the company of saints, and saints alone? The thing is impossible. It cannot be.

Never, never let it be forgotten, that our *tastes* on earth are a sure evidence of the state of our hearts; and the state of our hearts here on earth, is a sure indication of our eternal home hereafter. Heaven is a prepared place for a prepared people. He who hopes to be gathered with saints in Heaven, while he only loves the gathering of sinners on earth — is deceiving himself. If he lives and dies in that state of mind, he will find at last that it would have been better if he had never been born!

(3) If you are a true Christian, I exhort you to be often *looking forward*. Your best things are yet to come! Your redemption draws near! The *night* is far spent — the *day* is at hand. Yet in a little while, and He whom you love and believe on, will come, and will not tarry. When He comes, He will bring His *dead* saints with Him and change His *living* ones. Look forward! There is a "gathering together" yet to come!

The morning after a shipwreck is a sorrowful time. The joy of half-drowned survivors, who have safely reached the land — is often sadly marred by the recollection of shipmates who have sunk to rise no more. There will be no such sorrow when believers gather together round the throne of the Lamb. Not one of the ship's company shall be found absent! "Some on boards, and some on broken pieces of the ship — all will get safe to shore at last." (Acts 27:44.) *The great waters and raging waves shall swallow none of God's elect!* When the sun rises — they shall be seen all safe, and "gathered together."

Even the day after a great victory is a sorrowful time. The triumphant feelings of the conquerors are often mingled with bitter regrets for those who fell in action, and died on the field. The list of "killed, wounded, and missing," breaks many a heart, fills many a home with mourning, and brings many a grey head sorrowing to the grave! The great Duke of Wellington often said, "there was but one thing *worse* than a victory — and that was a defeat." But, thanks be to God, there will be no such sorrow in Heaven! The soldiers of the great Captain of our salvation shall all answer to their names at last! The muster-roll shall be as complete *after* the battle — as it was before! Not one believer shall be "missing" in the great "gathering together."

Does Christmas, for instance, bring with it sorrowful feelings and painful associations? Do tears rise unbidden in your eyes when you mark the empty places around the fireside? Do grave thoughts come sweeping over your mind, even in the midst of your children's mirth — when you recollect the dear old faces and much loved voices of some who sleep in the churchyard? Well, look up and look forward! The time is short. The world is growing old. The coming of the Lord draws near! There is yet to be a *meeting without parting*, and a *gathering without separation*. Those believers whom you laid in the grave with many tears are in good keeping — you will yet see them again with joy. Look up! I say once more. Lay hold by faith on the "coming of our Lord Jesus Christ, and our gathering together unto Him." Believe it, think of it, rest on it. It is all true!

Do you feel *lonely* and *desolate* as every December comes round?

Do you find few to *pray* with, few to *praise* with, few to open your heart to, few to exchange experience with? Do you learn increasingly, that Heaven is becoming every year more full — and earth more empty?

Well, it is an old story. You are only drinking a cup which myriads have drunk before. Look up and look forward. The *lonely* time will soon be past and over — you will have company enough by and by. "When you wake up after your Lord's likeness — you shall be satisfied." (Psalm 17:15.) Yet in a little while and you shall see a congregation that shall never break up, and a Sabbath that shall never end. "The coming of our Lord Jesus Christ, and our gathering together unto Him," shall make amends for all!

"Therefore comfort one another with these words!" 1 Thessalonians 4:18

THE GREAT SEPARATION!

"His winnowing fork is in His hand, and He will thoroughly cleanse His threshing floor. He will gather His **wheat** into the barn, but He will burn up the **chaff** with unquenchable fire!" Matthew 3:12

Wheat or chaff? You see *my question* — for *whom* do you think it is meant? Is it for corn merchants and farmers only, and for none else? If you think so, then you are much mistaken. It is meant for every man, woman, and child in the world. And among others, it is meant for *you*.

The question is drawn from the verse of Scripture which is now before your eyes. The words of that verse were spoken by John the Baptist. They are a prophecy about our Lord Jesus Christ, and a prophecy which has not yet been fulfilled. They are a prophecy which we shall all see fulfilled one day, and God alone knows how soon.

Reader, I invite you this day to *consider the great truths* which this verse contains. I invite you to listen to me, while I unfold them and set them before you in order. Who knows but this text may prove a word in season to your soul! Who knows but my question may help to make this day the happiest day in your life! Listen, before you begin once more your appointed path of duty. Listen, before you start once more on some round of business. Listen, before you plunge once more into some course of useless idleness and folly. Listen to one who loves your soul, and would sincerely help to save it, or draw it nearer to Christ. Who knows what a day may bring forth! Who can tell whether you will live to see tomorrow! Be still, and listen to me a few minutes, while I show you something out of the Word of God.

I. Let me show you in the first place, ***the two great classes into which the world may be divided.***

There are only two classes of people in the world, in the sight of God — and both are mentioned in the text which begins this tract. There are those who are called *the wheat* — and there are those who are called *the chaff*.

Viewed with the eye of man, the earth contains many different sorts of inhabitants. Viewed with the eye of God, it only contains two. Man's eye looks at the *outward* appearance — this is all he thinks of. The eye of God looks at the *heart* — this is the only part of which He takes any account. And tried by the state of their hearts, there are but *two classes* into which people can be divided — either they are *wheat*, or they are *chaff*.

Reader, **who are the WHEAT** in the world? Listen to me, and I will tell you.

The wheat means all men and women who are *believers* in the Lord Jesus Christ — all who are *led by the Holy Spirit* — all who have felt themselves *sinners*, and fled for refuge to the *salvation* offered in the Gospel — all who *love* the Lord Jesus, and *live* to the Lord Jesus, and *serve* the Lord Jesus — all who have taken Christ for their only confidence, and the Bible for their only guide, and regard sin as their deadliest enemy, and look to Heaven as their only home. All such, of every church, name, nation, people, and tongue — of every rank, station, condition, and degree — all such are *God's wheat!*

Show me men of this kind of people anywhere, and I know what they are. I know that they and I may not agree in all particulars — but I see in them the *handiwork* of the King of kings, and I ask no more. I know not whence they came, and where they found their religion — but I know where they are *going*, and that is enough for me. They are the children of my Father in Heaven. They are part of His wheat.

All such, though sinful, and vile, and unworthy in their own eyes — are the precious part of mankind. They are the sons and daughters of God the Father. They are the delight of God the Son. They are the habitation of God the Spirit. The Father beholds no iniquity in them — they are the members of His dear Son's body — *in Him* He sees them — and is well pleased. The Lord Jesus discerns in them, the fruit of His own travail and work upon the cross — and is well satisfied. The Holy Spirit regards them as spiritual temples which He Himself has raised — and rejoices over them. In a word, they are the *wheat* of the earth — God's wheat.

Reader, **who are the CHAFF** in the world? Listen to me once more, and I will tell you this also.

The chaff means all men and women who have no saving faith in Christ, and no sanctification of the Spirit — whoever they may be. Some of them perhaps are infidels — and some are *formal* Christians. Some are sneering Sadducees — and some self-righteous Pharisees. Some of them make a point of keeping up a kind of 'Sunday religion' — and others are utterly careless of everything except their own pleasure and the world. But all alike, who have the two great marks already mentioned — *no faith and no sanctification* — all such are *chaff*. From the *atheists* Paine and Voltaire — to the *formal* churchman who can think of nothing but outward ceremonies — to the unconverted admirer of sermons in the present day — all, all are standing in one rank before God all, all are chaff!

They bring no glory to God the Father. They honor not the Son, and so do not honor the Father who sent Him. They neglect that mighty salvation, which countless millions of angels admire. They disobey that Word which was graciously written for their learning. They listen not to the voice of Him who condescended to leave Heaven and die for their sins. They pay no tribute of *service* and *affection* to Him who gave them life, and breath, and all things. And therefore God takes no pleasure in them. He *pities* them — but He reckons them no better than chaff!

Yes — you may have rare intellectual gifts, and high mental attainments — you may sway kingdoms by your counsel, move millions by your pen, or keep crowds in breathless attention by your tongue — but if you have never submitted yourself to the yoke of Christ, and never honored His Gospel by heartfelt reception of it — then you are nothing but *chaff* in His sight. Natural gifts without saving grace, are like a row of *ciphers* without an *unit* before them; they look big — but they are of *no value*. The *vilest insect* that crawls in the filth — is a nobler being than you are! It fills its place in creation, and glorifies its Maker with all its power — and you do not. You do not honor God with heart, and will, and intellect, and members, which are all His. You invert His order and arrangement, and live as if time was of more importance than eternity, and body better than soul. You dare to neglect God's greatest gift — His own incarnate Son. You are cold about that subject which fills all Heaven with hallelujahs. And so long as this is the case, you belong to the *worthless* part of mankind. You are the *chaff* of the earth.

Reader, let this thought be deeply engraved in your mind, whatever else you forget in this volume. Remember there are only *two kinds* of people in the world. There are wheat — and there are chaff.

There are many **nations** in Europe. Each differs from the rest. Each has its own language, its own laws, its own peculiar customs. But God's eye divides Europe into two great parties — the wheat and the chaff.

There are many **classes** in England. There are nobles and commoners — farmers and shopkeepers — masters and servants — rich and poor. But God's eye only takes account of two orders — the wheat and the chaff.

There are many and various **minds** in every congregation that meets for religious worship. There are some who attend for a mere *form* — and some who really desire to meet Christ; some who come there to please others — and some who come to please God; some who bring their *hearts* with them, and are not soon tired — and some who leave their hearts behind them, and reckon the whole service as *weary work*. But the eye of Jesus only sees two divisions in the congregation — the wheat and the chaff.

There were millions of visitors to the Great Exhibition of 1851. From Europe, Asia, Africa, and America — from North, and South, and East, and West — crowds came together to see what human skill and industry could do. Children of our first father Adam's family, who had never seen each other before, for once met face to face under one roof.

But the eye of the Lord only saw two companies thronging that large palace of glass — the wheat and the chaff.

Reader, I know well the world dislikes this way of dividing professing Christians. The world tries hard to fancy there are *three* sorts of people, and not *two*. To be very godly and very strict does not suit the world — they *can*not, *will* not be holy. To have no religion at all does not suit the world — as that would not be respectable. "Thank God," they will say, "we are not so bad as that!" But to have religion enough to be respectable — and yet not go into extremes, to be sufficiently good — and yet not be peculiar — to have a quiet, easy-going, moderate kind of Christianity, and go comfortably to Heaven after all — this is the world's favorite idea! There is a *third* class, a *safe middle* class — the world imagines; and in this middle class — the majority of men persuade themselves they will be found.

Reader, I *denounce* this notion of a *middle class* as an immense and soul-ruining delusion! I warn you strongly not to be carried away by it. It is as vain an invention as the *Pope's purgatory*. It is a *refuge of lies*, a castle in the air, a Russian ice-palace, a vast unreality, an empty dream! This *middle* class is a class of Christians no where spoken of in the Bible!

There were two classes in the day of Noah's flood; those who were *inside* the ark — and those who were *outside*. There were two classes in the parable of the Gospel net; those who are called the good fish — and those who are called the bad. There were two classes in the parable of the ten virgins; those who are described as wise — and those who are described as foolish. There were two classes in the account of the judgment day; the *sheep* — and the *goats*. There were two sides of the throne; the *right* hand — and the *left*. There were two *abodes* when the last sentence has been passed; Heaven — and Hell.

And just so, there are only two classes in the world:
those who are in the state of nature — and those who are in the state of grace;
those who are in the narrow way — and those who are in the broad;
those who have faith — and those who have no faith;
those who have been converted — and those who have not been converted;
those who are *with* Christ — and those who are *against* Him;
those who *gather* with Him — and those who *scatter* abroad;
those who are *wheat* — and those who are *chaff*.
Into these two classes, the whole world may be divided. Beside these two classes, there is none.

Reader, dear reader, see now what cause there is for self-inquiry! Are you among the wheat — or among the chaff? *Neutrality* is impossible. Either you are in one class — or in the other. Which is it, of the two?

You attend church perhaps. You go to the Lord's table. You like good people. You can distinguish between good preaching and bad. You think Popery false, and oppose it firmly. You think Protestantism true, and support it cordially. You subscribe to religious societies. You attend religious meetings. You sometimes read religious books. It is well — it is all very well. It is good — it is all very good. It is more than can be said of many. But still, this is not a straightforward answer to my question: Are you wheat — or are you chaff?

Have you been born again? Are you a new creature? Have you put off the old man, and put on the new? Have you ever felt your *sins*, and repented of them? Are you *looking* only to Christ for pardon and eternal life? Do you *love* Christ? Do you *serve* Christ? Do you loathe heart-sins, and fight against them? Do you long for perfect holiness, and follow hard after it? Have you come out from the *world?* Do you delight in the *Bible?* Do you wrestle in *prayer?* Do you love Christ's people? Do you try to do good to the world? Are you vile in your own eyes, and willing to take the lowest place? Are you a Christian in business, and on week days, and by your own fireside? Oh, think, think, think on these things — and then perhaps you will be better able to tell the state of your soul!

Reader, I beseech you not to turn away from my question, however unpleasant it may be. Answer it, though it may prick your conscience, and cut you to the heart. Answer it, though it may prove you in the wrong, and expose your fearful danger. Rest not, rest not, until you know how it is between you and God! Better a thousand times find out that you are in an evil case, and repent in time — than live on in uncertainty, and be lost eternally!

Reader, remember my question. Begin to meditate on it this very day. *Are you wheat — or chaff?*

II. Let me show you, in the second place, ***the TIME when the two great classes of mankind shall be separated.***

The text at the beginning of this tract foretells a *separation.* It says that Christ shall one day do to His professing Church, what the farmer does to his corn. He shall winnow and sift it. "He will thoroughly cleanse His threshing floor." And then the wheat and the chaff shall be *divided.*

There is no separation *yet.* Good and bad are now all mingled together in the visible Church of Christ. Believers and unbelievers — converted and unconverted — holy and unholy — all are to be found now among those who call themselves *Christians.* They sit side by side in our assemblies. They kneel side by side in our pews. They listen side by side to our sermons. They sometimes come up side by side to the Lord's table, and receive the same bread and wine from our hands.

But it shall not *always* be so! Christ shall come the second time with His winnowing fork in His hand. He shall thoroughly purge His Church, even as He purified the temple. And then the wheat and the chaff shall be *separated* — and each go to its own place!

Before Christ comes, *separation is impossible.* It is not in man's power to effect it. There lives not the minister on earth, who can read the hearts of everyone in his congregation. About *some* he may speak decidedly — he cannot about *all.* Who have *oil* in their lamps — and who have not; who have grace as well as profession — and who have profession only, and no grace; who are children of God — and who of the devil. All these are questions which, in many cases, we cannot *accurately* decide. The winnowing fork is not put into **our** hands!

Grace is sometimes so weak and feeble — that it looks like nature. *Nature* is sometimes so plausible and well-dressed — that it looks like grace. I believe many of us would have said that *Judas* was as good as any of the apostles — and yet he proved a traitor! I believe we would have said that *Peter* was a reprobate when he denied his Lord — and yet he repented immediately, and rose again. We are but fallible men. We *know in part.* **We scarcely understand our own hearts. It is no great wonder if we cannot read the hearts of others.**

But it will not always be so. There is One coming, who never errs in judgment, and is perfect in knowledge. Jesus shall purge His floor. Jesus shall sift the *chaff* from the *wheat.* I wait for this. Until then, I will lean to the side of *charity* in my judgments. I would rather tolerate much chaff in the Church — than cast out one grain of wheat! He shall soon come who has His winnowing fork in His hand — and then the certainty about every one shall be known.

Before Christ comes, *I do not expect to see a perfect Church.* There cannot be such a thing. The wheat and the chaff, in the present state of things — will always be found together. I pity those who leave one Church and join another, because of a few faults and unsound members. I pity them, because they are fostering ideals which never can be realized. I pity them, because they are seeking that which cannot be found. I see chaff everywhere. I see *imperfections* and *infirmities* of some kind in every church on earth. I believe there are few tables of the Lord, if any, where all the communicants are converted. I often see *loud-talking professors,* exalted as saints. I often see holy and contrite believers, set down as having no grace at all. I think that if men are too scrupulous, they may go fluttering about, like Noah's dove, all their days, and never find *rest.*

Reader, do you desire a *perfect Church?* You must wait for the day of Christ's appearing. Then, and not until then — you will see a glorious

Church, having neither spot nor wrinkle, or any such thing. Then, and not until then — the floor will be purged.

Before Christ comes, *I do not look for the conversion of the world.* How can it be, if He is to find both wheat and chaff side by side in the day of His second coming? I believe some Christians expect that missions will fill the earth with the knowledge of Christ, and that little by little, sin will disappear, and a state of perfect holiness gradually glide in. I cannot see with their eyes! I think they are mistaking God's purposes, and sowing bitter disappointment for themselves. I expect nothing of the kind. I see nothing in the Bible, or in the world around me, to make me expect it. I have never heard of a single parish entirely converted to God, in England or Scotland — or of anything like it. And why am I to look for a different result from the preaching of the Gospel in other lands? I only expect to see a few raised up as witnesses to Christ in every nation — some in one place, and some in another. Then I expect the Lord Jesus will come in glory, with His winnowing fork in His hand. And when He has purged His floor, and not until then — His *kingdom* will begin.

No separation and no perfection until Christ comes! This is my creed. I am not moved when the infidel asks me why all the world is not converted — if Christianity is really true? I answer — It was never promised that it would be so in the present order of things. The Bible tells me that believers will always be few — that corruptions, and divisions, and heresies, will always abound — and that when my Lord returns to earth, He will find plenty of chaff.

No perfection until Christ comes! I am not disturbed when men say, "Make all the people good Christians at home, before you send missionaries to the heathen abroad." I answer, If I am to wait for that — then I will wait forever. When we have done all at home, the Church will still be a *mixed* body — it will contain some wheat, and much chaff.

But Christ will come again. Sooner or later there shall be a *separation* of the visible Church into two companies — and fearful shall that separation be! The wheat shall make up one company. The chaff shall make up another. The one company will be all godly. The other company will be all ungodly. Each shall be by themselves, and a *great gulf* between, that none can pass.

Blessed indeed shall the *righteous* be in that day! They shall shine like stars — no longer obscured with *clouds*. They shall be beautiful as the lily — no longer choked with *thorns*.

Wretched indeed will the *ungodly* be! How corrupt will corruption be — when left without one grain of *salt* to season it! How dark will darkness be — when left without one spark of light! Ah, reader, it is not enough to respect and admire the Lord's people; you must *belong* to them — or you will one day be parted from them forever. There will be no chaff in Heaven! Many, many are the families, where *one* will be taken — and *another* left.

Who is there now among the readers of these pages who loves the Lord Jesus Christ in sincerity? If I know anything of the heart of a Christian, your greatest trials are in the company of worldly people — your greatest joys in the company of the saints. Yes — there are many weary days, when your spirit feels broken and crushed by the *earthly tone* of all around you — days when you could cry with David, "Woe is me, that I dwell in Mesech, and have my habitation in the tents of Kedar." And yet there are hours when your soul is so refreshed and revived by meeting some of God's dear children, that it seems like *Heaven on earth.* Do I not speak to your heart? Are not these things true? See then, how you should long for the time when Christ shall come again. See how you should pray daily that the Lord would hasten His kingdom, and say to Him, "Come quickly, Lord Jesus!"

Then, and not until then, shall the church be a pure unmixed communion. Then, and not until then, the saints shall all be together, and shall go out from one another's presence no more. Wait a little. Wait a little. Scorn and contempt will soon be over. Laughter and ridicule shall soon have an end. Slander and misrepresentation will soon cease. Your Savior shall come and plead your cause. And then, as Moses said to Korah, "The Lord will show who are His!"

"This is certain — when the elect are all converted, then Christ will come to judgment. As he who rows a boat, stays until all the passengers are taken into his boat, and then he rows away; so Christ stays until all the elect are gathered in, and then He will hasten away to judgment!" — Thomas Watson, 1660.

Who is there among the readers of these pages, who knows that his heart is not right in the sight of God? See how you should fear and tremble at the thought of Christ's appearing. Alas, indeed, for the man who lives and dies with nothing better than a *cloak of religion!* In the day when Christ shall purge His floor, you will be shown and exposed in your true colors! You may deceive ministers, and friends, and neighbors — but you cannot deceive Christ! The *paint* and *varnish* of a *heartless Christianity* will never stand the *fire* of that day. The Lord is a God of knowledge, and by Him actions are weighed. You will find that the *eye*which saw *Achan* and *Gehazi* — has read your secrets, and searched out your *hidden* things! You will hear those awful words, "Friend, how did you get in here — not having a wedding garment?"

Oh, tremble at the thought of the day of sifting and separation! Surely *hypocrisy* is a most losing game! Surely it never is good, to try to deceive God. Surely it never answers, like Ananias and Sapphira, to *pretend* to give God something, and yet to keep back your heart. It all fails at last! Your joy is but for a moment. Your hopes are no better than a dream! Oh, tremble, tremble — tremble, and repent!

Reader, think on these things. Remember my question. Begin to meditate on it this very day. Are you wheat — or chaff?

III. Let me show you, in the third place, ***the portion which Christ's people shall receive, when He comes to purge His threshing floor.***

The text at the beginning of this tract tells us this in good and comfortable words. It tells us that Christ shall "gather His wheat into His barn."

When the Lord Jesus comes the second time, He shall collect His believing people into a place of **safety**. He will send His angels, and gather them from every quarter. The sea shall give up the dead that are in it, and the graves the dead that are in them — and the *living* shall be *changed*. Not one poor sinner of mankind who has ever laid hold on Christ by faith, shall be overlooked in that company. *Not one single grain of wheat* shall be missing, and left outside — when judgments fall upon a wicked world. There shall be a barn for the wheat of the earth — and into that barn *all* the wheat shall be brought.

Ah, reader, it is a sweet and comfortable thought, that "the Lord cares for the righteous." But how *much* the Lord cares for them, I fear is little known, and dimly seen. They have their trials, beyond question — and these both many and great. The *flesh* is weak. The *world* is full of snares. The *cross* is heavy. The *way* is narrow. The *companions* are few. But still they have strong *consolations* — if their eyes were but open to see them. Like Hagar, they have a well of water near them, even in the *wilderness* — though they often do not find it out. Like Mary, they have *Jesus standing by their side* — though often they are not aware of it for very tears.

Bear with me, while I try to tell you something about **Christ's CARE for poor sinners who believe in Him**. Alas, indeed, that it should be needful! But we live in a day of weak and feeble statements. The *danger* of the state of *nature* is feebly exposed. The *privileges* of the state of *grace* are feebly set forth. Hesitating souls are not encouraged. Disciples are not established and confirmed. The man outside of Christ is not rightly *alarmed*. The man in Christ is not rightly *built up*. The one sleeps on, and seldom has his conscience pricked. The other creeps and crawls all his days, and never thoroughly understands the *riches of his inheritance*. Truly this is a sore disease, and one that I would gladly help to cure.

Truly it is a melancholy thing that the people of God should never go up to *Mount Pisgah*, and never know the length and breadth of their possessions. To be brethren of Christ, and sons of God by adoption, to have full and perfect forgiveness, and the renewing of the Holy Spirit; to have a place in the *book of life* and a name on the breast-plate of the Great High Priest in Heaven — all these are glorious things indeed! But still they are not the *whole* of a believer's portion. They are upper springs indeed — but still there are lower springs beside.

The Lord *takes pleasure in His believing people.* Though filthy in their own eyes — they are lovely and honorable in His! They are altogether beautiful — He sees *no spot* in them. Their *weaknesses* and *shortcomings* do not break off the union between Him and them. He chose them, knowing all their hearts. He took them for His own, with a perfect understanding of all their debts, liabilities, and infirmities — and He will never break His covenant and cast them off. When they fall, He will raise them again. When they wander, He will bring them back.

Their *prayers* are pleasant to Him. As a father loves the first stammering efforts of his child to speak — so the Lord loves the poor feeble petitions of His people. He endorses them with His own mighty intercession, and gives them power on high.

Their *services* are pleasant to Him. As a father delights in the first daisy that his child picks and brings him — even so the Lord is pleased with the weak attempts of His people to serve Him. Not a *cup of cold water*shall lose its reward. Not a *word* spoken in love shall ever be forgotten. He told the Hebrews of Noah's *faith* — but not of his *drunkenness*; of Rahab's *faith* — but not of her *lie*. Oh, reader, it is a blessed thing to be God's wheat!

The Lord cares for His believing people in their *lives*. Their **dwelling place** is well known. The "street called strait," where Paul lodged; the "house by the sea-side," where Peter prayed — were all familiar to their Lord. None have such **attendants** as they have — angels rejoice when they are born again, angels minister to them, and angels encamp around them. None have such **food** — their bread is given them, and their water sure, and they have food to eat of which the world knows nothing. None have such **company** as they have — the Spirit dwells with them. The Father and the Son come to them, and make their abode with them. Their **steps** are all ordered, from *grace* to *glory*. Those who persecute them — persecute Christ Himself, and those who hurt them — hurt the apple of the Lord's eye.

Their **trials** and temptations are all measured out by a wise Physician — not a grain of *bitterness* is ever mingled in their cup, which is not good for the health of their souls. Their **temptations**, like Job's, are all under God's control — Satan cannot touch a hair of their head without their Lord's permission, nor even tempt them above that which they shall be able to bear. "As a father has compassion on his children, so the Lord has compassion on those who fear Him." He never afflicts them *willingly*. He leads them by the *right* way. He withholds nothing that is *really* for their good. Come what will, there is always a *needs-be*. When they are placed in the *furnace* — it is that they may be purified. When they are *chastened* — it is that they may become more holy. When they are *pruned* — it is to make them more fruitful. When they are *transplanted* from place to place — it is that they may bloom more brightly. All things are continually *working together* for their good. Like the bee, they extract sweetness even out of the bitterest flowers. Ah, reader, it is a blessed thing to be Christ's wheat!

The Lord cares for His believing people in their *deaths*. Their *times* are all in the Lord's hand. The *hairs* of their heads are all numbered, and not one can ever fall to the ground without their Father. They are *kept* on earth until they are ripe and ready for glory — and not one moment longer. When they have had sun and rain enough, wind and storm enough, cold and heat enough — when the fruit is perfected — then, and not until then, the sickle is put in. They are all *immortal* until their work is done. There is not a *disease* that can loosen the pins of their tabernacle — until the Lord gives the word. A thousand may fall at their right hand — but there is not a *plague* that can touch them — until the Lord sees fit. There is not a physician that can keep them alive — when the Lord gives the word for them to depart. When they come to their death-bed, the Everlasting Arms are round about them, and makes all their bed in their sickness. When they die, they die like Moses — according to the word of the Lord — at the right time, and in the right way. And when they breathe their last, they fall asleep in Christ, and are at once carried, like Lazarus, into Abraham's bosom.

Ah, reader, it is a blessed thing to be Christ's wheat! When the sun of other men is setting — the sun of the believer is rising. When other men are laying aside their honors, he is putting his on. Death locks the door on the unbeliever — and shuts him out from hope. But death opens the door to the believer — and lets him into Paradise!

And the Lord will care for His believing people in the dreadful day of His *appearing*. The flaming fire shall not come near them. The voice of the Archangel and the trumpet of God shall proclaim no terrors to their ears. Sleeping or waking, living or dead, moldering in the coffin, or standing at the post of daily duty — believers shall be *secure* and unmoved. They shall lift up their heads with joy, when they see redemption drawing near. They shall be changed, and put on their beautiful garments, in the twinkling of an eye. They shall be caught up to meet the Lord in the air. Jesus will do nothing to a sin-laden world — until all His people are *safe*. There was an *ark* for Noah when the flood began. There was a *Zoar* for Lot when the fire fell on Sodom. There was a *Pella* for early Christians when Jerusalem was besieged. There was a *Zurich* for English Reformers when Popish Mary came to the throne. And there will be a *barn* for all the wheat of the earth in the last day. Ah, reader, it is a blessed thing to be Christ's wheat!

I often wonder at the *miserable faithlessness* of those among us who are believers. Next to the hardness of the unconverted heart, I call it *one of the greatest wonders in the world.* I wonder that with such mighty reasons for confidence, we can still be so full of doubts. I marvel, above all things, how any can deny the doctrine that Christ's people persevere unto the end, and can imagine that He who loved them so as to die for them upon the cross — will ever let them be cast away! I cannot think so. I do not believe the Lord Jesus will ever lose *one* of His flock. He will not let Satan pluck away from Him — so much as *one sick lamb.*He will not allow one *bone* of His mystical body to be broken. He will not allow one *jewel* to fall from His crown. He and His *bride* have been once joined in an everlasting covenant, and they shall never never be put asunder!

The trophies won by earthly conquerors have often been wrested from them, and carried off — but this shall never be said of the trophies of Him who triumphed for us on the cross. "My sheep," He says, "shall *never* perish." (John 10:28.) I take my stand on that text. I know not how it can be evaded. If words have any meaning, the perseverance of Christ's people is there.

I do not believe when David had rescued the lamb from the paws of the lion — that he left it weak and wounded to perish in the wilderness. I cannot believe when the Lord Jesus has delivered a soul from the snare of the devil — that He will ever leave that soul to take his chance, and wrestle on in his own feebleness against sin, the devil, and the world.

Reader, I would be sure, if you were present at a shipwreck, and seeing some helpless child tossing on the waves, were to plunge into the sea, and save him at the risk of your own life — I would be sure you would not be content with merely bringing that child safe to shore. You would not lay him down when you had reached the land, and say, "I will do no more. He is weak — he is insensible — he is cold — it matters not; I have done enough. I have delivered him from the waters — he is not drowned." You would not do this! You would not say so. You would not treat that child in such a manner. You would lift him in your arms. You would carry him to the nearest house. You would try to bring back warmth and animation. You would use every means to restore health and vigor. You would never leave him until his recovery was a certain thing.

And can you suppose the Lord Jesus Christ is less merciful, or less compassionate? Can you think He would suffer on the cross and die for you, and yet leave it uncertain whether you would be saved? Can you think He would wrestle with death and Hell, and go down to the grave for our sakes — and yet allow our eternal life to hang on such a thread as our poor miserable endeavors?

Oh, no! He does not do so. He is a perfect and complete Savior. Those whom He loves — He loves unto the end. Those whom He washes in His blood — He never leaves nor forsakes. He puts His fear into their hearts — so that they shall not depart from Him. Where He begins a work — there He also finishes. All whom He transplants in His garden enclosed on earth — He transplants sooner or later into His Heavenly paradise. All whom He quickens by His Spirit — He will also bring with Him when He enters His kingdom. There is a barn for *every grain* of the wheat. All shall appear in Heaven with God.

From *false faith* men may fall — and fall both finally and foully. I never doubt this. I see proof of it continually. From true grace — men never do fall totally. They never did, and they never will. If they commit sin, like Peter — they shall repent and rise again. If they err from the right way, like David — they shall be brought back. It is not any strength or power of their *own* which keeps them from apostasy. They are kept because the power, and love, and promises of the Trinity are all engaged on their side! The *election* of God the Father shall not be fruitless; the *redemption* and *intercession* of God the Son shall not be ineffectual; the love of God the Spirit shall not be labor in vain. The Lord shall keep the feet of His saints. They shall all be more than conquerors through Him who loved them. They shall all conquer, and none die eternally.

Reader, if you have not yet taken up the cross and become Christ's disciple, you little know what *privileges* you are missing. Peace with God now — and glory hereafter; the Everlasting Arms to keep you along the way — and the barn of safety in the end; all these are freely offered to you without money and without price. You may say that Christians have *tribulations* — you forget that they have also *consolations*. You may say they have peculiar *sorrows* — you forget they have also peculiar *joys*. You see but *half* the Christian life. You see not all. You see the *warfare* — but not the food and the *wages*. You see the tossing and conflict of the outward part of Christianity — you see not the hidden treasures which lie deep within. Like Elisha's servant, you see the enemies of God's children — but you do not, like Elisha, see the chariots and horses of fire which protect them. Oh, judge not by outward appearances! Be sure that the least *drop* of the water of life, is better than all the *rivers* of the world. Remember the *barn* and the *crown!* Be wise in time.

Reader, if you feel that you are a weak disciple, think not that *weakness* shuts you out from any of the privileges of which I have been speaking. Weak *faith* is true faith — and weak *grace* is true grace; and both are the gift of Him who never gives in vain. Fear not, neither be discouraged. Doubt not, neither despair. Jesus will never break the bruised reed, nor quench the smoking flax. The **babes** in a family are as much loved and thought of as the elder brothers and sisters. The tender **seedlings** in a garden are as diligently looked after as the old trees. The **lambs** in the flock are as carefully tended by the good shepherd as the old sheep. Oh, rest assured it is just the same in Christ's *family*, in Christ's *garden*, in Christ's *flock*. ALL are loved. All are tenderly thought of. All are cared for. And all shall be found in His barn at last! Reader, think on these things. Begin to meditate on my question this very day. *Are you wheat — or chaff?*

IV. Let me show you, in the last place, ***the portion which remains for all who are not Christ's people.***

The text at the beginning of this tract describes this in words which should make our ears tingle — Christ shall "burn up the chaff with unquenchable fire!"

When the Lord Jesus Christ comes to *purge* His threshing floor — He shall *punish* all who are not His disciples with a fearful punishment. All who are found impenitent and unbelieving — all who have held the truth in unrighteousness — all who have clung to sin, stuck to the world, and set their affection on things below — all who are without Christ. All such shall come to an awful end! Christ shall "burn up the chaff!"

Their punishment shall be *most SEVERE.* There is no pain like that of *burning*. Put your finger in the candle flame for a moment, if you doubt this, and try. Fire is the most *destructive* and *devouring* of all elements. Look into the mouth of a blast furnace — and think what it would be to be there. Fire is of all elements most opposed to life. Creatures can live in air, and earth, and water — but nothing can live in fire! Yet fire is the portion to which the Christless and unbelieving will come. Christ will "burn up the chaff with unquenchable fire!"

Their punishment shall be *ETERNAL.* Millions of ages shall pass away, and the fire into which the chaff is cast, shall still *burn on*. That fire shall never burn low and become dim. The *fuel* of that fire shall never waste away and be consumed. It is "unquenchable fire."

Oh, reader, these are sad and painful things to speak of! I have no pleasure in dwelling on them. I could rather say with the apostle Paul, "I have great sorrow." But they are things written for our learning, and it is good to consider them. They are a part of that Scripture which is all profitable, and they ought to be heard. As painful as the subject of *Hell* is — it is one about which I dare not, cannot, must not be silent. Who would desire to speak of Hell-fire — if God had not spoken of it? When God has spoken of it so plainly — who can safely hold his peace?

I dare not shut my eyes to the fact, that a deep-rooted infidelity lurks in men's minds on the subject of Hell. I see it oozing out in the utter *apathy* of some — they eat, and drink, and sleep — as if there was no wrath to come! I see it creeping forth in the coldness of others about their neighbors' souls — they show little concern to pluck *brands* from the fire. I desire to denounce such infidelity with all my might. Believing that there are *terrors of the Lord*, as well as the recompense of reward — I call upon all who profess to believe the Bible, to be on their guard.

I know that some do not believe there is any Hell at all. They think it impossible there can be such a place. They call it inconsistent with the mercy of God. They say it is too dreadful an idea to be really true. The devil of course rejoices in the views of such people. They help his kingdom mightily. They are preaching up his favorite old doctrine, *"You shall not surely die!"*

I know furthermore, that some do not believe that Hell is *eternal*. They tell us it is incredible that a compassionate God will punish men *forever*. He will surely open the prison-doors at last. This also is a mighty help to the devil's cause. "Take your ease," he whispers to sinners — "if you do make a mistake, never mind, it is *not* forever."

I know also that some believe that there is a Hell — but never allow that anybody is going there! All people with them are 'good' as soon as they die — all were *sincere* — all *meant well* — and all, they hope, got to Heaven. Alas, what a *common delusion* is this! I can well understand the feeling of the little girl who asked her mother where all the *wicked* people were buried, "for she found no mention on the gravestones of any except the good."

And I know very well that some believe there is a Hell — but never like it to be spoken of. It is a subject that should always be kept back. They see no profit in bringing it forward, and are rather shocked when it is mentioned. This also is an immense help to the devil. "Hush, hush!" says Satan, "say nothing about Hell." The fowler wishes to hear no noise when he lays his *snare*. The wolf would like the shepherd to *sleep* while he prowls round the fold. Just so, the devil rejoices when Christians are *silent* about Hell.

Reader, all these notions are the *opinions of man*. What is it to you and I — what *man* thinks in religion? Man will not judge us at the last day. Man's *fancies* and *traditions* are not to be our guide in this life. There is but one point to be settled — "What says the Word of God?"

Do you believe the Bible? Then depend upon it, ***Hell is real and true***. It is as true as Heaven — as true as justification by faith — as true as the fact that Christ died upon the cross. There is not a fact or doctrine which you may not lawfully doubt — if you doubt Hell. Disbelieve Hell — and you unscrew, unsettle, and unpin everything in Scripture! You may as well throw your Bible away at once. From "no Hell" to "no God" there is but a series of *steps*.

Do you believe the Bible? Then depend upon it, ***Hell will have inhabitants***. The wicked shall certainly be turned into Hell, and all the people that forget God. These shall go away into *everlasting punishment*. The same blessed Savior who now sits on a throne of *grace*, will one day sit on a throne of *judgment* — and men will see there is such a thing as "the wrath of the Lamb!" The same lips which now say "Come — come unto Me," will one day say "Depart from Me, you who are cursed!" Alas, how awful the thought of being condemned by Christ Himself — judged by the Savior; sentenced to eternally misery — by the Lamb!

Do you believe the Bible? Then depend upon it, ***Hell will be intense and unutterable woe***. It is vain to talk of all the expressions about being only *figures of speech*. The pit, the prison, the worm, the fire, the thirst, the blackness, the darkness, the weeping, the gnashing of teeth, the second death — all these may be figures of speech if you please. But Bible figures *mean something*, beyond all question — and here they mean something which man's mind can never fully conceive. Oh, reader, the *miseries* of mind and conscience, are far worse than those of the body! The whole extent of Hell, the present suffering, the bitter recollection of the past, the hopeless prospect of the future — will never be thoroughly known, except by those who go there!

Do you believe the Bible? Then depend upon it, ***Hell is eternal***. It must be eternal, or words have no meaning at all. Forever and ever; everlasting; unquenchable; never-dying — all these are expressions used about Hell, and expressions that cannot be *explained away*. It must be eternal, or the very foundations of Heaven are cast down. If Hell has an end — then Heaven has an end too. They both stand or fall together. It must be, or else every doctrine of the Gospel is undermined. If a man may escape Hell at length without faith in Christ, or sanctification of the Spirit — then sin is no longer an infinite evil, and there was no such great need for Christ making an atonement.

And where is there warrant for saying that Hell can ever change a heart, or make it fit for Heaven? Hell must be eternal, or Hell would cease to be Hell altogether. Give a man *hope* — and he will bear anything. Grant a hope of deliverance, however distant — and Hell is but a drop of water. Ah, reader, these are solemn things!

FOREVER is the most solemn word in the Bible! Alas, for that *day* which shall have no tomorrow! That day when men shall seek death, and not find it, and shall desire to die — but death shall flee from them! Who shall dwell with devouring fire! Who shall dwell with everlasting burnings!

Do you believe the Bible? Then depend upon it, ***Hell is a subject that ought not to be kept back***. It is striking to observe the many texts about it in Scripture. It is striking to observe that none say so much about it as our Lord Jesus Christ, that gracious and merciful Savior; and the apostle John, whose heart seems full of love. Truly it may well be doubted whether we ministers speak of it as much as we ought. I cannot forget the words of a dying hearer of Mr. Newton's — "Sir, you often told me of Christ and salvation; why did you not oftener remind me of Hell and danger?"

Let others be silent about Hell if they will — I dare not do so. I see it plainly in Scripture, and I must speak of it. I fear that thousands are on that *broad way* that leads to it, and I would sincerely arouse them to a sense of the *peril* before them. What would you say of the man who saw his neighbor's house in danger of being burnt down — and never raised the cry of "Fire!" What ought to be said of us as ministers, if we call ourselves watchmen for souls, and yet see the fires of Hell raging in the distance — and never give the alarm? Call it *bad taste*, if you like, to speak of Hell. Call it *charity* to make things pleasant, and speak smoothly, and soothe men with constant lullaby of peace. From such notions of *taste* and *charity* — may I ever be delivered! My notion of *charity* is to warn men plainly of danger! My notion of *taste* in the ministerial office, is to declare all the counsel of God. If I never spoke of Hell — I would think I had kept back something that was profitable — and would look on myself as *an accomplice of the devil.*

Reader, I beseech you, in all tender affection, beware of false views of the subject on which I have been dwelling. Beware of new and strange doctrines about Hell and the *eternity* of punishment. Beware of *manufacturing a God* of your own: a God who is all mercy — but not just; a God who is all love — but not holy; a God who has a Heaven for everybody — but a Hell for none; a God who can allow good and evil to be side by side in time — but will make no *distinction* between good and evil in eternity. Such a God is an *idol of your own imagination!* It is as true an *idol* as any snake or crocodile in an Egyptian temple — as true an idol as was ever molded out of brass or clay! The hands of your own *imagination* and *sentimentality* have made him. He is not the God of the Bible — and beside the God of the Bible — there is no God at all. Your *Heaven* would be no Heaven at all. A Heaven containing all sorts of sinful people, would be miserable discord indeed. Alas, for the *eternity* of such a Heaven! There would be little difference between it and Hell! Ah, reader, there is a Hell! There is a *fire* for the chaff! Take heed, lest you find it out to your cost too late!

Beware of being wise above that which is written. Beware of forming fanciful theories of your own, and then trying to make the Bible square with them. Beware of making selections from your Bible to suit your taste — refusing, like a spoiled child, whatever you think bitter — seizing, like a spoiled child, whatever you think sweet. What is all this but taking *Jehoiakim's penknife?* What does it amount to but telling God, that you, a poor short-lived worm — know better than He? It will not do! It will not do. You must take the Bible as it is. You must read it all, and believe it all. You must come to the reading of it in the spirit of a little child. Dare not to say, "I believe *this* verse, for I like it. I reject *that*, for I do not like it. I receive *this*, for I can agree with it. I refuse *that*, for I cannot reconcile it with my views." Nay! but O man, who are you that replies against God? By what right do you talk in this way? Surely it were better to say over every chapter in the Word, "Speak, Lord, for your servant is listening!" Ah, reader, if men would do this, they would never deny *Hell*, the *chaff*, and the *fire!*

Think on these things once more. Meditate upon them. Remember my question, "Are you wheat — or chaff?"

I have shown you the **two great classes of mankind** — the wheat and the chaff.

I have shown you the **separation** which will one day take place.

I have shown you the **safety of the Lord's people**.

I have shown you the **fearful portion of the Christless** and unbelieving.

I commend these things to your conscience, as in the sight of God. And now, reader, let me say four things in **CONCLUSION**, and then I am done.

1. Settle it down in your mind, that the things of which I have been speaking are *all real and true*.

I do believe that many never see the great truths of religion in this light. I firmly believe that many never listen to the things they hear from ministers as realities. They regard it all, like Gallio, as a matter of names and words, and nothing more — a huge shadow — a religious play-acting — a vast sham! Macaulay's History of England, Dicken's last Novel, the latest news from France, India, Australia, California, or New York — all these are things they realize. They feel interested and excited about them. But as to the Bible, and Heaven, and the kingdom of Christ, and the judgment day — these are subjects that they hear unmoved. They do not *really* believe them.

Reader, if you have unhappily got into this frame of mind, I charge you to cast it off forever. Whether you mean to hear or forbear, awaken to a thorough conviction that the things I have brought before you are real and true. The *wheat*, the *chaff*, the *separation*, the *barn*, the *fire* — all these are great realities; as real as the sun in in the sky — as real as the paper which your eyes behold. For my part, I believe in Heaven — and I believe in Hell. I believe in a coming judgment. I believe in a day of *sifting*. I am not ashamed to say so. I believe them all, and therefore I write as I do. Oh, reader, take a friend's advice, *live* as if these things were true!

2. Settle it down in your mind, that the things of which I write *concern YOURSELF*. They are your business, your affair, and your concern. Many, I am am sure, never look on religion as a matter that concerns *themselves*. They attend on its *outward* part, as a decent and proper *fashion*. They hear sermons. They read religious books. They have their children christened. But all the time they never ask themselves, "What is all this to *me*?" They sit in our churches like *spectators* in a theater, or court of law. They read our writings as if they were reading a report of an interesting trial, or of some event far away. But they do not say to themselves, *"I am the man!"*

Reader, if you have this kind of feeling, depend upon it — it will never do. There must be an end of all this, if ever you are to be saved. *You* are the man I write to, whoever you may be who reads these pages. I write not specially to the rich. I write not specially to the poor. I write to everybody who will read, whatever his rank may be. It is on your soul's account that I am pleading, and not another's. You are spoken of in the text that begins this tract. You are this very day either among the wheat — or among the chaff. Your portion will one day either be the barn — or the fire. Oh, that men were wise, and would lay these things to heart! Oh, that they would not trifle, dally, linger, live on as *half-and-half* Christians, meaning well — but never acting boldly, and at last awake when it is too late!

3. Settle it down in your mind, that if you are willing to be one of the wheat of the earth — *the Lord Jesus Christ is willing to receive you.*

Does any man suppose that Jesus is not willing to see His barn filled? Do you think He does not desire to bring many sons to glory? Oh, you little know the depth of His mercy and compassion — if you can think such a thought! He wept over unbelieving Jerusalem. He mourns over the impenitent and the thoughtless in the present day. He sends you invitations by my mouth this hour. He invites you to hear and live, to forsake the way of the foolish, and to go in the paths of understanding. "As I live," He says, "I have no pleasure in the death of him who dies. Turn! Turn! Why will you die?"

Oh, reader, if you never came to Christ for eternal life before — come to Him this very day! Come to Him with the penitent's prayer for mercy and grace. Come to Him without delay. Come to Him while the subject of these pages is still fresh on your mind. Come to Him before another sun rises on the earth, and let the morning find you a new creature.

If you are determined to *have* the world, and the things of the world — its pleasures and its rewards — its follies and its sins — if you must have your own way, and cannot give up anything for Christ and your soul — if this is your case, there is but one end before you. I fairly *warn* you, I plainly tell you — *you will sooner or later come to the unquenchable fire!*

But if any man is willing to be saved, the Lord Jesus Christ stands ready to save him. "Come unto Me," He says, "weary soul — and I will give you rest. Come, guilty and sinful soul — and I will give you free pardon. Come, lost and ruined soul — and I will give you eternal life."

Oh, reader, let this message be a word in season. Arise and call upon the Lord! Let the angels of God rejoice over one more saved soul. Let the courts of Heaven hear the good tidings that one more *lost sheep* is found!

4. Settle it down in your mind, that if you have committed your soul to Christ — *Christ will never allow that soul to perish.*

The *Everlasting Arms* are round about you. Lean back in them, and know your safety. The same *hand* that was nailed to the cross — is holding you! The same *wisdom* that framed the Heavens and the earth — is engaged to maintain your cause. The same *power* that saved Israel from Egyptian bondage — is on your side. The same *love* that bore with and carried Israel from Egypt to Canaan — is pledged to keep you. Ah, reader, they are well kept — whom Christ keeps! Our faith may repose calmly on such a *bed*, as *Christ's omnipotence.*

Take comfort, doubting believer. Why are you cast down? The *love* of Jesus is no summer-day fountain — no man ever yet saw its bottom. The *compassion* of Jesus is a fire that never yet burned low; the cold, grey ashes of that fire have never yet been seen. Take comfort. In *your heart* you may find little cause for rejoicing — but you may always rejoice in the Lord.

You say that your *faith is so small.* But where is it said that none shall be saved except their faith is great? And after all, "Who gave you any faith at all?" The very fact that you have any faith, is a token for good.

You say that your *sins are so many.* But where is the sin, or heap of sins — which the blood of Jesus cannot wash away? And after all, "Who told you you had any sins? That feeling never came from yourself." Blessed indeed is that one, who really knows and feels that he is a sinner.

Take comfort, I say once more, if you have really come to Christ. Take comfort, and know your *privileges.* Cast every *care* on Jesus. Tell every *need* to Jesus. Roll every *burden* on Jesus — your sins, unbelief, doubts, fears, anxieties — lay them all on Christ! He loves to see you doing so. He loves to be employed as your High Priest. He loves to be trusted. He loves to see His people ceasing from the vain effort to carry their burdens for themselves.

I commend these things to your notice. Only be among Christ's *wheat* now — and then, in the great day of *separation,* as sure as the Bible is true — you shall be in Christ's *barn* forever!

ETERNITY!

"What is *seen* is temporary — but what is *unseen* is eternal." (2 Corinthians 4:18)

A subject stands out on the face of this text, which is one of the most solemn and heart searching in the Bible. That subject is *eternity*.

The subject is one of which the wisest man can only take in a little at a time. We have no *eyes* to see it fully, and no mind to grasp fully it — and yet we must not refuse to consider it. There is a depth of *stars* in the Heavens above us, which the most powerful telescope cannot pierce — yet it is well worth it to look into them and learn *something*, even if we cannot learn *everything*. There are heights and depths about the subject of eternity, which mortal man can never comprehend; but God has spoken of it, and we have no right to turn away from it completely.

The subject is one, which we must never approach without the Bible in our hands. The moment we depart from "God's written Word," in considering eternity and the future state of man — we are then likely to fall into error. In examining points like these, we must have nothing to do with *preconceived notions* as to what God's character is like, and what *we* think God ought to be, or ought to do with man after death. We only have to find out what is written. *What does the Scripture say?* What does the Lord say? It is foolish to tell us that we ought to have "noble thoughts about God," independent of, and over and above, Scripture. The noblest thoughts about God, which we have a right to hold, are the thoughts that He has been pleased to reveal to us in His "written Word."

I ask for the attention of everyone into whose hands this paper may fall, while I offer a few thoughts about eternity. As a mortal man, I deeply feel my own insufficiency to handle this subject. But I pray that God the Holy Spirit, whose strength is made perfect in weakness, may bless the words I speak, and make them *seeds of eternal life* in many minds.

I. The first thought that I bring to your attention is this — *we live in a world where all things are temporary and passing away.*

Surely, a man must be blind who cannot realize this. Everything around us is decaying, dying, and coming to an end. There is a sense, no doubt, in which "matter" is eternal. Once created, it will never entirely cease to exist. But in a popular practical sense, everything about us is dying except our souls. No wonder the poet says, "Change and decay all around me I see — O You who does not change, abide with me!"

We are all going, going, going — whether eminent or unimportant, gentle or cruel, rich or poor, old or young. We are all going — and will soon be gone!

Beauty is only temporary. Sarah was once the lovliest of women, and the admiration of the Court of Egypt; yet a day came when even Abraham, her husband, said, "Sell me some property for a burial site here so I can bury my dead." (Genesis 23:4)

Strength of the body is only temporary. David was once a mighty man of valor, the slayer of the lion and the bear, and the champion of Israel against Goliath; yet a day came when even David had to be nursed and ministered to in his old age like a child!

Wisdom and power of the brain are only temporary. Solomon was once a marvel of knowledge, and all the kings of the earth came to hear his wisdom — yet even Solomon in his latter days played the fool, and allowed his wives to "turn his heart after their gods." (1 Kings 11:2)

As humbling and painful as these truths may sound, it is good for all of us to realize them and take them to heart. The houses we live in, the homes we love, the riches we accumulate, the professions we follow, the plans we formulate, the relations we enter into — they are only for a time. "What is seen is temporary." "This world in its present form is passing away." (2 Corinthians 4:18; 1 Corinthians 7:31)

The thought is one which ought to awaken everyone who is living only for this world. If his conscience is not completely seared, it should stir in him a great searching of his heart. Oh, be careful what you are doing! Awake to see things in their true light, before it is too late. The things you live for now, are all temporary and passing away! The pleasures, the amusements, the recreations, the profits, the earthly callings, which now absorb all your heart and drink up your entire mind — will soon be over. They are poor fleeting things which cannot last. Oh, do not love them too much; do not hold on to them too tightly; do not make them your idols! You cannot keep them, and you must leave them. Seek first the kingdom of God, and then everything else will be given to you. "Set your minds on things above, not on earthly things." Oh, you that love the world, get wisdom! Never, never forget that it is written, "The world and its desires pass away — but the man who does the will of God lives forever." (Colossians 3:2; 1 John 2:17)

The same thought ought to cheer and comfort every true Christian. Your trials, crosses, and conflicts are all temporary! They will soon come to an end; and even now they are working for you "an eternal glory that far outweighs them all." (2 Corinthians 4:17) Receive them patiently; bear them quietly; look upward, forward, onward, and far beyond them. Fight your *daily fight* under a steadfast conviction that it is only for a little while, and that rest is not far off. Carry your daily cross always remembering that "what is seen is temporary." The *cross* will soon be exchanged for a *crown* — and you will sit down with Abraham, Isaac, and Jacob in the kingdom of God.

II. The second thought that I bring to your attention is this — *we are all moving towards a world where everything is eternal.*

That great unseen state of existence, which lies beyond the grave — is forever! Whether it is happy or miserable, whether it is a condition of joy or sorrow — we know that in one respect it will be utterly unlike anything in this world — it will be *forever*. There will be no change and decay, no end, no goodbye, no mornings and evening, no alteration, and no annihilation. Whatever there is beyond the tomb, when the last trumpet has sounded, and the dead are raised — we know it will be endless, everlasting, and eternal. "What is unseen is eternal."

We cannot fully realize this condition. The contrast between now and then, between this world and the next, is so very great that our feeble minds cannot grasp it all. How we live our lives in this world, brings consequences in the next, that are so tremendous, that they almost take away our breath, and we shrink back from looking at them. But when the Bible speaks plainly — we have no right to turn away from a subject; and with the Bible in our hands, we will do well to look at the "unseen things that are eternal."

Let us settle it then in our minds, for one thing, that **the future happiness of those who are saved is eternal**. However little we may understand it — it is something that will have no end — it will never cease, never grow old, never decay, and never die. "God will fill us with joy in His presence, with *eternal pleasures* at His right hand." (Psalm 16:11) Once they arrive in paradise, the saints will never ever leave that wonderful place. Their inheritance "can never perish, spoil or fade!" They will "receive the crown of glory which will never fade away." (1 Peter 1:4; 5:4) Their *warfare* is finished; their *fight* is over; their *work* is done. "Never again will they hunger; never again will they thirst."

They are traveling on towards an "eternal glory which far outweighs" all their struggles — towards . . .
a home which will never be broken up,
a meeting without a parting,
a family gathering without a separation,
a day without night.

Faith will be swallowed up in *sight*, and *hope* in *certainty*. They will see as they have been seen, and know as they have been known, and "be forever with the Lord!" I am not surprised that the apostle Paul adds, "Therefore, encourage each other with these words!" (1 Thessalonians 4:17, 18)

For another thing, let us settle it in our minds, that **the future misery of those who are lost is eternal**. I am aware that this is a dreadful truth, and flesh and blood naturally shrink from the contemplation of it. But I am one of those who believe it is clearly revealed in Scripture, and I dare not keep it back in the pulpit. To my eyes, eternal future happiness and eternal future misery appear to stand side by side. I fail to see how you can distinguish the duration of one, from the duration of the other. If the *joy of the believer* is forever — then the *sorrow of the unbeliever* is also forever. If Heaven is eternal — likewise so is Hell. It may be my ignorance — but I do not know how the conclusion can be avoided.

I cannot reconcile the concept of a "non-eternal" punishment with the language of the Bible. Its advocates talk loudly about love and kindness, and say that it does not harmonize with the merciful and compassionate character of God. But what does the Scripture say?

Who ever spoke such loving and merciful words as our Lord Jesus Christ? Yet His are the lips which three times over describe the consequence of refusing to repent of sin, as "the worm that does not die, and the fire that is not quenched." He is the Person who speaks in one sentence, of the wicked going away to "eternal punishment," and the righteous to "eternal life." (Mark 9:43-48; Matthew 25:46)

Who does not remember the Apostle *Paul's* words about love? Yet he is the very Apostle who says, the wicked "will be punished with everlasting destruction." (2 Thessalonians 1:9)

Who does not know the spirit of love that runs through all *John's* Gospel and Epistles? Yet the beloved Apostle is the very writer in the New Testament who dwells most strongly, in the book of Revelation, on the reality and eternity of future agony.

What will we say to all these things? Will we be wiser than that which is written? Will we admit the dangerous principle that *words* in Scripture do not mean what they *appear* to mean? Is it not far better to put our hands over our months and say, "Whatever God has written must be true!" "Yes, Lord God Almighty, true and just are your judgments!" (Revelation 16:7)

I lay no claim to any unusual knowledge of Scripture. I daily feel that I am no more *infallible* than the Pope of Rome. But I must speak according to the light that God has given to me; and I do not think I would be doing my duty if I did not raise a warning voice on this subject, and try to put Christians on their guard. Six thousand years ago sin entered into the world by the *devil's daring lie*, "You will not surely die!" (Genesis 3:4) At the end of six thousand years, the great enemy of mankind is still using his old weapon, and trying to persuade men that they may live and die in sin — and yet at some distant period may be finally saved. Let us not be ignorant of his devices. Let us walk steadily in the old paths. Let us hold fast the old truth, and believe that as the happiness of the saved is eternal — so also is the misery of the lost.

"There is nothing that Satan desires more than that we would believe that he does not exist, and that there is no such a place as Hell, and no such things as eternal torments. He whispers all this into our ears, and he rejoices when he hears any deny these things, for then he hopes to make them and others his victims." — *Wordsworth*

(a) Let us be faithful, in the interest of the whole system of the Christian religion.

What was the use of God's Son becoming incarnate, agonizing in Gethsemane, and dying on the cross to make atonement — if men can ultimately be saved without believing on Him? Where is the slightest proof that saving faith in Christ's blood can ever be achieved *after* death? Where is the need of the Holy Spirit, if sinners are can enter Heaven without conversion and renewal of heart? Where can we find the smallest evidence that after a person dies in an unregenerate state — that *later* he can still be born again, and have a new heart? If a man, without faith in Christ or sanctification of the Spirit, can escape eternal punishment — then sin is no longer an infinite evil — and there was no need for Christ making atonement.

(b) Let us be faithful, because of *holiness* and *morality*.

I can imagine nothing so *pleasant to our flesh and blood*, as the deceptive theory that we may live in sin — and yet escape eternal damnation; and that although we are "enslaved by all kinds of evil passions and pleasures" while we are on earth — we will somehow all eventually get to Heaven! Just tell the young man who "squandered his wealth in wild living" that Heaven is available even for those who live and die in sin, and he is never likely to turn from it. Why should be repent and take up the cross — if he can get eventually get to Heaven without repenting?

(c) Finally, let us be faithful, because of the common hopes of all God's people.

Let us distinctly understand that every blow struck at eternal punishment — is an equally heavy blow at the eternity of Heaven's bliss. It is impossible to separate the two things. No ingenious theological definition can divide them. They stand or fall together. The same *language* is used, the same *figures of speech* are employed, when the Bible speaks about either condition. Every attack on the duration of Hell — is also an attack on the duration of Heaven. It is true that if we take away the fear of Hell from sinners — then we also have taken away our own hope!

I turn from this part of my subject with a deep sense of its painfulness. I strongly agree with Robert McCheyne, that *"it is a hard subject to handle lovingly."* But I turn from it with an equally deep conviction that if we believe the Bible — then we must never give up anything that it contains. *Dear Jesus, deliver us from hard, austere, and unmerciful theology!* If men are not saved — it is because they "refuse to come to Christ." (John 5:40) But we must not be wise above that which is written. No morbid love of *liberality*, so called, must induce us to reject anything that God has revealed about eternity!

Men sometimes talk exclusively about God's *mercy* and *love* and *compassion* — as if He had no other attributes, and leave out His *holiness* and His *purity*, His *justice* and His *wrath*, and His *hatred of sin*. Let us beware of falling into this delusion. It is a growing evil in these last days. Low and inadequate views of the absolute vileness and filthiness of sin, and of the indescribable purity of the eternal God — are fertile sources of error about man's future state! Let us think about the *mighty Being* whom we are subject to, as He Himself declared His character to Moses saying, "The Lord, the Lord, the compassionate and gracious God, slow to anger, abounding in love and faithfulness, maintaining love to thousands, and forgiving wickedness, rebellion and sin!" But let us not forget the solemn clause that concludes the sentence, "Yet He does not leave the guilty unpunished!" (Exodus 34:6, 7) *Unrepented sin is an eternal evil,* and can never cease to be sin; and the One we are subject to is an eternal God!

The words of Psalm 145 are strikingly beautiful, "The Lord is gracious and compassionate, slow to anger and rich in love. The Lord is good to all; He has compassion on all He has made. The Lord upholds all those who fall and lifts up all who are bowed down. The Lord is righteous in all His ways and loving toward all He has made. The Lord is near to all who call on Him, to all who call on Him in truth. The Lord watches over all who love Him." Nothing can exceed the *mercifulness* of this language! But what a striking fact it is that the passage goes on to add the following *solemn conclusion*, "But all the wicked, He will destroy."

III. The *third* thought that I bring to your attention is this: our future state in the unseen world of eternity — depends entirely on what we are in the present!

The life that we live on the earth is short and soon gone! "We spend our years as a tale that is told." "What is your life? You are a *mist* that appears for a little while — and then vanishes!" (Psalm 90:9; James 4:14) The life that is before us when we leave this world, is an endless eternity, a *sea without a bottom*, and an *ocean without a shore*. "With the Lord a day is like a thousand years, and a thousand years are like a day." (2 Peter 3:8) In that world, there will be no more *time*. But as short as our life is here, and as endless as it will be in eternity — the life we now live will have a tremendous impact on eternity. Our lot after death depends, humanly speaking — on what we are while we are alive. It is written, God "will give to each person according to what he has done. To those who by persistence in doing good seek glory, honor and immortality — He will give eternal life. But for those who are self-seeking and who reject the truth and follow evil — there will be wrath and anger!" (Romans 2:6-8)

We must never forget, that every one of us, while we live, are in a state of *probation*. We are constantly *sowing seeds* which will spring up and bear fruit, every day and every hour in our lives. There are *eternal consequences* resulting from all our thoughts and words and actions, of which we pay too little attention to. "Men will have to give account on the Day of Judgment, for *every careless word* they have spoken." (Matthew 12:36) Our *thoughts* are all numbered; our *actions* are weighed. No wonder that Paul says, "The one who sows to please his sinful nature — from that nature will reap destruction; the one who sows to please the Spirit — from the Spirit will reap eternal life." (Galatians 6:8) In a word, what we sow in life — we will reap after death, and reap throughout all eternity!

There is no greater delusion than the common idea that it is possible to live wickedly — and yet rise again gloriously; to be without Christ in this world — and yet to be a saint in the next. When that great preacher George Whitefield revived the doctrine of conversion, in the last century, it is reported that one of his listeners came to him after a sermon and said, "It is all quite true, sir. I hope I will be converted and born again one day — but not until after I am dead." I fear there are many like him. I fear the false doctrine of the Roman Catholic *Purgatory* has many secret friends even within the confines Protestantism today! However sinfully and carelessly men may go on while they live, they secretly cling to the hope that they will be found among the saints when they die. They seem to embrace the idea that there is some *cleansing, purifying* effect produced by death, and that, whatever they may be in this life, they will be found "suitable for the inheritance of the saints" in the life to come. *But it is all a delusion!*

"The Scripture never represents the state of future misery, as a state of cleansing and purification, or anything analogous to a state of trial, where men may conform and qualify themselves for some better state of existence — but always as a state of retribution, punishment, and righteous vengeance, in which God's *justice* (a perfection of which some men seem to render no account) vindicates the power of His majesty, His government, and His love — by punishing those who have despised.

The Bible clearly teaches, that what we are when we die, whether converted or unconverted, whether believers or unbelievers, whether godly or ungodly — so we will be when we rise again at the sound of the last trumpet. There is no repentance in the *grave* — there is no conversion after the last breath is drawn. Now is the time to believe in

Christ, and to lay hold of eternal life. Now is the time to turn from darkness to light, and to make our calling and election sure. The night comes, when no man can work. *As the tree falls — there it will lie.* If we leave this world refusing to repent and believe — then we will rise in the same condition on resurrection morning, and find that it would have been "better for us if we had never been born!"

"This life is the time of our preparation for our future state. Our souls will continue forever what we make them in this world. Such a taste and disposition of mind as a man carries with him out of this life — he will retain in the next. It is absolutely true that Heaven perfects those holy and virtuous dispositions, which are *begun* here; but the eternal world alters no man as to his *main state.* He who is filthy — will be filthy still; and he who is unrighteous — will be unrighteous still." — Tillotson

I strongly advise readers of this paper to remember this, and to make a good use of their *time.* Regard it as the stuff of which life is made, and never waste it or throw it away. Your hours and days and weeks and months and years — all have something to say to your eternal condition beyond the grave. What you sow in this life on earth — you are sure to reap in a life to come. As holy Richard Baxter says, it is "now or never!" Whatever we do in religion — must be done now.

Keep this foremost in your mind, whenever you are tempted to do evil. When sinners entice you, and say, "It is only a *little* sin." When Satan whispers in your heart, "Never mind — what is the great harm in it? Everybody does it" — then look *beyond time* to the unseen world, and place *the thought of eternity* in the face of the temptation. There is a great saying by the martyred Reformer, Hooper, when someone urged him to recant before he was burned, saying, "Life is sweet and death is bitter." "True," said Hooper, "quite true! But eternal life is more sweet — and eternal death is more bitter!"

IV. The last thought which I bring to the attention of my readers is this — the Lord Jesus Christ is the great friend to whom we must all look to for help, both for now and eternity.

The reason why the eternal Son of God came into the world, can never be declared too fully, or proclaimed too loudly. He came to give us *hope* and *peace,* while we live among the "temporary things which are seen;" and *glory* and *blessedness* when we go to the "eternal things, which are unseen." He came to bring "life and immortality to light," and to "free those who all their lives were held in slavery by their fear of death." (2 Timothy 1:10; Hebrews 2:15) He saw our lost and bankrupt condition, and had compassion on us. And now, blessed be His name, a mortal man may pass through "temporary things" with comfort, and look forward to "eternal things" without fear!

Our Lord Jesus Christ has *purchased* these mighty privileges for us at the cost of His own precious blood. He became our Substitute, and bore our sins in His own body on the cross, and then rose again for our justification. "Christ died for sins once for all, the righteous for the unrighteous, to bring us to God." "God made Him who had no sin to be sin for us" — that we poor sinful creatures might have pardon and justification while we live, and glory and blessedness when we die. (1 Peter 2:24; 3:18; 2 Corinthians 5:21)

And all that our Lord Jesus Christ has purchased for us — He offers freely to everyone who will turn from his sins, come to Him, and believe. "I am the light of the world," He says, "whoever follows Me will never walk in darkness — but will have the light of life." "Come to Me, all you who are weary and burdened, and I will give you rest." "If anyone is thirsty, let him come to Me and drink." "Whoever comes to me — I will never drive away." And the *terms* are as *simple* as the offer is *free*, "Believe in the Lord Jesus — and you will be saved." "Whoever believes in Him — shall not perish but have eternal life." (John 8:12; Matthew 11:28; John 7:37; 6:37; Acts 16:31; John 3:16)

He who has Christ — has eternal life. He can look around at the "temporary things," and see change and decay everywhere — and yet have no fear. He has got treasure in Heaven, "where moth and rust do not destroy, and where thieves do not break in and steal." He can look forward to the "eternal things," and feel calm and composed. His Savior has risen, and has gone to prepare a place for him. When he leaves this world — he will have a crown of glory, and be forever with his Lord. He can look down even into the grave, as the wisest Greeks and Romans could never do, and say, *"Where, O death, is your victory? Where, O death, is your sting?"* (1 Corinthians 15:55)

Let us all settle it firmly in our minds, that the only way to pass through "what is seen" with comfort, and look forward to "what is unseen" without fear — is to have Christ for our Savior and Friend, to lay hold of Christ by faith, to become one with Christ and Christ in us, and while we live in the flesh to live the life of faith in the Son of God. (Galatians 2:20)

How vast is the difference between the state of him who has true faith in Christ — and the state of him who has none! Blessed indeed is that man or woman, who can say, with truth, "I trust in Jesus — I believe!" When the Catholic Cardinal Beaufort lay on his deathbed, our mighty poet describes King Henry as saying, "He dies — but gives no sign of comfort." When John Knox, the Scotch Reformer, was drawing to his end, and unable to speak, a faithful servant asked him to give some proof that the Gospel he had preached in life gave him comfort in death, by raising his hand. He heard; and raised his hand toward Heaven three times, and then departed. I say again, blessed is he who believes! He alone is rich, independent, and beyond the reach of harm! If you and I have no comfort among temporary things, and no hope for the eternal things — then it is completely our own fault. It is because we "refuse to come to Christ to have life." (John 5:40)

I leave the subject of eternity here, and pray that God may bless it to many souls. In conclusion, I offer to every one who reads this volume some food for thought, and material for **SELF-EXAMINATION**.

(1) First of all, how are you using your *time?* Life is short and very uncertain. You never know what a day may bring forth. Business and pleasure, making money, and spending money, eating and drinking, marrying and giving in marriage — all, all will soon be over and done with forever. And you — what are you doing for your immortal soul? Are you wasting time, or using it wisely? Are you preparing to meet God?

(2) Secondly, where will *you* be in eternity? It is coming, coming, coming very fast upon us. You are going, going, going very fast into it. But where will you be — on the right hand or on the left, in the Day of Judgment? Are you among the lost or among the saved? Oh, do not rest; do not rest until your soul is secured! Be prepared — leave nothing uncertain. It is a dreadful thing to die unprepared, and fall into the hands of the living God.

(3) Thirdly, do you want to be *safe* now and in eternity? Then seek Christ, and believe in Him. Come to Him just as you are. Seek Him while He may be found, call on Him while He is near. There is still a *throne of grace*. It is not too late. Christ waits to be gracious — He invites you to come to Him. Before the door is shut and the judgment begins, repent, believe, and be saved.

(4) Lastly, do you want to be *happy?* Cling to Christ and live a life of faith in Him. Remain in Him and live close to Him. Follow Him with heart and soul and mind and strength, and seek to know Him better every day. By doing so, you will have great peace while you pass through the "temporary things," and in the midst of a dying world you "will never die!" (John 11:26) By doing so you will be able to look forward to "eternal things" with unfailing confidence, and to feel and "know that if the earthly tent we live in is destroyed, we have a building from God, an eternal house in Heaven, not built by human hands!" (2 Corinthians 5:1)

www.ingramcontent.com/pod-product-compliance
Lightning Source LLC
LaVergne TN
LVHW041113080826
845145LV00007B/1789

* 9 7 8 1 6 4 4 3 9 1 3 7 2 *